PLANTATION POLITICS AND CAMPUS REBELLIONS

SUNY series, Critical Race Studies in Education

Derrick R. Brooms, editor

PLANTATION POLITICS AND CAMPUS REBELLIONS

POWER, DIVERSITY, AND THE EMANCIPATORY STRUGGLE IN HIGHER EDUCATION

Edited by

Bianca C. Williams, Dian D. Squire, and Frank A. Tuitt

Cover photo by Bach Nguyen on Unsplash.

Published by State University of New York Press, Albany

© 2021 State University of New York

All rights reserved

Printed in the United States of America

No part of this book may be used or reproduced in any manner whatsoever without written permission. No part of this book may be stored in a retrieval system or transmitted in any form or by any means including electronic, electrostatic, magnetic tape, mechanical, photocopying, recording, or otherwise without the prior permission in writing of the publisher.

For information, contact State University of New York Press, Albany, NY
www.sunypress.edu

Library of Congress Cataloging-in-Publication Data

Names: Williams, Bianca C., [date]- editor. | Squire, Dian (Dian D.), [date]- editor. | Tuitt, Frank (Franklin A.), editor.
Title: Plantation politics and campus rebellions : power, diversity, and the emancipatory struggle in higher education / Bianca C. Williams, Dian Squire, and Frank Tuitt.
Description: Albany, NY : State University of New York Press, [2021] | Series: SUNY series, critical race studies in education | Includes bibliographical references and index.
Identifiers: LCCN 2020023385 | ISBN 9781438482675 (hardcover : alk. paper) | ISBN 9781438482699 (ebook)
Subjects: LCSH: Racism in higher education—United States. | African Americans—Education, Higher—Social aspects. | African Americans—Social conditions. | Universities and colleges—United States—Sociological aspects.
Classification: LCC LC212.42 .P53 2021 | DDC 378.1/982996073—dc23
LC record available at https://lccn.loc.gov/2020023385

10 9 8 7 6 5 4 3 2 1

Contents

ACKNOWLEDGMENTS ix

INTRODUCTION
"Carving Out a Humanity": Campus Rebellions and the Legacy
of Plantation Politics on College Campuses 1
   Bianca C. Williams and Frank A. Tuitt

Part 1.
Capitalism and Colonial Vestiges of
White Supremacy in Higher Education

CHAPTER 1
Framing Plantation Politics: Allochronism's Pull on Contemporary
Formations of Higher Education 35
   Dian D. Squire

CHAPTER 2
Plantation Pedagogies in Contemporary Higher Education
Classrooms: Instruments of the Slave Society and Manifestations
of Plantation Politics 57
   Saran Stewart

CHAPTER 3
"Troubling the Waters": Unpacking and (Re)Imagining the
Historical and Contemporary Complexity of Historically
Black College and University Cultural Politics 77
   *Steve D. Mobley Jr., Sunni L. Solomon II, A. C. Johnson,
   and Patrick Reynolds*

CHAPTER 4
Fugitive Slave Act(s): The Emergence of Black Studies as an
Exemplar for Black Future(s) Insurrection 99
   Wilson Kwamogi Okello

Part 2.
Institutional Rhetoric and the
False Promises of "Diversity" and "Inclusion"

CHAPTER 5
Inclusion = Racial Violence? Time, Space, and the Afterlife
of the Plantation 119
   Armond Towns

CHAPTER 6
Future Thinking and Freedom Making: Antidiversity as an
Intervention to the Plantation Politics of Higher Education 141
   *Jesse Carr, Nicole Truesdell, Catherine M. Orr,
and Lisa Anderson-Levy*

CHAPTER 7
The Contemporary Chief Diversity Officer and the Plantation
Driver: The Reincarnation of a Diversity Management Position 171
   Frank A. Tuitt

CHAPTER 8
The Campus Underground Railroad: Strategies of Resistance,
Care, and Courage within University Cultural Centers 199
   *Toby S. Jenkins, Rosalind Conerly, Liane I. Hypolite,
and Lori D. Patton*

Part 3.
Resistance and Repression:
Campus Politics and Legislative Acts of Anti-Blackness

CHAPTER 9
Resistance In and Out of the University: Student Activist
Political Subjectivity and the Liberal Institution 227
   Kristi Carey

CHAPTER 10
Repurposing the Confederacy: Understanding Issues Surrounding the Removal and Contextualization of Lost Cause Iconography at Southern Colleges and Universities 249
    R. Eric Platt, Holly A. Foster, and Lauren Yarnell Bradshaw

CHAPTER 11
Codes of Silence: Campus and State Responses to Student Protest 273
    Kevin J. Bazner and Andrea Button

CHAPTER 12
"When Lions Have Historians": Black Political Literacy in the Carceral University 293
    Orisanmi Burton

AFTERWORD
Against Higher Education: Instruments of Insurrection 315
    D-L Stewart

ABOUT THE EDITORS 321

CONTRIBUTORS 323

INDEX 331

Acknowledgments

This book would not have been possible without the activism and organizing of so many—on university campuses and in the streets—who took risks to fight against anti-Black violence and declare that "Black Lives Matter!" In our classrooms, during community protests, and at conferences and city council meetings we saw you holding those in power accountable and pushing them to make amends and reparations for the harms institutions often perpetuate. We also saw you reimagining what emancipatory struggle and education can look like. Your community-building and collective resistance inspired us to labor alongside you in a multitude of ways, including writing this book. Since we started this project on plantation politics and campus rebellions in 2015, countless Black students, staff, community members, and faculty have shared their experiences in higher education with us, filling research meetings, town halls, panel discussions, and office hours with brave and vulnerable testimony. We thank you for your words and your hard work. We are grateful for you and the long legacy of Black protest and resistance that continues to push higher education to be better and do better. We hope that the provocations, questions, critiques, and goals offered in this text honor what you shared with us. We hope that the authors' contributions here will help in the fight to create academic institutions that will no longer kill Black people quickly or slowly, physically or psychologically. We look forward to dreaming and creating more liberatory education futures with you.

The editors would like to thank Ozy Aloziem, Shenhaye Ferguson, Patrice Greene, and Kahlea Hunt-Khabir for their research assistance and passion. Thanks to Rebecca Colesworthy, our editor at SUNY Press, for her guidance, encouragement, and patience. Finally, we are grateful for the long-term commitments and contributions the authors of each chapter gifted us.

Introduction

"Carving Out a Humanity": Campus Rebellions and the Legacy of Plantation Politics on College Campuses

BIANCA C. WILLIAMS AND FRANK A. TUITT

"I am reminded that our forebears—though betrayed into bondage—survived the slavery in which they were reduced to things, property, entitled neither to rights nor to respect as human beings. Somehow, as the legacy of our spirituals makes clear, our enslaved ancestors managed to retain their humanity as well as their faith that evil and suffering were not the extent of their destiny—or of the destiny of those who would follow them. Indeed, we owe our existence to their perseverance, their faith. In these perilous times, we must do no less than they did: fashion a philosophy that both matches the unique dangers we face, and enables us to recognize in those dangers opportunities for committed living and humane service. . . . Knowing there was no escape, no way out, the slaves nonetheless continued to engage themselves. To carve out a humanity. To defy the murder of selfhood. Their lives were brutally shackled, certainly—but not without meaning despite being imprisoned."

—Derrick Bell, *Faces at the Bottom of the Well*

Between 2012 and 2018, more than 100 US college and university campuses erupted in protests. Many used the #BlackLivesMatter declaration as a core message, connecting struggles on their campuses with the battles against police violence and anti-Black racism taking place in neighborhoods across the country. Black students were at the forefront of these campus rebellions, with actions ranging from minutes-long die-ins and street blockings to weeks of hunger strikes, building takeovers, and sit-ins. Students questioned the tenets and structures that formed the foundation of the universities of which they were community members. Similar to the protests of the 1960s and 1970s, these activists provided a list of demands to their administrations, requesting immediate action be taken to address hostile learning and living environments and institutional inequities. For as long as there have been universities, there has been resistance surrounding them, as their foundations have often been set on ideals of exclusion and the myth of meritocracy. Today the ideals remain but are wrapped in the rhetoric of diversity and inclusion (Ahmed, 2012). During the Movement for Black Lives (M4BL),[1] campus activists encountering the disconnect between this rhetoric and their lived experiences used multiple methods to get their demands and stories out, including photography, social media, street theatre, dance flash mobs, and various forms of digital storytelling.[2] University administrators had a range of responses to these rebellions, some physically violent, including using militarized security forces to pepper-spray, threaten, and arrest students; to refuse to allow food and water in protest spaces; and to remove students from the campus through suspension. These institutional responses supplemented the death threats, hate speech, and other forms of intimidation that campus activists received from their peers, alumni, residents living near campus, and white supremacists both on- and off-line. Campus rebellions such as these are sometimes the most public, spectacular manifestations of everyday protest by students, staff, and faculty; and they often explode when universities count Black *bodies* as present but are not ready to make the necessary changes to ensure Black *people* are welcome, safe, and treated equally.

In the epigraph above, law professor and activist Derrick Bell reminds us that fighting for liberation requires vision and faith. Alongside this, it helps if we have an appreciation for the resistance and resilience Black people have embodied throughout history; gratitude for struggles survived and hard-won victories achieved; and ownership of one's responsibility in the continuing fight for equity and justice. Acknowledging that responsibility, this book on plantation politics explores whether the university is a site where Black people can continue to "carve out a humanity." The authors examine who and what the barriers are to humanizing processes within higher education, and how an understanding of plantation politics might help us more effectively imagine and organize toward emancipatory futures. Here we zero in on the university as a microcosm of the larger struggles against white supremacy and anti-Blackness, recognizing that the protests and rebellions that erupted in places such as Ferguson and the University of Missouri (Mizzou) are deeply intertwined.[3] Though community organizers and campus activists are frequently discussed as separate entities, during the M4BL they were oftentimes one and the same, moving across spaces to engage in protests against exclusionary practices and police violence. The lines between the university and the community are often troubled when Black people are placed at the center of the analysis.

Bell's epigraph, however, is not only about the inheritance of resistance. It is a reminder that the systems of oppression that disempowered and disparaged enslaved Black peoples are still present—that the tentacles of violence, surveillance, and exploitation they lived through are entangled with the "unique dangers" Black people encounter today.[4] In her celebrated work *Lose Your Mother*, Saidiya Hartman echoes Bell, writing, "If slavery exists as an issue in the political life of [B]lack America, it is not because of an antiquarian obsession with bygone days or the burden of a too-long memory, but because [B]lack lives are still imperiled and devalued by a racial calculus and a political arithmetic that were entrenched centuries ago. This is the afterlife of slavery—skewed life chances, limited access to health and education, premature death, incarceration, and impoverishment" (2007, p. 6). Hartman pushes us to consider the afterlife of slavery, while Katherine McKittrick (2013) encourages us to think about how plantations continue to influence (Black) futures. As a result of the entanglements between plantations of the past and the establishment of many scholarly organizations and educational institutions, plantation politics are still embedded in the everyday life of the academy. Like McKittrick, we wonder what one might see, understand, and imagine they might do, if we recognize the haunting of plantation life as existing not only in the walls and structures that buttress the university but also in its operations, hiring practices, recruitment and attainment strategies, curriculum, and notions of sociality, safety, and community. Therefore, throughout this text, we use "plantation politics" to refer to the connections between historical policies, practices, and discourses in higher education and their new iterations, which are used to control, exploit, and marginalize Black people.

Moreover, we argue that plantation politics are often pushed to the forefront when institutional actors are confronted with Black people's resistance, such as during the Movement for Black Lives. Purposely, this book focuses on plantation politics *and* campus rebellions because we are aware of the relationship between the two. Through personal experience, hundreds of hours in committee meetings and classrooms, as "troublemakers" and researchers of racism and campus environments, we recognize the ways higher education institutions draw on strategies and ideologies of the plantation past to repress and fragment movements. So often these spaces and opportunities not only help us understand oppression better but also how the legacy of Black people's resistance has shaped the academy, and continues to shine a light on the racial violence that is present.

We call these instances of campus activism "rebellions" because we recognize that these multisited uprisings (sometimes spontaneous, but often organized) are socially, spatially, and temporally connected. "Rebellion" allows us to get a wide-lens view of campus activism, understanding how the work of residents and Dream Defenders in Sanford after Trayvon Martin was killed is not only linked to that of community members in Ferguson and students at Mizzou but also to the legacy of Black resistance during the 1960s and 1970s. Moreover, we use rebellion to note how these acts of disruption and open defiance against administrative and police authority trigger the fears of those in power at universities as they scramble to reestablish what they view as order, contain the movement and emotions of Black folx, and mitigate white anxiety. Though academic administrators can sometimes imagine they have dominion over their campus—viewing it as contained, privileged, and distant from the surrounding community—it is these rebellious acts of Black students that often disrupt this illusion. As Black students draw attention to the structural violence perpetuated by academic institutions, and call for things like reparations and equity, administrations mobilize to squash these rebellions and extinguish flames of resistance. An analysis of institutional responses to campus rebellions is useful for understanding how universities uphold white supremacy even as they pledge resources toward diversity and inclusion initiatives as remedies for these disruptions.

Teasing out a plantation politics framework has the potential to help us identify the machine of white supremacy in higher education[5]—how it operates, how it views us, how we act as assets and liabilities to it, who our accomplices or allies are, which entities act as barriers to equity and justice, what we need to tear down, and how we can build something new in its place. Putting a spotlight on university responses to campus rebellions during the Movement for Black Lives allows us to shift the attention from the protests that are viewed as symptoms of a problem to the conditions and individuals that assist in creating oppressive educational environments. Or a more favorable read may be that a plantation politics framework helps us see how institutions actually seeking to tackle inequities often end up perpetuating them by not directly addressing the root(s) of the problem.

Why a Plantation Politics Framework?

Although we started this project in 2015, there was a clear moment when we recognized the type of work a plantation politics framework could facilitate. Sitting in the room at the 2016 Association for the Study of Higher Education (ASHE) conference in Columbus, Ohio, the editors of this book waited for the appointed time for our panel session to begin. We were in a collective state of shock. Folx of color filled the seats around us, some speaking in whispers, as if speaking at a higher level would disrupt the grief and mourning permeating the space.[6] Others sat silently in their seats, staring off into the distance, with sadness coming off of them in waves. In the wee hours of the morning, it had been confirmed that Donald J. Trump had won the election for president of the United States. And we were here, in this room, committed to presenting on plantation politics in higher education. Some of us felt the words we planned to speak were necessary but also meant nothing. Urgent and weighty matters felt even more so, yet giving a presentation on them seemed inadequate. The stakes of valuing Black life, of maintaining safety and wellness in our environments, had increased exponentially overnight.

Staff, students, and faculty around the globe participating in the Movement for Black Lives had spent years engaging in activism and consciousness raising, declaring and demanding that "Black Lives Matter!" In multiple ways, voters, politicians, police, and university officials had replied that these lives, in fact, did not. With this in mind, several questions threaded the session's papers and comments together: How does one move the academy closer to its espoused aspirational goals of diversity, inclusion, and equality when a (white) majority has elected a white supremacist to lead the country?[7] Is a commitment to an equity-minded agenda within higher education even possible? In this political climate, how do we talk honestly about the ways oppression and dehumanization of Black people continue to be essential to higher education? How do we begin to value Black people and their labor when our experiences tell us that universities thrive using strategies from plantation pasts instead of working toward equitable futures? Finally, how do we imagine liberating spaces and emancipatory practices when our engagement with these institutions often results in us being implicated in our own oppression?

Though startling, the day after the election felt like a new phase on old terrain. As each presenter spoke about the various ways plantation politics show up on our campuses, the energy in the room shifted. People began to take notes, and their body language was attentive. Questions and comments were passionately expressed, and there was a general sense of recognition, confirmation, and validation. An exhale. A moment to breathe collectively at a time when it felt as though our breathing and our existence did not matter. There was also hopelessness. Anger. Rage. Sadness. Even helplessness. Audience members spoke about feeling stuck not only in their academic careers or training but also in spaces where fighting to make a difference, being dedicated to battling white supremacy and anti-Blackness, felt like a decision to suffocate one's self (Rushin, 1981; Evans, 2010).

In that room, "plantation politics" came to name something that had been weighing on many of us as Black folx in higher education: (1) the psychological warfare we experience in educational institutions whose histories make it clear that they were not made for us; (2) the creation of an active (but sometimes elusive) machine of racist rhetoric, policies, and procedures that fuel the academy; (3) the exploitation of Black people and Black labor that helps universities appear diverse enough for the sake of profit while devaluing Black voices when it comes to institutional change; and (4) a recognition of the emotional and pedagogical labor that marginalized people offer every day, but especially during periods of campus rebellions, which universities view as branding or reputation "crises." Naming these forces at ASHE, and the other conferences and universities we have presented at, has offered audience members and presenters alike some solace as white supremacy becomes more blatant everywhere. As many therapists teach, putting a name to a feeling or experience can allow a person to recognize what is happening to them and offers some space so they can work through it. We want this book to play a role in that affirming and healing process. Here, we name and mark plantation politics to contribute to the canon of research detailing how white supremacy and anti-Blackness were (and continue to be) central to the inner workings of higher education. We take seriously Black people's vernacular description of universities as "plantations" in order to tease out old and new dehumanizing practices and ideologies that universities implement to be profitable in the business of teaching, learning, and research.

It is our hope that readers will see how the technologies used to create plantation life are connected to those that sustain higher education, and the ways these produce racial inequities and hostile environments that give rise to campus resistance. In the next chapter, coeditor Dian Squire builds on Craig Steven Wilder and Thomas J. Durant's work to offer an analysis of the vestiges of plantation culture and life and their influence on modern university culture, climate, and structures of power. Each additional chapter offers a window into how employing control mechanisms to repress campus rebellions reinforces white supremacy, limits freedom, and continues to oppress Black people. The authors also open up possibilities for how actors within university structures and cultures may envision and work toward racial equity, justice, and liberation. The book acknowledges the physical and emotional costs Black people experience in the academy's mostly white spaces, while also speaking, dreaming, and strategizing steps toward more equitable futures.

To be clear—in this book we are not arguing that universities are actual plantations like those of the Antebellum South, nor are we arguing that Black people in academic institutions experience the type of physical, sexual, and psychological horrors our ancestors endured.[8] We will never know the violence of being treated solely as chattel, as a subhuman commodity, or the terror of such enslavement. As Black people's resistance chipped away at racist and otherwise unequal systems over generations, there has been greater mobility and access to housing, education, employment, and healthcare for many. However, in light of recent surges in raids within immigrant communities, a growing understanding of the intricate ways capitalist systems continue to disempower Black peoples, and a heightened awareness of the traumatizing effects of carcerality, surveillance, and police violence, many are asking whether the conditions of our current moment should be viewed as adaptations that present new terrors and challenges to freedom and liberation. As Black activists hold universities accountable and campaigns for reparations grow, some institutions excavate their racist histories from the archives and publicly share their stories. Here, we are made ever more aware of the interconnections between the plantations of the past and the establishment of many educational institutions. However, some unwisely believe that this history is distinct from current day operations and has no impact on the present.

As we spoke with Black folx in higher education throughout this project, it became clear that some had great concerns about the ways race, capital, and labor coalesce to perpetuate inequities in higher education.

Universities were critiqued for not valuing the pedagogical and emotional labor that staff and faculty of color invest to create welcoming environments that retain (tuition-paying and/or reputation-promoting) students of color; failure to honor the labor that Black student athletes contribute to both the university's coffers and the reach of the institution's brand (Hawkins, 2010); and the taken-for-granted ways Black faculty continuously drag institutions into the future through their theoretical and research innovations.[9] For universities to attempt to make campuses equitable or inclusive without explicitly working through the connections between race, capital, and labor, is to throw financial and work-energy resources at problems one does not honestly intend to solve. Some of the book's contributors ask if it is possible for educational institutions to be effective without exploiting Black labor or marginalizing those who are committed to being unapologetically Black. It may be that in order to respect and value Black people, the academy may be required to die to itself. In the wake of giving up the violence, exploitation, and exclusion that currently function as the motors of the academy, a rebirth will be necessary.

Campus Rebellions: From "I, Too, Am" to "#BlackLivesMatter"

One of the most prominent examples of the convergence of student and community organizing in recent years took place in February 2012 in Florida. A group now known as the Dream Defenders began organizing after 17-year-old Trayvon Martin was killed by neighborhood security person George Zimmerman on February 26, 2012. Students from Florida State University, Tallahassee Community College, and Florida A&M University marched from Daytona to Sanford (about 39 miles) and sat in governor Rick Scott's office for 31 days. They demanded that their representatives push back against the "Stand Your Ground" laws that Zimmerman used as part of his defense for killing Martin. Their demands and actions resulted in the legislature holding hearings on the law. Their organizing showed that students recognized how their experiences within higher education and on campuses were connected to a larger fight against police violence and the killing and surveillance of Black people. Their activism had the power to make a difference not only on their campuses but also in their state legislature.

Nationally, people took notice of the Dream Defenders' organizing and bold energy. As increased attention was paid to police shootings and killings of unarmed Black folx across the country, the organizing in Florida and many other states contributed to a politically intense climate. On July 13, 2013, George Zimmerman was found not guilty of killing Trayvon Martin. Outrage, disappointment, fear, and calls for justice fueled more rebellions nationwide. On that day, both Black Youth Project 100 (BYP100) and the global network of Black Lives Matter were birthed. Black Youth Project 100 is an affiliate organization of the national research endeavor called Black Youth Project, started by feminist political scientist Cathy Cohen and formerly led by founding national director Charlene Carruthers. Both BYP organizations were created in Chicago (Carruthers, 2018). That July, Cohen brought together 100 youth (including students ages 18 to 35) for a convening, and on the night of the 13th, they created BYP100 as an organizing body.

As the herstory goes, Black queer women community organizers Alicia Garza and Patrisse Cullors joined forces with Black woman immigration organizer Opal Tometi to cofound an online campaign using the rallying cry and hashtag "#BlackLivesMatter" (Khan-Cullors and Bandele, 2018). Eventually, Black Lives Matter (BLM) became a global network of over 45 chapters, filled with organizers who worked collectively at times, and autonomously during others.[10] Black Lives Matter became a central node in the even larger network called the Movement for Black Lives (M4BL), which was composed of over 50 organizing entities from places such as Ohio, New York, Missouri, Maryland, North Carolina, and California. Members of M4BL worked together to create what is commonly known as the policy platform for the movement. Prominent Black transwomen leaders in M4BL and the BLM global network, Elle Hearns went on to found the Marsha P. Johnson Institute, which focuses on policy and programming for Black transwomen, while Aaryn Lang helped lead Black Trans Liberation Tuesday, a national day of action. Protests and acts of resistance during the Movement for Black Lives generated national conversations about community safety, racialized and gendered violence, emotional wellness, prison abolition, voting rights, and economic empowerment. Students at universities across the United States were not only members of BLM chapters and M4BL organizations but also central actors in the alliances and partnerships created with student groups on college campuses.

In the shadow of the national mourning and organizing around Trayvon Martin and the ever-growing list of Black people who were victims of police violence, a photo campaign giving voice to Black students' experiences at Harvard College was created in March 2014. "I, Too, Am

Harvard" went viral, with students on multiple campuses describing their experiences with marginalization and belonging. Black Harvard students introduced the project by stating on their Tumblr page, "Our voices often go unheard on this campus, our experiences are devalued, our presence is questioned—this project is our way of speaking back, of claiming this campus, of standing up to say: We are here. This place is ours. We, TOO, are Harvard" (2014). Claiming that they, too, were essential members of their respective university communities, dozens of schools created photo campaigns and hashtags dedicated to the experiences of students of color on their campuses. At Harvard, the photo campaign was turned into a play based on interviews with Black students. In these interviews, and in other online conversations about inclusion, diversity, access, equitable resources, and surveillance, students began to identify some of the early demands for future campus rebellions.

In August 2014, Ferguson, Missouri, went up in a blaze. On the 9th, 18-year-old local resident Michael Brown was murdered by officer Darren Wilson. His body was left on the ground in the scorching sun for over four and a half hours, with family members, friends, and neighbors standing watch and comforting each other, unable to reach him as police investigating the scene barred their access. That night, and consistently for the next year, Ferguson residents led their neighbors and visitors in numerous rebellions, demanding justice for Brown's family, expressing rage at the death and disregard for Black life, and protesting for long-term change.[11] Some of the protestors were in high school, and others were campus activists from nearby colleges such as Saint Louis University and Washington University.[12] Streets and highways were shut down, city meetings disrupted, and buildings set ablaze while militarized police attacked protestors with Tasers, tear gas, sound cannons, and rubber bullets. Rebellions increased three months later when it was announced that the grand jury had decided not to indict Wilson. Many would argue that the killing of Brown, the nonindictment of Wilson, and the rage and bravery of Ferguson protesters and organizers was the central spark and motivating fuel of the international movement that would become popularly known as the Black Lives Matter movement. People all around the world watched the #FergusonUprising grow on the news and online live streams. Students at Howard University, the University of Pennsylvania, the University of California, Berkeley, the University of Maryland, and the University of North Carolina participated in die-ins, drawing attention to police disrespect of Brown's life as he laid dead in the street, and the trauma his community experienced as they were forced to watch him there. Since August 2014, protests, rebellions, and debates about police violence, surveillance, and the value and (in)significance of Black life have remained important parts of public discourse, political action, and classroom conversations.

While residents and community organizations such as BYP100, BLM, and Dream Defenders lit up the country with protests while publicly calling out presidential candidates, students on university campuses also engaged in an extended period of activism. One of the most prominent examples was the organizing of Black students at the University of Missouri in 2015, which eventually became the Concerned Student 1950 group. The "1950" refers to the year the first Black student was admitted to the university, and the group's name memorializes that moment. After several racist incidents took place on campus, and the administration failed to adequately address the concerns of the students these incidents targeted, a group of Black students began to organize. Taking lessons learned from the rebellion in Ferguson, which was two hours away from campus, students effectively mobilized using social media. In October, Black students blocked the car of university system president Tim Wolfe during a homecoming parade, demanding that he deal with the hostile campus environment. Videos of this confrontation went viral. Arguing that Wolfe should resign for his failure to effectively address the situation, Concerned Student 1950 increased the intensity of their organizing and offered eight demands. Graduate student Jonathan Butler went on a hunger strike, players on the football team threatened a labor strike (with the coaches' support), and students camped out on the quad. Administrators released statements and eventually met with students but offered little recourse as the organizing efforts gained national attention. This powerful demonstration of strategic organizing resulted in the resignation of Wolfe and the establishment of a system-wide diversity officer. Mizzou is a great case study not only of the effectiveness of student organizing but also of what can happen when the larger political context influences campus activism and vice versa.

The year 2015 was a particularly pivotal one as protests and acts of resistance took place around the globe. Though mostly ignored by US mainstream media, students in San Juan protested for over two months against proposed tuition increases and massive cuts in resources to the flagship campus of the University of Puerto Rico. They demanded that the administration address the university's accreditation crisis after it filed bankruptcy. The university shut its doors in response, with the president and many trustee members resigning in the midst of the crisis (Robles, 2017). In October 2015, students throughout South Africa protested the increase of school fees with #FeesMustFall. Police fired rubber bullets and stun grenades at the University of the Witwatersrand in Johannesburg in response to protests, while students were arrested at the University of Cape Town (Hauser, 2016). Calling for the abolition of tuition fees and "free education as a human right," students in London protested in November 2015, drawing attention to the great amount of debt students accumulate to attend university. Police and students confronted one another in the streets, resulting in the arrest of at least twelve students (Coughlan, 2015).

As rebellions exploded, the editors of this book focused their attention on the campus rebellions connected to Black Lives Matter in the United States in order to understand what was generating this energy for sustained, long-term protests, and how universities were responding to it. Each of us could feel the impact of these political encounters in our classrooms, in our conversations with colleagues and students, and on our own wellness. We asked how we could assist students in expressing themselves, in demanding what they needed from universities, and applying the critical thinking and action tools we offered in the classroom. We wanted to analyze this current moment to decipher what was happening at our universities, and to use this resistance to help move these institutions closer toward equity.

Coeditor Frank Tuitt pulled together a team of graduate students and postdoctoral researchers to analyze the demands of over 100 campus rebellions.[13] Many of the demands were almost exactly the same as the demands from Black student movements of the 1960s and 1970s: more Black faculty; a more inclusive curriculum; more resources for programming and residential issues. One of the few demands that stood out from the rest was the call for increased resources for mental health services, and professionals trained to be culturally responsive and culturally competent in order to assist Black students dealing with racism and anti-Blackness. Additionally, some students demanded reparations in the form of free tuition or other remedies to address present and historical campus inequity. During these rebellions, students were not simply asking for short-term fixes to the campus climate so they could feel more welcome. They were pushing all members of the community to question who was included or excluded from the stated purpose and values of their institutions.

The activism taking place on campuses and in nearby neighborhoods created an environment for one of the longest continuous anti–white supremacist, pro-Black movements in the United States. While campus administrators often think of these rebellions as activities that are contained by campus borders, this period of organizing shows us that (Black) students are affected by, participate in, and move across school boundaries in ways that some administrators are often unaware of. The alignment of rebellions on campus and in the streets was not surprising to many Black people, as universities have always been microcosms of the larger world. While academic institutions are sites of privilege and designed with borders to keep some without access, what happens in "the public" still affects what happens on campus. The academy may be distinct from "the public," but it is not free from the public's influence. In fact, in some political struggles, higher education is the frontline of ideological warfare. It is no surprise that debates about racism, freedom of speech, academic freedom, a living wage, sexual violence, immigration, and citizenship have significantly fueled student organizing in the past few years. And the tactics universities use to respond to these protests—the arming and militarization of campus police, the pepper-spraying and tear-gassing of students, strict disciplinary action against student activists, the banning of food and drink during sit-ins—demonstrate that universities are not sacred places held apart from the violence of police and security forces that surveil and punish society. They never have been. Being a student or staff member with university affiliation can bring with it a certain amount of privilege. However, for Black staff, faculty, or students, an ID with the emblem or crest of the university does not keep them safe in a world that does not see them as human. Black student organizers, faculty, and staff disruptors frequently understand this and take action accordingly.

Centering Black Lives in Higher Education

The recent surge of campus rebellions during the Movement for Black Lives serves as a reminder that Black people have always been central to the project and mission of education in the United States. Despite hundreds of years of systemic racism that barred access to educational institutions, generations of Black people have been actively present in college and university communities. Oftentimes they have pushed these institutions to become more equitable, just, and innovative. Texts such as Carter G. Woodson's *Miseducation of the Negro* (1933/2011) detail how efforts such as the Freedmen's Bureau attempted to provide education to Black people after emancipation, creating practices that would later be the foundation for public education. Black people were some of the earliest educators, architects, and laborers helping—willingly and unwillingly—to build academic institutions. Even today, Black feminist and Africana thought lead to programmatic and disciplinary innovations such as "intersectionality" and "interdisciplinarity," creating new ways of thinking and producing knowledge. Black students, faculty, and staff contribute greatly to academic institutions, often acting as their consciences whether they desire to or not. They contribute diversity, equality, and equity-based work, many times lifting the entire system up and improving it for everyone, while fighting for their own survival.

In their essay "A Case for Reparations at the University of Chicago," authors Caine Jordan, Guy Emerson Mount, and Kai Parker (2017) describe how essential Black people and their labor were to the university's establishment. They write,

> The University of Chicago does not exist apart from Julia Leakes and the suffering of her family—it exists because of them. Between 1848 and 1857, the labor and capital that [plantation owner Stephen A.] Douglas extracted from his slaves catapulted his political career and his personal fortune. Slavery soon provided him with the financial security and economic power to donate ten acres of land (valued at over $1.2 million in today's dollars) to start the University of Chicago in 1857. This founding endowment, drenched in the blood of enslaved African Americans, was leveraged by the University of Chicago to borrow more than $6 million dollars in today's terms to build its Gothic campus, its institutional structures, its vast donor network, and an additional $4 million endowment before 1881. In short, the University of Chicago owes it[s] entire presence to its past with slavery. (para 3)

The University of Chicago is not the only institution where this type of exploitation took place, nor was this exploitation simply used to establish the physical structures of the university. At some of the earliest established higher education institutions, foundational contributions to research disciplines were enabled by the labor and monetary "capital" of enslaved Black peoples. In "The Missing Link: Conservative Abolitionists, Slavery, and Yale," Eric Herschthal (2017) writes that letters from Benjamin Silliman,

Yale's first chemistry professor in 1802, "reveal how slave money helped build up Yale's science programs in particular. If scholars are to continue researching slavery's ties to universities, which they must, they need to pay closer attention not only to which universities profited from slavery, but what particular branches of knowledge within those universities gained from it" (para 3). As we seek to make Black Lives Matter in higher education, it might be helpful to center the contributions of Black peoples while documenting, valuing, and teaching about how their work helped shaped the physical and material conditions of the academy.

Many founders of academic institutions, fearful of how powerful Black learners would be if they had access to formal education, created policies and practices designed to keep Black folx out. Some of these white university founders, board members, and presidents made their fortunes from the slave economy and held Black people in captivity. We know that Black people's delayed access to these institutions and the research produced in them was not accidental but intentional. This is where the plantation politics in higher education truly began to crystallize. To be Black on a university's campus is to live with a contemporary version of W. E. B. Du Bois's "double-consciousness." It is to understand that the way you see yourself is different from how the institution views and values you, even as it recruits you, and highlights your experiences and achievements. Reading your institution's aspirational diversity mission statement, looking at the pictures of folx of color in the campus brochure dedicated to inclusion, or laboring on the university's diversity committee as a Black person is to endure a particularly insidious, long-term form of gaslighting. Here, the school promises to do better when it comes to issues of racism while arguing that the (unequal) access Black people have to the institution is an indicator that the necessary work has already been done. However, many Black students, staff, and faculty recognize that for the real work of equity to be completed, the institution will have to drastically change who and what it is. They know that the reality they are presented with in the university's materials isn't the reality of what they live each day on campus.

Having to fight tooth and nail to access higher education and then have our humanity degraded or threatened throughout the education process when we gain access is why so many Black students, staff, and faculty decided to protest and resist on campuses across the country. To be essential to the project of equality-based education yet be systemically marginalized from its fruits is enough to make anyone engage in rebellion.

However, having faith that things can be different, and desiring to demand and fight for that change, is some of the powerful work Black people continue to participate in. As we sit in classrooms, in libraries, and at the feet of our community members learning about our history and the ways we helped build the academic spaces that continue to try to diminish us, we grow ever more committed to creating new analyses, practices, policies, and visions of what education can look like.

Overview of the Book

Campus resistance during the Movement for Black Lives called universities to atone for their racist histories, create strategies that would generate institutional change, and clarify their commitment to the Black members of their communities. The disconnect between the university's values and commitments and the everyday experience of Black folx was made clear in the ways administrators decided to engage activists during these tense moments of disagreement and difference. As we examined universities' responses to students mobilizing around these incidents, one question we were interested in gaining insight into was, "What are the conditions that contribute to campus resistance?" Repeatedly, this question led us to the dual forces of white supremacy and anti-Blackness, and their manifestations in campus communities. Each part of the book addresses a particular instrument of plantation politics in the contemporary university, recognizing that these instruments and the forms of resistance that occur in response to them are all interconnected. Subsequently, there are inevitably—and, we hope, productively—connective threads running through the three sections. Part 1 of the book discusses how higher education can be used as a mechanism to control Black people while upholding whiteness, white supremacy, and anti-Blackness. Part 2 makes the case that instead of serving as a gateway to racial equality or justice, universities (especially traditionally white institutions) often design diversity and inclusion initiatives that neglect race and racism and reinforce whiteness. Finally, part 3 describes some of the forms of resistance students and instructors engage in as they call into question higher education's commitment to equity, and the narratives and policies administrators and government entities create in order to repress campus rebellions. By studying this system of plantation politics and the rebellions against it, we seek to illuminate the relationship between these experiences of oppression and resistance, showing how Black people pushing for change have always, and continue to, transform higher education for many.

PART 1: CAPITALISM AND COLONIAL VESTIGES OF WHITE SUPREMACY IN HIGHER EDUCATION

As we turned our collective focus to plantation politics, we saw the increasing tendency of white people calling campus police on Black folx as a clear example of the rising tide of white supremacist sentiment at traditionally white institutions (TWIs).[14] According to these complaints, working while Black, walking on campus while Black, sleeping while Black, teaching while Black, eating while Black, and standing in front of your residence hall while Black were code violations even though these were the very things Black people were invited to campus to do.[15] These complaints, and subsequent encounters with police and security authorities, were ways that (white) people and institutions made evident their notions about who they imagined Black people could be, how they thought Black people should act, and where they felt Black people should have limited access. Unfortunately, these racist incidents had real material consequences and served as reminders that many faculty, staff, and students still view Black people with contempt and are willing to do them harm. Thus, our book's discussion of plantation politics reinforces Michael Dumas's (2016) description of anti-Blackness, in which Black folx exist in a structurally antagonistic relationship with higher education institutions that repeatedly deny their humanity. Dumas suggests that institutions often employ technologies that affirm whiteness as humane while systematically excluding this as a reality for Black people. Accordingly, in the first part of this book, the chapters help us understand how Black people's most recent encounters with white supremacy and anti-Blackness on campuses are connected to those that grounded previous colonial and capitalist structures.

To this point, Dian Squire's chapter on allochronism opens part 1, making the case that the current white supremacist and anti-Black sentiments permeating college campuses should not be viewed as only recent acts of violence "but rather situated in material and nonmaterial realities of time and place [from] centuries ago." Specifically, Squire explores the characteristics of plantations as systems, connecting historic plantations and modern universities in order to offer greater detail about the plantation politics framework and its utility in understanding contemporary institutions. Correspondingly, Saran Stewart in chapter 2 describes three forms of plantation pedagogy in the Caribbean and the United States, demonstrating how instructors have inherited educational practices from the plantation and can push back against these in the classroom. Next, Steve D. Mobley Jr. et al. draw attention to the important point that white supremacy is not just a concern for TWIs. In chapter 3, the authors describe how the vestiges of white supremacy can be seen in institutions centered on Black education, making it possible for even our most revered HBCUs to uphold an anti-Black settler project. Finally, in chapter 4, Wilson Kwamogi Okello posits that education has been a training ground for submission and the passive acceptance of rules in society that prop up systems of dehumanization, oppression, and exploitation. He contends that the emergence of Black studies as an intellectual canon can be read as an act of insurrection—one that accounts for the legacy of violence inflicted on Black bodies while making room for the imagining of Black futures.

Taken together, the chapters in part 1 provide a historical overview and insight into theoretical groundings of the plantation politics framework. The chapters suggest that higher education operates as a system to maintain and perpetuate white supremacy and anti-Black racism as well as other forms of racial formation projects that subjugate Black people for capitalist gains. Moreover, they build a compelling argument for situating recent campus rebellions as an intentional response to the instruments of social control and exploitation employed by ruling elites in the academy.

Part 2: Institutional Rhetoric and the False Promises of "Diversity" and "Inclusion"

Another aspect of plantation politics that contributed to contemporary campus rebellions is a growing suspicion of diversity and inclusion (D&I) initiatives that are divorced from, or in conflict with, racial equity and racial justice goals. In part 2, the authors argue that diversity initiatives have been operationalized in a manner that positions the inclusion of Black people into higher education as a means to further the aims of whiteness and white supremacy. Oftentimes at the center of the false promises of inclusion are diversity workers—for example, staff at cultural centers and chief diversity officers, or faculty representatives on diversity committees. These individuals are required to provide disproportionate amounts of labor as they are exploited, and then punished and discarded for doing the work they were hired to do. Unfortunately, one consequence of the widespread adoption of diversity initiatives, such as inclusive excellence (IE), is that it allows universities (particularly TWIs) to move away from a focus on race and racism as a central component of diversity and inclusion efforts (Tuitt, 2016). Frequently, universities will focus on, and invest resources in, programming around gender, class, sexuality, or even diverse political ideologies at the expense of institutional change around race, racism, and white supremacy. The authors warn that if we are not vigilant, many will continue to be seduced by IE and diversity-driven initiatives that mask the plantation politics of representation, and become complicit in the management of difference and the suppressing of resistance. Additionally, in this context, D&I initiatives become a sort of Trojan horse that results in the exploitation and minimization of staff and resources that are theoretically supposed to help Black people successfully move in, through, and out of academic institutions.

Collectively, the chapters in part 2 highlight how diversity and inclusion efforts have become co-opted as sophisticated instruments of plantation politics that protect white interests and privilege. Universities advance D&I rhetoric while simultaneously limiting opportunities for real transformation. Armond Towns sets the conversation off in chapter 5, as he makes the case that D&I efforts function as a plantation politic in which Black folx are not included as promised in inclusivity policies. He describes how the interconnection between racism, capitalism, and higher education functions in ways that not only render D&I policies ineffective but call for an investigation of whether violence against people of color is necessary for the establishment and maintenance of US institutions, including educational ones. In chapter 6, Jesse Carr et al. further demonstrate the limits of D&I initiatives by suggesting that diversity efforts at TWIs are a means of branding and crisis management that seek to assimilate nonwhite folx into primarily and historically white spaces without disrupting institutional investments in whiteness. In these efforts, "diversity workers" are often exploited for the reputation and profit of the institution, even while their labor is framed paternalistically as a charitable benefit to those who exist at the margins.

The remaining two chapters in this part provide concrete examples of the ways diversity workers are potentially set up to be agents of plantation politics. In chapter 7, Frank A. Tuitt explores the eerie similarities between the contemporary chief diversity officer (CDO) and the plantation driver during slavery, highlighting the roles these two positions play in the management of Black people in traditionally white institutions. He argues that the CDO position is a descendent of the plantation driver, and as such has the potential to be complicit in the systematic and often violent dehumanization of Black and Brown people in TWIs. Toby S. Jenkins et al. expand this discussion of the exploitation of diversity workers by analyzing how cultural center directors create strategies to resist the subjugation of racially marginalized communities. The authors bring an intersectional analysis to plantation politics by highlighting the precarious position that women of color who serve as cultural center directors inhabit as they are expected to advocate for racially marginalized students in a manner that often results in their own marginalization. Overall, the four chapters in part 2 illuminate the limits of institutional diversity and inclusion efforts. They warn that if universities are not critical of their implementation of D&I initiatives, their programs intended to facilitate equality can actually act as barriers to antiracist campus environments and can reinforce whiteness.

PART 3: RESISTANCE AND REPRESSION: CAMPUS POLITICS AND LEGISLATIVE ACTS OF ANTI-BLACKNESS

As the national conversation about violence against Black people took center stage during the Movement for Black Lives, Black staff, students, and faculty increasingly aired their grievances and concerns on university campuses. Some expressed their frustrations not only with feeling unsafe but also with being viewed as responsible for diversifying campuses, then experiencing a lack of institutional support once those efforts challenged the status quo. Campus rebellions grew, and university administrators and local government officials became fearful in the face of being held accountable for institutional racism. Demands from young leaders organizing a national movement scared board members and various stakeholders concerned not only with campus safety but also with university reputations and ranks. A series of campus policies and legislative acts were revisited or newly instated in an attempt to extinguish the tensions.[16]

A recent report by the American Council on Education (2016) noted that a climate of fatigue develops as racially marginalized peoples expend significant emotional and physical labor to respond to campus needs during a racial crisis. The report acknowledges that often this labor exists outside of explicit job responsibilities, and the feelings of fatigue are greater when this labor does not result in any significant change nor is valued by campus leadership. Correspondingly, Black people who experience racial battle fatigue are frustrated, shocked, angry, filled with anxiety, and at times feel a sense of hopelessness with each new racist incident. According to Phanuel Antwi (2018), Black folx at TWIs are prone to attacks because their praxis, their work, and the very presence of their Blackness challenges white security, and they carry burdens white people are never called upon to bear. Consequently, when Black people advocate for racial equity they are often subject to intense inaction or backlash—a sort of fragility in which there is a breakdown in the social contract (acceptable rules of engagement) with the institutions they attend or work (Lindborg, 2017). Many times this institutional fragility results in a set of intentional, strategic, and systematic measures to repress campus resistance and reinforce whiteness. Thus, the chapters in part 3 bring us full circle to the reality that any attempt to disrupt plantation politics—business as usual—will frequently result in institutional responses to repress rather than engage campus resistance.

Buttressing many of the arguments presented in the preceding chapters, the authors in this part fortify the notion that the modern-day university is influenced by white supremacist colonial and capitalist ideologies that are central to its existence. However, they extend the analysis to the reality that when rebellions push universities to transform into more racially inclusive and equitable campus environments, instead of acquiescing, an institution will resist, sometimes doubling down on its resolve to be what it has always been. As an example of this, in chapter 9, Kristi Carey offers a case study of the University of Missouri, arguing that universities are historicopolitically mapped geographies of white supremacy, racial capitalism, and global imperialism, and as such respond to student activists by attempting to sanitize their movements. She suggests that student movements need to be understood in their own multiplicity, as encounters with the university that are always active within and against the violent colonial histories of the plantation that haunt their existence.

Chapter 10 continues the discussion of the university's struggle with its colonial past as R. Eric Platt et al. examine Lost Cause (Confederate) icons on Southern campuses. The authors draw attention to some of the complexities of dealing with plantation pasts as TWIs seek to respond to protests and assuage concerns regarding Confederate memorabilia but are reluctant to do so out of fear of the potential legislative backlash or the loss of support from wealthy white alumni and influential political figures. In chapter 11, Kevin J. Bazner and Andrea Button reveal that as TWIs face more criticism from policymakers for their inability to manage campus rebellions, legislative proposals have been introduced to regulate student protest and control institutional responses to racist speech. They compare these recent legislative proposals to earlier attempts in which plantation owners and political leaders designed "slave codes" to maintain social control and prevent resistance among enslaved and freed Black persons. Finally, in chapter 12, Orisanmi Burton posits that in this current context of plantation politics, universities and prisons include an assemblage of ideologies and social practices that maintain racial capitalist systems that exploit the labor of racially marginalized people. As a result, he declares that student activists must develop a Black political literacy that enables them to navigate these oppressive politics and write alternative scripts that imagine and enact Black liberatory futures.

Cooperatively, the chapters in part 3 reveal the third instrument of plantation politics to be the mode in which campus administrators and state politicians use policies, practices, and legislation to repress campus rebellions. Whether it is out of fear of displeasing their alumni base or external stakeholders, universities often delay or resist doing the right thing, sending the message to Black campus community members that equity is not in the best business interests of the institution.

Overall, this book provides a conceptual framework illuminating three instruments of plantation politics that are prevalent in higher education institutions today.[17] All three instruments require a critical understanding of how white supremacy, colonialism, capitalism, and anti-Blackness are fundamental to the current day-to-day operations of the university. Regarding the first instrument of plantation politics, the authors direct change agents to recognize how education continues to be a vehicle of social control that results in the dehumanization, oppression, and exploitation of Black people. The second instrument highlights how diversity and inclusion efforts often function as institutional mechanisms that center and reinforce whiteness, while simultaneously protecting universities from critics concerned with the lack of progress. Finally, the third instrument shows how educational institutions and local governments use policies and legislation as tools to repress and dismantle rebellions when Black campus community members experience a racial crisis and organize around their anger, frustration, and distrust with the university.

Conclusion

While the contributors in this volume address a variety of important issues, including police violence, campus climate, pedagogy, and diversity initiatives, there are of course themes and topics that are not included. Productive dialogues about pertinent issues such as academic freedom, freedom of speech, unionization, abolition, the experiences of contingent faculty, disability and accessibility, and the role of international students as allies emerged as we presented on plantation politics at conferences and universities. Each time we presented, we said, "We hope you submit that proposal for the next volume!" Though a number of these pertinent themes are not discussed at length in the book, we hope readers will take up this framework and interrogate the connections between these topics and plantation politics in the future.

In particular, a gendered analysis of how plantation politics operate would be beneficial. A deep dive into the ways patriarchy and sexism work through plantation politics to uphold white supremacy would offer more insight into the gendered dynamics of higher education. Some of these issues include the disproportionate amount of emotional and pedagogical labor for which Black women are deemed responsible; patriarchy and misogynoir in administration and the classroom; #MeToo and sexual violence against Black peoples, especially Black women; feminist praxis and campus organizing; and the hypervisibility *and* invisibility of trans and gender-nonconforming folx within campus communities. Moreover, the relationship between Black women and white women at universities, and how they are differently positioned within these systems of power, should be interrogated.[18] In the past few years, scholars such as Daina Ramey Berry (2017) and Marisa J. Fuentes (2016) have written about the different monetary values white people placed on Black folx and their bodies during slavery, and how focusing on gendered experiences offers us greater insight into the ways white colonial power (in the United States and the Caribbean) operated. If our argument is that vestiges of this power still haunt higher education, then we must investigate how patriarchy is a prominent factor in the white supremacy that anchors these institutions of learning.

In spite of the reality of plantation politics, this book provides some insight into how Black change agents and their allies might begin to imagine emancipatory practices within higher education. For example, authors point to the importance of employing radical pedagogical frameworks that connect the mind, body, and soul. These transformative and inclusive pedagogies, combined with culturally relevant curricula, can lead to the creation of educational experiences that nurture Black people instead of dehumanizing them. Moreover, they make possible the opportunity for Black folx to possess the critical political literacy necessary to navigate the destructive instruments of plantation politics identified in this volume. Authors also call for an antidiversity movement in which universities move away from their false promises of inclusion and begin to reimagine new concrete modalities of praxis that result in racially inclusive and equitable campus environments. For this to happen, academic institutions will need to ensure that *all* of their employees, not just their diversity workers of color, have the capacity, skills, knowledge, and courage to support the development of antiracist campuses. Finally, this book indicates that if we have any chance of destroying instruments of plantation politics, campus leaders and external stakeholders must be dedicated to not repressing campus rebellions and instead must embrace the resistance as a diagnosis of what is not working—a beacon lighting the way to a more just and equitable future.

Plantation Politics and Campus Rebellions allows for a turning of the lens from those who are often marked as troublemakers, violent, problematic complainers to the actual institution and actors that perpetuate the issues related to inequities within the academy. Accordingly, we feel strongly that this book would be useful reading for current and future faculty, staff, administrators, trustees, policymakers, and other external stakeholders who have the ability to influence the upholding or disruption of plantation politics in higher education. University administrators could use this text to understand the larger historical factors that influence their campus's environment, while students could also understand the psychosocial and historical contexts for some of their experiences. State political leaders and systemwide chief diversity officers could glean the larger meaning of their surveillance and hiring strategies, including how Black people feel about safety and inclusion, and the ways that state policies influence university campuses. Alumni and other stakeholders could use the plantation politics framework to understand the implications of increasingly privatizing many aspects of education and creating long-lasting partnerships with private corporations that are also frequently in the business of exploiting Black labor. Finally, in our conversations with diversity workers at conferences such as the National Conference on Race and Ethnicity (NCORE) and the National Association of Diversity Officers in Higher Education (NADOHE), we heard from staff and teachers in K–12 schools that plantation politics was a framework also applicable to their environments, especially as one considers how school boards, private school trustees, and principals sometimes function within these institutions.

While we recognize the utility of change in individual action, we want to place emphasis on the call for new practices and policies that might lead to cultural and institutional transformation. Throughout our work together on this book, the editors and contributors recognized that even among ourselves there was a wide range of desired strategies and practices for changing higher education—including calls for everything from reform to abolition. As texts such as *The Third University* (la paperson, 2017) and *The Undercommons* (Harney and Moten 2013) powerfully demonstrate, it will take extraordinary, paradigm-shifting thinking and action in order to create a new education system. This requires knowledge of the historical and current roles white supremacy and settler colonialism play in higher education, while pressing forward toward something that is beyond simplistic reform. By marking and disrupting plantation politics, we hope that readers follow the lead of some of the most dedicated activists and organizers within movements such as the Movement for Black Lives. The end goal is not to only diversify universities benefiting from plantation politics; the goal is to deconstruct, interrupt, and build something anew in its place that enables Black people to be free.

Once readers complete the book, we hope we can all engage in a long-term, vibrant discussion about some of the following questions: How can we shift from condemning Black campus activists and organizers to analyzing the impact of white supremacy and anti-Blackness in higher education? What do we see if we understand campus rebellions as moments for deep reflection and analysis of a university's purpose, an assessment of whether it is reaching its goals, and an opportunity to investigate if it is moving away from plantation politics? What role does the university play in the fight for equity and against racism if we understand how closely related to the plantation system it remains?

Black feminist geographer Katherine McKittrick states that "the legacy of slavery and the labor of the unfree both shape and are part of the environment we presently inhabit" (2013, p. 2). We cannot escape the hauntings of our history, particularly since it played such a foundational role in the processes and capital accumulation that enabled academic institutions to exist. McKittrick reminds us that not only are plantation roots significant in understanding how power currently operates but that it is also essential to remember the multiple forms of resistance and acts of survival that Black people in these environments generated. We are the ones who can carry that work forward, and a plantation politics framework may help us identify the steps required. For, as Derrick Bell (1992/2018) reminds us, the mission is to "carve out a humanity. To defy the murder of selfhood" (p. 197). To get ourselves free.

Notes

1. We recognize that the "origin moment" of social movements are frequently highly debated, and it has been no different with the "Movement for Black Lives." We offer some insight into our framing of this movement later in the chapter. However, it is important to note here that unless indicated, when we reference the "Movement for Black Lives" we are speaking about more than the umbrella organization for 50-plus entities that formally came together in Cleveland, Ohio, in 2015. We are often referencing the events and resistance that stretched spatially and temporally from the killing of Trayvon Martin in Florida to Ferguson and the killing of Michael Brown to the international movement that manifested in various sites around the globe.

2. Shamell Bell, one of the leaders of the Los Angeles chapter of Black Lives Matter, wrote about the significance of joy, storytelling, and parenting in her dissertation on "street dance activism." In "Street Dance Activism: From Krumping to the Black Lives Matter Movement (2019)," Bell theorizes dance as resistance using footage of choreographed group dancing in protests in city streets and on UCLA's campus.

3. For further discussion of how the push and pull between student protests and the university can lead to social change and/or the perpetuation of inequity, see Demetri L. Morgan and Charles H. F. Davis's *Student Activism, Politics, and Campus Climate in Higher Education* (2019) and Roderick Ferguson's *We Demand: The University and Student Protests* (2017).

4. We found the community-sourced document created by senior slavery scholars titled "Writing about Slavery / Teaching about Slavery? This Might Help" (Foreman 2019) to be helpful as we discussed appropriate ways of naming various aspects of the institution of slavery and its actors throughout the writing process. The document offered great suggestions for language to both avoid and utilize, while teaching some of the racialized, nationalized, and gendered politics of multiple terms.

5. When we use the term "white supremacy" we are speaking about more than the racist stereotypes and rhetoric people often point to, such as that of the Ku Klux Klan or neowhite supremacists. Throughout the book, "white supremacy" references an entire system of power that controls economic, social, and political resources (often fueled by capitalism) and categorizes people and ideas based on a racialized hierarchy. It perpetuates the notion that whiteness is superior, and that which is closest to whiteness is best. Within this system, whiteness is

the (sometimes unspoken) norm, and those seeking to be included in campus community and culture must not call attention to the inequities and institutional violence white supremacy depends on. Anti-Black racism and white supremacy are often interconnected, with white supremacy deeming whiteness as powerful, and anti-Blackness marking the violence directed at peoples of African descent that is white supremacy's cornerstone. Throughout the text, contributors discuss how anti-Black practices and language are used by white people and folx of color to dehumanize and exploit Black peoples in order for the university to remain elite, exclusive, and profitable.

6. We use the term "folx" to be as inclusive as possible regarding gender and sexual diversity within Black communities, and to note the politics that surround gendered and sexualized identities. For us, "folx" points to queer, gender-nonconforming, nonbinary, trans, cis peoples, recognizing the different experiences and positionalities these communities and individuals have in relation to gendered and sexualized systems of oppressions, such as transphobia, heteronormativity, and heterosexism. It also emphasizes peoples marginalized by racism, and how their race influences their experiences of, and within, white supremacy. For a brief explanation of the term, read the description by the Radical Copyeditor (2016).

7. This is not to ignore his sexism, ableism, homophobia, transphobia, or xenophobia.

8. We recognize that those engaging in heated discussions about whether or not the prison industrial complex is a continuation of enslavement may have critiques of our framework also. But our experiences and observations of the tools university administrations used to shut down campus resistance during the Movement for Black Lives, the emotions and rhetoric expressed by university officials, and the types of violent environments activists endured pushed us to consider the potential relationship between this moment of white supremacy and previous ones. The system that saw our ancestors as inhuman, as only bodies for laboring and reproductive purposes, as a means to an end for profit, is connected to the one that teargases Black student activists, kills them for driving while Black near campus, and views their calls for equity as dangerous disruptions. Moreover, we recognize that a significant portion of the capital that helped establish academic institutions, and the policies of exclusion that were essential to them, were deeply rooted in plantation society. Here we seek to decipher how this history taints and acts as a motor for the contemporary life of higher education.

9. See concepts such as "intersectionality" (coined by Kimberlé Crenshaw), ethnographic methods for community engagement and social innovation, notions of interdisciplinarity, and the creation of new canons, such as critical race theory, hip-hop studies, and queer of color critique.

10. In honor of transparency and naming one of the positionalities she is writing from, it should be noted here that one of the authors of this chapter, Bianca Williams, was a cofounder and colead of Black Lives Matter 5280 (the

Denver chapter of BLM) alongside cofounders Amy E. Brown and Reverend Dr. Dawn Riley Duval, and 15 other committed organizers. The chapter was established on May 21, 2015.

11. Five years after the #FergusonUprising, Bakari Kitwana spoke with a few of the local activists to get their reflections on events and the personal and professional costs of organizing, including Traci Blackmon, Johnetta "Netta" Elzie, and Ashley Yates. Joshua Williams, a young protestor, is still serving part of his eight-year sentence for burglary and arson. Many Ferguson activists say Williams was given a disproportionate sentence for his crime in order to make an example of him and discourage other folx from protesting and organizing. Finally, at least six men who were active in Ferguson during the protests have been found dead—Edward Crawford Jr., Danye Jones, Deandre Joshua, Bassem Masri, MarShawn McCarrel, and Darren Seals. While some of these deaths have been ruled suicides, local residents believe that the deaths of these men are connected, and possibly punishment for participating in the uprising. Melissa McKinnies, the mother of Jones, who was found hanging from a tree in his yard, has been quoted as saying, "They lynched my baby" (Salter, 2019). These men paid the ultimate price for their activism.

12. For an idea of how campus rebellions such as the one in Ferguson help us reimagine these communities as resistance spaces, see Dache-Gerbino et al. (2018), "Re-Imagined Post-Colonial Geographies: Graduate Students Explore Spaces of Resistance in the Wake of Ferguson."

13. Bianca Williams was cofacilitator of this research team, while Dian Squire was one of the researchers. The website http://www.thedemands.org/ was very useful in this initial analysis, as it archived the demands of over 80 of the campus rebellions. While we never formally wrote up our findings from this preliminary team exercise, the review and assessment of these demands confirmed that our next step should be teasing out a framework for plantation politics. A study that offers useful analysis of these and other university demands during this period of protests is one by Hollie Chessman and Lindsay Wayt (2016) in "What Are Students Demanding?" Here the authors lay out seven major themes among student demands: reviews and revisions of institutional policies and practices regarding campus climate and diversity practices; more active participation by senior administrators in acknowledging institutional histories of racism and advocating for more effective diversity initiatives; more resources allocated for needs related to marginalized students; representation diversity across campus community; cultural competency or other diversity-related training for community members, including police; curriculum revisions or additions; and, finally, support services for marginalized students.

14. The American Council on Education reported that since 2016 there has been a rise in the number of incidents of hate symbols and verbal and physical abuse.

15. If one were to go to the *Journal of Blacks in Higher Education*, you would find a running list of recent racist incidents targeting Black folks in 2019, including "Black Doll Found Hanging from a Shower Rod in a Residence Hall at Eastern Michigan University" (2019, February); "Two University of Oklahoma Students in Blackface Post Video on Social Media" (2019, January); and "Vandals Deface a Memorial to Enslaved Black Workers at the University of North Carolina" (2019, April). See https://www.jbhe.com/incidents/.

16. Sports journalist Dave Zirin offers a great example of this when he writes about the state legislation that was proposed when Mizzou football team refused to play while demanding the resignation of systemwide president Tim Wolfe. State representative Rick Brattin proposed House Bill 1743, which stated, "Any scholarship athlete who refuses to play for a reason unrelated to health, shall have his or her scholarship revoked" (Zirin, 2015). In the article titled "'Plantation Politics': Racist Legislation Stalks the Mizzou Football Team," Zirin cites a football player who texted him, "We joke about the NCAA plantation politics but this wild. What's next? We lose scholarships if we go to a protest, or if we speak in class?"

17. While we have intentionally structured the book around these three facets of plantation politics, it is important to keep in mind that many of the chapters in the book touch on multiple aspects of the framework.

18. In chapter 6, Carr et al. examine (the lack of) solidarity between white women and women of color in campus communities, suggesting that within a plantation politics framework, white women are often tapped to function as contemporary "overseers" within university administrations.

References

Ahmed, S. (2012). *On being included: Racism and diversity in institutional life*. Duke University Press.

American Council on Education. (2016). Speaking truth and acting with integrity: Confronting challenges of campus racial climate. https://www.acenet.edu/Documents/Speaking-Truth-and-Acting-with-Integrity.pdf

Antwi, P. (2018). On labor, embodiment, and debt in the academy. *Auto/Biography Studies, 33*(2), 301–26. DOI: 10.1080/08989575.2018.1445577

Association of American Colleges and Universities. Making excellence inclusive. https://www.aacu.org/making-excellence-inclusive

Bell, D. (2018). *Faces at the bottom of the well: The permanence of racism*. Basic Books. (Original work published 1992)

Bell, S. (2019). *Street dance activism: From Krumping to the Black Lives Matter Movement* (doctoral dissertation). Accessed June 1, 2020, https://www.shamellbell.com/scholar

Berry, D. R. (2017). *The price for their pound of flesh: The value of the enslaved, from womb to grave, in the building of a nation.* Beacon Press.

Carruthers, C. (2018). *Unapologetic: A black, queer, and feminist mandate for radical movements.* Beacon Press.

Chessman, H., & Wayt, L. (2016, January 13). What are students demanding? *Higher Education Today.* https://www.higheredtoday.org/2016/01/13/what-are-students-demanding/

Coughlan, S. (2015, November 4). Students protest against tuition fees. *BBC News.* https://www.bbc.co.uk/news/education-34721681

Dache-Gerbino, A., Aguayo, D., Griffin, M., Hairston, S., Hamilton, C., Krause, C., Lane-Bonds, D., & Sweeney, H. (2018, March 9). Re-imagined post-colonial geographies: Graduate students explore spaces of resistance in the wake of Ferguson. Research in Education. *The Demands.* http://www.thedemands.org/

Du Bois, W. E. B. (1994). *The souls of black folks.* Dover Publications. (Original work published 1903)

Dumas, M. J. (2016). Against the dark: Anti-blackness in education policy and discourse. *Theory into Practice, 55*(1), 11–19.

Evans, D. (2010). *Before you suffocate your own fool self.* Penguin Books.

Ferguson, R. (2017). *We demand: The university and student protests.* University of California Press.

Foreman, P. Gabrielle, et al. "Writing about Slavery / Teaching about Slavery: This Might Help" (community-sourced document). Accessed June 1, 2020, https://docs.google.com/document/d/1A4TEdDgYslX-hlKezLodMIM71My3KTN0zxRv0IQTOQs/mobilebasic

Fuentes, M. J. (2016). *Dispossessed lives: Enslaved women, violence, and the archive.* University of Pennsylvania Press.

Harney, S., & Moten, F. (2013). *The undercommons: Fugitive planning and black study.* Minor Compositions.

Hartman, S. (2007). *Lose your mother: A journey along the Atlantic slave route.* Farrar, Straus, and Giroux.

Hauser, C. (2016, September 23). "Fees must fall": Anatomy of the student protests in South Africa. *New York Times.* https://www.nytimes.com/2016/09/23/world/africa/fees-must-fall-anatomy-of-the-student-protests-in-south-africa.html

Hawkins, B. (2010). *The new plantation: Black athletes, college sports, and predominately white NCAA institutions.* Palgrave Macmillian.

Herschthal, E. (2017, March 23). The missing link: Conservative abolitionists, slavery, and Yale. *The African American Intellectual History Society's Black Perspectives.* https://www.aaihs.org/the-missing-link-conservative-abolitionists-slavery-and-yale

I, Too, Am Harvard. (2014, March 1). A photo campaign highlighting the faces and voices of black students at Harvard. Retrieved from https://itooamharvard.tumblr.com/

Jordan, C., Mount, G. E., & Parker, K. (2017, May 22). A case for reparations at the University of Chicago. *The African American Intellectual History Society's Black Perspectives*. https://www.aaihs.org/a-case-for-reparations-at-the-university-of-chicago/

Journal of Blacks in Higher Education. (2017) Many instances of racial hate on college campuses. *Journal of Blacks in Higher Education*. https://www.jbhe.com/2017/09/many-instances-of-racial-hate-on-college-campuses/

Khan-Cullors, P., & Bandele, A. (2018). *When they call you a terrorist: A Black lives matter memoir*. St. Martin's Press.

Kitwana, B. (2019, August 9). Message from the Ferguson grassroots: 5 years after Michael Brown's death. *Colorlines*. https://www.colorlines.com/articles/message-ferguson-grassroots-5-years-after-michael-browns-death

la paperson. (2017). *A third university is possible*. University of Minnesota Press. https://manifold.umn.edu/read/a-third-university-is-possible/section/ba50806d-ff18-4100-9998-784aecb42ae4

Lindborg, N. (2017, July 31). Handle with care: The challenge of fragility. *Brookings Institute*. https://www.brookings.edu/research/handle-with-care-the-challenge-of-fragility/

McKittrick, K. (2013). Plantation Futures. *Small Axe, 17*(3): 1–15.

Morgan, Demetri L., & Davis III, Charles H. F. (2019). *Student activism, politics, and campus climate in higher education*. Routledge.

Movement for Black Lives. (2017). Platform. https://policy.m4bl.org/platform/

Patton, L., & Njoku, N. (2019). Theorizing black women's experiences with institution-sanctioned violence: A #BlackLivesMatter imperative toward black liberation on campus. *International Journal of Qualitative Studies in Education, 32*(9), 1162–82.

Radical Copyeditor. (2016, September 12). Ask a radical copyeditor: "Folx." https://radicalcopyeditor.com/2016/09/12/folx/

Robles, F. (2017, May 25). Puerto Rico's university is paralyzed by protests and facing huge budget cuts. *The New York Times*. https://www.nytimes.com/2017/05/25/us/puerto-ricos-university-is-paralyzed-by-protests-and-facing-huge-cuts.html?login=email&auth=login-email

Rushin, D. K. (1981). The bridge poem. *History is a weapon*. https://www.historyisaweapon.com/defcon1/thebridgepoem.html

Salter, J. (2019, March 18). A puzzling number of men tied to the Ferguson protests have since died. *Chicago Tribune*. https://www.chicagotribune.com/nation-world/ct-ferguson-activist-deaths-black-lives-matter-20190317-story.html

Sharpe, C. (2016). *In the wake: On blackness and being*. Duke University Press.

Taylor, K.-Y. (2016). *From #Black Lives Matter to Black liberation*. Haymarket Books.

Thomas, D. (2016). Time and the otherwise: Plantations, garrisons and being human in the Caribbean. *Anthropological Theory, 16*(2–3), 177–200.

Tuitt, F. (2016, Spring). Making excellence inclusive in challenging times. *Liberal Education, 102*(2), 64–68.

Woodson, Carter G. (2011). *Miseducation of the Negro*. Tribeca Books. (Original work published 1933.

Zirin, Dave. (2015, December 15). "Plantation politics": Racist legislation stalks the Mizzou football team. *The Nation*. https://www.thenation.com/article/archive/plantation-politics-racist-legislation-stalks-the-mizzou-football-team/.

Part 1

Capitalism and Colonial Vestiges of White Supremacy in Higher Education

Chapter 1

Framing Plantation Politics

*Allochronism's Pull on
Contemporary Formations of Higher Education*

DIAN D. SQUIRE

In the newest edition of *Critical Race Theory in Education*, Garret Albert Duncan (2017) wrote, "Contemporary forms of racial oppression and inequality are expressions of allochronic discourses that inform 'ontological Blackness,' or the Blackness that whiteness created as Western civilization began to emerge as a prominent force in the world" (p. 67). Allochronism rejects the contemporaneous existence of object and subject, and therefore places the object in another time. That is to say that Black people are seen, understood, and treated by others as existing in a space that is not contemporary but rather situated in material and nonmaterial realities of time and place as originally defined by their captors centuries ago. In essence, Black people are seen as savage, and nonhuman, and having a "debilitated mental capacity" (John, 1999, p. 45). As a result, the policies, programs, and realities of today's white supremacist society act and reproduce in accordance to the racist epistemologies of another.

Duncan brings this anthropological concept into the educational fold to provide us an apt language to explore the phenomenon more clearly. The goal of revealing and critiquing allochronism is to bring into better alignment time and place, or coevalness. The project of a plantation politic is to define the ways in which the organization of a plantation society instructs higher education as a system to maintain and perpetuate white supremacy and anti-Black racism as well as other forms of racial formation projects that subjugate people of color.

As Bianca Williams, Frank Tuitt, and I (2018) wrote previously:

> The vestiges of those colonial, imperialist mindsets still exist in the many "neos," that scholars and experts speak of today, namely, neoliberalism, neoconservativism, neocolonialism, and neofascism. Each has transformed across time (indubitably appropriating the preface neo-) and continue to influence policy, behavior, and culture within the United States. . . . Furthermore, they are connected to the many ways in which universities reach beyond borders and engage in economic globalization. Recently, The Movement for Black Lives and the Indigenous communities that organized at Standing Rock repeatedly made visible the legislative and economic linkages between the not-so-long-ago past and the colonial and imperialist present. We follow the lead of these organizers, arguing that the institutional logics of colonialism and imperialism—which were essential to the establishment of this country, and led to the creation of plantations and the enslavement of Black bodies—exists within our higher education institutions today. (n.p.)

A project such as this allows one to begin to paint parallels between time and place and illuminate the ways that allochronism works to make normal the dehumanization of Black people in modern times. Craig Steven Wilder (2013) provided us with an extensive history of the ways that higher education was quite literally built on the backs of Native peoples and enslaved Black people starting in the 1600s (this book should be required reading for all students of the field). Wilder (2013) wrote that "colleges were imperial instruments akin to armories and forts, a part of the colonial garrison with the specific responsibilities to train ministers and missionaries, convert indigenous peoples and soften cultural resistance, and extend European rule over foreign nations" (p. 33). This project is not an extension of Wilder's but rather an epistemological exploration of the ways that anti-Black racism of the 1600s and beyond continues to poison the waters of today's colleges and universities.

Katherine McKittrick (2013) called the plantation the "ongoing locus of anti-Black violence and death that can no longer analytically sustain [dehumanizing violence]" (p. 2) and posited that a "spatial continuity between the living and the dead, between science and storytelling, and between past and present" (p. 2) exists and must be "unearthed" in an effort to restore Black people's respect, dignity, and humanhood. In her formation of a "Plantation Future," McKittrick (2013) argued that the linkage between Blackness, violence, and resistance to dehumanization has always been present and continues to exist today in racialized geographies. In her analysis of these "racial geographies" (p. 3), the "socioeconomic logic of plantocracies" (p. 3) transcends the time of the enslaved Blacks' emancipation and creates racist anti-Black logics that infuse contemporary society ideologically and materially. Additionally, it creates what is understood to be normal; this normality is not linked to Blackness. With normal comes its antithesis, abnormal, deviation, and aberration. Through this lens, one may explore the role of historically Black colleges and universities and how their racial geographies link to a plantation politic, as Steve Mobley Jr. et al. do in chapter 3.

The project of white supremacy in this country, and globally, was born out of colonial competition between European nation-states. This project aimed to extend religious rule, build economy, and redefine politics based in Machiavellianism that defined "state" as a "sovereign body politic ruled by a government exerting definite power over its people" (Dessens, 2003, p. 9). This project is multimodel and mobile, thereby integrating itself in a variety of institutions, including universities.

The globalized capitalism that created colonial structures around the world has transformed itself into what may now be encapsulated by the term "neoliberalism." And much like the capitalism of early times, neoliberalism is inextricably linked to racist ideologies that work to exploit Black bodies in the name of economic production and excellence, including on the college campus (see Hamer & Lang, 2015; Osei-Kofi et al., 2013; Squire et al., 2018). In their exploration of structural violence, Jennifer Hamer and Clarence Lang (2015) identify the "conditions and arrangements embedded in the political and economic organization of social life that cause injury to individuals and populations or put them in harm's way" (p. 899). Neoliberalism as a set of ideologies, practices, and policies that leverage a free market, privatization, co-optation of diversity, profit-driven culture, an erosion of public goods, and an increase of contingent labor degrades the potential for the liberatory possibilities of education and creates a dependency culture, or involuntariness of membership, by restricting the option of leaving the system and imposing consequences on those who try (Wilson Okello discusses as much in chapter 4; Giroux, 2002, 2015a; Hamer & Lang, 2015).

Unlike slave plantations, which created conditions that restricted movement outside of the boundaries of property, modern universities create the circumstance that socially stratify, ostracize, and minoritize those who leave its system. The long-running narrative of education as the great equalizer and a necessity for upward mobility implores anybody wishing for "'success'" to engage the university and makes one a slave to "anyone who would feed them" (Morgan, 1972, p. 11). "Them" in this case being the university as a place that defines itself as the only place that can provide higher learning, thereby creating a dependence on the University (capital U, a system). Those who leave the system are made to believe that they cannot succeed (and they might not); but the narrative prescribes only one pathway of purpose and success, and makes one believe that one is not enough without it. The university is a technology of domination in this case, a domination that is then internalized (Foucault, 1977), normalized, and defined and redefined as an economic driver of this country. As Cheryl Matias (2015) wrote about faculty of color in a "neoplantation" state, "Under the surveilling eyes of the college's administration, like trained dogs we are expected to bark a false truth about the romance of being faculty of color in the academy" (p. 60). The false truth is rooted in the involuntariness of membership.

This dependency must be maintained in order to reproduce and grow the academic enterprise, including the academic-capitalist knowledge-regime (Cantwell & Kauppinen, 2014; Slaughter & Rhoades, 2004), the military-industrial-academic complex (Giroux, 2015b), and, most glaringly related to Black bodies, the athletic-industrial complex (as an example of modern day slavery; Hawkins, 2013), and must be maintained by larger social systems that strip people of their opportunities for upward social mobility economically and social stratification racially. Beverly John (1999), in her analysis of slave plantations, noted that white people created a hegemonic understanding of "the power of the slaveholding planter class to construct reality in a fashion that justified their every action" (p. 45). In this example, the slaveholding planter class is the university, and its actors and their construction is the narrative linking prosperity to university. This is to say that the parallels that are drawn within this book do not explicitly derive themselves from the physical manifestations of plantations but rather from the paradigmatic threads that run across time and space. It is the sinews of that anti-Black racism that continue to structure the web of neglect, exploit, hate, death, pain, and fear for people of color widely and Black people specifically.

At this point, I must acknowledge that this book will not spend significant time discussing plantations in the Caribbean or South America (outside of Saran Stewart's chapter); however, it is important to recognize that the trade of Black people is the beginning of modern capitalism and the global economic market (see Dessens, 2003; Mintz, 1969; Morgan, 1972; Trouillot, 2016). We recognize that economics, politics, social norms, imaginings, and even emotions (e.g., longing, trauma, fear, sadness) are diasporic and transnational and cross and transcend (ever-changing) imagined national boundaries. Enslaved Africans were aware of this in ways that the white people who captured them were not, as Africans were forced to imagine, yearn, fantasize, and create culture across national boundaries, from Africa to the Americas, and throughout the Middle Passage. The structures, traditions, and cultures that were created and institutionalized on US plantations were influenced by the cultures, traditions, and structures that took place on plantations in the Caribbean and South America. These plantation locales were not completely separate. While they were distinct, they were also interconnected. Culture and power are not bounded entities, and all involved became ever more aware of this. These realities are true today in our globalized world and on our internationalized campuses.

For example, policies and legislation that influenced how US plantations operated were influenced by the fear white people had about the possibility of the Haitian Revolution happening in the United States. Enslaved Africans freeing themselves in Haiti led to changes in strategy and policies in the United States (such as miscegenation laws, and laws around literacy/education), particularly in the South, where white plantation enslavers were afraid of insurrection and rebellion, a major theme and site of analysis of this book. And enslaved Africans on these Southern plantations heard the rumors of this Haitian Revolution and reimagined their own plantation lives with the knowledge of this case study in rebellion. This might parallel the ways that contemporary campus rebellions in South Africa, Puerto Rico, Colombia, Brazil, Argentina, and the United States are connected, particularly as the neighborhoods surrounding these campuses engage in Black Lives Matters protests against police violence and state-sanctioned violence (Maira & Sze, 2012). In discussing transnational coordinated responses to rebellion, these rebellions are reactions to "contemporary globalization of policing as a technology of repression that is part of the transnationalization of the security state apparatus in which models of securitization are shared and developed collaboratively among repressive nation-states" (p. 324). While the language and culture of protests and resistance on college campuses in the United States may be distinct (particularly with respect to a US brand of racial politics), the ideologies, strategies, and imaginings of rebellion and resistance are interconnected. The neoliberalism that runs rampant in US institutions is also at the heart of many of the plantation politics that are at play in these other countries, even if they are different forms of plantation politics (Squire et al., 2018). The globalization of higher education and the labor exploitation of people of color for capitalistic gain is undoubtedly a legacy of a plantation politic (Maira & Sze, 2012; Lee & Rice, 2007; Squire, 2019).

Additionally, we must acknowledge the fact that people of color (as an entire community) are being exploited by institutions, and that plantation politics puts a particular emphasis on anti-Black racism. Despite the ways that people of color individually and collectively are subjugated, there is an underlying foundation to these forms of racism that are built upon anti-Black racism. For example, OiYan Poon et al. (2015) explored the ways that the model minority myth is a tool of anti-Black racism utilized as a racial wedge to uphold white supremacy and maintain Black oppression. In my work with multiracial students and their desires for acceptance by both white and racially minoritized group, colorism and phenotypic superiority are all based in the need to be seen as both white enough and Black enough, for example, a harkening to ongoing racial formation project based in white supremacy and the subordination of Black people (Omi & Winant, 2014). So, while all people of color are exploited and oppressed, they are experiencing these oppressions differently in relation to anti-Black racism, which is essential to an understanding of plantation politics. This is not to say that an oppression Olympics must ensue; rather, there is a contested racial hierarchy, and the analysis of the ways racialized oppression operates in higher education requires a focus on the Black experience in relation to the plantation system. The buying and selling of Black bodies, the extraction of their labor, the constant threat of Black death, and the fear of Black resistance are central to plantation politics, which is different (and yet not more important), for example, than the colonization, displacement, and genocide of Native Indigenous peoples who helped build some of the first universities some of whom were slave-holding themselves, complicating a racialized and classed society (Durant & Moliere, 1999).

In the next section, I spend some space exploring the characteristics of plantations as systems and begin to connect the lines between historic plantations and modern universities in order to support the reader in their conceptualizations of contemporary institutions under this framework. This is not meant to be a deep, or even complete, dive into the framework, but rather a jumping off point for the rest of the authors to construct their analyses. Elinor Miller and Eugene D. Genovese (1974) urge us to recognize the technologies of domination of the past in order to deconstruct the technologies of the present and to test our understandings of plantation life. An explication of the system allows for an apt foundation to engage those understandings.

Plantation as System

As hinted earlier, plantations existed differently depending on size and demography of plantation, slave population, topography, culture (e.g., management style), geography, crop, local culture, and colonial rule (Dessens, 2003; Durant, 1999; Miller & Genovese, 1974; Pargas, 2010). This is not unlike the university system. Therefore, the purpose of this section is not to explain all plantations but rather to explore the characteristics of the system as a whole.

Importantly, the university can be defined as a city in and of itself, and thereby understood as having a defined economy, much like plantations were microcosms of a broader burgeoning republic. Plantations had homes (residence halls), offices (main administration and academic buildings), barns, pastures, and crops (agriculture, particularly at land grant institutions), kitchens (dining halls), and gardens, among other entities. Universities are also linked to major economic structures outside of campus, such as other forms of commerce and corporation, and are part of a broader statewide, nationwide, and worldwide enterprise. McKittrick (2013) argues that this is important to keep in mind that it "compels us to think about the ways the plantation became key to transforming the lands of no one [Native lands] into the lands of someone [white elites], with Black forced labor propelling an economic structure that would underpin town and industry development" (p. 8). As such, she argues that the racial economy is linked to an agricultural, industrial, transportation, religious, and labor economy. Schools such as Georgetown, Yale, the University of Georgia, and others have begun to quite literally dig up skeletons of the past in order to explore the linkages of their schools to the slavery. I argue that the university is a machine of the racial economy.

The plantation as a social system, as defined by Thomas J. Durant Jr. (1999), is an "orderly and systematic social unity composed of identifiable and interdependent parts (social structure) and social processes" (p. 5). Born out of economic, cultural, and political "necessity," as defined by multiple waves of colonial rulers, slave plantations burgeoned to maintain colonial dominance at the sake of Black humanhood and body. This social system, perpetuated for decades, may be defined as one of the origins of race relations in the United States (Durant, 1999), including white supremacy, interracial conflict, a white upper class, racial segregation, and the institutionalized racial norms that exist in higher education today.

Broadly speaking, Durant (1999) argued that slave plantations are characterized by (a) importation of Black Africans and social and physical control of those people by whites as fixed capital (Anderson & Gallman, 1977); (b) exploitation of labor by force, which resulted in acquired wealth, power, profit, and prestige for whites; (c) enslaved Black people as chattel property; (d) racialized caste systems with minimal chance of upward mobility; (e) a racially stratified division of labor with whites at the top and Black people at the bottom; (f) strict systems of governance that employ technologies of control; (g) "slave and non-slave subsystems, represented by emerging social institutions such as family, economy, education politics, and religion" (p. 5); and (g) a system requiring adaptation to internal and external forces. The parallels are incriminatory, and it is clear that plantation politics can serve as an apt framework from which to view the university.

STRUCTURAL ELEMENTS

In his work, Durant defines structural and social systems, and I aim to spend a little room exploring how each one might show up on today's campuses. Understanding the organization of plantations involves understanding nine structural elements.

Knowledge or the belief of what is thought to be true. At the basis of slave plantations was the ontological Blackness that Duncan (2017) described forming the widely shared understanding that whites were superior and that enslaved Blacks were subordinate property. Durant (1999) argued that plantations were the origins of race relations and governed these relations through mechanisms of control and pattern, thereby embedding within society a racial caste. This caste perpetuated the wealthy white elite and maintained a dehumanized and enslaved Black population. However, these beliefs were not without contradiction.

Beverly John (1999) called these contradictions the oxymoronic existence of whites. I write about how this plays out in another manuscript (Squire et al., 2018). On the one hand, whites treated enslaved Black people as inhuman, dangerous, and unintelligent, while on the other, they required enslaved Black people to care for children and family, tend crops (the white industry), and maintain house and home, keeping them at once distant ontologically but close physically. For instance, they made it unlawful to teach enslaved Black people how to read (keeping some families illiterate for generations) in an attempt to avoid repeating previous victories in effective strategizing and rebellion. Neoliberalism is also fraught with contradictions in theory and practice. For example, modern universities utilize bodies of color for economic gain through neoliberal ideologies that exploit image and likeness for the "smile of diversity" (Ahmed, 2012, p. 164; Hamer & Lang, 2015; Osei-Kofi et al., 2013) while at the same time calling them at-risk, marginalizing and ostracizing them, segregating their social activities, and using their labor in myriad ways with little recognition or remuneration. Therefore, in a current analysis of higher education, it is important to analyze both the ways Black communities are understood as being, what we know and think about Black communities, and the contradictory ways that we at once use them and also uphold them (albeit in limited capacities).

Sentiment or expressive feelings between two people. Some plantation enslavers expressed a paternal superiority over their enslaved, and enslaved Black people reciprocated via victimization and powerlessness or resistance (Durant, 1999). Paternalism in this case reinforced the fact that enslavers had goods and wares (e.g., clothing, food) that enslaved Black people were dependent on, and only by following the rules of the house could enslaved Black people receive these goods. Paternalism also manifested by breaking with the traditional cultural norms of maternalism under which many enslaved Black families operated (Jack Jr., 1999). This "non-violent form of social control" (Durant, 1999, p. 12) reified interracial dependence and destroyed independent forms of functioning and social organizing (including resistance).

We want to be clear that these "nicer" forms of coercion that were sometimes present on the plantation did not exist without more dominant forms. These paternalistic relationships still partnered within a more prominent context of punishment, torture, and "paternalism" that disciplined Black peoples with various forms of psychological terror as forms of "nonviolent" social control. This form of potential terror, punishment, and surveillance (or an offshoot of it) is still present in the academy, especially if one thinks of how campus police departments/security function in campus environments (e.g., the checking of IDs of Black folx, including staff/faculty) on campus to make sure they "belong" or the hyperpolicing of Black parties on campus. While the administration may make the rules and act out of paternalistic urges (as enslavers), the campus security act as enforcers who threaten with punishment, terror, and potential violence.

In today's universities, the overregulation of space, including policing for what purpose of use and at what times Black student groups can use facilities, and the increasing bureaucracy related to when and how one can organize on campus, may be seen as a form of social control. When administrators leverage their power by way of regulatory mechanism to reduce the ability for groups of color to organize while at the same time provide ample space for white groups (e.g., fraternities, sororities, guest speakers), they reinforce the racial hierarchy and interdependence of community to organization. Undoubtedly, many campuses utilize free speech as a way to reify whiteness as normal and paint those who are opposed to oppressive (psychologically and sometimes physically) violent hate speech as deviant in the name of "hearing from all sides." In these cases, it is often fear of reproach from dominant upper-class conservative whites in the media that works to maintain whiteness (and Blackness) as property (Harris, 1993).

Goals or the objective of slavery. Simply put, the goal of slavery was profit for the slaveholders. The goal of profit in higher education may be examined by institutional type, but it is inarguable that as state funding of institutions continues to decline, the role of grants, private donations, tuition dollars, and austerity measures to broader historically bestowed public good benefits (e.g., insurance and benefits, tuition remission) remains of great concern to administrators. These profits are seen through athletics and the massification of athletic sports, often through the exploitation of student-athletes (Hawkins, 2013) and an increasing push for international graduate student enrollment to the tune of $44.7 billion in 2018 (Institute of International Education, 2019)

Norms or the rules that govern and control behavior. The norms or rules of plantations maintained that enslaved Black people were not allowed to leave the land, and that they were to serve the enslaver. These two forms of controlled behavior reduced property loss and maintained social dominance. There were rules for particular groups of people, for instance, where certain people worked (e.g., women in the home, though not exclusively), and rules against insubordination or rebellion. As discussed earlier, the role of the success narrative in maintaining higher education as the sole source of upward mobility may be determined to be a normative control mechanism governing behavior. In thinking about faculty, systems and structures such as tenure and merit pay may be used to control behavior.

Status or position in a social unit. On plantations there were enslavers, managers, overseers, drivers, house slaves, and field slaves. Within these divisions one might expect to also find specific skills or traits that provided varying levels of freedom of movement. For instance, Black men were allowed to be drivers and would maintain the field slaves' labor while experiencing fewer restrictions. Some enslaved Black people held special skilled positions as carpenters or metal workers but remained diminutive in the power structure and certainly were not free.

Jack Feldman (2012) called the university the new plantation and defined various actors as such: for example, undergraduates as livestock who are raised and sold for profit. Keep them docile, he wrote, and they "fatten up nicely" (para. 8). Feldman laid out that research grants and contracts were crops, not the research itself, but the research that wins awards; faculty were sharecroppers; and graduate students were apprentices to the sharecroppers. One may take this position; however, I think it lacks the nuance required to truly analyze the plantation system in modern universities.

In a more succinct formation we might say that enslavers are boards of trustees; managers are executive administrators, including the president; the overseer is provost; the driver is chief diversity officer; house slaves are faculty and staff of color; and field slaves are students. As noted, each plantation existed as an individual entity, dependent on a variety of factors, and there are many different types of universities, including teaching and community colleges, thereby making the application of grants and contracts to crops, for instance, a moot parallel. In total, it is important to explore the threads of association and power between these varying levels of administration and community. I think it is also critical to examine the role of poor whites and other nonenslaved communities who interacted with plantations. For instance, what can an examination of the actions of Melissa Click, a white professor who placed herself in between journalists and Black students at the University of Missouri during the Concerned Student 1950 protests and had recourse taken against her by the university, tell us about the role white people played in supporting plantation uprisings? Richer white landowners would often buy the land owned by poorer whites in order to create distance between two groups (enslaved Blacks and poor whites), who may wish to rebel against an elite white class. Once again, what does a raced/classed analysis of racial solidarity tell us about the goals of current university actions in relation to deeply embedded racially classed hierarchies formed hundreds of years ago?

Rank or the arrangement of power into a social hierarchy. Rank refers to the power bestowed among the varying positions within the social order. Enslaved Black people were given differential power and prestige. Feldman (2012) recognized that not all students were crops, including those who received elite grants and scholarships. These might be known as the "good ones," while others are deemed "at risk" or "remedial." As a result, they are placed in special programs, to do special work to survive, sometimes on behalf of the university.

Durant and Moliere (1999), in exploring the relations between Native peoples, enslaved Black people, and whites, discuss the new racialized and classed hierarchies that formed as a result of white colonizing of Native peoples. In this analysis, they discuss a new racial hierarchy, with elite whites at top followed by poorer whites, "reds," and then enslaved Black people. This hierarchy existed dependent on tribe, but the fact remained that some Native tribes enslaved Black people as a way to survive in a new economy and engaged in whiteness to the extent that they were placed in a higher racial order than Black people. In a modern arrangement of racial formation, as discussed previously, Asian Americans were used as a racial wedge to maintain Black oppression at the bottom of the hierarchy, with Asian Americans existing just below whites (Poon et al., 2015). This is to say that an exploration of the placement of people of color in a hierarchy and the power afforded to some of them is of valid concern, especially as it relates to racial solidarity in campus rebellion projects against a unified white supremacist structure (Poon et al., 2017).

Power or the capacity to control others. Existing on an enslaver-to-enslaved continuum, power to control others most certainly existed in the hands of the enslavers, managers, drivers, and overseers. However, power could be bestowed on well-behaved Black people in the form of house slaves and most notably as drivers who controlled the plantations. But the power extended only so far. Ulrich Phillips (1974) wrote, "In frequent instances the financial interests of the master lay in giving his capable slaves as much industrial freedom as they could use; but it was a social necessity to keep under complete control every black who could possibly incite or take part in a servile insurrection or otherwise promote disorder" (p. 13). This meant giving enslaved Black people certain jobs or opportunities, but only enough as to not cause harm to the order of the plantation. It should also be understood that although whites had power of enslaved Black people, there were limitations to this power. Particularly, there was never enough supervisory oversight, the enslaver would resist killing his property by way of starvation or torture, the enslaver could make his enslaved Black people do only so much as he would like, and enslavers were often "too lazy, too stupid, or away too often . . . to maintain strict surveillance over their slaves" (Blassingame, 1972, p. 172).

Sara Ahmed (2012) discusses similar modern arrangements in her discussion of diversity workers on college campuses whose bodies exist only as racially diverse bodies of color to be used for profit. In existing as bodies to be utilized as an extension of the university through representative measures (e.g., brochures), the university then does not need to do equity work to improve the material conditions for those communities. That is, people of color who do the work of diversity (in student support services, as chief diversity officers, or others) have the freedom to do diversity as much as their bodies represent diversity externally (as a number or visual) but cannot do the work of diversity to change the system itself. One's being a Black driver does not give the driver power to change the system but only to give the hint of freedom while still being enslaved to the system. If drivers are chief diversity officers of color who act at once as representations of diversity, then they are asked to control the plantation, muffle campus uprisings, and put in place in menial programs and policies that do not change the nature of how the university operates but give a façade of change. Frank Tuitt explores this more in chapter 7.

Sanctions or the allocation given based on conformity or nonconformity. Sanctions exist as positive or negative allocations based on conformity to the rules. Enslaved Blacks are given either rewards or punishments.

Today's administrators often place "good" students of color in outward-facing opportunities to show the public that they appreciate diversity and that they have good Black people (Osei-Kofi et al., 2013). They are put on panels, in booklets, and on websites. This might also be the case with faculty or staff who do research in line with the outcomes and rewards of the university, namely large grant-funded research. Those who act out of line by way of rebellion or who publish or do work that is deemed too critical may be punished via forced solitude and marginalization within a faculty department or threat of loss of housing, enrollment, or engagement opportunity, among others.

Facility. These are the "tools and implements, land, labor, capital, and production strategies and techniques" (Durant, 1999, p. 6). In modern universities, land is often bought up and gentrified as a way to extend the reach of campuses (Hamer & Lang, 2015). Campuses engage in globalizing and neocolonial behaviors when they create extension campuses in other countries and teach only in English using US-centric ideologies. Corporations are invited to "sponsor" classrooms and athletic centers or research institutes (providing funds to the universities), in exchange for their brand and name on spaces of classroom learning or athletic profit. Other technologies of production are research grants and contracts, extension relationships, publications, and programming and services such as enrollment management functions. Labor, knowledge, and skills are explored later in this book.

Processual Elements

There are six social processes that I will explain briefly and provide a linkage to modern universities. Processual elements lay out the ways in which decisions are made, people are punished, communication is transmitted, and systems are maintained.

Communication or how information, decisions, or directives are transmitted. Certainly when Africans were first brought into enslavement, language existed as a barrier to communication. Over time, through force and learning basic language and then future education, enslaved Black people were able to communicate with enslavers.

As the British colonized the world, they spread the English language. English is utilized across much of the world and is considered dominant and necessary. It is normalized and associated with whiteness, especially "proper" or "academic" English. Modern-day language can be analyzed as the language of the elite, white, professional class. Accessibility to education and the rhetoric of the academy has often been a critique of the academy. However, in this social process, a more apt analysis probably requires critical discourse analyses of mission statements and diversity statements, campus email responses to critical racial incidents, and social analyses of interactions between administrators and communities of color to understand the ways that social control maintains whiteness and oppresses people of color and those who wish to dissent (Squire et al., 2019).

Boundary maintenance or attempts to protect the system from the outside. Boundary maintenance explores the need to preserve property and maintain a labor, knowledge, and skill supply. Two ways to analyze this function might be enrollment management functions around racialized bodies and diversity hires. That is, exploring the ways that people think about bodies of color are used in the admissions and hiring processes.

An example of this derives from the work around affirmative action as a policy implemented to atone for the generational disadvantages that African Americans experienced because of slavery. Unfortunately, affirmative action has been challenged or dismantled in many states through continued legal and social attacks removing its equitable potential. The contemporary admissions process on many campuses recruits Caribbean and African immigrant students in order to recruit more Black students, in many ways keeping out African American descendants of slaves. Because these immigrants are usually of middle-class status, and of a different relationship to the history of plantations and racism in the United States, it may be argued that they are recruited to provide phenotypic racial diversity, but stay invested in middle-class values that align with the university. Lani Guinier (2015) stated,

> Students at elite colleges, for example, who are the beneficiaries of affirmative action tend to be either the children of immigrants or the children of upper-middle-class parents of color who have been sent to fine prep schools just like the upper-middle-class white students. The result? Our nation's colleges, universities and graduate schools use affirmative-action-based practices to admit students who test well, and then they pride themselves on their cosmetic diversity. Thus, affirmative action has evolved in many (but not all) colleges to merely mimic elite-sponsored admissions practices that transform wealth into merit, encourage overreliance on pseudoscientific measures of excellence and convert admission into an entitlement without social obligation. (p. 23)

Additionally, one might examine how the removal of troublemakers by way of dissolving certain academic programs, particularly in the humanities and social sciences; the reduction of tenured faculty and the power they hold; the increasing fear of litigation against the university by way of dissident opinion; and the lack of hiring more racialized bodies in certain positions at the highest ranks may be of import. For instance, Ralph Anderson and Robert Gallman (1977) wrote that there was no need for slave "labor redundancy" (p. 38). Might this lead to having representation in one position, for instance chief diversity officer, being enough for the university to meet its visible quota and reduce the need for other people of color in high ranks who might disturb the system?

Systematic linkages or the way multiple systems are linked together. Durant (1999) wrote that systematic linkages are those that link together multiple plantations, exchange labor, techniques, management, and production to control enslaved Blacks. In higher education, the use of best practices, benchmarking, standards, and competencies all speak to institutional isomorphism. Additionally, neoliberal practices require the privatization of previously public services and goods, and on campuses has resulted in the outsourcing of campus safety, police militarization, housing, transportation, dining, and corporate partnership/sponsorship, among others. These can all be critiqued for the ways they continue to dehumanize Black bodies and communities of color (see Hamer & Lang, 2015).

Socialization or norm transmission. Socialization consists of processes by which people are acculturated to a system. This includes learning rules, roles, status, and culture of a plantation. Universities engage in these behaviors from the moment a prospective student visits a campus website, continuing through orientation and transition programming, which sets the norms for behavior on campus and presents students with rules and regulations for engaging in scholarly and social activity. As Feldman (2012) noted, graduate students are apprentices to their faculty and are socialized to engage in the structures of the university that privilege grants, scholarship, and service that profit the university system while dehumanizing and removing individuality from the student.

Social control or the way deviancy is eliminated, reduced, or rendered harmless. Slave codes, or rules and regulations against certain behaviors for enslaved Black people, were commonplace. Slave codes determined how, when, and if one was able to leave a plantation and for what purposes. This control of conduct was integral to maintaining order and minimizing the chance for rebellion. As Squire, Williams, and Tuitt (2018) wrote:

> Today, universities tout diversity and inclusion policies despite the continued cultural environments that perpetuate white supremacy and the dehumanization of people of color aptly rendering those policies powerless. . . . This is how neoliberalism acts as slave codes. Neoliberal action and policy—policy that is guided by economic interest and fierce individualism—determines the types of coursework Black faculty and staff teach on campuses (e.g., often "diversity" related) and the presence they hold (e.g., the "token" on committees, university marketing). This controlling of body and mind works through many mechanisms including alumni giving-power and scholarly publishing normativity (n.p.).

Anderson and Gallman (1977) also discussed the role of enslaved Blacks as "fixed capital" (p. 25), that is, capital that is not diminished as a result of the creation of a product. Fixed capital does not lose its value in the process of producing its product. If enslaved Black people are viewed as fixed capital, they can be purchased, leased, and rented, and are counted as assets in accounting of wealth. Therefore, it stands to reason that in order to get more product out of their enslaved, enslavers would not want idle hands or uprisings. Additionally, because the product was fixed and enslaved Black peoples' purpose malleable, they could be used to diversify outputs (Anderson & Gallman, 1977). Therefore, one can analyze the role of people as technologies, products, and diversified mechanisms of production such as student-athletes, the hyphen remaining an important signifier of both/and status in such that they both provide physical representation for neoliberal gains in the enrollment management process and create a multimillion-dollar athletic-industrial-complex on the backs of a predominantly Black body.

Institutionalization. Durant (1999) defined institutionalization as the "process through which organizations are made stable, persistent, and predictable" (p. 6). Institutionalization is the process of making ordinary the everyday events of an organization, including change. Therefore, making the abnormal normal, or the deviant normal, is encompassed under institutionalization. One can explore how the reproduction of education as an oppressive structure is reified in the tenure policies, the implementation on nonworking diversity programming, and the ongoing creation of diversity task forces and repetitive diversity actions that lead to little structural change.

Conclusion

If we look at campus environments through the structural and processual lens of Durant's slave plantation, this helps us better understand (1) the ways plantations and their communities are fundamental to contemporary iterations of organizations, namely universities by way of racial hierarchy, interracial conflict, white supremacy, and Black domination; (2) how the exploitation of the labor, knowledge, and skills of Black, Indigenous, and People of Color continues to be central to the economy of the university; and (3) how the vestiges of plantation culture and life influence modern university culture, climate, and structures of power.

Durant concluded that "many of the patterns of contemporary black/white relations, which still can be found in varying degrees in America . . . have their origins in the primordial slave plantation system. . . . The slave plantation left a legacy of race relations and social inequality that have shown remarkable resistance to change and, thus, helped shape and define contemporary patterns or black/white relations and social inequality" (p. 14). Using this framework, we are able to examine the interactions between institutional leaders and campus protestors (students, faculty, and/or staff) in order to understand the power differentials embedded in these interactions. We can explore how the technologies used to create plantation life are similar to those technologies used to sustain higher education institutions, and the ways these work to produce racial inequities and hostile racial environments that give rise to campus rebellions. Finally, we can better understand how employing control mechanisms that seek to repress campus rebellions may reinforce white supremacy, limit freedoms, and continue to oppress Black lives. While plantation life has been vigorously studied for its heterogeneity of system determined by geography, crop, individual slave owner, and time (Blassingame, 1972), there are broad commonalities and trends, much as there are broad characteristics and movements in today's higher education system. The nuance of place, time, and purpose opens up interstices for future exploration.

References

Ahmed, S. (2012). *On being included: Racism and diversity in institutional life.* Duke University Press.

Anderson, R. V., & Gallman, R. E. (1977). Slaves as fixed capital: Slave labor and Southern economic development. *The Journal of American History, 64*(1), 24–46.

Blassingame, J. W. (1972). *The slave community: Plantation life in the antebellum South.* Oxford University Press.

Cantwell, B., & Kauppinen, I. (2014). *Academic capitalism in the age of globalization.* Johns Hopkins University Press.

Dessens, N. (2003). *Myths of the plantation society: Slavery in the American South and the West Indies.* University Press of Florida.

Duncan, G. A. (2016). Critical race ethnography in education: Narrative, inequality, and the problem of epistemology. In C. K. Rousseau and J. K. Donner (Eds.), *Critical race theory in education: All God's children got a song* (pp. 65–86). Routledge.

Durant, T. J. (1999). The slave plantation revisited: A sociological perspective. In T. J. Durant & J. D. Knottnerus (Eds.), *Plantation society and race relations: The origins of inequality* (pp. 3–16). Praeger.

Durant, T. J., & Knottnerus, J. D. (1999). *Plantation society and race relations: The origins of inequality.* Praeger.

Durant, T. J., & Molier, N. (1999). Plantation slavery among Native Americans: The creation of a red, white, and Black America. In T. J. Durant & J. D. Knottnerus (Eds.), *Plantation society and race relations: The origins of inequality* (pp. 113–24). Praeger.

Feldman, J. (2012, August 20). *The new plantation.* Provocateur at large. http://www.provocateuratlarge.com/2012/08/the-new-plantation.html?showComment=1346258915425

Foucault, M. (1977). *Discipline and punish.* Random House.

Giroux, H. (2002). Neoliberalism, corporate culture, and the promise of higher education: The university as a democratic public sphere. *Harvard Educational Review, 72*(4), 425–63.

Giroux, H. (2015a). Democracy in crisis, the specter of authoritarianism, and the future of higher education. *Journal of Critical Scholarship on Higher Education and Student Affairs, 1*(1), 101–13.

Giroux, H. A. (2015b). *University in chains: Confronting the military-industrial-academic complex.* Routledge.

Guinier, L. (2015). *The tyranny of meritocracy: Democratizing higher education in America.* Beacon Press.

Hamer, J. F., & Lang, C. (2015). Race, structural violence, and the neoliberal university: The challenges of inhabitation. *Critical Sociology, 41*(6), 897–912.

Harris, C. I. (1993). Whiteness as property. *Harvard Law Review, 106,* 1707–91.
Harvey, D. (2005). *A brief history of neoliberalism.* Oxford University Press.
Hawkins, B. (2013). *The new plantation: Black athletes, college sports, and predominantly white NCAA institutions.* Palgrave Macmillan.
Institute of International Education (IIE). (2019). *Open doors 2019 executive summary.* https://www.iie.org/en/Why-IIE/Announcements/2019/11/Number-of-International-Students-in-the-United-States-Hits-All-Time-High
Jack Jr., L. (1999). "I looked for home elsewhere": Black Southern plantation families, 1790–1940. In T. J. Durant & J. D. Knottnerus (Eds.), *Plantation society and race relations: The origins of inequality* (pp. 77–88). Praeger.
John, B. M. (1999). The construction of racial meaning by Blacks and whites in plantation society. In T. J. Durant & J. D. Knottnerus (Eds.), *Plantation society and race relations: The origins of inequality* (pp. 41–52). Praeger.
Knottnerus, J. D., Monk, D. L., & Jones, E. (1999). The slave plantation system from a total institutional perspective. In T. J. Durant & J. D. Knottnerus (Eds.), *Plantation society and race relations: The origins of inequality* (pp. 17–28). Praeger.
Lee, J., & Rice, C. (2007). Welcome to America? International student perceptions of discrimination. *Higher Education, 53,* 381–409.
Maira, S., & Sze, J. (2012). Dispatches from Pepper Spray University: Privatization, repression and revolts. *American Quarterly, 64*(2), 315–30.
Matias, C. E. (2015). "I ain't your doc student": The overwhelming presence of whiteness and pain at the academic neoplantation. In K. Fasching-Varner, K. A. Albert, R. W. Mitchell, & C. Allen (Eds.), *Racial battle fatigue in higher education* (pp. 59–68). Rowland & Littlefield.
McKittrick, K. (2013). Plantation futures. *Small Axe, 17*(3), 1–15.
Miller, E., & Genovese, E. D. (1974). *Plantation, town, and country: Essays on local history of American slave society.* University of Illinois Press.
Mintz, S. W. (1969). Slavery and emergent capitalism. In L. Foner & E. D. Genovese (Eds.), *Slavery in the New World* (pp. 27–37). Prentice Hall.
Morgan, E. S. (1972). Slavery and freedom: The American paradox. *The Journal of American History, 59*(1), 5–29.
Omi, M., & Winant, H. (2014). *Racial formation in the United States.* 3rd ed. Routledge.
Osei-Kofi, N., Torres, L. E., & Lui, J. (2013). Practices of whiteness: Racialization in college admissions viewbooks. *Race Ethnicity and Education, 16*(3), 385–405.
Pargas, D. A. (2010). *The quarters and the fields: Slave families in the non-cotton South.* University Press of Florida.
Phillips, U. B. (1974). The slave labor problem in the Charleston district. In E. Miller & E. D. Genovese (Eds.), *Plantation, town, and country: Essays on local history of American slave society* (pp. 7–28). University of Illinois Press.

Poon, O., Squire, D., Kodama, K., Byrd, A., Chan, J., Manzano, L. . . . and Bishundat, D. (2015). A critical review of the model minority myth in selected literature on Asian Americans and Pacific Islanders in higher education. *Review of Educational Research, 86*(2), 469–502.

Slaughter, S., & Rhoades, G. (2004). *Academic capitalism and the new economy: Markets, states, and higher education.* Johns Hopkins University Press.

Squire, D. (2019). The neoliberal and neoracist potentialities of international doctoral student of color admissions in graduate education programs. *Philosophy and Theory in Higher Education, 1*(2), 29–53.

Squire, D., Nicolazzo, Z., & Perez, R. (2019). Institutional response as nonperformative: What

university communications (don't) say about movements toward justice. *Review of Higher Education, 42,* supplement, 109–33.

Squire, D., Williams, B., & Tuitt, F. (2018). Plantation politics and neoliberal racism in higher

education: A framework for reconstructing anti-racist institutions. *Teachers College Record, 120*(14), n.p.

Trouillot, M. R. (2016). *Global transformations: Anthropology and the modern world.* Springer.

Wilder, C. S. (2013). *Ebony and ivy: Race, slavery, and the troubled history of America's universities.* Bloomsbury Press.

Chapter 2

Plantation Pedagogies in Contemporary Higher Education Classrooms
Instruments of the Slave Society and Manifestations of Plantation Politics

SARAN STEWART

> He imitates as a monkey does a man . . . he is idle, unambitious as to worldly position. . . . Intellectually, he is apparently capable of but little sustained effort; but singularly, enough, here he is ambitious. He burns to be regarded as a scholar, puzzles himself with fine words, addicts himself to religion for the sake of appearance. . . . I do not think that education has as yet done much of the black man in the Western World. He can always observe, and often read; but he can seldom reason.
>
> —Anthony Trollope, *The West Indies and the Spanish Main*

Knowledge was and is espoused as a form of oppression, and for those who controlled knowledge, also controlled power. What would follow from this observation by Anthony Trollope (1860), a nineteenth-century English novelist, of the qualities of the emancipated West Indian Negro was the conclusion that "the white man is the god present to his eye, and he believes in him—believes in him with a qualified faith, and imitates him with a qualified constancy" (p. 57). Trollope later alludes to the fact that although religious education has done some good to "civilize" the emancipated Negro, there is no true understanding of the scripture because "what he lacks is a connecting link between these doctrines and himself" (p. 58). The connecting link Trollope failed to explain was the purposeful ideological severing of the Jamaican Negro from ways of truly knowing his emancipated self. The slave society model, using multiple tools of ideological, physical, and psychosocial dismemberment, perfected the art and process of conditioning the enslaved mind to be forever enchained, even centuries after Emancipation through education. I will argue in this chapter that the tools used and still practiced today are manifestations of plantation pedagogies.

The legacies of slavery and the resulting effects of colonial rule on the emancipated Negro led to the emergence of plantation pedagogy (Bristol, 2010) in which teaching was an inherited educational practice of oppression and subservience constructed out of the plantation society or plantocracy. Furthermore, the plantation society operated on plantation politics that provided a capitalist social oligarchy of governance, reinforcing the division of labor by race and gender for supply and production of agricultural profits. It was a society that resembled capitalist authoritarianism not by a single dictator but by multiple white supremacists parading as civilized entrepreneurs. As a framework, I argue that plantation politics is a product of Western colonization that provides a webbing of events, activities, theories, and concepts formed spatially and temporally, across geographical and sociopolitical eons that inform both the past and modern-day conceptions of power and status in society. For the purpose of this chapter, the framework informs the historical analysis of educational practice and the ways in which the relationship between education and plantation politics is replayed within contemporary higher education classrooms.

Accordingly, this chapter seeks to answer the following questions: How do plantation pedagogies function within the modern conceptualization of plantation politics in higher education? How can educators disrupt these forms of pedagogical oppression through radical emancipatory imaginings? To answer these questions, I present an educational critique of plantation politics to understand contemporary education practice, and forms of pedagogy in particular. The critique begins off the shores of the Caribbean and travels north to the United States. The chapter tracks the exportation of the slave society model from Barbados to the Carolinas. Thereafter, I juxtapose the past and present by exploring three forms of plantation pedagogies: (1) removal, isolation, and unlearning of the self;

(2) acculturation, adaptation, and survival lessons; and (3) resistance teaching, subversion planning, and emancipatory understanding. To disrupt these forms of pedagogical oppression, I argue for an emancipatory pedagogical matrix of the transgressional and transformational arts of teaching and learning. I argue for a typology of pedagogies that question the official hegemonic view of ahistorical educational change that teaches the collective power to overcome the inimical forces of capitalism and the commodification of one's soul (McLaren, 2016). Radical in nature and transformational in praxis, revolutionary critical pedagogy produces comrades committed to realizing "pedagogy as the practice for freedom" (Giroux, 2010, p. 715).

Slave Society Model

Plantations existed and still exist as both a reminder and as loci of oppression and resistance, spaces in which systems of subservience and subversion operated simultaneously. To better understand the plantocracy, the slave society model provides a historical, socioeconomic, and political guide to the proliferation of colonial white supremacy based on the plantation economy. Within a slave society, slavery forms the epicenter of the socioeconomic and political foundation of the society, in which social relations are codified through master-slave relations (see Berlin, 2003; Goveia, 1965). Unlike other colonial societies that had varying forms of servitude in which slavery was one, a slave society was predominantly dependent on enslavement for capital accumulation and colonial enterprise. By 1660, Barbados had become the first slave society in the Americas, not solely because of the population of enslaved people but because of the social and political governance of the society (Beckles, 2016). In 1661, the Slave Code was passed, providing a legal constitution for the slave society model. This act, titled An Act for the Better Ordering and Governing of Negroes, would later become the blueprint for other colonies to follow (Beckles, 2016). By all socioeconomic terms the model was very successful and provided England with a competitive advantage in the sugar industry. Hilary Beckles (2016) explains, "Sugar planters and large slave-owners constructed a complex legal system for public governance and an elaborate machinery for political administration. All of it was shaped by and infused with the needs of the slave economy" (p. 3). He goes on to further explain the philosophical underpinnings of the society, in which "the cultural and ideological forces that held the slave society together as a distinct civilization reflected a hegemonic white supremacy value system" (p. 3). By the end of the seventeenth century, Barbados was known as the leading sugar trader and had developed an effective labor supply chain model throughout British America (Beckles, 2016). It would only be a matter of time before other colonies sought to employ the slave society model and develop pockets of racialized chattel societies (see Beckles, 2016).

Exportation of the Chattel Model

In 1655 the British overthrew the Spanish in Jamaica, and in 1664, Sir Thomas Modyford arrived from Barbados as the new governor, and with him came a copy of the 1661 Slave Code (Beckles, 2016). In his first assembly, Modyford issued the Slave Code in Jamaica, and with it plans to scale up the slave economy. Throughout the seventeenth century, there was an increasing distribution of sugar exports from Barbados and Jamaica. By the eighteenth century, Jamaica had surpassed all other West Indian colonies in sugar exportation (Beckles, 2016).

Having mastered the implementation of the slave society model in Jamaica, the British looked north to expand their economic empire. However, establishing the slave society model in the Carolinas would take more time, resources, planning, and influence from the first knights of Barbados and investors from the Crown. By 1665 Sir John Colleton and Sir John Yeamans both allies and core financiers of Sir Thomas Modyford, would devise a plan to establish a Barbados-like settlement in the Carolinas. Yeamans was appointed lieutenant governor, and by 1667 had arranged for a fleet of settlers, including enslavers, enslaved Africans, and laborers, to arrive in the Carolinas (Beckles, 2016). Adaptations of the 1661 Slave Code would govern the new settlement and growing population of enslaved Africans. Between the 1690s and 1720s rice instead of sugar became the main crop, which led to the outnumbering of Africans to whites by two to one. This rapid shift created fear among the whites and led to stricter acts of punishment for petty crimes, namely murder. Based on control of power, wealth, and economic profiteering, the acts and legislations would be amended to benefit the planters, making it impossible for enslaved persons to understand and follow the codes. For the enslaved, life on the plantation depended on how well one could quickly acculturate and adapt to plantation politics.

Plantation Politics in Higher Education

Within British American slave societies, there were systems of governance that replicated those in England, such as the appointment of the governor to the Crown, his executive committee, the Most Honourable Privy Council, the House of Assembly, and so on. Mainly planters of large and small estates occupied government and parliamentary roles within the slave society, essentially forming an oligarchy system in which few possessed most of the wealth and power in society. Ironically today, we have substituted oligarchy for democracy and traded in the plantation mercantilist economy for capitalism, operating within the same political ideology that white supremacy serves as an ideological framework rooted in the minds of both the oppressed and the oppressor. White supremacy describes the system and series of (educational) practices, policies, and behaviors that reinforce oppressive hierarchical structures to subjugate racially minoritized persons (see Haynes, 2017).

Furthermore, plantation politics meant that legislations at large were written and voted in to satisfy the interests of the planters and their estates. Wealth, power, and influence were built on the backs of enslaved women, men, and children. Plantation politics was intricately intertwined within the psychosocial and economic fabric of the slave society in which owning enslaved people was not solely for the accumulation of capital but also for free Blacks to manumit their kin. It served as a path to emancipation from an oppressive chattel system. Free Blacks who understood and knew how to manipulate the system well could purchase businesses, small plots of land, and eventually their kin. Most notable is the case of Patience Graham, who was born enslaved but accumulated enough capital for self-purchase, and with her savings purchased several businesses (Beckles, 2016). Her children were born free. Although free, they were born within a system of plantation politics, a racist and sexist systemic web of power and oppression.

Plantation politics provided a bureaucratic blueprint for a racist, gendered, and sexist social class system: a system of hierarchical, race, and class stratification. This system created the conditions in which divisions between Black enslaved and free coloreds were based on education and class status. As Trollope (1860) wrote, "Both the white men and black dislike their coloured neighbours" (p. 73) because they sit at the governor's table and at the House of Assembly. Trollope further acknowledged the reason for the contempt between and within races by the levels of acquisition of education, civilization, and power. More specifically, he stated, "Those who are educated and civilized and powerful [i.e., coloreds] will always, in one sense, despise those who are not [i.e., Black]; and the most educated and civilized and most powerful [i.e., whites] will despise those who are less [i.e., coloreds]" (p. 74). Internalized oppression within and between races was a by-product of the system that suggested that Blacks and coloreds might gain some benefit if they rejected their own. Colonial whites had designed a system of institutionalized racism based on power, education, race, and sex that would transcend time and remain as a formidable force within modern-day British America.

A postsecondary critique of plantation politics informs an understanding that the systems of higher education, although built by enslaved people and the descendants of enslaved people, were not created with them in mind. And centuries of interloping identities have done little to help Black people to overcome and emancipate their minds but instead fall in line and remain complicit with plantation pedagogies at the peripheries of knowledge construction. Systems of higher education within British America originated from the Oxbridge structure of multiple colleges and faculties of disciplines. Some colonial institutions originated as offshore colleges of universities based in England, such as the University College of the West Indies, now known as the University of the West Indies. These colleges were controlled by their mainland institutions, and the approval of the syllabus, the administration of exams, and the conferral of degrees were managed by the host institution (see Hall, 1998; Stewart, 2013). Oftentimes these institutions serving in a majority Black populace would be in constant "political and ideological struggle for the soul of the university" (Howe, 2000, p. 15). The fact that some of these very institutions were bequeathed from former estate and plantation owners and established on former plantations provides a modern-day historical oxymoron. The very system of institutionalized learning and oppression was created on the lands of slave societies, and although higher education institutions operate today in an era of emancipation, most function within the principles of plantation politics. These principles include (1) the exploitation of Black labor, identity, and emotions at the expense of the self but for the economic benefit of the institution; (2) the institutionalized hierarchy and stratification of race, class, and gender that inform the climate and structures of power within the institution; (3) policy guidelines and regulations designed for and to reinforce the structure of power and wealth of an institution; and (4) the practice and reward of plantation pedagogy to support the ideological subservience of the plantation (i.e., the institution). Keeping with the purpose of this chapter, only the fourth principle is deconstructed in detail below.

Plantation Pedagogies as Instruments of Colonization

Plantation pedagogies, though born out of colonization, are heavily practiced and rewarded today in the form of higher education teaching, often disguised as institutional ideology, lectures, and tutorials. The resulting effects of colonial rule on the emancipated Negro led to the emergence of plantation pedagogy (Bristol, 2010) in which teaching in Trinidad and Tobago (and the wider Caribbean) was an inherited educational practice of oppression and subservience constructed out of the plantation society or plantocracy. Plantation pedagogy during colonization was a system of teaching and learning colonial practices and customs. For the whites, it was teaching order and control reinforced by legislation. For the enslaved, it was both teaching and learning how to survive, adapt, and resist within plantation life. Depending on the teacher, the lessons changed daily. This point is critical, as I will argue below that the first two forms of planation pedagogy were taught by white slave owners, and the last form by the enslaved. From the analysis of the slave societies and building from Laurette Bristol's (2010) seminal work in Trinidad and Tobago, plantation pedagogies have three main forms: (1) removal, isolation, and unlearning of the self; (2) acculturation, adaptation, and survival lessons; and (3) resistance teaching, subversion planning, and emancipatory understanding.

Plantation Pedagogy as a Form of Removal, Isolation, and Unlearning of the Self

The first form of plantation pedagogy was often taught by white enslavers through the ideological severing of the African from their continent, countries, tribes, families, language, culture, ways of knowing, and sense of self. The pedagogical practice of isolating enslaved Africans from their communal tribes was meant to ideologically suppress their minds, break their spirit, and in many ways strip them of an identity of their own. The regenderization or *seasoning* of the enslaved was purposeful for "the reproduction of the gender order" (Beckles, 1999, p. 9) to emasculate enslaved Black men; place Black enslaved women "at the head of the pecking order of human exploitation and subjection" (p. 40); revere white womanhood as "a symbol of white supremacy, moral authority, and sexual purity" (p. 7); and fear white men as the closest semblance and replica of God. Enslaved women and their bodies were a central edifice in slavery, more so the "using up of the body—day and night" (p. 158) at the pleasure, demand, and discard of Black and white men.

This form of plantation pedagogy was designed to be cyclical and have long-lasting, perennial effects. For example, the emancipated Negro was viewed by colonizers as stateless: "They have no country of their own . . . they have no language of their own, nor have they yet any language of their adoption for they speak their broken English as uneducated foreigners always speak a foreign language" (Trollope, 1860, p. 55). Trollope continues by stating that the emancipated Negro has "no pride of race . . . and no religion of their own" (p. 9). I argue that plantation pedagogical practices of removal, isolation, and unlearning of the self-contributed to the dehumanization and cleansing of the African identity from enslaved and emancipated persons, a severing practice that contributed to William Cross's (1991) modern-day preencounter stage of nigrescence model, in which attitudes and behavior "range from low salience to race neutrality to anti-Black[ness]" (Ritchey, 2014, p. 101).

Within Caribbean higher education classrooms, the first form of plantation pedagogies is experienced through the preencounter stage, tokenism, and invisibility syndrome paradigm (Franklin, 1999), whether by race, sex, or class. In particular, in the Caribbean, with a predominantly Black populace, "people do not acknowledge race as something that has affected their lives thus far" (Ritchey, 2014, p. 102). Students, being the first generation in their family to attend higher education, oftentimes from a lower social class and attending prestigious universities, grapple with a sense of belonging and questioning of their identity. The experience of leaving one's family and community for the first time to attend a university or college can lead to feelings of isolation and identity self-defamation, especially if those communities are laden with high incidences of violence, gross poverty, and poor living conditions.

In the context of the modern-day higher education classroom, the learning environment easily becomes a space for lecturers to intentionally or unintentionally sever students' ways of knowing and understanding. In these cases, students' experiential knowledge is seldom used within the learning space and curriculum, and students often piece and parcel themselves to suit or "fit in" to the classroom space. As Walter Rodney (1972) debated, colonial education at all levels serves the interest of the dominant class and co-opts the children of the exploited and oppressed classes. Some of these children grow up to be university lecturers and learn how to navigate and survive a system that was not designed with them in mind, often leaving that very system intact and whole.

Plantation Pedagogy as a Form of Acculturation, Adaptation, and Survival Lessons

The second form of plantation pedagogy, acculturation, adaptation, and survival lessons, arguably make up the most enduring pedagogical process to learn and master. These lessons focus on how to endure by subordination, not how to thrive. This form takes place after the enslaved have been broken in to the slave society, survived the passage, built up their immunity to the new diseased environment, and understood their newly adopted identity as subhuman: a slave. For example, Black enslaved women and their enchained wombs were forced to learn how to straddle two competing masculinities: the white hegemonic and the marginalized Black (Beckles, 1999). Black women had to understand that they were neither women nor were they human, as they were intentionally defeminized and their wombs were treated as rental properties to temporarily house future labor supply. Child bearing became so politicized that slave owners' natal policies were forms of torture for enslaved women in ways that Beckles (1999) states "historians may never comprehend" (p. 159). Arguably, this phase required a level of conscious numbing in which lapses in consciousness would have to take place in order to cope with the daily lessons of torture and the uncertainty of life. The barbarity of daily life enforced by slave codes made conformity a necessity to survival.

Even after the 1834 declaration of emancipation, the brutal and torturous crimes committed on apprenticed freed slaves were more heinous than during slavery. Historically, one can argue that white-interest convergence (Bell, 1980) started with the emancipation proclamation and the era of apprenticeships. As a condition of emancipation, there was an agreed-upon system of apprenticeship coupled with the compensation of labor losses to white plantation owners (Act for the Abolition of Slavery, 1833). Freedom of slaves was conditional, based on the compensation and power control of whites for years after. The implementation of apprenticeships was an incremental approach for white planters to continue their slave societies long after the emancipation proclamation. Apprenticed laborers or freed slaves would essentially succumb to inconceivably more brutal genocidal punishments than during slavery. For petty crimes, the correction (workhouse) house in Jamaica was used to punish and work apprentices who "walked" the mill while being flogged with the "cat." Important to note was the use of Negro overseers to inflict the floggings (Patton, 2001). The conditioning process of the apprenticeship period further forced freed slaves to adapt, acculturate, and engage in lessons of survival. Finally, the stratification of classes and oppressive roles within the Negro population further divided apprenticed populations and embedded an internalized oppression.

Bristol (2010), in her analysis of plantation pedagogy as a form of oppression, stated, "Consequently, plantation pedagogy as a form of oppression may serve as a therapeutic form of survival in a post-colonial society. The colonizing conditions which gave birth to this version of plantation pedagogy prevent the teacher from recognizing that she/he has become an agent of colonization" (p. 174). As an agent of colonization, the teacher most resembles an overseer who reinforces the ideological severing discussed earlier. Furthermore, the form of therapy described mimics how Caribbean academic staff acculturate in the region's higher education institutions. They must often code switch, assimilate, and become complicit to earn tenure and promotion, and to remain at the institution. Some lecturers, having been reared within the Caribbean higher education system, endured forms of what Lori Patton and Nadrea Njoku (2019) name as institution-sanctioned violence, in which institutional policies and practices reinforce and allow for epistemological, emotional, and psychological harm to persons within the institution. I have described (Stewart, 2019) a series of microaggressions that go unabated while navigating the Caribbean academy as an Afro-Caribbean female faculty. I argue that lessons of survival for Black, female academic staff who are also mothers include balancing motherhood, service, and research while never complaining. Because in predominantly heteronormative patriarchal societies such as those in the Caribbean, there is a common belief that a mother's primary responsibility is that of childbearing and household management. These intersecting identities, especially for Black women faculty, normally leave them at the "intersections of multiple oppressions" (Edwards & Thompson, 2016, p. 42) and in need of creating survival strategies. This form of plantation pedagogy is often didactic, sometimes punitive, and resembles what Paolo Freire (1973) terms "the banking system of education" in which students enter the learning environment completely empty to be filled by those knowledge elites. This form of pedagogy reinforces the status quo and the idea that knowledge starts with Western colonization.

Plantation Pedagogy as a Form of Resistance Teaching, Subversion Planning, and Emancipatory Understanding

The third form of plantation pedagogy differs from the first two, as it is taught for and by enslaved persons in a form of communal learning that attempts to disrupt plantation politics. In this respect, resistance teaching and subversion planning are made up of acts of purposeful opposition, in which enslaved persons would plan revolts, strategize forms of resistance, and collectively organize. Slave rebellions were common across the British Caribbean plantations, as enslaved Africans originating from the former Gold Coast (now Ghana) had an inherent warrior spirit (Mathurin Mair, 1975). Colonies such as Jamaica and Guyana, "each of which had a long history of black protest, also had a high percentage of Gold Coast people in their slave populations," amounting to 39 percent in the eighteenth century (p. 2). As a result, white planters refused to buy Africans from that region, especially the Koromantyns, Ashantis, and Akans. In the eighteenth century, Barbados "made it illegal for Gold Coast blacks to enter the island" (Mathurin Mair, 1975, p. 2). Although the number of imported enslaved Gold Coast Blacks fell, rebellions and ideology of resistance were reinforced among the enslaved who remained on the plantations. Plantation pedagogy as emancipatory understanding occurred in acts of rebellions such as the Haitian Revolution in 1804, Bussa's Rebellion in 1816 (Beckles, 2016), and the Morant Bay Rebellion in 1865 led by former slave and current Jamaican national hero Paul Bogle (Bacchus, 1994; Rose, 2002). Emancipatory understanding is the purposeful strategic planning and collective organization to orchestrate rebellions and disrupt plantation societies.

A controversial form of resistance on the plantation is learned from sociosexual relations between enslaved women and white men. One can argue that, when successful, these relations yield symbolic achievement—ultimately in the purchase of freedom, but also as the bearing of lighter-skinned children to absolve the next generation of enslaved children from field labor (Beckles, 1999). The strategy of sociosexual relations is further exemplified in the narratives of enslaved women such as Phibbah, the creole housekeeper in a Jamaican sugar plantation who later became the wife of the infamous slave owner Thomas Thistlewood. Thistlewood was most notably known as a vile, ruthless, sexual sadist and rapist. And although he had 265 sexual partners between 1751 and 1754, Phibbah was known to be his muse. However, depending on the colonial orientation of the historian, Phibbah's narrative was either revered or despised. Afro-Caribbean historian Hilary Beckles (1999) noted, "Phibbah's freedom was the end product of a domestic mission that stands as evidence of the overriding value placed upon liberty by enslaved blacks. . . . She, at once, accepted and rebelled against their relationship. She wrestled with his [Thistlewood's] crudeness and sexual permissiveness, challenged the limits of his social control over her, and kept her autonomy by significantly determining the terms of his 'real' power" (p. 57). Resistance teaching is understanding how other enslaved women learned of the hidden costs of Phibbah's freedom and the resilience it took to earn her freedom.

Another form of resistance teaching is the overt act of seeking formal court justice while enslaved, as illustrated in Kitty Hilton's slave narrative, which was documented as a part of the abolitionists' papers and letters to end slavery (Jamaica, 1831). In 1829, Hilton was brutally flogged by order of her massa (Rev. Mr. Bridges, Rector of St. Ann) and left for dead, when she escaped and ran to the nearest magistrate, only to be turned away and sent back to her massa (Jamaica, 1831). Hilton did not receive justice in the formal sense, because the house of magistrates ruled 14 to 4 that Mr. Bridges should not be prosecuted (Jamaica, 1831). However, Hilton took her massa to court, and thereby the court proceedings were recorded and used in defense of the abolitionist movement to end slavery. These acts of resistance were much more than forms of survival, as in many cases they were conscious and purposeful decisions to oppose and fight against slaver owners. This form of plantation pedagogy is not to be confused with dismantling systems of oppression but is instead about how to transgress the system of plantation politics. Admittedly, this form leaves the system of oppression intact.

This form of plantation pedagogy within higher education teaches the ways in which one can move in and out of the system leaving it intact. However, it provides the tools with which to create subversions—subversions that may not change the system but still form pockets of student liberation through campus rebellions such as student protests. Caribbean student protests and movements have been at the helm of historical social revolutions, such as the Cuban Revolution and its heritage in the halls of the University of Havana, or the Rodney riots at the University of the West Indies. These forms of subversion attempt to dismantle systems of oppression; however, many dissipate, leaving the institution's hegemony unbroken.

For academic staff, these forms of subversion take shape in the ways in which critical and inclusive pedagogical approaches are used to create emancipatory learning environments. In predominantly white and Western-post/colonial institutions, Black and Brown academic staff engage in pedagogical activism that calls for a decolonial approach to white supremacy teaching. White supremacy teaching supports and reinforces dominant, Western philosophies, ideologies, and epistemologies as the primary source of knowledge production. In the United States, the hashtag #citationpolitics is used to represent the racial politics of citations in academia. There is a growing movement for Black and Brown faculty to cite knowledge that is decolonized and written for and by Black and Brown scholars. These forms of pedagogical liberations are designed as transgressional, transformational, and power-retaining forms of constructing, receiving, and disseminating knowledge.

Implications for Dismantling Plantation Politics through Radical Emancipatory Imaginings

In an attempt to provide specific takeaways that enable one to push back against plantation politics in higher education, I present counterpedagogical framings designed to dismantle the massa's narrative. Below I give a more expansive view of the emancipatory pedagogical frameworks that can be used to dismantle white hegemonic-style teaching in higher education institutions. I use this framing to answer the second question of this chapter, How can educators disrupt these forms of pedagogical oppressions through radical emancipatory imaginings?

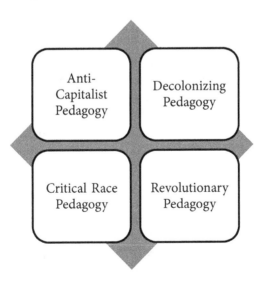

Figure 2.1. A Collectivist Matrix of Various Classifications of Empancipatory Pedagogies. Courtesy of the author.

The figure represents a collectivist matrix of various classifications of emancipatory pedagogies designed to disrupt modern-day forms of pedagogical oppressions in higher education classrooms. The overarching frame, emancipatory pedagogy, "supports a radical change in the power relationships in the classroom" and consists of the following key principles: (1) education broadens the students' view of reality; (2) education is transformative; (3) education is political; (4) education is empowering; and (5) education is based on true dialogue (Nouri & Sajjadi, 2014, p. 81). My analysis and interrogation of the literature encapsulated the following pedagogical frames within emancipatory pedagogy: (a) anticapitalist pedagogy, (b) decolonizing pedagogy, (c) revolutionary pedagogy, and (d) critical rage pedagogy.

Anticapitalist Pedagogy

The first aspect of the matrix is anticapitalist pedagogy, which dismantles education as the commodification of knowledge operating within free-market capitalism and in most twentieth-century, postcolonial countries, involves the exchangeability of a product to the wealthiest. An anticapitalist pedagogy promotes the dissemination of free and quality education to all within society, despite power or wealth. In reading and researching for this chapter, I better understood that the epistemological chain of knowing oneself starts with owning oneself. Are we not chained to the new versions of the slave model that is the capitalist model of higher education? The cultural and ideological forces that held the slave society together as a distinct civilization reflected a hegemonic white supremacy value system (Beckles, 2016, p. 3). This type of pedagogy requires an understanding of the self within a Marxist epistemology: an understanding of the differences between an economic good and a human right. Engaging the classroom from this pedagogical space affords the students a social responsiveness to each other and posits that education is a right and not a commodity.

Decolonizing Pedagogy

Following the development of social responsiveness, decolonizing pedagogy calls for the dismantling of "neoliberal policies and practices, imperialism and militarism" (McLaren, 2015, p. 231). Decolonizing pedagogy is more than a set of activities aimed at deconstructing heteronormative systems of oppression; it is also the abstract understanding that "the teacher's thinking is authenticated only by the authenticity of the students' thinking" (Freire, 1973, p. 63). It is a rehistoricizing of knowledge and history for and by the decolonized, Indigenous, and Native people to make sense and meaning of their own ontology. It is further, the critical reflection and unlearning of one's own past, including memories, moments, feelings of surety and therefore safety that master narratives and "truths" can be deconstructed and if needed relearned. In this respect, decolonized knowledge becomes the subject of onto-epistemologies and not objections to knowing.

REVOLUTIONARY PEDAGOGY

Similar to decolonizing pedagogy, revolutionary pedagogy is a pedagogical praxis that questions the official hegemonic view of ahistorical educational change that "does not call for violence but civil disobedience" (McLaren, 2015, p. 60), and that teaches the collective power to overcome the inimical forces of capitalism and the commodification of one's soul. What we have learned from slave rebellions and are currently learning from campus rebellions is that Black and Brown lives need spaces of hope and possibility. As professors, we must transform higher education classrooms as spaces of resistance and transformation. Peter McLaren (2015) reminds us that we are not going to lead the oppressed; we are creating spaces where the oppressed can lead themselves. Campus rebellions and movements are richly steeped in the praxis of revolutionary pedagogy, and our continued labor as Black educators is not to become complicit with the oppressor within but to learn from, embed within, and create more spaces for marginalized comrades in this struggle. By exposing the link between plantation politics and revolutionary praxis, this form of emancipatory pedagogy prompts those "squatting on their academic bed pans until they overflow" to do more than engage in resistance rhetoric (McLaren, 2015, p. 448).

CRITICAL RAGE PEDAGOGY

On January 12, 2018, the news was replete with expletives from the president of the United States saying Africans and Haitians are from "S***hole countries" (Vitali, Hunt, & Thorp, January 12, 2018). Sadly, such news becomes widespread "knowledge," and the attack on Black and Brown nations drives rage and anger to critically make sense out of nonsense. Critical rage pedagogy becomes a necessary form of dialectical praxis that derives from McLaren's (2015) *Pedagogy of Insurrection* and starts with a critical catharsis of self and social transformation. I build on McLaren's work by understanding it from a decolonized perspective, from Marcus Garvey who stated, "There can be no peace among men and nations, so long as the strong continues to oppress the weak, so long as injustice is done to other people, just so long we will have cause for war, and make a lasting peace an impossibility" (Garvey, 2013, p. 12).

Black and Brown bodies and minds have been under siege for centuries, conditioned to invisibility and a sense of powerlessness. Critical rage pedagogy becomes necessary to fiercely teach a dialectical reconditioning of truth telling and sense of knowing, informed for and by the decolonized. This form of pedagogy is fueled with a sense of fury and wrath for all the lies taught and the manner in which knowledge was and is espoused as a form of oppression, an attack on the self. Critical rage pedagogy denounces hate but equips students and faculty to become racially woke and intersectionally armed with the levels of critical consciousness needed to disrupt the curriculum and the academy.

Conclusion

Having straddled four systems of higher education in the Caribbean, the United States, the United Kingdom, and Europe as a student, faculty member, and an administrator—I argue that my experiences as a PhD candidate in the United States first introduced me to forms of audacious hope (Duncan-Andrade, 2009). This is where I believed I could change the system by first mastering my understanding of higher education and disrupting it from within. However, I have learned that a system rooted in oppression for centuries can only be incrementally changed over generations as the truest form of oppression is rooted within the colonial gaze of the people trained within the system. The system ran on its Slave Code–style policies that promoted access through meritocracy and white-interest convergence-type apologies for affirmative action practices. Members of my PhD cohort and I found solitude in other Black and Brown faculty and defied the deficit-thinking outcomes by obtaining our degrees *despite* our race and gender. We also did exactly what we shouldn't have: we bought into a narrative that was never written for or by us that if we worked hard, graduated, and entered the academy, we could dismantle the very same academy that trained us. Most of us have learned that it is difficult to dismantle the master's house with the master's tools (Lorde, 1983), and that Black and Brown faculty were educated to operate as the oppressor in the academy while being simultaneously oppressed. Frantz Fanon (1952) echoed similar sentiments in describing what it meant to be Black faces in white masks living as the oppressor within. Arguably, there is a concerted movement by Black and Brown faculty to become critically conscious of the oppressor within and disrupt what Frank A. Tuitt (2019) argues is the colonial academic gaze within us.

Throughout our schooling, my cohort and I were challenged to answer the question, What are you willing to lose with what you will gain?, because true re/imaginings of the future of the academy without plantation politics is revolutionary in thought, action, and purpose. It is understanding the sacrifice of academic martyrdom without the promise of the reward. Back in 1968, Walter Rodney echoed similar words when, challenged to present a radical re/envisioning of education, he explained that the minds of the students must be re/oriented and the "need for committed socialist staff" realized (Rodney, 1968, p. 84). However, in 1972 Rodney went on to express that "it is dialectically impossible for profound change to take place in the old educational system" (p. 98). The re/envisioning of education through counter narratives and radical imaginings is critical to realize modern-day higher education institutions without plantation politics.

From Trollope to Trump, white supremacists have been at the helm of knowledge creation, dissemination, and propagation. The emancipatory pedagogical matrix provides a critical dialectical framing to dismantle forms of plantation pedagogies that were designed to sever the mind and dismember the soul. It further allows for the reclamation of knowledge by and for Black and Brown people. The plantation owners and planter economy heavily influenced the system of governance. As a result, there were little to no sustainable education policies to build upon or contribute to the education sectors of enslaved and freed Blacks. The influence of the planters' policy to not instruct the masses and the government's lack of interest in encouraging education ultimately plagued the economic growth of the freed societies. Religious and moral education continued to be the primary and foundational basis of the curriculum, the aim of which was to enforce the role and place of the emancipated Negro in the social and economic hierarchy of society. Consequently, when education was philosophically understood as "fitting" for a society, what that essentially meant was that education was expected to create a local citizen for a society structured along the supply chains of a plantation economy (Bristol, 2010). If we are to remove ourselves from these supply chains, we must be willing to sacrifice, lose, demand more of ourselves and our comrades, and engage in a pedagogy of resistance (McLaren, 2015). This chapter was designed not to present pedagogical frameworks confined to brick-and-mortar institutions of higher learning but to present emancipatory forms of pedagogy to decolonize the academy, where knowledge is not owned by a university press, nor the impact factor(ed) in to change, but is constructed and valued from "the bottom of the global capitalist hierarchy" (McLaren, 2015, p. 142).

References

Act for the Abolition of Slavery. (1833). 3 & 4 Will. IV c. 73. https://www.pdavis.nl/Legis_07.htm

Bacchus, M. K. (1994). *Education as and for legitimacy: Development in West Indian education between 1846 and 1895.* Wilfred Laurier University Press.

Beckles, H. (1999). *Centering woman: Gender discourses in Caribbean slave society.* Ian Randle Publishers.

Beckles, H. (2016). *The first black slave society: Britain's "barbarity times" in Barbados, 1636 1876.* University of the West Indies Press.

Bell, D. (1980). Brown v. board of education and the interest-convergence dilemma. *Harvard Law Review 93,* 518–33.

Berlin, I. (2003). *Generations of captivity: A history of Afro-American slaves.* Harvard University Press.

Bristol, L. (2010). Practising in betwixt oppression and subversion: Plantation pedagogy as a legacy of plantation economy in Trinidad and Tobago. *Power and Education 2*(2), 167–82.

Cross, W. (1991). *Shades of black: Diversity in African-American identity.* Temple University Press.

Duncan-Andrade, J. (2009). Note to educators: Hope required when growing roses in concrete. *Harvard Educational Review 79*(2), 181–94.

Edwards, K. T., & Thompson, V. J. (2016). Womanist pedagogical love as justice work on college campuses: Reflections from faithful Black women academics. *New Directions for Adult & Continuing Education, 2016*(152), 39–50.

Fanon, F. (1952). *Black skin, white masks.* Pluto Press.

Franklin, A. (1999). Invisibility syndrome and racial identity development in psychotherapy and counseling African American men. *The Counseling Psychologist 27,* 761–93.

Freire, P. (1993). *Pedagogy of the oppressed* (new rev. 20th anniversary ed.). Continuum Books.

Garvey, A. (2013). *The philosophy and opinions of Marcus Garvey: Africa for the Africans*. Routledge.
Giroux, H. (2010). Rethinking education as the practice of freedom: Paulo Freire and the promise of critical pedagogy. *Policy Future in Education, 8*(6),
Goveia, E. (1965). *Slave society in the British Leeward Islands at the end of the eighteenth century*. Yale University Press.
Hall, D. (1998). *The University of the West Indies: A quinquagenary calendar, 1948-1998*. University of the West Indies Press.
Haynes, C. (2017). Dismantling the white supremacy embedded in our classrooms: White faculty in pursuit of more equitable educational outcomes. *International Journal of Teaching and Learning in Higher Education, 29*(1), 87–107.
Haynes, C., Stewart, S., & Allen, E. (2016). Three paths, one struggle: Black women and girls battling invisibility in U.S. classroom. *The Journal of Negro Education, 85*(3), 380-91.
Higman, B. (1988). *Jamaica surveyed: Plantation maps and plans of the eighteenth and nineteenth centuries* (pp. 121-24). Institute of Jamaica Publications.
Howe, G. D. (2000). *Higher education in the Caribbean: Past, present, and future directions*. The University of the West Indies Press.
Jamaica. (1831). *Papers relating to the treatment of a female slave in Jamaica*. Colonial Department, Downing Street. Archives of the House of Commons Papers, Great Britain.
Lorde, A. (1983). The master's tools will never dismantle the master's house. In C. Moraga & G. Anzaldua (Eds.), *The bridge called my back: Writing by radical women of color* (pp. 94-101). Kitchen Table Press.
Mathurin Mair, L. (1975). *The rebel woman in the British West Indies during slavery*. Institute of Jamaica Publications Limited.
McLaren, P. (2015). *Pedagogy of insurrection: From resurrection to revolution*. Peter Lang Publishing, Inc.
McLaren, P. (2016). Critical pedagogy and class struggle in the age of neoliberal terror. In R. Kumar (Ed.), *Neoliberalism, critical pedagogy and education* (pp. 19-67). Routledge.
Nouri, A., & Sajjadi, S. (2014). Emancipatory pedagogy in practice: Aims, principles and curriculum orientation. *International Journal of Critical Pedagogy 5*(2), 76-87.
Patton, D. (Ed.). (2001). *A narrative of events, since the first of August, 1834, by James Williams, an apprenticed labourer in Jamaica*. Duke University Press.
Patton, L., & Njoku, N. (2019). Theorizing black women's experiences with institution-sanctioned violence: A #BlackLivesMatter imperative toward black liberation on campus. *International Journal of Qualitative Studies in Education, 32*(9), 1162-82.
Ritchey, K. (2014). Black identity development. *The Vermont Connection 35*(12), 99-105.

Rodney, W. (1968). Education and Tanzanian socialism. In I. Resnick (Ed.), *Tanzania: Revolution by education* (pp. 71–84). Tanzania: Longman Group.

Rodney, W. (1972). Education in Africa and contemporary Tanzania [Monograph]. In *Education and black struggle—Notes from the colonized world*, special issue, *Harvard Education Review, 2*, 82–99.

Rose, E. (2002). *Dependency and socialism in the modern Caribbean: Superpower intervention in Guyana, Jamaica, and Grenada, 1970–1985*. Lexington Books.

Stewart, S. (2013). *Everything in di dark muss come to light: A postcolonial examination of the practice of extra lessons at the secondary level in Jamaica's education system* [Doctoral dissertation]. ProQuest, Order No. 3597983.

Stewart, S. (2016). Advancing a critical and inclusive praxis: Pedagogical and curriculum innovations for social change in the Caribbean. In F. Tuitt, C. Haynes, & S. Stewart (Eds.), *Race, equity and the learning environment: The global relevance of critical and inclusive pedagogies in higher education* (pp. 9–22). Stylus Publishing.

Stewart, S. (2019). Navigating the academy in the post diaspora: #Afro-Caribbean Feminism and the intellectual and emotional labour needed to transgress. *Caribbean Review of Gender Studies, 13*, 147–72. https://sta.uwi.edu/crgs/june2019/documents/CRGS_13_Pgs147-172_SStewart_Navigatingthe Academy.pdf

Stewart, S. Deal, K., Hubain, B., Hunt, C., & Bowlby, N. (2013). Who am I? An exploration of role identity formation and socialization throughout the U.S. doctoral process. *Journal of Student Affairs, 22*, 77–84.

Sue, D. W., Capodilupo, C. M., Torino, G. C., Bucceri, J. M., Holder, A. M. B., Nadal, K. L., & Esquilin, M. (2007). Racial microaggressions in everyday life: Implications for clinical practice. *American Psychologist, 62*, 271–86. http://dx.doi.org/10.1037/0003-066X.62.4.271

Trollope, A. (1860). *The West Indies and the Spanish main*. Chapman and Hall. https://books.google.com.jm/books?id=Ir8NAAAAQAAJ&printsec=frontcover&source=gbs_ge_summary_r&cad=0#v=onepage&q&f=false

Tuitt, F. (2019). Disrupting the colonial gaze: Emancipatory imaginings of a Caribbean centered research praxis. In S. Stewart (Ed.), *Decolonizing qualitative approaches for and by the Caribbean* (pp. 205–20). Information Age Publishing, Inc.

Vitali, A., Hunt, K. & Thorp V, F. (2018, January 12). Trump referred to Haiti and African nations as "shithole" countries. NBC News. https://www.nbcnews.com/politics/white-house/trump-referred-haiti-african-countries-shithole-nations-n836946

Young, K., Anderson, M., & Stewart, S. (2014). Hierarchical microaggressions in higher education. *Journal Diversity of Higher Education, 8*(1), 61–71. DOI: 10.1037/a0038464

Chapter 3

"Troubling the Waters"

Unpacking and (Re)Imagining the Historical and Contemporary Complexity of Historically Black College and University Cultural Politics

STEVE D. MOBLEY JR., SUNNI L. SOLOMON II,
A. C. JOHNSON, AND PATRICK REYNOLDS

For over a century the complexities and tensions that surround how Black students are engaged within educational spaces have been a source of contentious debates. The ways in which Black communities have been relegated to the margins, silenced, *and* indoctrinated within K–12 and higher education environments has called particular attention to "how" and "why" these instances have and continue to occur. What is striking is that education scholars largely situate instances of anti-Blackness and Black degradation within a Black-white paradigm—particularly as it pertains to the presence of white supremacy within historically white institutions.[1] Within higher education discourses we constantly contend with and contemplate how US colleges and universities must atone for and recognize how they knowingly participate in and perpetuate the ills of systemic racism. However, we rarely discuss how the roots of Black education have been so thoroughly entrenched in the lessons and rules of white supremacy that continue to live beneath the surface of even our most revered historically Black colleges and universities (HBCUs).

The colonialism and imperialism that played a major part in founding this country led to the enslavement of Black bodies within plantation cultures (Squire et al., 2018). What is unfortunate is that the remnants of this toxic residue have affected and still currently exist within HBCU environments. In this chapter we argue, nuance, and extend the arguments surrounding how the heritage of US colleges and universities (including HBCUs) embodies an anti-Black settler colonial state and resembles the politics of the Southern American plantation (Anderson, 1988a; Thelin, 2011; Dancy et al., 2018).

(Re)Viewing HBCU Histories

Ever since African Americans arrived on American soil as involuntary minorities, they fought to acquire knowledge and deemed fierce educational pursuit as their key to freedom during numerous eras of tumultuous peril, uncertainty, and discord (Gasman, 2016; Mobley, 2017).[2] Though enslaved on plantations, Black communities still found a way to exist and pursue myriad forms of education despite laws enforced in all of the Southern states that forbade them from learning to read and write (Gasman, 2016). During this time Black colleges were being founded, including Cheyney University (1837) and Lincoln University (1854) in Pennsylvania, and Wilberforce University (1856) in Ohio. These institutions paved the way for the establishment of more than 100 colleges and universities dedicated to the education of Black people (Anderson, 1988b; Williams, 2018; Williams & Ashley, 2004). Indeed, prior to the Civil War, Black Americans were using their agency to become educated—this is of critical importance.

While there was groundbreaking movement to establish some of the oldest HBCUs in the nation in the North, the great majority of our nation's Black colleges and universities were founded in the Deep South. At the conclusion of the Civil War, the nation, and the South in particular, was forced to contend with integrating Blacks into the "new" social order. Education became a critical part of this process as African Americans insatiably pursued educational pursuits at *all* levels (Williamson, 2004). The "Negro Problem," also known as the "Black Menace," is a term often used to describe the plight of newly freed enslaved Blacks in the United States. With emancipation came the "right" for Blacks to legally pursue education; however, the remnants of slavery and the ever-present social politics of the Southern American plantation still lingered. Coupled with segregation and the overwhelming number of Blacks in the United States who were illiterate, the task of educating this population was overwhelming (Anderson, 1988a; Brazzell, 1992; Williams & Ashley, 2004). Southern institutions of higher education and the majority of Northern institutions operated exclusively for whites and excluded Blacks from full participation in postsecondary education (Brown & Davis, 2001). M. Christopher Brown and James Earl Davis (2001) contend that HBCUs were created to provide African Americans with access to higher education, and as a result served as *social equalizers* (Mann, 1848/1903). These institutions have distinct historical foundations that require a nuanced unraveling. They have been controversial since their founding. The institutional cultures of HBCUs "have been shaped in the womb of a country that has and continues to struggle with how and if it values and invests in the education of Black Americans" (Commodore, 2017, p. 4). Furthermore, due to the diverse stakeholders that played major parts in establishing these postsecondary spaces, there are many facets that should be explored regarding how whiteness and the presence of Southern American plantation cultures have been *and* are ever-present within these "seemingly" homogenous educational spaces.

Loaded Pasts: Interest Convergence and White "Benevolence"

Before delving further into the histories of historically Black colleges and universities, it is important to recognize that their definitions and institutional names are loaded designations (Mobley, 2017).[3] We must not ignore the fact that the word "Black" is included in the designations of these colleges and universities or the inherent racial implications that this association creates. There are considerable effects "when race is tied to territory in a way that mimics the white's only/colored only designations of the past" (hooks, 1992, p. 15). Historically Black colleges and universities are viewed through highly racialized lenses within the broader societal context and, due to their status as minority serving institutions, have been and are perceived as academically inferior (Minor, 2004). These prejudices were particularly inherent in HBCUs foundings, and are *still* felt today.

Upon reviewing the manner in which these schools came into existence, a critical race theory lens can definitely be applied to highlight their implicit and explicit cooperation in the United States' anti-Black plantation politics model. A "plantation politics" lens allows for the deliberate opportunity to enumerate how contemporary campus culture norms model antebellum slave plantations. It is essential to underscore that racist ideologies were in play during the establishment of HBCUs. Acknowledgment of this is critical, especially because racism is normalized within the American societal context and "is so enmeshed in the fabric of our social order, it appears both normal and natural to people in this culture" (Ladson-Billings, 1998, p. 11). Thus, when discussing HBCUs in historical and contemporary discourses, the unmasking and exposing of racism in its myriad forms is vital.

In the Jim Crow South, the Morrill Land-Grant Act of 1862 was passed and further perpetuated a divisive educational system based on race.[4] African Americans' access to higher education required intervention from the military branch of the federal government (i.e., the Freedmen's Bureau and the passing of the Morrill Act of 1890[5]). White Northern missionary aid societies, white industrial philanthropists, and various factions of the Black church also assisted in providing Blacks in the United States with access to higher education through HBCUs (Anderson, 1988b; Brazzell, 1992; Redd, 1998). As HBCUs were established, many of their white founders not only sought to educate newly freed enslaved Blacks but also instilled the values of white morality (Nguyen et al., 2018).

Interest convergence was also an unmistakable force. Derrick Bell (1980) introduced "interest convergence" as a tenant of critical race theory and asserted that strides in racial equity and equality are reached only when the interest of communities of color converge with the concerted and viable interests, wants, anticipations, and ideologies of whites. In other words, "racism always remains firmly in place but social progress advances at the pace that white people determine is reasonable and judicious" (Lopez, 2003, p. 84). The various white factions in the North (e.g., white Northern philanthropists and missionaries) were quite paternalistic and empathetic toward Southern whites; there was an understanding that they were bonded through racial ties (Decker, 2014; Peeps, 1981). White status and rank played major roles in HBCU campus cultures early on. And white investiture came with hidden costs that are still felt today.

W. E. B. Du Bois (1903/2003) alluded to the aforementioned when he referred to HBCUs as "social settlements." HBCU cultures often embody conservative ideals that manifest as a result of respectability politics (Higginbotham, 1993) via a specific brand of teaching and enculturation that are derivative of these schools' attempts to thwart stereotypes that derived from Southern plantation cultures (Mobley & Hall, 2020; Mobley & Johnson, 2019; Njoku et al., 2017).

Du Bois (1903/2003) contends that "had it not been for the Negro school and college, the Negro would have been driven back to slavery" (p. 121). He also explains that "[HBCUs] were social settlements; homes where the best of the sons of the freedmen came in close and sympathetic touch with the best traditions of New England" (p. 69). Many of the founders of these institutions "sought to divest Blacks of their 'peculiar' cultural past and to teach them the ways of middle-class white Americans" (Allen & Jewell, 2002, p. 246). Northern abolitionists and white philanthropists provided financial funding to HBCUs in an effort to educate Black populations in the South; however, "this benevolence toward the former slaves was not without its disturbing side" (Decker, 2014, p. 235). White HBCU investors held the belief that education was important for newly freed Blacks, but they also used education as a means of control and to ensure that Blacks would maintain a subordinate stature in the postbellum social order, as they would now have to navigate and participate in a white "civilized" society (Anderson, 1988b; Decker, 2014).

Ultimately, in order to act in the interest of white people who played major roles in the founding of HBCUs and to also survive and thrive in their tumultuous social contexts, Black students who matriculated at these schools were ultimately viewed as individuals who needed to be "delivered" and made "worthy" citizens through the lenses of white Protestant ideology (Decker, 2014; Ferguson, 2005; Nguyen et al., 2018). While Northern missionaries thought that the newly freed enslaved Black people should be "free," they also believed that these free Black people had been tainted by slavery and needed to be "saved" from their own moral savagery (Decker, 2014). According to E. Franklin Frazier (1957), "The missionaries from New England who founded the first schools for Negros left their Puritan background upon Negro education . . . when the Negroes themselves began to assume control of their schools they tried to maintain the same tradition of piety" (pp. 71–72). This raises several questions: Have white norms grown on the Southern American plantation shaped HBCU cultures by determining *which* representations of Blackness are deemed acceptable, marketable, or worthy (hooks, 1996)? Were "exploited Black folks all too willing to be complicit in perpetuating the fantasy that ruling-class white culture is the quintessential site of unrestricted joy, freedom, and pleasure" (hooks, 1996, p. 281)? The Puritan evangelical mores that were being put in place on many HBCU campuses "rigidly defined 'appropriate' behavior, dress, speech, and extracurricular activity for the future 'leaders' of the Black race" (Allen & Jewell, 2002, p. 246). For example, some of the aforementioned can be seen contemporarily in many highly regarded HBCU campus traditions (e.g., the former Spelman College white dress tradition) and the fact that many of these campuses still have single-sex residence halls, enforce curfews, and have strict policies regarding visitation between male- and female-identified students.

Confronting How White Supremacy Seeks to Dominate "Blackness" within HBCU Environments

The fact that various forms of white supremacy exist within HBCU environments and that these systemic impediments are unconsciously carried forward and forced on Black students by HBCU administrations and faculty under the guise of tradition must be fully acknowledged and confronted (Sullivan, 2006). Shannon Sullivan (2004, 2006) describes a process in which individuals receive messages that are in direct opposition to their existence or their sociocultural upbringing (e.g., the pervasive stereotypical images that appear in U.S media that Blacks are lazy, inferior, criminals, etc.) and that are embedded in their subconscious by way of constant exposure and reinforcement. How does this occur on HBCU campuses?

Franz Fanon's *Black Skin, White Masks* (1952/2008) introduces the revolutionary concept of ethical slippage, in which the morals, expectations, and values of white society become unconsciously embedded and accepted in the minds of Black people as a result of the constant introduction to and immersion in Eurocentric social constructs and codes of ethics (Sullivan, 2004). In his autobiographical account, Fanon tells how he was raised as a French citizen in the predominantly Black Antillean island of Martinique but did not "realize" that he was a Black man until he visited France. As a citizen of the French West Indies, an officially recognized region of France, Fanon describes the constant bombardment of classroom teachings, textbooks, music, magazines, and movies that influenced not only his views but also those of many previous generations of Black Martiniqueans. While he always understood that whiteness translated to being virtuous, cultured, and pure, and that Blackness was understood to be bad, savage, evil, flawed, tainted, and undesirable, he assumed that this related to character and state of mind and not skin color (Fanon, 1969; Sullivan, 2004, 2006). Similar to the unconscious French/Western European indoctrination of the Black people of Martinique, HBCU cultures have also been unconsciously indoctrinated by the values and beliefs that ruled US slave plantations, resulting in anti-Black practices manifesting on these campuses (Commodore, 2019; Mobley & Hall, 2020). Ethical slippage and plantation politics have affected and continue to affect HBCU cultures—as evidenced in aspects of their curricula, intraracial tensions among their students, and policies that are enacted.

The Enforcement of Respectability Politics within HBCU Contexts

> In the push toward middle-class respectability, we wanted tongue depressors sticking from every Black man's coat pocket and briefcases swinging from every Black hand . . . the old verities that made being Black and alive in this country the most dynamite existence imaginable—so much of what was satisfying, challenging and simply more interesting—were being driven underground—by Blacks. In trying to cure the cancer of slavery and its consequences, some healthy as well as malignant cells were destroyed.
>
> —Toni Morrison, "Rediscovering Black History"

Toni Morrison (1974) contends that many Blacks of her generation, the one that preceded hers, and the one(s) that would ultimately follow have embodied respectability politics (Higginbotham, 1993) in an effort to be accepted by the majority. Historically Black colleges and universities have long upheld their role as prominent agents of ideological indoctrination regarding issues within Black communities (Grundy, 2012). This includes the socialization of their students' nuanced assumptions surrounding Black sexuality, gender, and gender identity—through the enforcement of Black respectability politics (Grundy, 2012; Mobley & Hall, 2020). While these institutions seek to embody an ideal of racial uplift and service to the Black community via higher education, they subtly send a message that if students do not adhere to these values, they may not belong. Frazier (1957) expressed that within HBCU environments, "The Negro student should strive to be respectable . . . the best and worst of the race should guide the masses away from the worst" (p. 77). This ideal resembles that of Du Bois's (1903/2003) "Talented Tenth" concept, in which he argues that a small educated elite group of Blacks would lead and elevate the majority of Black communities away from the ideals and mores that "contaminated" the community during slavery. Both of these beliefs are deeply laden with respectability politics.

A concept first theorized by Evelyn Brooks Higginbotham (1993), Black respectability politics promotes certain traits and behaviors that Black communities are expected to adhere to in order to be seen as worthy of occupying space in the white world. Style of dress, cleanliness, sexuality, self-control, clarity of speech, and educational background are all areas in the Black community in which respectability politics has helped to set both policies and norms that guide how people show up and the way they engage one another. Respectability politics at HBCUs results from the collision of racial uplift/cultural pride and the negative biases, stereotypes, and myths about Blackness, which subsequently results in a clinging to the concepts of assimilation, self-improvement, recognition, and avoiding difference as coping strategies to combat anti-Blackness (Njoku et al., 2017). This particular approach seeks to provide Black people with a tangible tool they can employ to combat racism and dehumanization while also empowering them to define how they are seen, heard, and received by an unforgiving society (Patton, 2014). But respectability politics are complex, because while these norms were created as a form of protection against white supremacy, they have also caused harm intraracially within many Black communities.

In their attempts to instill the ideologies of respectability within their students, many HBCU communities have also produced a hidden curriculum that permeates their campus cultures, thus affecting HBCU students, staff, faculty, and their alumni (Njoku et al., 2017). With regard to how and why HBCU communities infuse respectability politics as hidden curriculum, Nadrea Njoku, Malika Butler, and Cameron C. Beatty (2017) further assert that "the hidden curriculum in education refers to the unwritten, unofficial, and often-unintended lessons, values, and perspectives that students learn in school. The result has been a graduate that has not only obtained a Bachelor's degree but also, from the perspective of the gatekeepers of HBCU traditions, is equipped with tools to combat the social attitudes and stereotypes levied against them in a society that maintains a system of patriarchy, white supremacy, and capitalism" (p. 786). It appears that an essentialist approach is being taken with regard to how "Blackness" is being monitored within these environments via respectability politics. A (re)defining of "respectable" standards and approaches that are inherent within HBCU cultures should be (re)visited.

An antiessentialist approach that underscores the depth and uniqueness of Black experiences within HBCU contexts is absolutely necessary to combat the Southern plantation politics that were historically rooted in these unique educational spaces. Antiessentialist approaches would serve to recognize that Black intraracial differences are often fashioned within specific institutions, social relations, and histories that serve to establish available options for myriad identities (Warnke, 2005). There is a presence of both history and power with regard to how "Blackness" is performed in relation to whiteness even within HBCU environments. A prominent example of how the aforementioned plays out is at Hampton University in Virginia. The founders of this institution used an industrial curriculum infused with respectability politics as a means to strip Blacks of their cultural past and racial pride, and in return they were indoctrinated with the traditions and expectations of white society (Allen, & Jewell, 2002).

The Hampton Institute Negro Education Model

The United States' rise to worldwide prominence as the chief producer of cotton and other agricultural wares was made possible by the incalculable amounts of stolen labor, knowledge, and skills provided by chattel slavery (Watkins, 2001). Essential to this form of slavery were the concepts of white supremacy and racial subservience, which outlined the relationships, communications, and power dynamics that existed between white plantation enslavers and their Black enslaved people (Watkins, 2001). Part of what made the practice of chattel slavery so successful was the extreme mental abuse and manipulation that included the denial of any form of education to the enslaved that would allow them to assert their independence. This most notably meant that enslaved Black people were prohibited from learning how to write, read, and learn mathematics. Still, many enslaved people still found ways to acquire education even against their enslaver's wishes, and they were brutally punished as a result.

However, there were many cases where the essentiality of those who were enslaved were quite critical in ensuring that plantations would remain in operation. As such, in the economic interests of whites enslavers, some enslaved Black people were informally taught how to read, write, and perform mathematic tasks such as bookkeeping and budgeting (Watkins, 2001). These enslaved people were valued and became a sort of "enslaved aristocracy," in turn transmitting the message to other enslaved people that formal education was power. Booker T. Washington, founder of Tuskegee University and a former enslaved man who was mentored by general Samuel Chapman Armstrong, once spoke of this power and referred to the slave plantation as a "industrial school," implying that even though Black people had endured horrible atrocities as a part of plantation life, they had also acquired valuable concrete skills and experiences that they now were able to leverage to make better lives for themselves (Watkins, 2001). Well before the Civil War there were signs that Black education was considered to be the great equalizer that determined whether an enslaved person could live, think, and thrive in a white society that held no love or affection for Black men and women (Anderson, 1988b). Following the Civil War it became very clear that in order to maintain white dominance, the education of this massive population of newly freed enslaved people had to be managed in a particular manner.

The newly freed enslaved community's collective thirst for knowledge after the Civil War left them vulnerable to white educational influence, because they did not yet possess the education or resources necessary to create and control their own curriculums and schools. At the same time, the reduction of free Southern labor crippled the agriculture industries' stronghold on the United States and made way for Northern businessmen to become wealthy industrialists by creating factories and processes that were unrivaled around the globe. Blacks knew only hard labor, so it would seem that this was a perfect fit given where the nation was headed. Still, there was a persistent commentary from whites suggesting that "learning will spoil the nigger for work" (Anderson, 1988a, pp. 21–21).

Industrial philanthropists saw the thirst for education exhibited by former enslaved people as an opportunity to engage in social engineering, and in turn began to use their substantial financial resources to shape and influence Black education in hopes of solving the "Negro problem" (Watkins, 2001). The most popular and well-supported model that emerged is known as the "Hampton Institute Model" or the "Hampton-Tuskegee Idea." Designed by General Armstrong, it was extremely successful at perpetuating ethical slippage and injecting respectability into the psyche of newly freed Blacks in the form of education following the Civil War (Anderson, 1988a; Sullivan, 2004).

The Hampton Model was more focused on creating skilled Negro teachers that could promote white societal values and structures than it was on classically educating formerly enslaved people and their descendants in the arts and sciences (Anderson, 1988a). Armstrong's vision for and founding of the Hampton Normal and Agricultural Institute (now Hampton University) was not driven by what was in the best interest of newly freed Blacks; quite the contrary, it was built by a white man from a foundation of realism that took into account where the nation was at that time and how whites were receiving the idea of having educated the formerly enslaved as part of society (Watkins, 2001; Anderson, 1988a). A carefully crafted curriculum was designed and implemented at Hampton from the very start. One of the main objectives was to imbed the idea of subservience in the minds of Black students, and to teach them their role in society. As such, manual labor was a pervasive part of both classroom instruction and cocurricular activities at the institute (Anderson, 1988b). Students did not attend the institute for free: male students were required to work on the farm, and female students performed domestic duties for the school. Each student was paid eight cents per hour of work, which was banked and used to cover their room and board (Watkins, 2001). The need to reinforce the subordinate and docile role expected of the newly freed enslaved seeking education was precipitated by Southern states' desire to maintain rules, regulations, and a social order similar to that which existed prior to the Civil War (Anderson, 1988a). Formerly enslaved people were used for hard labor, knowledge, and skills, and they held a tremendous respect for education, so the exploitation of their experiences in bondage, coupled with the promise of becoming a learned people, helped to mask the white supremacist ideology that was being promoted by Hampton's founder and first president. As a producer of Black teachers, Hampton became a sort of propaganda machine that was able to transmit its message far and wide by simultaneously setting the standard for Black education and indoctrinating Black students to stay in their "place" within a larger white society.

Interestingly, W. E. B. Du Bois, an ardent opponent of the Hampton-Tuskegee idea, strongly criticized the Hampton-Tuskegee Model and highlighted the extreme limitations it placed on Black education and the HBCU curriculum by white oppression (Mobley, 2015). Du Bois (1903/2003) was unsatisfied with the notion that Blacks were suited only for industrial education and realized the limitations this put on the upward mobility of educated Black communities writ large. Instead, he was an ardent advocate of Black people's rights to expand their horizons and become deep, critical thinkers by way of receiving the classic liberal arts education that was being offered to white students. Here it is important to note that Du Bois's focus on creating a Black intelligentsia was not a goal but a method he saw as essential to advancing the race (Dunn, 1993). Through the building of a community of competent Black intellectuals that were permitted to dream and achieve at levels previously unavailable to Black people, Du Bois believed that Black people would never be in a position to be enslaved again (Dunn, 1993). With these demands and aspirations that were so far ahead of his time, Du Bois established himself as a radical thinker that was willing to constantly step outside of what was considered respectable for a Black man to publicly write and speak. Unsatisfied with the mobility-limiting fundamental components of the Black industrial education model that was championed by Armstrong at Hampton and Washington at Tuskegee, Du Bois's radical counterarguments placed him in a position to be labeled as an example of "bad" Blackness that did not know its place in a white society during this time period.

#BlackLivesMatter: Seeking Freedom in Rebellion and Resistance within HBCU Contexts

Deliberate and concerted social justice movements are deeply embedded within the historical and contemporary cultural fabrics of HBCU contexts. Historically Black colleges and universities have been the premiere postsecondary environments where many of the world's most influential Black leaders and activists have been and are being cultivated. Steve D. Mobley (2017) expressed that HBCUs and their students were major forces during the civil rights movement in the 1950s and early 1960s, the Black Power movement of the 1970s, and even during the fight to end apartheid in South Africa in the 1980s and 1990s. In unpacking this culture of resistance there is a (re)calling of the past in a powerful manner.

The successive waves of African enslaved people that were brought to the United States and that now make up the very fabric of HBCU cultures brought with them varied notions of freedom and justice—even in the midst of immense terror and turmoil. Ultimately, Black American who were enslaved "fought tenaciously, by all available means, including the ultimate confrontation of revolt, to enforce their own view of social relations" (Genovese, 1992, p. xvi). Amid the overt and covert semblances of plantation politics that are present among these institutions, there also lies a spirit of resistance and rebellion. This spirit of resistance mirrors that of the plantation slave rebellions that occurred during the antebellum period.

The contexts for HBCU have been noted as being conservative educational spaces due to their authoritarian regulation of faculty and student expression (Commodore, 2019, Harper & Gasman, 2008; Mobley & Johnson, 2019). However, "throughout the history of Black colleges, students have rebelled against institutional policies and practices they found too restrictive and aligned with the status quo" (Harper & Gasman, 2008, p. 337). There have always been student and faculty critics within HBCU contexts who were displeased with how these institutions were acting *and* being purveyors of Black education (Miles, 1973; Rosenthal, 1975). Significant strikes, revolts, and boycotts occurred during the 1920s at several HBCUs, including Fisk University, Hampton Institute, and Howard University (Harper & Gasman, 2008; Lamon, 1974; Rosenthal, 1975). These deliberate acts of resistance were sparked mostly by students who became disillusioned with white administrative leadership structures, which sought to control student sexuality, free speech in campus media outlets, enforce strict codes of student conduct, and provided pervasive support of Jim Crow standards on and off campus (Harper & Gasman, 2008; Logan, 1969; Wolters, 1975).

Another generation of rebellion appeared during the civil rights movement. North Carolina Agricultural and Technical State University students integrated a Woolworth counter on February 1, 1960 in Greensboro, North Carolina. There was also Diane Nash, a Fisk University student who was active in the Freedom Rider movement and a founding member of the Student Nonviolent Coordinating Committee (Carter, 2013; Mobley, Solomon, & Johnson, 2017). However, during this time period, HBCU students who took an active role in civil rights activism often received lukewarm support from HBCU administrations. There were some HBCU presidents who expelled or reported these student activists to authorities for their participation in the Black freedom struggle (Wheatle & Commodore, 2019; Williamson, 2004).

The Black Power movement during the 1970s evoked resistance on HBCU campuses. What is telling is that during this time, HBCUs students inspired and sparked pan-African movements nationally (especially at historically white universities) with their efforts to effectuate change to preserve Black colleges (Biondi, 2012). This was especially evident at Grambling State University and Southern University, where in the eyes of the students on these campuses their administrators were "tools of the white power structure in the state, who were in turn the authors of the segregationist policy" (Aiello, 2012). Thomas Aiello (2012) expresses that during this era, "student protests at Southern and Grambling—and at Black universities in general—were neither the result of a seamless transition from candlelight vigils for voting rights nor an inherent continuation of or dependency on white college radicalism. They were a combination of those realities, additionally feeding from a long history of the contradictory nature of Black colleges themselves and the historical frustration Black students often expressed at those schools" (p. 263). This culture of rebellion and protest is quite distinct within HBCU cultures. There are intraracial tensions present. The conflict that arises within *this* brand of resistance is driven by asserting and fighting for Blackness within Black spaces. This friction persists today.

HBCUs campuses have also been at the forefront of the Black Lives Matter movement. The Sandra Bland case unfolded on an HBCU campus. She was stopped mere feet from her alma mater, Prairie View A&M University, before meeting her unfortunate demise at the hands of police. Also, during the infancy of the Black Lives Matter movement, the Trayvon Martin case called HBCU communities to action. Kevin Cunningham, a Howard University Law School alumnus, spearheaded a vital initiative and utilized social media to bring attention to the Martin case, garnering 2,271,988 signatures of support for the arrest and criminal prosecution of George Zimmerman (Mobley, Solomon, & Johnson, 2017). Trayvon Martin's mother, Sybrina Fulton, referencing the media attention and public interest in the death of her son, stated, "Whenever I'm asked about how all of this started, I mention that it started at Howard" (The Jurist, 2013). This brand of activism shows how these campuses can erupt while seeking justice and freedom for our most vulnerable populations (Mobley, Solomon, & Johnson, 2017).

Also, queer and trans* HBCU students have also been at the fore in the wake of the Black Lives Matter movement. Students fueled by a desire for change have been less inclined to acquiesce to institutionally-minded leaders, and as a result protests have rocked these institutions nationwide (Mobley et al., forthcoming). Recent highly publicized protests at Howard University, Morehouse College, Spelman College, and Clark Atlanta University, have signaled to HBCUs how Black queer and trans* students have been relegated to the margins and silenced on their campuses. These recent protests provided space for Black queer and trans* students to call attention to the ways that HBCU communities must begin to atone for and recognize how they have been affected by and complicit in reifying white supremacy and anti-Blackness. Black queer HBCU student activists are demanding that HBCUs begin to embrace free and bold Blackness that is not stifled by the convergence of race, gender, gender identity, religion, sexuality, or social class (Mobley, 2017).

These student activists "no longer want to pass as heterosexual or 'cover' or de-emphasize their sexuality in Black spaces" (Moore, 2015, p. 15). Instead, queer and trans* HBCU students are insisting that their peers, professors, and administrators move toward complete acceptance. The discourse surrounding queer and trans* students across HBCU contexts is evolving, and there are promising policy changes and interventions being put into place at the administrative level to better serve queer students. Of note, Morehouse College's "Appropriate Attire Policy" has been amended, all of the traditionally single-sex HBCUs now have trans* admissions policies, and there are a handful of HBCU presidents (e.g., at Morgan State University, Dillard University, and Virginia State University) that have formed task forces or working groups to directly confront how they can better engage their queer and trans* students (Mobley, McNally, & Moore, 2019). Many of these advancements have been student driven and are a result of Black queer HBCU student activism. These activists should be celebrated for their tremendous efforts.

The Need to (Re)Visit HBCU Histories in the Present

Within this chapter we (re)situate the history of HBCUs and address how their pasts have had an indelible impact on how they function contemporarily. There is profound power in unveiling the past to uncover the complexities of the present so that we may effectuate change in the future. One must approach this opportunity with care and humility. To admit and address how these schools have the potential to embody an anti-Black settler colonial state and resemble the politics of Southern American plantations is an uncomfortable discourse—but a necessary one. It is essential to name and even confront a past *and* present that has celebrated and disgraced HBCU communities. In uncovering truth there is no room to twist the past in order to serve the present. When we realize that what is done effects our present, we are then free to influence the future. The present and the past both should be recognized as formidable forces. What we hope has been uncovered is that HBCU communities are extremely complex educational spaces. They have been quite intentional in directing a Black cultural pulse *and* the shifts that have occurred in Black communities and in wider society (Douglas, 2012). The Herculean tasks that these institutions have successfully accomplished in such a short period of time often lead many internal and external to the Black community to assume that HBCUs occupy a position beyond reproach or critical examination. This is not so. However, due to the "raced" positions that these schools hold in higher education discourses, there is a need to be thoughtful and careful with regard to how they are nuanced. With the critical information and concepts provided within this chapter, we offer a nuanced perspective that will hopefully begin broader conversations about "Blackness" within higher education spaces that do not have to ever include normative white standards.

Notes

1. We use "historically White institutions" instead of predominately White institutions to acknowledge that arguments surrounding structural diversity with regards to the exact numbers of White students versus students of color has less to do with the "appearance" of diversity than the historical and contemporary racial infrastructures that are in place that still overwhelmingly advantage Whites at the expense of communities of color who attend these institutions (Mobley, 2017; Mobley & Johnson, 2019; Smith et al., 2006).

2. Ogbu and Simons (2008) contended that "involuntary (non-immigrant) minorities are communities that have been conquered, colonized, or enslaved. Unlike immigrant minorities, non-immigrants have been made to be a part of the U.S. society permanently against their will. Two distinguishing features of involuntary minorities are that (1) they did not choose but were forced against their will to become a part of the United States, and (2) they themselves usually interpret their presence in the United States as forced on them by White people" (pp. 165–66).

3. The Higher Education Act of 1965, as amended, defines an HBCU as "any historically Black college or university established prior to 1964, whose principal mission was, and is, the education of Black Americans" (White House Initiative on Historically Black Colleges and Universities, 2018).

4. The Morrill Act of 1862 established public universities throughout the United States. These institutions were established to provide access to members of the working class so that they could gain a liberal and practical education (Lee & Keys, 2013; Thelin, 2011).

5. The Freedman's Bureau was a United States federal government agency that provided financial subsidies to newly freed Blacks during the Reconstruction period. This agency is most noted for their work and influence in establishing colleges and universities created for the sole purpose of educating Blacks and providing funding to these institutions (Anderson, 1988a; Thelin, 2011). The second Morrill Act (1892) was established to further expand access to postsecondary

education by barring governmental funding to states that upheld the distinction of race in their admissions practices. States were, however, provided separate funds to create colleges and universities for Blacks. Many of these institutions are now known as many of our public HBCUs (Lee & Keys, 2013; Thelin, 2011).

References

Aiello, T. (2012). Violence is a classroom: The 1972 Grambling and Southern riots and the trajectory of Black student protest. *Louisiana History: The Journal of Louisiana Historical Association, 53*(2), 261–91.

Allen, W. R., & Jewell, J. O. (2002). A backward glance forward: Past, present and future perspectives on historically Black colleges and universities. *The Review of Higher Education, 25*(3), 241–61.

Anderson, J. D. (1988a). *The education of Blacks in the South*. University of North Carolina Press.

Anderson, J. D. (1988b). Northern foundations and the shaping of Southern Black rural education, 1902–1935. *History of Education Quarterly, 18*(4), 371–96.

Bell, D. A. (1980). Brown v. Board of Education and the interest convergence dilemma. *Harvard Law Review, 93*(3), 518–33.

Biondi, M. (2012). *Black revolution on campus*. University of California Press.

Brazzell, J. C. (1992). Bricks without straw: Missionary-sponsored Black higher education in the post-emancipation era. *Journal of Higher Education, 63*(1), 2649.

Brown, M. C., & Davis, J. E. (2001). The historically Black college as social contract, social capitol, and social equalizer. *Peabody Journal of Education, 76*(1), 31–49.

Carter, D. T. (2013). *Rebellion in black and white: Southern student activism in the 1960s*. Johns Hopkins University Press.

Commodore, F. (2017). The tie that binds: Trusteeship, values, and the decision-making process at AME-affiliated HBCUs. *The Journal of Higher Education*, 1–25. DOI: 10.1080/00221546.2017.1396949

Commodore, F. (2019). Losing herself to save herself: Perspectives on conservatism and concepts of self for Black women aspiring to the HBCU presidency. *Hypatia, 34*(3), 1–23. doi:10.1111/hypa.12480

Dancy, T. E., Edwards, K. T., & Earl Davis, J. (2018). Historically white universities and plantation politics: Anti-Blackness and higher education in the Black Lives Matter era. *Urban Education, 53*(2), 176–95.

Decker, T. N. (2014). Not in my backyard: Puritan morality versus puritan mercantilism and its impact on HBCUs. In M. Gasman & F. Commodore (Eds.), *Opportunities and challenges at historically Black colleges and universities* (pp. 235–52). Palgrave Macmillan.

Douglas, T. M. O. (2012). HBCUs as sites of resistance: The malignity of materialism, western masculinity, and spiritual malefaction. *The Urban Review*, 44, 378–400.

Du Bois, W. E. B. (2003). *The souls of black folk*. W. W. Norton & Company. (Original work published 1903)

Dunn, F. (1993). The educational philosophies of Washington, DuBois, and Houston: Laying the foundations for Afrocentrism and multiculturalism. *The Journal of Negro Education*, 62(1), 24–34.

Fanon, F. (1969). *Toward the African revolution: Political essays*. Grove Press.

Fanon, F. (2008). *Black skin, white masks* (R. Philcox, Trans.). Grove Press. (Original work published 1952)

Ferguson, R. A. (2005). The stratifications of normativity. *Rhizomes*, 10. http://www.rhizomes.net/issue10/ferguson.htm

Frazier, E. F. (1957). *Black bourgeoisie*. Simon & Schuster.

Gasman, M. (2016). Historically Black colleges and universities. In Stone, J. Rutledge, D. M., Smith, A.D., Rizova, P. S., & Hou, X. (Eds.), *The Wiley Blackwell encyclopedia of race, ethnicity, and nationalism* (pp. 978–982). Wiley-Blackwell.

Genovese, E. D. (1992). *From rebellion to revolution: Afro-American slave revolts in the making of the modern world*. Louisiana State University Press.

Grundy, S. (2012). "An air of expectancy": Class, crisis, and the making of manhood at a historically Black college for men. *The ANNALS of the American Academy of Political and Social Science*, 642(1), 43–60.

Harper, S. R., & Gasman, M. (2008). Consequences of conservatism: Black male undergraduates and the politics of historically Black colleges and universities. *The Journal of Negro Education*, 77(4), 336–51.

Higginbotham, E. B. (1993). *Righteous discontent: The women's movement in the black Baptist church, 1880–1920*. Harvard University Press.

hooks, b. (1992). *Black looks: Race and representation*. Boston, MA: South End Press.

hooks, b. (1996). *Reel to real: Race, sex, and class at the movies*. Routledge.

Ladson-Billings, G. (1998). Just what is critical race theory and what's it doing in a nice field like education?. *International Journal of Qualitative Studies in Education*, 11(1), 7–24.

Lamon, L. C. (1974). The Black community in Nashville and the Fisk University student strike of 1924–1935. *The Journal of Southern History*, 40, 225–44.

Lee, J. M., & Keys, S. W. (2013). Land-grant but unequal state one-to-one match funding for 1890 land-grant universities. Washington, DC: Association of Public and Land-Grant Universities.

Logan, R. W. (1969). *Howard University: The first hundred years, 1867–1967*. New York University.

Lopez, G. R. (2003). The (racially neutral) politics of education: A critical race theory perspective. *Educational Administration Quarterly*, 39(1), 68–94.

Mann, H. (1903). *Education and prosperity*. Directors of the Old South Work. (Original work published 1848)

Minor, J. T. (2004). Decision making in historically Black colleges and universities: Defining the governance context. *Journal of Negro Education, 73*, 40–52.

Mobley, S. D., Jr. (2015). *Difference amongst your own: The lived experiences of low-income African-American students and their encounters with class within elite historically Black college (HBCU) environments* [Doctoral dissertation]. University of Maryland, College Park. ProQuest Digital Dissertations (3725526).

Mobley, S. D., Jr. (2017). Seeking sanctuary: (Re)Claiming the power of historically Black colleges and universities as places of Black refuge. *International Journal of Qualitative Studies in Education, 30*(10), 1036–41.

Mobley, Jr., S. D., & Hall, L. (2020). (Re)Defining queer and trans* student retention and success at Historically Black Colleges and Universities. *Journal of College Student Retention: Research, Theory & Practice, 21*(4), 497–519.

Mobley, Jr., S. D., & Johnson, J. M. (2019). "No pumps allowed": The "problem" with gender expression and the Morehouse College "Appropriate Attire Policy." *Journal of Homosexuality, 66*(7), 867–95.

Mobley, Jr., S. D., Johnson, R. W., Sewell, J. P., Johnson, J. M., & Neely, A. J. (forthcoming). "We are not victims": Un-masking the narratives of HBCU Black queer student activism. *About Campus*.

Mobley, Jr., S. D., McNally, T., & Moore, G. (2019). (Re)Centering the narrative: Revealing the potential for HBCUs to be liberatory environments for queer students. In E. M. Zamani Gallaher, D. D. Choudhuri, & J. L. Taylor (Eds.), *Rethinking LGBTQIA students and collegiate contexts: Identity, policies, and campus climate.* (pp. 99–119). Routledge.

Mobley, Jr., S. D., Solomon II, S. L., & Johnson, A. C. (2017). Securing the future: Creating "social engineers" for societal change at historically Black college and university law schools. In T. F. Boykin, A. A. Hilton, & R. T. Palmer (Eds.), *Professional education at Historically Black Colleges and Universities: Past trends and future outcomes* (pp. 29–46). Routledge.

Moore, M. (2015). LGBT populations in studies of urban neighborhoods: Making the invisible visible. *City and Community, 14*(3), 245–48.

Morrison, T. (1974, August). Rediscovering Black history. *New York Times Magazine, 11*, p. 220.

Nguyen, T., Samayoa, A. C., Gasman, M., & Mobley, S. D., Jr. (2018). Challenging respectability: Student health directors providing services to lesbian and gay students at historically Black colleges and universities. *Teachers College Record, 120*(2), 1–44.

Njoku, N., Butler, M., & Beatty, C. C. (2017). Reimagining the historically Black college and university (HBCU) environment: Exposing race secrets and the binding chains of respectability and othermothering. *International Journal of Qualitative Studies in Education, 30*(8), 783–99.

Ogbu, J. U., & Simons, H. D. (2008). Voluntary and involuntary minorities: A cultural-ecological theory of school performance with some implications for education. *Anthropology & Education Quarterly, 29,* 155–88.

Patton, L. D. (2014). Preserving respectability or blatant disrespect? A critical discourse analysis of the Morehouse Appropriate Attire Policy and implications for intersectional approaches to examining campus policies. *International Journal of Qualitative Studies, 27*(6), 724–46.

Peeps, J. M. S. (1981). Northern philanthropy and the emergence of Black higher education—do-gooders, compromisers, or co-conspirators? *Journal of Negro Education, 50*(3), 251–69.

Redd, K. E. (1998). Historically Black colleges and universities: Making a comeback. *New Directions for Higher Education, 102,* 33–43.

Rosenthal, J. (1975). Southern Black student activism: Assimilation vs. nationalism. *The Journal of Negro Education, 44*(2), 113–29.

Sybrina Fulton one year later: Mother of Trayvon Martin visits Howard. (2013). *The Jurist: Howard University School of Law News Journal, 22*(1). Retrieved December 8, 2019, from http://www.law.howard.edu/dictator/media/230/2013_jurist.pdf

Smith, W. A., Yosso, T. J., & Solórzano, D. G. (2006). Challenging racial battle fatigue on historically white campuses: A critical race examination of race-related stress. In C. A. Stanley (Ed.), *Faculty of color: Teaching in predominantly white colleges and universities* (pp. 299–327). Anker.

Squire, D., Williams, B, & Tuitt, F. (2018). Plantation politics and neoliberal racism in higher education: A framework for reconstructing anti-racist institutions. *Teachers College Record, 120*(14), 1–20.

Sullivan, S. (2004). Ethical slippages, shattered horizons, and the zebra striping of the unconscious: Fanon on social, bodily, and psychical space. *Philosophy & Geography, 7*(1), 9–24.

Sullivan, S. (2006). *Revealing whiteness: The unconscious habits of racial privilege.* Indiana University Press.

Thelin, J. (2011). *A history of American higher education.* The Johns Hopkins University Press.

Warnke, G. (2005). Race, gender, and antiessentalist politics. *Signs, 31*(1), 93–116.

Watkins, W. (2001). *White architects of Black education: Ideology and power in America, 1865–1954.* Teachers College Press.

Wheatle, K. I., & Commodore, F. (2019). Reaching back to move forward: The historic and contemporary role of student activism in the development and implementation of higher education policy. *The Review of Higher Education, 42*(5), 5–35.

White House Initiative on Historically Black Colleges and Universities. (2018). http://www2.ed.gov/about/inits/list/whhbcu/edlite-index.html

Williams, J. L. (2018, March 14). What about Cheyney University? We rose first! *Diverse Issues in Higher Education.* http://diverseeducation.com/article/112097/

Williams, J., & Ashley, D. (2004). *I'll find a way or make one: A tribute to historically Black colleges and universities.* Harper Collins.

Williamson, J. A. (2004). "This has been quite a year for heads falling": Institutional autonomy in the civil rights era. *History of Education Quarterly, 44,* 554–76.

Wolters, R. (1975). *The new Negro on campus: Black college rebellions of the 1920s.* Princeton University.

Chapter 4

Fugitive Slave Act(s)

The Emergence of Black Studies as an Exemplar for Black Future(s) Insurrection

WILSON KWAMOGI OKELLO

Setting the Scene

In 1851, Dr. Samuel Cartwright named a disease he claimed was unique to Black bodies.[1] He termed it "Drapetomania" (Drapetomania, n.d.), a disorder that creates within the Negro an uncontrollable desire to escape. Cartwright's thesis, and others like it, were issued to justify the enslavement of Black individuals. Additionally, laws such as the Fugitive Slave Act (1793), authorized governments to "seize and return escaped slaves to their owners and imposed penalties on anyone who aided in their flight." (Fugitive Slave Act, n.d.). Controlling mechanisms that function to keep the Black body in its place (Hartman, 2008), part of a long transcript of surveillance tactics inscribed on the American cultural text by way of plantation politics, have had the cross-generational effect of instructing how Blackness is understood in higher education. While Cartwright and his proponents' reasoning was debunked as scientific racism, their observations were not wrong. The Negro earnestly desires to be free. Given the ubiquity of plantation politics, that is, those colonial vestiges designed to maintain and perpetuate white supremacy and anti-Black racism (see

Dian Squire's chapter in this volume), this chapter endeavors to explicate *fugitive acts*, specifically the desires of Black bodies to escape surveillance in and through higher education by challenging epistemic violence and engaging in knowledge production.

To accomplish this, the first part of this chapter theorizes on the captive/enslaved Black body (Spillers, 1987) with a Black feminist framing that starts from the beginning (i.e., the pressures of colonization, the Middle Passage, and the establishment of institutional slavery). I read this history alongside Cheryl Harris's (1998) thesis of white property, which situates slavery as a system that facilitated the merger of white identity and property. The second part of this chapter illustrates how fugitive acts built on the insubordinate praxis of antebellum Black epistemology. To clarify this praxis, I lean on the pragmatic futurism of Maria Stewart, David Walker, and Ida B. Wells. As ministers of public insurrection, I submit that their exposure of plantation politics (control, assimilation, etc.), reconstitution of Black subjectivity, and rupture of surveillance charted new territory for Black dignity and livelihood. The third part of this chapter, an outgrowth of insurrection legacies, investigates the public emergence of the Black (studies) intellectual cannon as an academic discipline. I argue that this was an act of insurrection designed to expose and reverse irrationality projected onto Black bodies (epistemic violence), and continues to be central in imagining alternative futures for Black lives.

Captive Beginnings

The notion of Black bodies as property was not a spontaneous idea; rather, it was a deliberate rendering from the architects of the United States. According to James Baldwin (1985), these architects decided that the priority for property took precedence over the possibility of some lives being seen as human. With this extrapolation, one is able to identify the benefits of securing whiteness, and the racism that engenders its reproduction. Harris's (1998) thesis on *whiteness as property* buttresses this point, denoting whiteness as that "which meets the functional criteria of property. Specifically, the law has accorded 'holders' of whiteness the same privileges and benefits accorded holders of other types of property . . . the exclusive rights of possession, use, and disposition" (p. 281). To draw a sharp distinction between the experiences of Black lives, white people in higher education are thus granted the exclusive rights of possession, use, and disposition. According to Harris (1998), the right to disposition holds that the entitlement of whiteness cannot be taken away or separated from those who hold it. The right to use and enjoy whiteness references its ability to be both experienced and deployed as a resource. Whiteness "can move from being a passive characteristic as an aspect of identity to an active entity" (Harris, 1998, p. 282), to fulfill, will, and exercise power. Possession, as rights bestowed upon whiteness, adds to these principles the absolute right to exclude those deemed not white from the privileges of whiteness.

Legal statutes have been the fulcrum by which Black bodies are (re)membered in their (non)being. Saidiya Hartman (2008) agreed, declaring that "if slavery persists as an issue in the political life of black America . . . it is because black lives are imperiled and devalued by a racial calculus and a political arithmetic that were entrenched centuries ago" (p. 6). Importantly, this is not because of an obsession with tales of history or due to the burden of a "too long memory" (p. 6) but because of the ways in which Black bodies live histories of trauma in the present as the grounds they walk on everyday. Hortense Spillers (1987) described the order of sequence that represents the African presence in the Western cultural imagination as one of "mutilation, dismemberment, and exile" (p. 67). This tragic terrorism marked a definitive moment of constitution, a point in the arc of history where parameters were outlined as to whom or what one was signified as, and capable of becoming.

This arrangement marked "a theft of the body—willful and violent severing of the captive body from its motive will, its active desire" (Spillers, 1987, p. 67). Under these estranged conditions the body lost its nominative properties and became the territory of cultural and political imposition of dominant communities. At this point of convergence, the body was relegated to specific uses and meaning. First, the captive body became the source of an irresistible, destructive sensuality. Secondly, the captive body was reduced to a thing for the captor. In the absence of a subject position, the captured sexualities provided a physical and biological expression of otherness. Finally, as a category of otherness, the enslaved embodies sheer physical powerlessness that slides into a more general powerlessness, resonating through various centers of human and social meaning (Spillers, 1987). Under this constitution, the body came to represent a metaphor for values thoroughly entrenched in the American memory—a hieroglyphics of the flesh whose branding, symbolically, transfers across hers/history, from one generation to another.

In a US context, the enslaved, and the offspring of the enslaved, had an identity undefined until or unless awarded by those who dominated them. Unrecognized in slavery and thus absent of meaning, Black bodies held no dominion, which extended but was not limited to naming. Spillers (1987) notes, "The captivating party does not only 'earn' the right to dispose of the captive body as it sees fit, but gains consequently, the right to name and *name it*" (p. 69). The powers of distortion that are owned by the dominant community act as levers of citizenship under their prerogative. Situated acutely in an her/historical context, the captive body surrenders to a governing episteme that remains, however muted or disguised, in the originating metaphors of captivity and dismemberment "so that it is as if neither time nor history, nor historiography and its topic, show movement, as the human subject is 'murdered' over and over again" (Spillers, 1987, p. 68). This order of symbolism and hers/historical tracing represents what Spillers (1987) calls an *American grammar*.

It has become popular to think about narratives of Blackness in Western culture as a story of triumph. While not untrue, Spillers's projection delimits a fuller, more nuanced story than what emerges in progressive discourse. A framing of the Black body that starts from the beginning, under the pressures of events consisting of colonization of an indigenous Africa, the Middle Passage, and the establishment of institutional slavery, necessitates a rupture of contemporary cultural understandings of dignity and personhood, while also demonstrating the effectual power of the plantation ethos to move across time and space.

Taking Spillers's thesis on American grammar to be true raises several critical questions, the first of which asks, How should we understand the metamorphosis from chattel to person, vis-à-vis, freedom? The unfortunate truth is that the advent of freedom in the Western, US imagination was put forth with constraints that placed limitations on conceptions of liberty, sovereignty, and equity. Emancipation did not mirror the desires of the enslaved, alternatively leading to a "resubordination of the emancipated, the control and domination of the free black population, and the persistent production of blackness as abject, threatening, and irrational" (Hartman, 1997, p. 116). The achievement of freedom, against plantation politics that frame the Black body as described above, signaled a transition from the indiscriminate technologies of enslavement to the "burdened individuality" of the freed person (p. 117). This is to say, the graduated body out of enslavement represents diminutive elevation, and the disingenuous extension of mobility found in plantation politics. This precarious and newly born autonomy resulted in the paradoxical construction of free persons as self-determining and burdened, and whose existence was still heavily regulated and policed in the interests of a growing capitalist state. The double-bound nature of freedom was such that it created notions of Black personhood with all of the burdens and a few of the entitlements that came to characterize white humanity in the Western, US context. Higher education, in effect, offers similar claims of freedom for Black lives, promising that in exchange for their assimilation—framed as a privately owned decision to attend an institution by an autonomous adult—they will be granted sociopolitical power and mobility, equivalent to that of white humanity, upon graduation. The paradox of contemporary freedom is that it masquerades narrow choice(s) as the acceptance of ongoing domination.

A second question raised against the backdrop of Spillers's American grammar asks, How have plantation politics truncated and circumscribed notions of freedom through the apparatus of higher education? Again, if we take Spillers's thesis to be true, can Black and minoritized students on college campuses experience freedom through rational apportionments? Moreover, what should the curricula of emancipation entail, such that it does not simply reproduce or democratize the entitlements conferred upon whiteness? The next section takes up these questions by pointing to the radical praxis of Maria Stewart, David Walker, and Ida B. Wells and how they might direct educators in a politics of disruption.

The Formation of Insubordinate Praxis

Fugitive: a person who has escaped from a place.

—Lexico, n.d.

Plantation politics was and is about control. *Keep the body, take the mind.* In this statement, readers witness principles of colonialism that have endured generations and seeped into higher education (Duran & Okello, 2018). This familiar plantation phrase serves as an entrée into versions of schooling that tranquilize the psyche by taming the body, ensuring that students cooperate with the agenda of the status quo. Schooling in many ways has become a training ground for acquiescence (Duran & Okello, 2018) and the passive acceptance of rules in society that prop up systems of dehumanization, oppression, and exploitation; these directives are replenished through epistemic violence and are fashioned to monitor disruption.

"Epistemic violence" should be understood here as that which interrupts opportunities to take hold of ways of knowing and being that would otherwise engender power for minoritized people. Kyra T. Shahid (2015) discusses the term as "numerous projects in history, philosophy, and literature that endorsed claims to knowledge that identified colonized communities as other" (p. 63). Thomas Teo (2008) states that epistemic violence can "range from misrepresentations and distortions, to a neglect of the voices of the *Other*, to statements of inferiority, and to the recommendations of adverse practices or infringements concerning the *Other*" (p. 58). This displacement has the intended effect of sustaining hegemony in its many forms. The evidence of this pattern is recognizable in curricula design (Soto & Joseph, 2010), in disciplining styles of pedagogy (Freire, 1970; Ladson-Billings, 1995), and in efforts to quell student voices (Hope et al., 2016). This brand of domination, however, has not gone unchallenged. There are those who embody noncompliance, most readily observed in the fugitive event.

To label someone disobedient or insubordinate is to determine that they meet some qualification as property. Implicit in the fugitive event is that one (a subordinate) has violated the terms of their apportioned status. The perceived subordinate has evaded the constraints intended to legislate their actions. They are in a transient space. They have upset panoptic powers, and thus they are criminal. Breaches of these social contracts typically assume that escapees are fleeing from their pursuers (those who desire to maintain control).

Fugitives, I argue, were not simply those who escaped the various assaults on their captive flesh but those who had passed over and through psychological barriers that were supposed to keep both the mind and the flesh chained. Fugitives in the plantation context harbored a deep desire to experience freedom beyond the panoramic view of the captor's porch. Their longing to escape the tyranny of surveillance and the miseries of bondage are evident in micro- and macro-level resistance strategies that held political significance (Hartman, 1997; Scott, 1990). Most often, these moments of disobedience were disguised by public performances of deference, loyalty, prudence, and circumspect behavior, which conveyed to power holders an agreement with the terms of their condition. The safest displays of this political discourse were enacted as flattering self-images of those in power.

The enslaved, according to James C. Scott (1990), were able to make use of this small rhetorical space to appeal for better food and human treatment without appearing seditious. In contrast to these representations, the hidden transcript, or offstage speech and gestures, captured the true feelings of those enslaved outside of the intimidating gaze of the controlling elite. Enslaved persons also made use of shielded strategies such as folk tales, songs, and rituals to openly disguise their freedom rumblings. Rare were the moments of open rebellion that could swiftly be met with the strokes of repression. Though "infrapolitics" (Scott, 1990, p. 19), or the low-profile forms of resistance were more frequent, the rupture between the public and the hidden transcript will be the focus of this section. Maria Stewart, David Walker, and Ida B. Wells were coconspirators in the disruption of plantation politics and the epistemic violence that accompanied it.

Though Stewart, Walker, and Wells were born *free*, their bodies carried a historical memory that would not let them forget their systematically inscribed place in the social hierarchy. More pointedly, the designation of free for Black bodies should be met with suspicion at best, and disregard at worst, because the concept was laced with parameters, caveats, and a disingenuous allotment of sociopolitical power for the freed. Notwithstanding these markers, Stewart, Walker, and Wells masterfully employed text and speech toward the exposure of plantation politics, the reconstitution of Black subjectivity, and an uncompromising rupture of surveillance.

Insubordinate acts gain their social force by virtue of their roots in the hidden transcript of a subordinate group. These transcripts are the archives that make the public act of insubordination possible. Walker and Stewart were judicious in their excavation of the social, cultural, and political artifacts that orchestrated life for many Black people. In full recognition of the consequences that might await them, they opted to expose plantation politics by speaking directly to the controlling elite, thereby *rupturing the surveillance* that called for Black bodies to remain in silence; they refused to comply with hegemonic performance. Walker (1830) repudiated, "I am fully aware, in making this appeal to my much afflicted and suffering brethren, that I shall not only be assailed by those whose greatest earthly desires are, to keep us in abject ignorance and wretchedness, and who are of the firm conviction that Heaven has designed us and our children to be slaves and *beasts of burden* to them and their children" (p. 4). In the same spirit, Stewart (1835) declared, "Many will suffer for pleading the cause of oppressed Africa, and I shall glory being one of her martyrs; for I am firmly persuaded, that the God in whom I trust is able to protect me from the rage and malice of mine enemies, and from them that will rise up against me; and if there is no other way for me to escape, he is able to take me to himself" (as quoted in Richardson, 1987, p. 30). More than just breaches of procedure and order, acts of public insubordination necessarily call into question the collective's subordination and cannot be written off, or repaired, by the controlling forces as a lapse in conformity. Most times, the enslaved exercised "tight control over the impulses either to verbal or physical defiance" (Scott, 1990, p. 208). Walker and Stewart rupture this surveillance agenda by placing their bodies and voices on the line, in public. Loosening the voice is key here, but not to be missed is the principle warring over the body. If we understand the body as property, then it is essential that we see it as a site of ongoing struggle: "When a slave cannot be flogged, they are more than half way free" (Douglass, 1855, p. 152). Insubordination pressed against the disciplining prowess of what the enslaved body was supposed to do, which invited new questions of what was probable. How the body performs, what it enacts, and what it reenacts is in itself a dialogue with witnesses that gives way to what George J. Sefa Dei (2017) calls embodied knowledge.

Dei (2017) stated that knowledge is gained by somatically sitting with what our bodies feel when engaging with others in a particular setting and context. Walker and Stewart in this way serve as the existential nexus, that is, the canvas on which definitions rotate, deviate, and come to life as they reflect the corporeal sentiment of their articulated speech. Plainly, they embody the very theories of dignity that they profess. Walker did this by textually scripting: "My object is, if possible, to awaken in the breasts of my afflicted, degraded and slumbering brethren, a spirit of inquiry and investigation respecting our miseries and wretchedness in this *Republican Land of Liberty*" (Walker, 1830, p. 4). For Stewart, her presence served the dual deliberate purpose of challenging the dominant elite and empowering women of color: "How long shall the fair daughters of Africa be compelled to bury their minds and talents beneath a load of iron pots and kettles? . . . We have never had an opportunity of displaying our talents; therefore the world thinks we know nothing. And we have been possessed of by far too mean and cowardly a disposition" (as quoted in Richardson, 1987, p. 30). Walker and Stewart facilitate an unlearning of oppressive order and instigate the arousal of what Black feminist theorist Alexis Pauline Gumbs calls "livable and loving logics" (Gumbs, 2010, p. 4). Their work survives an intergenerational archive that turns the (re)presentation of language into life, and serves as an intervention into contemporary understandings of subjectivity that offer alternative forms of sociality for minoritized bodies and dominant bodies alike.

Similarly, Wells, surviving in the postemancipation and Reconstruction era, offers a portrait of fugitivity that serves not only as an exemplar of insubordinate praxis but also as a curriculum for confronting epistemic violence by recapturing the subjugated body (Royster, 2016). Embodying a fearless iconoclasm, Wells facilitated an unrelenting critique of plantation logics, which were largely facilitated through material violence as an auxiliary of epistemic violence. As a controlling mechanism, lynching existed in the aftermath of slavery largely as a barbaric form of collective punishment meted to and against Black communities to maintain white dominance and prevent Black economic mobility and political power (James, 1999). The basis for this ritual was rooted in the mythology of Black men's obsession with white women. For this reason, Well's antilynching insurgency battled against racial-sexual terror, laying the groundwork for future iterations of Black antiracist feminism.

Wells exposed the racial inversion of sexual violence as a rationale for white supremacist hostility and obfuscation of sexual assault toward Black women (James, 1999). This praxis functioned to create a viable political language that could critique the standard rational moralism of a white-dominated culture. This work is pivotal because "during slavery, blacks were generally denied the right to testify against whites, because they were not seen as credible witnesses, so when the only (willing) witnesses to white crimes were black, these crimes would not be brought to light" (Mills, 2007, p. 32). Thus, if publicizing knowledge is one way to confront epistemic violence, Wells was a forerunner. Due in large part to her journalistic sensibilities and investigative reporting, the public was made aware of facts of lynching terror that were sanitized by white courts and the press (Royster, 2016). This model of indicting rationality, rupturing silence, and establishing a record of disproportionality brought Black feminism into conversation with the tradition of Black nationalism (James, 1999), a legacy that would serve as an approach to freedom in and through the cultivation of Black studies curricula. Insubordinate praxis provides a *cite* (captive beginnings) and *sight* of possibilities (Stewart, Walker, and Wells) for Black lives that have been trained into docility. Bringing about alternative futures, however, must locate emancipatory sensibilities in a *site*. Higher education offers one such spatiality by which Black fugitives would stage and (re)present their insurrection(s).

Act(s) of Insurrection

Under the guise of holistic outcomes, *schooling* takes place in and throughout institutions of higher education. As mentioned above, schooling represents the regulation and training of human capital to reproduce the status quo. In cases of higher education, Black bodies, through curricular and conditioning strategies, are trained away from themselves through submission to contemporary data-driven outcomes of education. This is different from education, which should be conceptualized as that which exists to empower, liberate, and transform. Plantation politics are weakened by the thought that Black bodies might be able to (re)member (Dillard, 2012) themselves, that is piece themselves back together at the core, which would disaffirm rationality and objectivity as the true basis of holistic education (Walton, 1969). Black studies was to be an intervention occurring inside the gates.

Historians cite the emergence of Black studies as "the refusal to give over our lives, our creativity, our history, our future into the hands of white America, for have they proved themselves totally inadequate" (Biondi, 2012, p. 178). Articulating a broad condemnation of old perspectives, Black studies sought to create a viable ideological alternative to the epistemic violence taking place in higher education. Black young people of the 1960s, in the United States, were inheriting a burden that, regardless of their moral, social, or political orientation as conservative, moderate, or liberal, situated their bodies as marked, the very absence of humanness (Holland, 2000), an inheritance that, while heavy, menacing, and egregious, has been carted for generations.

Due to the nature of this inscribed inheritance, in a culture that demands acquiescence, respectability, and assimilation, the marked body has a decision to make. The genesis of the Black student movement locates its root of life in the gardens of Black nationalism. Black Power, its most seasoned fruit, was a sociopolitical text whose rhetoric, strategic analysis, and tactics were a break from the politics of civil disobedience, nonviolence, and integration that directed much of the civil rights movement of the times. For those advocating Black Power, "nonviolence" was an approach to civil rights that "Black people could not afford and a luxury white people did not deserve" (Carmichael & Hamilton, 1967, p. 53). Alternatively, Black Power summoned a revised, critical consciousness that was deconstructive and reconstructive in nature. The goal of Black Power, as communicated by Stokely Carmichael and Charles Hamilton (1967), was "full participation in the decision making processes affecting the lives of Black people, [and] recognition of the virtues in the themselves" (p. 47). Black Power would name, with consistency and vigor, the contradictions of American values.

Given the turmoil of the 1950s and 1960s that included deaths of Emmett Till (1955), Addie Mae Collins (1963), Denise McNair (1963),

Carole Robertson (1963), Cynthia Wesley (1963), Medgar Evers (1963), Malcolm X (1965), and Martin Luther King (1968), there was profound questioning of integrationist philosophies that counseled patience and long-suffering. Black Power was reconstructive in the sense that there would be an emphasis placed on self-reliance and self-determination, which would manifest in the creation of institutions and the management of economics in the community. It was Malcolm's Black Nationalist position, prominently, that convinced students of the failure of old modes of change, and that if there were to be a critical rise en masse, a new mode could be demanded. Black students heard him. With the moderate gains of Black student enrollment into historically white universities in the mid- to late 1960s, higher education was set to become an extension of the broader movement.

Rejecting Assimilation

Instructed by plantation politics to concede identifiers associated with Blackness, for safety, security, and the possibility of mobility, students began to question these de facto moral codes and their fidelity to them. "The false concept of basic Negro inferiority is one of the curses that still lingers . . . we were taught a pretty lie—excel and the whole world lies open before you. I obeyed the injunction and found it to be wishful thinking" (Carmichael & Hamilton, 1967, p. 52). Budding in their activism, students began to narrate their objections, resolving, "They wanted us to pretend we were just like them . . . we began to see that whites weren't supermen" (Biondi, 2012, p. 17). Demystifying whiteness assisted Black students in recognizing their own humanity.

At Amherst College, for example, students described standards of marginalization that banned them to the periphery of the college community and the curriculum. Interestingly, the stated goal of the institution was the "preparation of the whole man," the mirror of a cultural ideology that upheld paternalistic versions of manhood and piety (Williams, 2014, p. 21). Acute in their analysis, Black students at Amherst found the "whole man" ideology uncomfortable because it sought to "produce men who were analytical . . . and believed in very little except themselves and their . . . position in a world of privilege created by their forefathers and mothers" (Williams, 2014, p. 91). When encouraged by deans to "be your own man," Horace Porter (2003), a student at the college, asked rhetorically, "How could we be our own men in a system that is racially and politically rigged? How could we be our own men when the courses we took were basically the same ones taken by the men who sat in our nation's highest councils of power?" (p. 67). Implied in this redress is an argument that university curriculums and climates were threatening the self-concept of Black students by waging what preeminent scholar Harold Cruse and Black Power advocates called domestic colonialism (Carmichael & Hamilton, 1967; Cruse, 1967).

Domestic colonialism, as noted by historian Kabria Baumgartner (2016), "characterized the exploitative relationship of white (domination) to black (subjugation)" (p. 299), a mirror of the plantation politics. Language such as this armored Black students with a vocabulary for understanding their experiences under a Eurocentric curriculum at a predominantly white liberal arts curriculum college. Another student of the era, Rusan Wilson, added, "We were these nice little Southern girls, who had probably even brought white gloves with us. This was a period where, literally, you started off as a colored girl and ended up four years later a Black women" (Biondi, 2012, p. 18). Apparent in these testimonies, and in many others like them, was a natural politicization being brought to the fore through the insertion of Black Power to the Black college student ethos. Coming to understand that the state was lacking in integrity, while simultaneously recognizing the dignity they deserved, students surmised no one could be "healthy, complete and mature" if they were being asked to deny a part of the themselves—and this denial, they believed, was simmering under the banner of colonialism and concession of integration (Carmichael & Hamilton, 1967, p. 55). Black Power was a rejoinder to the logic that reinforced a sense of pride and self-acceptance, a language long elusive to students.

Accentuated in these reorientations of personhood was the question of humanness. More to the point, there was a burgeoning public solicitation by students to be seen and recognized for their humanity, a task that the American establishment was considerably sidestepping. Resentment of this ideal induced general suspicion and distrust of the objectives of the university structure and society. Actively reframing a Blackness that would enable them to push back against the deceit of whiteness, a Berkeley student aptly noted, "They never let us forget we were Black . . . so we decided to remember we were black." Another student resolved, "We refuse . . . to jeopardize four years of our lives becoming socialized to fit a white dominant cultural pattern" (Biondi, 2012, p. 22).

This general disposition raises questions about the expectations that Black and minoritized students had of higher education institutions. One could assume from their displeasures that there was, at one time, a sense of optimism that propelled student's ambitions into the annals of higher education, particularly in the wake of the *Brown v. Board of Education* decision. Seemingly waking up from that dream, many Black students came to associate higher education with the replication of white citizenship.

Reconstituting Subjectivity

In step with the social frustration engulfing the nation was the press to uncover new ideologies that would undergird, guide, and propel Black students' emerging ethos. The current structuring of society, and the ideologies that upheld it, were no longer viable. Coinciding with the Black Power movement, a host of revolutionary leaders were engaged in liberation struggles, both domestically and abroad, that captured students' attention. In their search to explain society, Black students read, debated, and would engage in endless hours of ideological discussion, weighing the merits and positions of thought leaders such as Fidel Castro, the socialist president of Cuba and supporter of the African American freedom struggle; Robert F. Williams; Harold Cruse; Nathan Hare; W. E. B. Du Bois; Karl Marx; E. Franklin Frazier; and Franz Fanon (Biondi, 2012; Rojas, 2007). Black Power was establishing an intellectual dimension, and it was made possible through Black students' veracity and efforts to make sense of their existential situation. Remembering students' gravitation to and identification with colonized peoples internationally, faculty mentor George Henderson (2010) recalls, "Fanon was our fire" (p. 37). Stemming from an in-depth critique of colonialism, which can be understood as the patriarch of the plantation model, Fanon's strategies for achieving solidarity and the manner in which he promoted positive self-images was appealing to Black students at the University of Oklahoma and across the United States. Here we see students' desire for and attachment to not just the rhetorical/textual fervor of Fanon but also what the writings might be able to show them about themselves and the world around them that was specific to their condition.

Thus, the strength of Fanon was in how his writings captured the "psycho-affective realm" (Fanon, 1961, p. xviii) of the colonized subject. In advancing this realm, Fanon is pointing to a line of thinking that privileges neither the subjective nor objective but rather a location that functions between the multiple domains of the self. Using the context of the colonization, Fanon discusses the psycho-affective as "the body, dreams, psychic inversions and displacements . . . it involves the emotions, the imagination or psychic life, but is only ever mobilized into social meaning and historical effect through an embodied and embedded action . . . a performance of agency in the present tense" (p. xix). Fanon maneuvers between the psychic body and the body politic, suggesting that confronting colonialism "is not a rational confrontation of viewpoints. It is not discourse on the universal, but the impassioned claim by the colonized that their world is fundamentally different" (p. 6). In the tradition of Stewart, Walker, and Wells, Fanon's indictment of rationality and ability to name the epistemic violence at bay under colonialism resonated deeply with students who had new found evidence for how erasure from the curriculum contributed to a devalued consciousness.

Seeing this sort of psycho-affective rumination as critical, Fanon discussed it as "the focal point where citizen and individual develop and grow" (Fanon, 1961, p. 40). As reflected above, this explication resonated with the evolving sensibilities of students and with generations of students to follow. As an example of the influence of Fanon on Black futures, historians note that Bobby Seale and Huey Newton both read *The Wretched of Earth*. Supplemented by their engagement with the Afro-American study group meetings on campus at Berkeley, they would lay the groundwork for what would become known as the Black Panther Party.

Black Studies as the Redemption of Western Society

In an era when the image and understanding of the Black body was still deeply historicized (i.e., the subject of terror, mutilation, lynching, subservience)—knowledge production and distribution were methods of reclamation; textual embodiment was the procedure for agency. Demanded, and earned, in Black student advocacy was an assertion of dignity in the curriculum. Black studies anchored this restoration, serving three wide purposes, according to Manning Marable (2000), as descriptive, corrective, and prescriptive: descriptive in that it attempts to provide detail of the materiality of Black life; corrective such that it challenges normative interpretations and assumptions of Black peoples, "raising fundamental questions with regard to the objectivity of social knowledge" (Biondi, 2012, p. 177), troubling the universal applicability of Western theory; and prescriptive in that it presents theoretical and pragmatic models for the purpose of empowering Black bodies in the real word.

As a site of insurrection, it is important to note that Black studies still exists, predominantly, within white institutions, which begs the question of potentialities. In what ways are Black studies programs under the watchful gaze of overseers? What possibilities survive after Black studies courses meet general education requirements? Is it possible to completely reject plantation politics in and through Black studies, inside institutions of higher education? These are hard questions, and Audre Lorde's (1984) parable on the master's tools, perhaps, leaves us with harder answers. I submit, however, that the answers may not be as important as what the insurrection of Black studies teaches us about the link between Black creativity and futurity.

New worlds—places not yet—must be dreamed before they can be made. Black bodies in a Western, US context have always imagined ways to return to themselves, to experience self-definition. Black studies curricula, because of their partnership with the university enterprise, will never be a utopia. Not to be lost, however, is its service as a model for nurturing Black creativity/imaginings through recall, (re)membering, and (re)presentation (Durham, 2014; Okello & Quaye, 2018). Recall (citing), the retracing of captive histories within Black studies, is able to illuminate the many meanings of the Black body as a dynamic entity that is always and already mediated through history. (Re)membering (sight) allows witnesses to place themselves in conversation with artists, thinkers, and doers of histories for the purpose of acting on the present. (Re)presentation (site) calls for a reconfiguring of the body against plantation politics. Stated differently, creativity is how Black bodies wrestle with a real past, an imagined future, and an active, shifting present. How does Black studies inspire other *rehearsal* spaces (Okello & Quaye, 2018), where educators and students alike have the opportunity to practice ownership of their voices and bodies through various aesthetics, with the understanding that the work starts upon leaving the classroom? Examples of this work might include advancing and supporting publishing channels outside of traditional, *high-impact* journals in higher education; educators and students hosting a Black feminist futures conference; and facilitating critical, creative, and interdisciplinary knowledge(s) as core curricula instead of supplemental readings.

Plantation politics is about relations of domination and subordination, and thus the work of living and imagining alternative futures begins with a recognition and examination of one's existential situation. The first part of this chapter spelled out the investment and purpose of plantation politics to the perpetual benefit of dominant parties. Educators owe students an honest and critical assessment of plantation logics (which should presently be understood as *whiteness and white supremacy*) within their scope and how it has functioned historically to debilitate the mobility of some students. This rendering opens the gate for the fugitive event. Confronting epistemic violence, the bold next step, has a long memory that can support transformative acts in the present. Embodying fugitivity, or actively displacing comfort and placing one's body on the line as a site and sight of critique, is a political claim that can rupture surveillance mechanisms, making room for alternative discourses and retheorization of one's subjectivities in a white, Western, context (Dei, 2017). Alternative knowledge production upends the colonial inventions of Black subjectivity and the hegemonic interests they serve. Black studies, a manifestation of insurrection legacies, offers but one example of how Black peoples might creatively take up the work of *escape*, which is to say, surviving the improvisation and adaptability of plantation politics in the present, and scripting possibilities and futures in an anti-Black world.

Notes

1. I borrow Black girlhood scholar Dr. Dominique Hill's language to frame the body (bodies) in this chapter as a dynamic entity with personal and collective manifestations. It is interlaced as mental, emotional, spiritual, and spatial construct that is always mediated through history. (D. Hill, February 7, 2018, personal communication.)

References

Baumgartner, K. (2016). "Be your own man": Student activism and the birth of Black studies at Amherst College, 1965–1972. *The New England Quarterly*, *89*(2), 286–322.

Baldwin, J. (1985). *The price of the ticket: Collected nonfiction, 1948–1985*. Macmillan.

Bay, M. E., Griffin, F. J., Jones, M. S., & Savage, B. D. (Eds.). (2015). *Toward an intellectual history of Black women*. UNC Press Books.

Biondi, M. (2012). *The Black revolution on campus*. University of California Press.

Carmichael, S., & Hamilton, C. (1967). *Black power: The politics of liberation in America*. Random House.

Cruse, H. (1967). *The crisis of the Negro intellectual: A historical analysis of the failure of Black leadership*. New York Review of Books.

Dei, G. J. S. (2017). *Reframing Blackness and Black solidarities through anticolonial and decolonial prisms*. Springer International Publishing.

Dillard, C. B. (2012). Dillard, C. B. (2012). *Learning to (re)member the things we've learned to forget: Endarkened feminisms, spirituality, and the sacred nature of research and teaching.* Peter Lang.
Douglass, F. (1855). *My bondage and my freedom.* Courier Corporation.
Drapetomania. (n.d.). Diseases and peculiarities of the Negro race. *PBS.* https://www.pbs.org/wgbh/aia/part4/4h3106.html
Duran, A., & Okello, W. (2018). An autoethnographic exploration of radical subjectivity as pedagogy. *Journal of Curriculum and Pedagogy, 15*(2), 158–74.
Durham, A. (2014). *Home with hip-hop feminism: Performances in communication and culture.* Peter Lang Publishing Group.
Fanon, F. (1961). *The wretched of the earth.* Maspero.
Freire, P. (1970). *Pedagogy of the oppressed.* Continuum.
Fugitive Slave Act. (n.d.). The fugitive slave act. *History.com.* http://www.history.com/topics/black-history/fugitive-slave-acts
Gumbs, A. P. (2010). *We can learn to mother ourselves: The queer survival of Black feminism 1968–1996* [Doctoral dissertation]. Duke University.
Guy-Sheftall, B. (Ed.). (1995). *Words of fire: An anthology of African-American feminist thought.* The New Press.
Harris, C. (1998). Whiteness as property. In D. Roediger (Ed.), *Black on white: Black writers on what it means to be white* (pp. 103–18). Shocken Books.
Hartman, S. (1997). *Scenes of subjection.* Oxford University Press.
Hartman, S. (2008). *Lose your mother: A journey along the Atlantic slave route.* Macmillan.
Henderson, G. (2010). *Race and the university: A memoir.* University of Oklahoma Press.
Holland, S. P. (2000). *Raising the dead: Readings of death and (Black) subjectivity.* Duke University Press.
Hope, E. C., Keels, M., & Durkee, M. I. (2016). Participation in Black Lives Matter and deferred action for childhood arrivals: Modern activism among Black and Latino college students. *Journal of Diversity in Higher Education, 9*(3), 203.
James, J. (1999). *Shadowboxing: Representations of Black feminist politics.* St. Martin's Press.
Ladson-Billings, G. (1995). Toward a theory of culturally relevant pedagogy. *American Educational Research Journal, 32*(3), 465–91.
Lexico dictionary. (n.d.). https://www.lexico.com/en/definition/fugitive
Lorde, A. (1984). *Sister outsider: Essays and speeches.* Crossing Press.
Marable, M. (2000). Black studies and the racial mountain. *Souls: Critical Journal of Black Politics & Culture, 2*(3), 17–36.
Mills, C. W. (2007). *The racial contract.* Cornell University Press.
Okello, W. K., & Quaye, S. J. (2018). Advancing creativity for pedagogy and practice. *Journal of Curriculum and Pedagogy, 15*(1), 43–57.

Porter, H. (2003). *The making of a Black scholar: From Georgia to the Ivy League.* University of Iowa Press.

Richardson, M. (1987). *Maria W. Stewart, America's first Black woman political writer: Essays and speeches.* Indiana University Press.

Rojas, F. (2007). *From Black power to Black studies: How a radical social movement became an academic discipline.* Johns Hopkins University Press.

Royster, J. J. (2016). *Southern horrors and other writings: The anti-lynching campaign of Ida B. Wells, 1892–1900.* Macmillan Higher Education.

Scott, J. C. (1990). *Domination and the arts of resistance: Hidden transcripts.* Yale University Press.

Shahid, K. T. (2015). Eating from the tree of life: Endarkened feminist revelation. In V. E. Evans-Winters & B. L. Love (Eds.), *Black feminism in education: Black women speak back, up, and out* (pp. 61–70). Peter Lang.

Soto, S. K., & Joseph, M. (2010). Neoliberalism and the battle over ethnic studies in Arizona. *Thought & Action,* 45–56.

Spillers, H. J. (1987). Mama's baby, papa's maybe: An American grammar book. *diacritics, 17*(2), 65–81.

Teo, T. (2008). From speculation to epistemological violence in psychology: A critical hermeneutic reconstruction. *Theory & Psychology, 18*(1), 47–67.

Walker, D. (1830). *David Walker's appeal, in four articles; together with a preamble, to the coloured citizens of the world, but in particular, and very expressly, to those of the United States of America. National Humanities Center.* http://nationalhumanitiescenter.org/pds/triumphnationalism/cman/text5/walker.pdf

Walton, S. F., Jr. (1969). *The Black curriculum: Developing a program in Afro-American studies.* Black Liberation Publishers.

Williams, J. (2014). *Unfinished agenda: Urban politics in the era of Black power.* North Atlantic Books.

Part 2

Institutional Rhetoric and the False Promises of "Diversity" and "Inclusion"

Chapter 5

Inclusion = Racial Violence?

Time, Space, and the Afterlife of the Plantation

ARMOND TOWNS

Across the United States, institutions of higher education have been implementing "inclusivity" policies. The vast majority of these policies concern themselves with increasing student, faculty, and staff of color at historically white institutions. These policies have been attempts to diversify knowledge and to provide comfortable transitions into higher education for people of color. The University of North Carolina at Chapel Hill (UNC), for example, defines its "inclusivity & diversity" policy as an attempt to build "[understanding] across differences, create conditions to ensure the equitable educational and social benefits of diversity, and cultivate a welcoming and supportive environment for undergraduate students, graduate and professional students, faculty, and staff, positioning them to reach their greatest potential" (UNC, 2017). Likewise, the University of Denver (DU) promotes "inclusive excellence" based on the "recognition that a community or institution's success is dependent on how well it values, engages and includes the rich diversity of students, staff, faculty, administrators, and alumni constituents" (DU, 2017). Similar inclusivity policies show up at institutions throughout the United States (Dartmouth College, 2017; Saint Mary's College, 2017; University of Colorado Boulder, 2017; University of Wisconsin–Green Bay, 2017; University of Arizona, 2017).

Each of the aforementioned policies begins with a simple, yet debatable, premise: that "diverse populations" that is, people of color, are "excluded" from higher education. It stands to reason, then, that we diverse populations require "inclusion." However, if one goes slightly deeper into an examination of these universities, then people of color's exclusion becomes far more complicated. The establishment of the UNC, for example, owes its legacy to racial slavery, as many buildings on campus were built by enslaved people that the university contracted from local North Carolina enslavers (Ballinger et al., 2006; Wilder, 2013). Likewise, DU was founded on land inseparable from the Sand Creek massacre of the Arapahoe and Cheyenne in 1864 (John Evans Study Committee, 2014). Indeed, one will be hard-pressed to find a university in the United States that has not directly benefited from racial violence, whether it is genocide, Native removal acts, or racial slavery. Multiple forms of such violence were necessary for the foundation of US institutions of higher education (Wilder, 2013).

In such a context, are the Arapahoe and Cheyenne excluded from DU? Or are their deaths necessary, always already included in the foundation of the university? If one answers affirmative to the first question, then DU is an entity that has made mistakes in the past but is attempting to rectify them via including and welcoming all its students, particularly those who have been historically excluded, such as the Arapahoe and Cheyenne. Here, higher education is an inherent good, and in order to succeed, one must engage the ivory tower. Indeed, as Dian Squire, Bianca Williams, and Frank Tuitt (2018) argue, such a logic fits into the neoliberal "college-degree-is-the-new-high-school-diploma" rhetoric (p. 13), which situates inclusion as a step not to rectify the history of racism but to increase the bottom lines of institutions. This is the position of the inclusivity policies. But if one answers affirmative to the latter question—that the deaths of the Arapahoe and Cheyenne are necessary for DU's foundation—then DU is part of the longer narrative of the inability of US institutions to understand the centrality of racial violence to their establishment. Here, DU is *not* enacting racial violence via excluding students of color. The University of Denver *is* racial violence. From plantations to universities, US institutions require racial violence. If racial violence against people of color is essential to US institutions, then we, people of color, have never been excluded from higher education; instead, history fails to acknowledge our violent inclusion. Contemporary inclusivity policies continue this legacy.

I contend that many universities' inclusivity policies begin with a problematic assumption: that people of color are excluded from the project of higher education. However, the exclusionary logic brushes over the necessity of racial violence to the establishment of what the West has called an institution to begin with. Instead, I show that US higher education begins by legitimizing/including two related forms of racial violence: (1) anti-Blackness and settler colonialism as of necessity to clear land for universities; and (2) Western constructs of knowledge, which begin with conceptualizations of time (progress, civilization, "man," etc.) and space (nature, fixity, the Negro, the Native, etc.) as distinct spheres. Drawing from Tiffany Lethabo King (2016), the plantation exceeds the material practice of racial slavery to encompass the interrelation between "Black fungibility" and settler colonial violence,[1] both of which are essential to "clear spaces" for universities to sit on. Those who claimed people as property not only enslaved Africans but their plantations were set up on illegitimate land grabs; this linked white self-determined capacity with "pioneerhood."

In this chapter, I take a cultural studies approach to inclusivity policies to consider the way that these policies remain complicit within the plantation politics from which they emerge. Pulling from Squire et al. (2018), I consider plantation politics as the "parallel organization and cultural norms between contemporary higher education institutions and slave plantations" (p. 2). In short, due to the centrality of race and racism to US institutions, Squire et al. (2018) argue that higher education is not immune to race and racism. Instead, the structural and processual elements of plantations hold contemporary relevance for US higher education (Squire et al., 2018, pp. 7–9). The two universities I have selected are structured around my own familiarity with them as a graduate student (UNC) and as a faculty member (DU). I neither think one is worse than the other, nor do I think they are special cases; rather, they are the rule of how inclusivity always speaks back to previous structural and processual organizing principles of the plantation. This chapter proceeds by illustrating that inclusivity on college campuses cannot be distinguished from interrelations between racism and capitalism. It then moves on to examine the Western conceptions of time and space and their implications for academic knowledge. Next, I apply both relations to UNC's and DU's inclusivity policies. I conclude with thoughts on the plantation and the university.

Contextualizing the Neoliberal University

In *On Being Included*, Sara Ahmed (2012) provides a cultural studies reading of higher education. Rather than institutional assumptions that people of color are always already in debt to the institution (static), Ahmed calls for us to think about institutions as "processual," as always in flux. Thus, she wonders, why inclusivity now? Her work suggests that we ask more questions around the context of higher education. This is a context that I argue cannot be disconnected from the inability to separate racism from capitalism in Western societies, what Cedric Robinson (2000) calls "racial capitalism." Robin D. G. Kelley (2017) elaborates on Robinson's term: Robinson challenged the Marxist idea that capitalism was a revolutionary negation of feudalism. Instead capitalism emerged within the feudal order and flowered in the cultural soil of a Western civilization already thoroughly infused with racialism. Capitalism and racism, in other words, did not break from the old order but rather evolved from it to produce a modern world system of "racial capitalism" dependent on slavery, violence, imperialism, and genocide. Capitalism was "racial" not just because of attempts to divide workers or justify slavery and dispossession, but because racialism had also already permeated Western feudal society (Robinson, 2000, p. 17). Race and capitalism are not distinct entities but processes that work together, particularly in institutional formats. Thus, contemporary higher education and its calls for inclusivity are not immune to racial capitalism but must be considered as complicit within it.

If one cannot separate race from capitalism, in line with Squire et al. (2018, p. 13), I contend that contemporary higher education admits more people of color not because of a benevolent reach for inclusion but due to new modes of profit seeking in a post–civil rights context. Likewise, Martha Biondi (2012) suggests that the conjuncture of higher education must be put into conversation with the larger context of "the Black revolution on campus." For Biondi (2012), largely Black campus protests in the late 1960s and early 1970s "set in motion a period of conflict, crackdown, negotiation, and reform that profoundly changed college life" (p. 1). Some of the demands from the protests were responded to with the creation of programs such as Black studies but *not* with a transformation in the institution of higher education on the whole. Put differently, the establishment of Black studies programs did not mean that philosophy or political science had to address racism in their own programs. It meant that white scholars pushed the work of race and racism onto Black studies, with no self-interrogation about what race meant for their own academic disciplines and ultimately misunderstanding Black studies on the whole. Further, it meant that institutions could profit off of student protests by offering new courses but without full transformation.

Relatedly, historically white institutions in the mid-twentieth century admitted more people of color and created new departments and programs within the context of the shifting economy, one now popularly called "neoliberalism." Under neoliberalism, for Henry A. Giroux (2003), profit making is positioned as equivalent to democracy. Rather than trust people of color with their own critiques of racism, neoliberalism assumes that the market can fix all social problems: "The development of all aspects of society should be left to the wisdom of the market" (Giroux, 2003, p. 196). In arguments about the market's neutrality, people of color are positioned as either not working hard enough to gain entrance into college or are seen as attending college only as a result of biased handouts. Here, higher education is positioned as either purely merit-based (ignoring the financial benefits historically given to white people) or as degraded because of governmental assistance supposedly provided disproportionately to students of color ("big government's" intrusion in market neutrality).

Ahmed (2012), Biondi (2012), and Giroux (2003) all point to two interesting yet seemingly contradictory points. At the same time that colleges and universities across the Western world acknowledged their limitations (i.e., that they were extremely white and male), neoliberalism individualized higher education's limits by brushing over the history of systematic racism. Put simply, rather than the institutions admitting they were at fault for the lack of people of color in higher education, people of color were now positioned as not working hard enough to get there. Further, the few people of color who were on campuses were *monetized* and *tokenized*, set up as individualized proof that there was no fault in the institution, and that the fault lay in the individuals who could not make it. This ensured two things: that from the 1970s to the present there have been more people of color on historically white campuses, but no drastic increases; and that those few people of color required social, political, economic, and emotional support in an economy in which white people doubted the legitimacy of their presence and the capacity of their individual work ethic.

Institutions of higher education, then, situate themselves as judge and jury, as neutral figures in a way that shuns responsibility. This shunning of responsibility is no monolith. On the one hand, it can occur as institutions loudly proclaim they are not at fault for racism. On the other, if there is some responsibility taken, then the institution can argue it is the measure of what is necessary for "societal success," so responsibility in previous forms of racial violence must be minimized in the contemporary context.

The problem with the former is that the institutions deny responsibility, and thus openly continue racism. This is not surprising to people of color. The problem of the latter may be more insidious because it incorporates people of color as its biggest champions, under the guise of inclusivity. In the process, the institutional gatekeepers cannot comprehend why people of color are protesting when they have been *given* so much. Indeed, people of color *owe* the institution. Yet this is also a shunning of responsibility. The institution rests on the Western necessity of violence against people of color. So who owes whom here?

The Plantationization of "Western Knowledge"

The problem of benevolent institutions hinted at above is compounded by the form of education doled out in Western academia. While few disagree that the United States and its institutions are structured on Native land, it is more difficult for people to accept that Western knowledge constructs are connected to racial violence. This relates to an equal assumption that knowledge equates to freedom and is an inherent good. However, as Squire et al. (2018, p. 7) illustrate, knowledge and racial violence seem detached only if one ignores how Black bodies are positioned in Western political and academic concepts: as the "slave," "commodity," "object," and "nonbeing." Each of these concepts signifies space, and the relationship of the Black body to space predates the United States. For example, at the 1705 General Assembly in Williamsburg, Virginia, also called the "Middle Plantation" (Gruber, 2016), the colonial state admitted that it was suffering from a crisis of recognition, as "race mixing" supposedly made it increasingly difficult to know who was Black and who was white. The colonial state's solution to the crisis of recognition? "An act declaring the Negro, Mulatto, and Indian slaves within this dominion, to be *real estate*" (Erikson, 2015; emphasis added). The equation of Negroes, Mulattos, and enslaved Indians with "real estate" should not be taken lightly. Real estate, as in property consisting of land, buildings, and any natural resources on such property, links people of color to *space*. Politically and economically speaking, then, there was no distinction between the Negro, the Native, and an acre of land.

While the Williamsburg General Assembly may be deemed far from the domain of higher education,[2] Katherine McKittrick (2006) suggests that such knowledge constructs exceeded political classifications, and found their way into the halls of academia. McKittrick (2006) argues that the concept of space described within the field of geography has mirrored the description of people of color throughout the West: both have been imagined as fixed, natural objects open to scientific inquiry. Similarly, the work of Denise Ferreira da Silva (2007) and Sylvia Wynter (2003) suggest that time has also often been associated with Westernism. The assumption here is that the ontological concept of Western being is related to linear progress (time). Indeed, this situates the Western construct of being, the self, the enslaver, or *man*, as capable of manipulating, studying, observing, selling, and classifying the object, the fixed, or the spatial. In short, the dynamic temporality of Western man is what allows him to study the set fixity of the spatial. This brings Ferreira da Silva to argue that Darwin's study of the Negro differs very little from Newton's study of matter (2007, p. 110): both assumed that Western science's study of bodies (space, but also "nature," the Negro and the Native) have always been situated outside the domains of change, transformation, and progress (or time).[3] In short, to have *time* one must be able to study, manipulate, observe, and classify the spatial. The Negro and the Native, as real estate, are not *excluded* from Western self-conceptions but are already *included* in Western conceptions of being and knowledge constructs.

What we find, then, is that gendered and racialized conceptions of time and space are materialized in what we now call "academic disciplines," such as biology (science) and philosophy (humanities), and what we can call "higher education" for the rest of this chapter. Isaac Newton (1846) argued that space and time were absolute (science); not long after, Immanuel Kant (1965) argued that space was separate from, and subordinate, to time (humanities). Similar arguments continued during the height of US racial slavery, justifying the setup of the plantation. Later, Friedrich Hegel (2001) noted that Western Europe, particularly Germany, was the first "place" (or the nation-state) where self-consciousness developed and, therefore, its progress was measurable against Africa—the *dark continent*, that space which "lacks history." Hegel (2001) argued that there was a "geographical basis of history," and there was no reason to "return" to Africa, as the African (particularly the Negro) had no capacity for consciousness, outside of what Western Europe could provide/gift. Western academic divisions between time and space were less neutral and more justifications of long-held power relations, many of which replicated the structural elements of a plantation politic.

The plantation equated the Negro and the Native with space, with real estate, with "nature," while the enslaver was the self-determined, temporal figure; likewise, the university houses self-determined (largely white) scholars, students, and administrators, who "study nature," who contemplate their own being—all "others" who enter into its fold must follow suit, or enter history, as per Hegel. As the figures most closely equated with space, or nature, people of color are *not* the populations that receive recognition of ourselves as human in the institution, because to study nature is historically to study *me*. Thus, we, as people of color, as studiable objects, are necessary to maintain Western academia's continued distinctions between knower and known. Whether inclusivity policies exist or not, we, as people of color, are already included because we are what made Western knowledge constructs possible to begin with. Further, our inclusion via inclusivity policies into the hallowed halls where these distinctions are taught *does not* guarantee the destruction of the racial violence of Western academia but may make us its accomplices.

The plantation, the Negro, the Native, and "nature" are spatial constructs from which man creates knowledge and politics. What this means is that if higher education, and the presumable distinctions between humanities and sciences, begins by separating time from space, then we as people of color must question our capacity to inclusively enter such structures in any neutral fashion that does not always already implicate our social death. This is not to say people of color should not pursue higher education. Instead, it is to argue that higher education, like the plantation, has always held raced and gendered implications. We should ask why.

The Plantationization of Higher Education

Both the University of North Carolina at Chapel Hill and the University of Denver illustrate that inclusivity has functioned along a plantation politics that has yet to be interrupted. What this means is that people of color are not included in the way promised via inclusivity policies. Instead, the interconnection between racism, capitalism, and higher education ensures that we, as people of color, are necessary to maintain institutions antithetical to our being. Again, this is a consistency of a plantation politics. There are two violent functions of inclusion that go largely unmentioned in higher education inclusivity policies: these dominant inclusivity policies equate inclusion with the market; and they cannot recognize Black and Native life because we are too closely linked to Western constructs of space, that which has no self-determination, no history, and thus makes no sense in the Hegelian conception of being.

The University of Denver is an interesting case to think about inclusivity, especially because the university admits it was structured on the violent settler colonial relationship with the school's founder and former Colorado territorial governor, John Evans. Thus, DU's foundation is based on its associations of "manifest destiny," of "American" territory as empty and awaiting Western advancement. Today, DU sits on Cheyenne and Arapaho land, two Indigenous populations that were under the "protection" of Evans during the mid-nineteenth century. Still, on November 29, 1864, after much instigation from Evans's fabricated distinctions between "friendly" and "hostile Indians," troops from the 1st and 3rd regiments of the US Colorado Volunteers killed the Cheyenne and Arapaho who were displaced to Sand Creek, mostly women and children: "The killing went on for nine hours," and "when darkness fell, over two hundred Cheyennes and Arapahos lay dead, and a like number wounded" (John Evans Study Committee, 2014, pp. 7–8). Unlike the Northwestern University report (also a university Evans founded), the DU report argued that Evans was directly culpable in the killing that occurred, what is now known as the Sand Creek massacre. The report concludes, "Nearly every situation involving Native people in Colorado—from the confused and neglected situation at the Upper Arkansas Agency; to the failed treaty council of September, 1863; to the orchestration of the only successful treaty signing during Evans's tenure as superintendent, which occurred without his involvement; to the inability to scale back suspicion and hostility toward Cheyennes and Arapahos in order to ensure their security rights; to the outright rejection of conciliation—reflects Evans's superintendency, as a function of his governorship, as a failed undertaking" (John Evans Study Committee, 2014, p. 88). In addition, Evans notes that the territory itself must be "cleared" of the hostile Native population to make way for Western progress; yet he does not draw strict distinctions between friendly and hostile Natives but instead often conflates them. The Native, then, is tantamount to what the General Assembly in Virginia concluded over 100 years before Evans's statement: they were like *land*, "real estate," that must be cleared for the establishment of Denver and any institutions the city might house. The Native is a spatial construct, removed for the inevitability of Western progress (time).

It is easy to conclude that Evans's words and actions were from "another time," and that the processes of old hold no sway on contemporary thought. However, the structure of DU suggests otherwise. Not only is DU on Cheyenne and Arapaho territory, but its "inclusive excellence" policies continue a trajectory that situates the concept of temporal progress (financial, political, intellectual, etc.) over and against the spatial stasis that plantation politics always associate with Natives and people of color. If the Native is a Western spatial construct (that which is imagined by Western Europe and North American white people as in need of "clearing" to make way for progress), then, as Glen Coulthard argues, this is not a population that received, or currently receives, "recognition" of themselves as human by the state or its institutions. Recognition by the state as "human" is an impossibility because it legitimizes the same state that instituted the social death of the Native to begin with. In the process, there are different forms of oppression, and "without transformative struggle constituting an integral aspect of anticolonial praxis the Indigenous population will not only remain subjects of imperial rule insofar as they have not gone through a process of purging the psycho-existential complexes battered into them over the course of their colonial experience—a process of strategic *desubjectification*—but they will also remain so in that the Indigenous society will tend to come to see the forms of structurally limited and constrained recognition conferred to them by their colonial 'masters' *as their own*: that is, the colonized will begin to *identify* with 'white liberty and white justice'" (Coulthard, 2014, p. 39). I contend that inclusive excellence continues in the same vein as the Hegelian recognition that Coulthard outlines: it requires that Native students, staff, and faculty accept the terms of inclusivity as an always already legitimate form of recognition, without ever questioning the legitimacy of DU itself or its right to legitimately recognize. Rather than question the fact that DU is structured on an illegitimate land grab, its inclusive excellence policies begin with the assumption that DU is inherently good, with the legitimate capacity to recognize those students, faculty, and staff worthy of inclusion in its fold. Yet because recognition exists within Western registers that benefit DU, its inclusive policies must also benefit itself.

One component of DU's "Strategic Plan for Inclusive Excellence" illustrates this point perfectly. The policy was first imagined under then chancellor Robert Coombe in 2007. In particular, the policy notes that diversity, while utilized in reference to racial, ethnic, and gender minorities, *must be expansive beyond such categories*: "While the University understands diversity as encompassing 'race, ethnicity, gender identity, socio-economic background *and other salient social dimensions*' this document will address compositional diversity by focusing primarily on historically underrepresented groups—racial and ethnic minorities and women—for which data have been collected to meet federal reporting requirements. *Going forward, we must also address additional identity groups whose federal reporting and/or internal tracking may be different and/or non-existent*" (DU, 2011, p. 1; emphasis added). Inherent in DU's own definition of diversity is the potential for diversity to be appropriated by "other salient social dimensions." This is, in part, due to the same federal reporting requirement that makes it illegal to hire or admit someone into an institution based on their race. The federal government's categorizations of race, class, and gender that were utilized to hurt the minority population is now abstracted from its original purpose to remake the categorization of the "minority." In the process, white, male, heterosexual, conservative Christian is now argued as a minority position, despite the fact that this is the position central to DU's foundation and, relatedly, the physical enactment of Native death that DU is founded on.

Likewise, the chancellor who followed Coombe, Rebecca Chopp, also extended diversity "*beyond just race and gender*—including sexual orientation, gender identity and expression, socioeconomic status, religion, *political and ideological viewpoints*, and more" (Chopp, 2017; emphasis added). This nod to political and ideological (and I add economic) views is not random but systemic. Thus, DU's inclusivity policy not only opens space for the inclusion of conservative populations but also seems to position inclusion as for those populations who can increase the university's bottom line—often these are the same groups. For example, according to the policy, under one of its "Goals for Structuring Change," DU notes that it will begin to engage in a "screening process" for its third-party vendors. This entails the university reserving the right to prevent vendors who rent space on campus from coming, especially if they are perceived as harmful to university members. The university will thus: "Implement systemic review of and policy for holding vendors and third-party partners to University's high standards of non-discrimination. For example, restricting our business relationships to companies that share our commitment to a broad definition of diversity, much as some schools have done (re: sweatshop labor, sustainability, lending discrimination, etc.)" (DU, 2011, p. 8). This stated goal was not enough to prevent the 2016 Pipeline Leadership Conference from coming to DU. The university's own stated mission to not partner with third-party vendors who pose a threat to its population was thrown out, as this conference was coordinated in relation with the now-infamous Dakota Access Pipeline, "a shale oil pipeline, beginning in the Bakken oil fields of North Dakota, and running underneath the Missouri River" (#Resist—Student Activism @ DU, 2017). Thus, oil companies "decided to route the pipeline under the river on the Standing Rock Sioux reservation" (#Resist—Student Activism @ DU, 2017), a controversial practice that has seen protests and violent state responses to those same protests (Meyer, 2016). Despite DU's attempt to include its Native population, for the second straight year the pipeline conference was "sponsored by Michels Corporation and Enbridge Energy Partners, two of the companies involved in the Pipeline" (#Resist—Student Activism @ DU, 2017), hosted by DU's Daniels College of Business. The university is not neutral but consistent with the neoliberal economy: the profits from the Pipeline Leadership Conference are presented as beneficial for all. Who DU classifies as *all* is irrelevant here. Further, the violence assumed in both the physical pipeline itself and in the conference suggests that the Indigenous population is not excluded from DU or from larger US institutions. Instead, their harm is fundamental to paying for the pipeline, the conference, and DU's well-being.

Indeed, if we follow DU's statement on inclusive excellence, the Pipeline Leadership Conference is no anomaly but an alternative, "salient dimension." And within this context, that dimension most "salient" is that which has paid the most to reserve campus space. At the same conference, students, faculty, staff, and community members organized a #NoDAPL protest in solidarity with the Native Student Alliance and Standing Rock. Yet while voicing their dismay of the conference in protest form, the response of DU's campus safety department and, by extension, the university itself, was violence *against* protestors. This protest ultimately ended when the Denver SWAT Team mowed through unarmed protestors in militarized form in order to escort members of the conference off campus. For multiple people, DU remained Denver's elite, private institution, distinct from its surrounding community that day. Furthermore, on its own campus, DU *appeared* more concerned with increasing its bottom line than with the concerns of some of its people. If we follow this to its end, the conference equals forward, temporal progress because it garners money, while the people protesting racial violence could not see the forest for the trees. This is not to argue that DU was unconcerned with its university or community members—but appearances matter. Whether intended or not, student, faculty, staff, and local community member concerns appeared to matter less than the money paid by the Pipeline Leadership Conference to DU and its campus security.

At the University of North Carolina at Chapel Hill there are similar yet different problems. The university has recently acknowledged that enslaved Black people were central to the physical construction of the university, contributing "mightily to the construction of Old East, the Old Chapel (Person Hall), Old West, the New Chapel Gerrard Hall) and additions to Old East and Old West" (Ballinger et al., 2006). One memorialization of the university's slavery past exists in McCorkle Place, the Unsung Founders Memorial table, dedicated by the class of 2002 (Crisp at al., 2017). The black granite table is held up by figurines of enslaved Black people raising the table top above their heads. The table was strategically located in the same quad as *Silent Sam*, the Confederate statue dedicated by the United Daughters of the Confederacy on June 2, 1913.[4] Unlike the table, *Silent Sam* memorialized the failing yet "strong" actions of the Confederacy's attempt in the US Civil War to maintain the "rights" of states to keep the enslaved in bondage. Despite the US Civil War being over, the "heroic" narrative of the Confederacy was kept alive in *Silent Sam*, who stood "quiet but firm," facing the North, ready to continue the fight against what North Carolina students used to call "the War of Yankee Aggression" (aka the US Civil War). Nearly 50 years after the war's end, at the dedication speech in 1913, industrialist Julian Carr celebrated anti-Black racism against a Black woman to connect slavery, violence, and the memorialization of the Confederacy: "I trust I may be pardoned for one allusion, howbeit it is rather personal. One hundred yards from where we stand, less than ninety days perhaps after my return from Appomattox, I horse-whipped a negro wench until her skirts hung in shreds, because upon the streets of this quiet village she had publicly insulted and maligned a Southern lady, and then rushed for protection to these University buildings where was stationed a garrison of 100 Federal soldiers. I performed the pleasing duty in the immediate presence of the entire garrison . . ." (Carr quoted in Green, 2017).

If we take Carr's words to heart, then UNC's long backing of *Silent Sam*, which ended only when students forcefully pulled the statue down (Grubb, 2019), does not provide safe harbor for Black women in particular, or for Black people in general. It never has. This is not a matter of inclusion for Black women. Instead, anti-Black women's violence is central to the foundation and maintenance of the university—the garrison who did not intervene against Carr backs this position. The dedication of the statue, the whipping of a "negro wench," along with the enslaved who built UNC, suggests that Black people are not excluded from UNC but rather that UNC is itself consistent with a long-lasting plantation economy that structures what the Black body means.

Long before I attended UNC, students of all races had been protesting *Silent Sam*'s presence on campus and, thus, Black fungibility. Students such as myself have acknowledged the discomfort of attending an institution that celebrates the legacy of enslaving our ancestors. This is compounded by the fact that, in my own case, as my family was enslaved in the state of North Carolina, and because UNC "rented" the enslaved from plantations in the state to complete the university's construction, one of my ancestors could have actually built the university I received my PhD from. Yet if we follow UNC's actions and statements about the statute, it remained more important than its psychological impact on students, particularly students of color. Thus, UNC mirrors DU's policy on including nondominant voices: inclusion is *for* the United Daughters of the Confederacy and those conservative voices who back *Silent Sam*. To go a step further—like the Black people who built the school, though very different from them—UNC suggests that the descendants of the Confederacy have *never* been excluded. The university, supposedly overrun with too many liberals, who are "too sensitive" to slavery, needs to *include* those who promote it. It notes a complicity with racial violence, as its foundation rests *not* on a recent realization of excluded Black people who now must be benevolently included but on the inability to function *without Black social death*. The university's former chancellor, Carol Folt, provided a definition of "diversity & inclusion" that backs such a position: "We are determined to chart a course where we can all work together to create and sustain the kind of community where we all feel welcomed, respected and free to pursue our goals and dreams and to become our best and truest selves. To realize that course, we must create a diversity structure that is coordinated and integrated, that celebrates all forms of diversity, and which ensures equitable and inclusive educational and social benefits for all" (Folt, 2017). The potential of us "all feeling welcomed" is not all-inclusive (no pun intended). These policies were instituted because people of color do not feel welcomed on campus, with or without these policies. Thus, a diversity and inclusion policy open for all is doomed to fail its students of color because it assumes that the dominant population must also feel welcomed to institutions that are made for them. This is not a call for the dominant population to feel unwelcomed but an attempt to point out that the reason they are dominant in the first place is structured on the normalization of their connection to institutionality on the one hand, and racial violence on the other. If a diversity and inclusion policy that welcomes nondominant people is possible (and I do not think it currently is), then it must be based on the discomfort of some people. The racial violence that structures UNC is not *comfortable* for people of color, whether students or their enslaved ancestors.

Diversity and inclusion cannot play both sides without the discomfort of *someone*. For Black students to feel remotely comfortable at UNC, they require a simple request: their school's lack of hesitation in removing a Confederate statue that celebrates the state's rights to own their ancestors. To add insult to injury, this is a request granted by UNC's neighboring school, Duke University (NPR, 2017). The University of North Carolina's status as a state school matters because the state continues to be politically and financially controlled by those who disarticulate state's rights from racial slavery. Of course, UNC's students *do not ask that they do so*. They ask that UNC, the flagstaff state school, the "public ivy," remove statues without hesitation that represent the maintenance of racial slavery.

Further, UNC's approach to recent protests of *Silent Sam* mirrors DU's approach to the #NoDAPL protests. In the process, the "danger" to diversity and inclusion appears not to be from those who continue to celebrate a group that openly promoted the need to maintain racial slavery (i.e., those who continue to fund the school with money that cannot be separated from that racial slavery) but from the students, faculty, and staff who disagree with such a position. In late 2017, UNC students were camping outside of *Silent Sam* to demand the removal of the statue. UNC's response was to engage in tactics similar to those of the Federal Bureau of Investigation, what UNC professor John McGowan (2017) calls "J. Edgar Hoover tactics." While camping one day, students recognized the familiar face of a man with the UNC police department, who had initially presented himself as a protestor, sympathetic to their efforts. As McGowan (2017) reported, "Last Friday, the university community learned that an undercover policeman spied on the students who participated in an eight-day vigil to protest the continued presence of Silent Sam, UNC's Confederate monument. Claiming to be an auto mechanic named Victor, sympathetic to their cause, the undercover policeman from UNC's Department of Public Safety chatted up those at the vigil." McGowan argues that the undercover police officer suggests that it was not the students who required protection but university and conservative dollars.

The placement of an undercover police officer to monitor students protesting for the removal of a statue should be shocking, but not when situated within a larger plantation politics. Indeed, it suggests that those protesting the statue are antithetical to progress and to any sort of "inclusive dialogue" mutually beneficial to *all*: they are stuck in the past (the construct associated with Western space) and must become more forward focused. The student protests are considered not routes to dialogue but antithetical to it. This is because UNC has already decided what the dialogue *must look like*. McGowan (2017) asks, "Is this the message we want to send to prospective and current students: you attend a university that instead of talking with you will accord itself the right to spy on you?" This level of suspicion was not aimed at the group that continued to fight *for Silent Sam*. The assumption of being stuck in the past was not a descriptor used for the population who continued to celebrate a war lost over 150 years ago. Instead, the true danger lay with those populations who *protested* the celebration of slavery. To protest this was to challenge the foundation of UNC's legitimacy for academic study. Even in the wake of the recent removal of *Silent Sam*, UNC has shown a propensity to protect those who backed the statue over those who protested it (Grubb, 2019).

The problem with diversity and inclusion, as it is currently defined by UNC and other universities, is that it cannot fulfill its promise. It begins with the assumption that inclusivity is for all, which functions, ironically, to erase the history of all people upon entrance to the campus. In its most crass form, UNC allots the potentiality for a Black lesbian from a low socioeconomic background to be placed on the same footing as a white heterosexual male who promotes racist and homophobic rhetoric, as both are deemed nondominant positions by the institution. Forget the politics behind race, gender, and sexuality that has negatively affected the Black lesbian *off campus*, prior to admission; once at UNC, her voice deserves just as much airplay as all others. This only makes sense at an institution that views itself as neutral and somehow distinct from the larger society that enacts violence. At UNC, a school dedicated to protecting the legacy of the Confederacy's proclamation of "state's rights," a Black lesbian is not fully excluded. Instead, such a student does not make sense in the institution of higher education. Indeed, a "Black student" is a contradiction (ask Carr's whip). The need to say the words "Black student" ("white student" is a redundancy) suggests that such populations were not meant to be students in the first place. Historically, all that are Black *are enslaved*, spatial constructs that built UNC so that those Confederate descendants could become "correct educational subjects."

The Limits of Inclusivity

Something strange is happening on college campuses across the country as inclusivity comes to mirror the larger trend of conservative appropriations of civil rights discourse. As one early version of DU's free speech policy noted, conservative pundits recently added to college speaking tours for the promotion of "diversity," such as Milo Yiannopoulos, can be compared to Martin Luther King Jr.—as if King's fight to end racism were the same as Yiannopoulos's fight to keep it. In the process, the policies that are coming out of college campuses engage in flattening power relations. This ensures that inclusivity discourses are just as deceptive (which is *not* to say just as physically violent) as the plantation. Of course, no one dared question who had the power on the plantation: the white enslavers and overseers. However, today higher education officials appear increasingly confused about who has the power at their predominantly white institutions—which continue to be financially structured mostly by white trustee members; inhabited mostly by white students, staff, faculty, and administrators; and cleaned and serviced predominantly by workers of color. This is deeper than a pipeline conference; it includes an uncritical inputting of people of color into the university as if you were doing us a benevolent favor. Recruiting more "nature" to study other forms of "nature" does not undo the institution that fabricated nature to begin with.

Further, if we rethink the campus's relation to a plantation politics, as suggested throughout this chapter, we must also rethink what activism is. Most people who read this, I hope, agree that the plantation was rightfully destroyed. Yet I would guess that just as many people see the university as a space of hope. I, however, return your attention to the title of this edited volume. If the university is a plantation, where does that leave us? We must rethink Black and Indigenous forms of activism not as inside versus outside the university but as related to larger critiques of Western institutionality. The university is no neutral space where thought is formulated but is structured on a confluence of racial violence that must be challenged within and beyond itself. From the American Indian movement to #BlackLivesMatter, community activism must not be distinguished from its college variants; instead, community and campus activism are consistent fights toward liberation.

Notes

1. My use of the terms "Black fungibility" and "settler colonialism" pull directly from King. For King, Black fungibility is about the violent replaceability associated with all Black bodies, or that which links Black bodies with Western concepts of space. Specifically, King argues, that thinking of Black bodies "as forms of flux or space in process" enables "at least a momentary reflection upon the other kinds of (and often forgotten) relationships that Black bodies have to plants, objects, and non-human life forms" (King, 2016, p. 1023). One of those other nonhuman life forms includes Indigenous people, and the violence they face via settler colonialism, another Western conception of flux or space. Indeed, King argues that Blackness becomes a feature of the conquistador/settler spatial imagination, informing and informed by the racial violences enacted against Indigenous peoples in the "New World." Both the violence associated with Blackness and settler colonialism are closely associated with Western concepts of space.

2. Although it is important to note that even this assumption is not true, as the Williamsburg General Assembly was held not far from the second oldest institution of higher education in the United States, William & Mary.

3. This is not to say that Darwin's reading of race is not more complicated but to say that he is building off an older model of time and space that often replicates these older problems. See Ferreira da Silva (2007) for more information on this.

4. In August 2018, Silent Sam was physically pulled down by a number of protestors, which included students, faculty, staff, local community members, and friends of mine, some of whom faced legal ramifications for their actions (Grubb, 2019). Building on the legacy of protesting Silent Sam at UNC, this group of people felt that the university would never take down the statue, so they took matters into their own hands, tying ropes around the statue and pulling it until it toppled (Svrluga, 2018). The university's reaction to this move further backs this chapter's argument: their goal was to rehouse Silent Sam in a 5.3-million dollar history center (Johnson, 2018). This goal was only stopped due to a "grade strike." Local activists sent a letter to graduate students, instructors, and faculty asking them to not release student grades in the fall of 2018 if the university built the history center (Johnson, 2018). Through the power of organizing, UNC halted the history center and also decided not to return Silent Sam to its original pedestal (Debruyn et al., 2018; Michaels et al., 2019). Currently, Silent Sam has been left down, and is being kept in an unrevealed location.

References

#Resist—Student Activism @ DU. (2017). NoDAPL Pipeline Conference Protest + "Day of Action." *University Libraries Online Exhibits.* http://digital.library.du.edu/librariespresents/exhibits/show/resist/2000s/nodapl-pipeline-conference-pro

Ahmed, S. (2012). *On being included: Racism and diversity in institutional life.* Duke University Press.

Ballinger, S., Helms, B., & Holder, J. (2006). Slavery and the making of the university. *UNC Libraries.* https://exhibits.lib.unc.edu/exhibits/show/slavery/introduction

Biondi, M. (2012). *The Black revolution on campus.* University of California Press.

Chopp, R. (2017). Chancellor's statement on diversity, equity, and inclusive excellence. The University of Denver. https://www.du.edu/about/our-leadership/chancellor/university-vision/equity-diversity-inclusive-excellence.html

Coulthard, G. (2014). *Red skin, white masks: Rejecting the colonial politics of recognition.* University of Minnesota Press.

Crisp, W., Hertel, A. L., & Leloudis, J. (2017). The unsung founders and their memorial deserve better. *The Daily Tar Heel.* http://www.dailytarheel.com/article/2017/09/the-unsung-founders-and-their-memorial-deserve-better

Dartmouth College. (2017). Inclusive excellence. https://inclusive.dartmouth.edu

Debruyn, J., Michaels, W., & Baier, E. (2018). Board of Governors rejects plan to build history center to house *Silent Sam. WUNC.* https://www.wunc.org/post/board-governors-rejects-plan-build-history-center-house-silent-sam

Erikson, M. (2015). Defining, then defying the bonds of slavery in Virginia's colonial capital. *The Daily Press.* http://www.dailypress.com/features/history/our-story/dp-defiining-then-defying-slavery-in-virginias-colonial-capital-20150212-post,amp.html

Ferreira da Silva, D. (2007). *Toward a global idea of race.* University of Minnesota Press.

Folt, C. (2017). University commitment to diversity and inclusion. *The University of North Carolina.* https://diversity.unc.edu/about/statement/

Giroux, H. A. (2003). Spectacles of race and pedagogies of denial: Anti-Black racist pedagogy under the reign of neoliberalism. *Communication Education, 52*(3/4), 191–211.

Green, H. N. (2017). Julian Carr's speech at the dedication of *Silent Sam. Dr. Hilary N. Green, PhD.* http://hgreen.people.ua.edu/transcription-carr-speech.html

Grubb, T. (2019). 2 guilty, 2 cases dismissed in toppling of UNC's *Silent Sam* statue. And a knife charge. *The News & Observer.* https://www.newsobserver.com/news/local/article229620599.html

Gruber, K. E. (2016). Williamsburg during the colonial period. *Encyclopedia Virginia.* https://www.encyclopediavirginia.org/Williamsburg_during_the_Colonial_Period#start_entry

Hegel, G. W. F. (2001). *The philosophy of history*. Batoche Books.
John Evans Study Committee. (2014). Report of the John Evans Study Committee. https://portfolio.du.edu/evcomm
Johnson, S. (2018). *Silent Sam* protesters at Chapel Hill embrace a new tactic: A "grade strike." *Chronicle of Higher Education*. https://www.chronicle.com/article/Silent-Sam-Protesters-at/245288
Kant, I. (1965). *The critique of pure reason*. St. Martin's Press.
Kelley, R. D. G. (2017). What did Cedric Robinson mean by racial capitalism? *The Boston Review*. http://bostonreview.net/race/robin-d-g-kelley-what-did-cedric-robinson-mean-racial-capitalism
King, T. L. (2016). The labor of (re)reading plantation landscapes fungible(ly). *Antipode, 48*(4), 1022–39.
McGowan, J. (2017). Opinion: UNC goes fishing, hook, line and stinker—John McGowan. *The Herald Sun*. http://www.heraldsun.com/opinion/article 183309671.html
McKittrick, K. (2006). *Demonic grounds: Black women and the cartographies of struggle*. University of Minnesota Press.
Meyer, R. (2016). The legal case for blocking the Dakota Access Pipeline. *The Atlantic*. https://www.theatlantic.com/technology/archive/2016/09/dapl-dakota-sitting-rock-sioux/499178/
Michaels, W. Baier, E., & Philip, L. (2019). On her way out, UNC chancellor orders removal of *Silent Sam* pedestal. *NPR*. https://www.npr.org/2019/01/15/685442684/on-her-way-out-unc-chancellor-authorizes-removal-of-silent-sam-pedestal
Newton, I. (1846). *The mathematical principles of natural philosophy*. Daniel Adee.
NPR. (2017). Duke University removes Robert E. Lee statue from chapel entrance. *National Public Radio*. https://www.npr.org/sections/thetwo-way/2017/08/19/544678037/duke-university-removes-robert-e-lee-statue-from-chapel-entrance
Robinson, C. (2000). *Black Marxism: The making of the Black radical tradition*. University of North Carolina Press.
Saint Mary's College. (2017). Inclusive excellence. https://www.stmarys-ca.edu/about-smc/our-commitments/inclusive-excellence
Squire, D., Williams, B. C. & Tuitt, F. (2018). Plantation politics and neoliberal racism in higher education: A framework for reconstructing anti-racist institutions. *Teachers College Record, 120*(14), 1–20.
Svrluga, S. (2018). UNC in turmoil over *Silent Sam*, the Confederate monument toppled by protesters. *The Washington Post*. https://www.washingtonpost.com/education/2018/12/13/unc-turmoil-over-silent-sam-confederate-monument-toppled-by-protesters/?utm_term=.c4a34ec8bfc7
University of Arizona. (2017). Diversity and inclusion. *Office for Diversity and Inclusive Excellence*. http://diversity.arizona.edu/inclusive-excellence-0.

University of Colorado Boulder. (2017). Inclusive excellence. https://www.colorado. edu/studentsuccess/inclusive-excellence

University of Denver (DU). (2011). Strategic plan for inclusive excellence. *Center for Multicultural Excellence.* https://www.du.edu/cme/media/documents/du-IEStratPlan-2011.pdf

University of Denver (DU). (2017). Inclusive excellence at DU. *Center for Multicultural Excellence.* https://www.du.edu/cme/resources/inclusive-excellence.html

University of North Carolina at Chapel Hill (UNC). (2017). Mission. *University Office for Diversity and Inclusion.* https://diversity.unc.edu/about/office/

University of Wisconsin-Green Bay. (2017). Inclusive excellence. https://www.uwgb.edu/inclusive-excellence/

Wilder, C. S. (2013). *Ebony and ivy: Race, slavery, and the troubled history of America's universities.* Bloomsbury Press.

Wynter, S. (2003). Unsettling the coloniality of being/power/truth/freedom: Towards the human, after man, its overrepresentation—an argument. *CR: The New Centennial, 3*(3), 328–29.

Chapter 6

Future Thinking and Freedom Making

*Antidiversity as an Intervention
to the Plantation Politics of Higher Education*

JESSE CARR, NICOLE TRUESDELL, CATHERINE M. ORR,
AND LISA ANDERSON-LEVY

In *The Transformation of Plantation Politics*, Sharon Wright Austin (2006) describes the plantation economy as a complex set of relationships organized around the interests of a white "power elite" (p. 5). She describes this power elite as "plantation bloc millionaires" who inherit wealth and privilege from their families and reap ongoing benefits from the cheap labor of a racialized workforce (p. 5). Furthermore, the plantation encompasses a larger political economy in which the white and wealthy power elite control and govern through carefully selected and cultivated politicians and civil servants. Austin explains that the plantation economy extends beyond the distribution of wealth and labor in particular economic sectors (such as agriculture). It includes as well the power to determine how public monies are spent, to create legislation and regulation, and to direct law enforcement, all in accordance with elite interests. Following Bianca Williams, Dian Squire, and Frank Tuitt's discussion of how "the vestiges of plantation culture and life influence modern university culture, climate, and structures of power" (see introduction to this volume), if we see and understand the plantation as a technology of colonization, settler colonialism, and enslavement, then we must also acknowledge that this form of control has not ended, as institutions of higher education are another location where plantation politics are maintained and enacted. This chapter argues that the politics of diversity plays a key role in maintaining the plantation political economy described in the introduction to this volume. We dig deeper into how diversity relates to the plantation structure, and offer a framework of what a decolonial pedagogy might look like when viewed through an "antidiversity" lens.

The resonance between the plantation political economy and the operation of US colleges and universities is not necessarily surprising. Many institutions of higher education did indeed start as plantations or include plantations on their grounds; even more relied on enslaved labor, admitted only or mostly white students, and amassed fortunes from the donated estates of their power-elite alumni (Wilder, 2013). Even the most humble public institutions, not to mention prestigious research universities, located in states and territories that never permitted slavery, originated in land grants made possible by the theft of land from and displacement of Indigenous populations, what Glen Coulthard (2014) describes as "accumulation by dispossession."[1] In other words, the terminology of "plantation" is not mere analogy or polemic; this seemingly anachronistic term, as Squire et al. explain, is actually allochronistic, or utilizing a frame from another (*allo-*) time (*chrono-*) to understand a group of people today (p. 5). Understanding the history of plantation politics is crucial to understanding the ongoing operation of higher education in the United States.

Our goal, then, is to (re)imagine how students, staff, and faculty who sit at the margins can intervene and resist these exploitative dynamics, creating decolonial spaces within colonial/plantation university settings, what la paperson (2017) describes as the "third world university" (pp. 43–44). Getting to this future thinking and making entails the examination and dismantling of the ways "diversity and inclusion" have become a technology of plantation politics within higher education. We reject the predominant model found at most institutions (including our own) and propose instead a practice of "antidiversity" that draws on women of color and Black feminist, decolonial, and antiracist praxis. This praxis integrates academic knowledge production with activist strategies such as grassroots organizing, community building, consciousness raising, and binary breaking. Implementing these strategies requires collaboration across boundaries of power that usually divide college communities: staff versus faculty, faculty versus administrator, and student versus everyone. The university's hierarchical divisions of rank, which are classed, gendered, and racialized, tend to reinforce the cycle of wealth extraction that is central to the plantation's political structure. Coalition across these boundaries—expressed through concrete acts of mutual solidarity—is necessary if this structure is to be destabilized.

The remainder of this chapter will first offer a more detailed description of the plantation political economy described above, focusing on the ways colleges and universities use diversity and inclusion initiatives as both alibis (Truesdell et al., 2018) and brand management, often in response to student protests and uprisings. To speak back against the cooptation of diversity and return to the social justice roots of concepts such as equity, antiracism, and decolonization, we advance the decolonial intervention of "antidiversity." We situate what an antidiversity lens could look like through two praxis examples. The first is a disciplinary case study of the shift from women's and gender studies to what is now called critical identity studies (CRIS). The second is the Decolonizing Pedagogies Project, a Mellon-funded faculty and professional development project that seeks to proliferate new models of teaching and governance by subversive means through the centering of marginalized people, voices, and experiences. For us, these projects show how to conceptualize and enact future thinking and making in the present. Taken together, they also demonstrate the limits and possibilities offered by various forms of institutionalization—by which we mean the acceptance (or rejection) of particular forms of structural support, which are often accompanied by the promise of security and the peril of cooptation. When we shift our lens to see the ways decolonial possibilities are always already present within colonial institutions such as higher education, we can disrupt ideas of time to show the ways that past, present, and future exist simultaneously, and that histories and futures of liberation are therefore within our reach right now (la paperson, 2017). In other words, the process of decolonization does not follow a "progress narrative" that proceeds neatly from the status of "colonized" through various stages to an outcome of "decolonization." Rather, the process of decolonization is both iterative and generative—continuously building decolonial spaces and seeking to expand them. As such, the chapter concludes with reflection on major challenges we have faced in doing this work (and which you might face if you attempt something similar).

Part 1: Diversity and/as Plantation Politics

Whether one regards the concept of "plantation" in terms of the historical and material connections between universities, enslavement, and settler-colonialism, or as a metaphorical gesture toward universities' role in reproducing racial inequality in the present, it's worth elaborating more on what we mean when we describe institutions of higher education as "plantations" and assert that "diversity" has been incorporated into, and used as a technology of, this colonial plantation system. Following Squire, we draw on the idea of plantation as a system that functions as the "origins of race relations in the United States . . . including . . . the institutionalized racial norms that exist in higher education today" (see chapter 1 of this volume). Readers will recognize the structural elements he lays out in our descriptions of how diversity operates—or fails to operate—across various higher education contexts. In particular, we believe the white "knowledges" and "sentiments" (see chapter 1) he recounts align with our observations of administrators' oxymoronic desires, where people of color are seen as nothing more than bodies that are cast as immature, unintelligent, and dangerous. The chief value of keeping such a dangerous body in the faculty and administrative ranks of the college is in pressuring them to fulfill the role of overseer—for example, by calling on directors and chief diversity officers to clean up the messes that inevitably result when institutional violence against marginalized people erupts in protest or self-extraction. Both "ontologically distant" and "physically close," Black bodies at small Midwestern colleges in particular—where niceness and paternalism operate as the dominant modes of address—are too often the hypervisible yet invisible racial alibis for the institution.

In short, we observe that diversity is all too often put into the service of whiteness, used to prop up the myth of meritocracy and to further the liberal notion of a universal human. This ideological misapplication of diversity intersects with the notion of education as a "great equalizer" in pursuit of the American dream (Growe & Montgomery, 2003). Put into the service of whiteness and capitalism, "diversity" becomes a form of social control or, in the words of Squire, a method by which "deviancy is eliminated, reduced, or rendered harmless." "Diversity" simultaneously disciplines and placates the underclasses by ensuring that upward mobility is available to some members of "minority" groups, albeit only to the extent that their demographic representation in the larger (white) population might call for. Indeed, the notion of education as a good that is inherently, well, "good," is a staple of white class mythology that insists that personal attributes such as intelligence and responsibility, applied through hard work, are all it takes to succeed under American capitalism (Castagno, 2014; DiAngelo, 2012; McKenzie & Phillips, 2016). This myth of meritocracy takes on new meaning in an era of "color-blind racism," in which seemingly race-neutral laws, policies, and public discourse nonetheless operate to reproduce racialized and gendered hierarchies (Bonilla-Silva, 2009). Even in the face of this violent social reproduction, the myth of meritocracy combined with a superficial commitment to "diversity" naturalizes the hierarchies it produces while also insisting that explicit white supremacist politics are a thing of the distant past.

"Diversity," as currently constituted in institutions of higher education, plays a central role in the function of these myths of postracialism and meritocracy. At the institutional level, diversity operates as a tool of appeasement and crisis management (Stewart, 2017). From our perspective as antiracist scholars and administrators, the "crisis" of diversity in higher education centers on the marginalization of students of color, LGBTQ+ students, students with disabilities, female students, first-generation students, and students who are low-income or poor, as well as the intersectional barriers faced by people who experience multiple systems of oppression simultaneously. For many high-level administrators, however, the "crisis" of diversity centers on institutional reputation and profitability, and incidents of harassment, violence, exclusion, hate crime, microaggression, and so on, are a crisis for the "brand" of the institution. For example, the publication and consulting firm DiversityInc describes the danger of a "diversity crisis" as affecting "whether your leadership stays or goes and whether the public loses faith in your organization (causing plummeting stock price, for example)" (DiversityInc, 2013; see also Wilkinson, 2014). Since the demographic profile of US college presidents continues to be "a white male in his early 60s with a doctoral degree," and contains a disproportionate number of millionaires, there is little question what the "you" looks like when diversity consultant firms market their services toward the preservation of "your leadership" (American Council on Education, 2017; Kessler & McDonald, 2016; Bauman, 2017).

While many participants in "diversity"-related initiatives, offices, academic departments, and so on may see themselves as carrying on a radical tradition of transforming higher education through the infusion of intellectual work from people and places that have historically been excluded, the actual institution(s) where these offices/departments are located treat them as a dumping ground for all diversity-related "crises"—which they perceive primarily as crises of "brand," "reputation," or "marketing." The institution continues to treat students, staff, and faculty who are associated with these realms as "less than"—intellectually and politically. Indeed, they tend to frame these locations through a deficit-based lens, as serving students in need of remediation, populated by staff/faculty who have nothing to offer the institution beyond embodying a particular identity. The particularity of this embodiment is called on in moments of crisis even while it is denigrated in the day-to-day operations of the institution.

This might be unremarkable if it happened only in a few institutions; but this describes how many institutions of higher education approach diversity, particularly at predominantly white institutions such as our own (Iverson, 2007; Stewart, 2017). In other words, this approach to diversity is not just "institutionalized" in the sense of specific individual institutions, it is also a systemic technology used across the domain of higher education as a whole. The structural element has its own set of consequences, then. It transforms diversity into a mere metric, what some have called "the body count" method, which conflates diversity with parity of representation (Stulberg & Weinberg, 2011). Although representation is of course important, it can also manifest as tokenization (in which selected "diverse" individuals are used as institutional mouthpieces), as well as diversity-without-inclusion (in which substantive numbers of a marginalized group exist, but they do not experience genuine "belonging" or possess the power to set institutional norms). Moreover, diversity metrics focused on representation can sometimes mask less superficial forms of discrimination, such as when women or people of color are being concentrated in low-level positions, or when "diversity numbers" remain high overall, even as there are issues with turnover and retention.

When the "crisis" of diversity is framed as a crisis of brand management, and when the "solution" for diversity is to increase the body count of underrepresented groups, an overarching discourse emerges for broader public consumption in which diversity is perceived as little more than paternalism. This predictable discourse plays out again and again on social media and in op-ed columns: something happens to embarrass an institution (such as students at the margins protesting the injustices they see and experience in these spaces), thus the institution makes "concessions" related to representation. The results of these "concessions"—which might include new programs, new people, new policies—are then stigmatized as profiteers that distract from the "true" purpose of higher education. A representative article in the *Atlantic*, for example, blamed "diversity officers" for administrative bloat and thus rising tuition rates. The author bemoaned what he considered to be the onus of hiring diversity workers as a "response to the wave of racial incidents that convulsed campuses," and went on to describe the increased focus on "diversity" as an example of "institutions generating a perpetual cycle of employment in specialties for which there would otherwise be no demand at all" (Frum, 2016). Education scholar Benjamin Ginsberg makes similar arguments in his influential book *The Fall of the Faculty: The Rise of All-Administrative University and Why It Matters* (2011).

To the extent that diversity has been used by higher ed administrators as a tool of crisis management and appeasement, these critics have a point. Painting universities as places where "diversity obsession" drives up administrative costs while adding nothing of genuine value fuels broader public antipathy toward the democratization of higher education, as evidenced by growing opposition to affirmative action, antistudent narratives ("special snowflakes," etc.), and political attacks on the humanities and social sciences (Ahmed, 2015). In this vein, colleges and universities placate demands for a focus on "diversity and inclusion," while at the same time ensuring such initiatives are siloed in locations that can easily be removed, cut, or disassembled when their brand is no longer in crisis and/or when student populations turn over. The cynical manipulation of diversity replicates numerous structural elements described by Williams, Squire, and Tuitt. With the goal of extracting profit from student tuition while minimizing costs, administrators use "diversity" to express paternalism and reinforce divisions of rank and status.

Lower-ranking diversity workers are never allowed to forget that their tools, resources, and facilities are owned and controlled by the institution; they are rewarded when they cooperate and punished when they do not. When diversity efforts themselves and the workers who are brought in to "do" that work are no longer seen as valuable (bringing in actual capital and maintaining the silence of marginalized students), then institutions are quick to dispose of such initiatives and/or people. This keeps diversity and inclusion work and officers who do that work in subjugated roles within the plantation economy of higher education and ensures that the foundations of this plantation remain the same. Or, read another way, these diversity initiatives and officers provide just enough color to the plantation without diluting the foundational whiteness colleges and universities are founded on and invested in maintaining. Even worse, these dynamics sometimes induce "diversity workers" into the role of plantation "overseer" (Squire, Williams, Tuitt). Administrators might expect them to use their identity as a tool against students rather than as a tool to represent and advocate for students—as when an African American chief diversity officer tells Black students they don't realize how easy they have it, or when female administrators are put in charge of powerless "sexual assault task forces." Unfortunately there are too many who comply, either because they have internalized these norms of whiteness or because they fear economic or professional sanctions.

Here, Austin (2006) and Williams, Squire, and Tuitt's formulation of plantation politics proves useful once again (see the introduction to this volume). Austin describes a historical cycle in which the plantation system starts out based on the complete exclusion of colonized subjects, but eventually incorporates those subjects as comanagers. Exclusion begets resistance and demands for inclusion, but subjugated communities are often disappointed to find that "increased representation does not lead to more concrete benefits" (Austin, 2006, p. 14). Instead, as Squire et al. describe, elite control of the system is maintained through less recognizable means. "Representation" is concentrated in the positions of least power; the higher up the hierarchy one goes, the less "representation" there is to be found. Moreover, the potential for using representation subversively is undercut by "the ability of the elite class to exclude certain issues from the decision making process" (p. 15), meaning essentially that elites still set the agendas and frame the discourse of what is possible, even while sharing narrow forms of power with nonelite "representatives."

Part 2: Antidiversity and/as the Politics of Equity and Liberation

What possibilities of liberation can one find in these spaces then? To engage this question, one has to believe what la paperson (2017) argues, that "within the colonizing university also exists a decolonizing education" (p. xiii). We adhere to this logic and focus on the ways we can use the technologies of the plantation in general, and within colleges and universities specifically, to reassemble and repurpose them for decolonizing means. Diversity is one such technology that we seek to repurpose into what we deem to be "antidiversity" thought and praxis.[2] In a nutshell, the central practice of antidiversity is the decentering and disrupting of whiteness. To do this one must first be willing to commit to deep self-reflective work on the intricate and embedded ways whiteness maintains a tight grip on institutional, disciplinary, and personal ways of knowing and being.

When we talk about "whiteness" in this context, we are talking not only about a group of people but also about a space of colonization, capitalism, and oppression, as well as an ideology. Whiteness is an unimaginative location that knows only how to take and never to cooperate. Whiteness prioritizes individualism through the constraints of narrow binaries and stereotypes that prevent us from knowing ourselves or building new ways of operating in the world. The history of whiteness in the West is a history of movement away from collective humanity, a movement toward inhumanity, dehumanization, spiritual, and ecological destruction. Whiteness is killing us all, because it has the power to define, even as it denies and erases; the power to marginalize and violate, even as it claims helplessness and demands pity; the power to denigrate and murder, even as it claims rationality and intellectual objectivity. White people are not the only ones invested in and possessed by the inhumanity of whiteness; whiteness has many allies among communities of color and colonized communities, as it seems to offer the promise of safety (perhaps the worst will be visited on someone else rather than on me). This false promise enabled by the insidious and devastating effects of the power of whiteness destroys communities of color and colonized communities, from the inside, by turning us against each other, so that we fight each other rather than unite against the terror of whiteness. Yet the promise of whiteness (safety achieved through domination) remains alluring to many, even as it proves time and time again that the ultimate end game of whiteness is mass devastation and destruction of the world.

Antidiversity is our response to the ways in which these toxic patterns of whiteness have poisoned "diversity" in higher education. The goal of this reframing is to push back on the cooptation of "diversity," through the mechanisms of whiteness, niceness, and liberalism. Many institutions of higher education are dominated by friendly white liberal elites who understand that racism is "a problem" but who invariably locate the problem somewhere else. These institutions devote much lip service to the concept of "wanting" to be more welcoming, or "aspiring" toward equity. They create abstract statements celebrating "diversity," and form task forces to study "the issues." Sometimes new policies are implemented, and new mission statements are articulated and voted on. It is rare for institutions to undertake the kind of deep self-reflection that is required to engage with what actually makes them unwelcoming, particularly in the context of an oppressive atmosphere of self-congratulatory white liberalism. White liberalism often weaponizes niceness to dismiss concerns that emerge from the margins. After all, if everyone at our institution is nice, how could it possibly be unwelcoming? Furthermore, because everyone is so nice, and interested in "advancing diversity," calling attention to racism and inequity at the level of the institution or at the individual level will inevitably be interpreted as uncivil, uncollegial, uncharitable, and making personal attacks.

Decentering whiteness requires putting aside white ego-driven patterns of conflict. By this we mean conflicts that primarily center on the reputational concerns of white-dominated departments, divisions, and boards, which would prefer to cast themselves as "advancing diversity" without ever having to acknowledge or discuss how universities were maintained as white spaces to begin with. White egos require whiteness to be seen as benevolent, and for white supremacy to be seen as a historical accident. As on the plantation, this assumed benignness protects whiteness by obscuring the violence that is inherent in its emergence and reproduction over time. This normalization and even naturalization of whiteness in higher education makes it difficult for those invested in its benevolence to even "see," let alone radically critique, its operation. It is essential that staff, faculty, and administrators understand how and why their institutions are unwelcoming, rather than using niceness as an alibi to avoid these difficult conversations. This starts with the practice of believing students, staff, and faculty who sit at the margins—giving them at least the same benefit of the doubt one would give to a more powerful white administrator.

When we believe and support those who are structurally positioned at the margins of power, it is easier to understand why institutions are unwelcoming despite their commitment to diversity. Marginalized folks' experiences are supported by a growing literature. Though each institution has its own idiosyncrasies, research and experience lead us to highlight seven major patterns that reproduce toxic whiteness in educational spaces. These patterns are distressing but not surprising when viewed through the plantation politics theoretical framework. As we will discuss further in part 3, our Decolonizing Pedagogies Project aims to identify and disrupt these patterns. Although these items might be familiar to many readers, some elaboration is worthwhile:

1. Microaggressions. The seemingly small but frequent interactions that reinforce one's status as an "other" (Wong et al., 2014). Microaggressions are an expression of "knowledge" and "sentiment" (Squire et al.) that communicate whites' belief in their own superiority while provoking feelings of victimization and powerlessness among students, staff, and faculty of color.

2. Deficit-based thinking. "Diversity" is paternalistically framed around the need to "help" the "disadvantaged" "overcome" their background. Students, staff, faculty, and administrators who sit at the margins are told that success requires a fundamental alienation from who you are and where you come from (Sharma, 2016; Clycq et al., 2013). Deficit-based thinking is both discursive and structural, a manipulation of academic norms that reinforces educators' bias and prevents marginalized people from perceiving their own worth.

3. Curricula. The ways in which course content and progression reflects how academic disciplines developed concurrently with European and American colonialism, settler colonialism, enslavement, segregation, Jim Crow, etc. As we elaborate below in our case study, these progress narratives have profoundly negative methodological and epistemological effects on what counts as knowledge and who counts as knowledge producer; who is seen as intelligent and scholarly versus who is seen as an object of study; what major concepts, theories, and texts constitute "the canon"; and what is considered "required" knowledge for an educated person with a specific major or concentration. For students who sit at the margins, the majority of their required coursework can feel, at best, irrelevant, and at worst outright hostile to their existence (Smith, 2012). In the academic context, knowledge is a "facility"—both a production and an outcome—that is ultimately "owned" by the university. Decolonial knowledge and methods of knowledge production are consistently undermined and squeezed out.

4. Purpose. Squire et al. note that rhetoric on the lack of possibilities for success without a college degree is one

means by which marginalized students who do attend university are disciplined. This partly works because people from marginalized backgrounds view the individual and social purpose of education differently from people from white middle- or upper-class backgrounds (Banks-Santili, 2014). For many privileged people a university education is, at least in part, a status symbol—the entire purpose is to achieve social superiority and a competitive edge over others. In contrast, marginalized students (especially those from lower incomes or who are the first in their family to attend college) are more likely to approach higher education with the idea of giving back to their communities or helping their families. When the purpose of education is consistently framed in terms of achieving economic mobility *away* from community and family, marginalized people are put in a bind between changing their values or being alienated from those around them.

5. Location. Both physically and intellectually, at most institutions "diversity" is siloed into specific administrative offices and perhaps one or two academic departments. It is not institutionalized across the whole campus and all its offices and departments. The result is that certain options are foreclosed as students must either survive in locations that are hostile or seek "home" in the few places where they are valued (Hartwell et al., 2017).

6. Criminalization. Racial profiling, campus judicial-board, and town-gown dynamics, typically reinforce the criminalization of blackness and inequities in the broader justice system. Black students experience racial profiling from both public and campus security forces, while residential segregation patterns affect students of color differently than their white counterparts. (Jascik, 2017; Pelfrey et al., 2016; Schmidt, 2014). Similar to racial profiling outside of university settings, the criminalization of blackness is firmly rooted in the plantation history of enforcing special codes aimed specifically at monitoring and controlling populations of enslaved people.

7. Major incidents. Finally, major incidents such as hate crimes, harassment, and assault (JBHE, 2017) must be mentioned.

We purposely left "major incidents" until last because usually it's the first thing people cite when asked to describe why minorities find their institutions unwelcoming. In the view of nice white liberalism, hate crimes are exceptional, tragic incidents; we have likely all received the predictable campus-wide email from the President's Office asserting that such incidents "don't represent who we are or what we stand for." Although these incidents can be traumatic and damaging to the campus climate, the problem with this fetishization of hate crimes is that the response misses an important point, namely, that they *do* represent who we are and what we stand for, if "we" is the colonial/plantation institution. A white liberal perspective misinterprets why these major incidents are so often a catalyst for protest and activism—it's not because they are so exceptionally horrible, but because they are in fact generic, predictable, and a mere extension of the more normalized day-to-day racism that already defines the campus life (Caplan & Ford, 2014).

The simple fact is, underrepresented groups were not present or permitted to be part of shaping the cultures of institutions of higher education. As we seek to push back against the violent rhetoric of diversity, decenter whiteness, and believe what those who sit at the margins tell us about what it is like to navigate these colonial spaces, a new question emerges: What would it look like if marginalized groups were not just "welcome" as bodies in an institution but their exercise of power was also welcome? It would require, at minimum, a reversal of the factors listed above:

1. The assets of people who have faced marginalization would be valued and prioritized; experiences of privilege would be reframed as deficits to be overcome because of the negative effects of unearned privilege on people's personal, social, and intellectual development.

2. As historically marginalized people are prioritized, they will begin to feel "at home" in institutions of higher education; colleges and universities would become places of comfort, nurturance, and constructive criticism. All aspects of the institution, and all its resources, would be attuned to the demands of equity—not just the offices, student clubs, or courses specifically set aside for "diversity."

3. The histories, values, communities, cultures, and politics of marginalized groups would be core to the curriculum rather than add-ons; courses that focus only on European and/or "Western" traditions, or only on men, would be labeled as such to denote the narrowness of content and, thus, lack of generalizability.

4. Institutions would be consciously abolitionist in their internal procedures and their relationship to law enforcement. As "sanctuary campuses" in the broadest sense possible, institutions of higher education would also become laboratories of restorative and transformative justice practices that seek to address interpersonal harm while dismantling systems of oppression that foster the conditions in which harm occurs (Wang, 2016).

5. Institutions of higher education would have mutually beneficial rather than extractive relationships with the communit(ies) in which they are located and where research takes place. This would extend to include reparations and land repatriation for past reliance on enslaved labor and/or settler-colonial land grants.

6. The purpose of education would be geared toward the problems and concerns of those who have been historically shut out: the economic success of *their* communities, the production of knowledge that is valued by and will serve the people they come from.

7. Rather than treating higher education as a way to overcome and escape from marginalization, higher education would become a place to examine and challenge the structures that produce marginalization in the first place.

The theoretical framework of antidiversity is ambitious because we are asking institutions of higher education to be actual intellectual spaces and not indoctrination locations. The conundrum of developing an antidiversity praxis is that whiteness is centered and deeply embedded in disciplinary knowledge and in broader institutional spaces and practices, and the allies of whiteness will fight to maintain the status quo. This reality has an impact on the work we're trying to do. After all, even our theorization of antidiversity relies on disciplinary or interdisciplinary knowledge production, in a system that is hostile to the knowledge we are trying to produce; and the practical tools we use to do the work are part of the structures of power we are trying to dismantle. This paradox has caused us to return to Audre Lorde's famous caution: "The master's tools will never dismantle the master's house" (Lorde, 1983). It is worthwhile to engage in deep reflection on this oft used but perhaps underanalyzed phrase. All too often, in the rush to avoid "the master's tools," people committed to social justice engage in a fruitless search for some pure or innocent space from which to undertake radical work. We end up discarding items of value, ironically ceding to the master the stolen goods of colonialism, even though it is the blood, sweat, and labor of colonized peoples who built most of these artifacts in the first place.

We argue for a more subtle reading of Lorde's (1983) words, in which the phrase "the master's tools" is understood within the context of her prolific life's work and refer to dysfunctional and violent engagements with difference. The master's tool is to exploit difference in order to produce hierarchies for the enrichment of some at the expense of others—that is, the plantation political economy. That is the tool we must never pick up lest we merely recreate the master's house. The rest of the world, though perhaps built to the master's specifications, nonetheless does not rightfully belong to the master. It is all stolen goods—the land, the buildings, the technologies, the medicines, the food, the utilities—all of it. The project of decolonization requires these tools to be recaptured, returned to their rightful owners, and repurposed for liberatory ends. In this way, we draw upon the past in the present to make future spaces that we can thrive in, here and now.

This repurposing requires constant vigilance along with deliberate critical reflection; we are flying the plane as we build it, and that is part of this work as well. Rather than being discouraged by this, we believe that it only highlights the importance and immediacy of creating decolonial spaces within the colonial plantation of higher education.

Part 3: The Decolonizing Pedagogies Project: Future Making in the Present

What does antidiversity look like in practice? For us, it is the ongoing, quotidian work of calling out whiteness, unapologetically, and of repurposing the tools of our colonized trade (knowledge production and dissemination) to center the margins within our classes, programming, and administrative bureaucracies, using activist and organizing strategies. These strategies draw upon the past, calling in the work of our ancestors and placing them in the present context for the purpose of future thinking and making. This means treating institutions of higher education as sites of serious grassroots organizing, community and coalition building, consciousness raising, binary breaking, and collaboration across structures of power. This work drew us together from our different locations (faculty and staff) and led to two "interventions" at the institution where we worked: the development of our Critical Identity Studies Department and our Mellon Decolonizing Pedagogies Project.[3] These projects illustrate the pervasive cooptation of "diversity," the need for "antidiversity" or decolonizing work, and the possibilities we seek to create within often impossible spaces.

Decolonizing Women's and Gender Studies

As Squire et al. (2018) note, a key structural element of the plantation is knowledge—or "the beliefs of what are thought to be true" (p. 7). We contend that in the case of the contemporary university, these "true thoughts"—or mindsets—come to life through the production, maintenance, and policing of academic disciplines. As indigenous scholar Linda Tuhiwai Smith (2012), argues, disciplines "are deeply implicated in each other and share genealogical foundations in various classical Enlightenment philosophies . . . that have no methodology for dealing with other knowledge systems" (p. 65). From physics to literature to art history to anthropology, the very organization of knowledge into academic disciplines constitutes a subject/object binary that is profoundly racialized and directly connected to beliefs that justified centuries of enslavement of peoples across the Americas (p. 66). This understanding of university-based knowledge production means that any and every discipline can, if its practitioners so choose, trace its history back to the structural and processual elements of the plantation. There is no disciplinary innocence.

For example, for the past 50 years the discipline of women's and gender studies (WGS) has been seeking to understand the production of marginalization based on gender, along with race, class, nation, and other axes of identities. Even though WGS is oriented around social justice and has made intersectionality a foundational disciplinary artifact, it too has continued to be a fraught location in its reproduction of whiteness in the curriculum. Therefore, we believe in the use value of excavating the historical conditions of any particular disciplinary knowledge project, understanding how it centers whiteness, and thereby tracing its methods for reproducing contemporary anti-Blackness in university classrooms, curricula, operations, and cultures.

In the case of WGS, almost any cross-section of textbooks, syllabi, or curricula makes it obvious just how insidiously disciplinary artifacts—especially at the introductory level—still reproduce an origin story of something called "The Women's Movement," even while any number of WGS scholars pointed out decades ago the extremity of its white-centeredness (Thompson, 2002; Sandoval, 2000; Gluck et al., 1997; Baxandall, 2001). This narrative investment categorically invisiblizes histories of organizing and activism by Black, Indigenous, Asian, and Latinx women around welfare reform, sterilization, public health, tribal sovereignty, US imperialist wars, and so on, as something "other" that "the" women's movement to which the discipline aligns. As a result, significant numbers of WGS practitioners who might prefer to emphasize different histories, intellectual traditions, or political movements (e.g., womanist, Black nationalism, trans, Xicanista, antiracism, or queer) are questioned as to whether they are actually doing the work of the discipline (Braithwaite and Orr, 2013).

Furthermore, the insistence on feminism as the foundational—and, for most WGS scholars, singular—paradigm of the field typically disavows the racialized origins of that term as it was embedded in nineteenth century ideologies that included "civilization-work," social evolution, eugenics, and imperialism to argue for white women's perceived rights to empire via suffrage (Newman, 1999). Such aspirations are not far from what historian Stephanie Jones-Rogers (2019) has recently described as the "many freedoms" white women enslavers sought to mobilize in previous eras of US history. For them, "slavery was their freedom. They created freedom for themseves by actively engaging and investing in the economy of slavery and keeping African Americans in captivity" (p. xvii). Thus, WGS is, among other things, a disciplinary project born of the structural and processal elements of plantations, or what Amy Brandzel (2012) has described as an investment in "whitenormative citizenship" that begins at the introductory level and carries through to the WGS PhD. They argue that "despite the attempts to centralize intersectionality and transnationality, women's studies is haunted by the historical telos of rights claims and citizenship aspirations of white women" (p. 505).

Analyses of disciplines that contain within them understandings of race that reverberate across these historical eras is one way to construct counternarratives with the potential to decenter whiteness in the everyday reproduction of those disciplines. In other words, telling one story means not telling another, and making space for different stories of the discipline to be told is a form of antidiversity work. For example, in "How Does It Feel to Be a Problem? A Conversation between Two Feminist Black Queer Femme Chairs," WGS scholars Mel Michelle Lewis and Shannon J. Miller (2018) use their informal "margin talk" (they literally hit "record" on their phones at an "antidiversity" workshop led by the authors) to capture, transcribe, and publish "what happens when we find each other, talk about what's been happening to us, and how we continue to 'make it over' at all levels and roles in academia" (p. 80). In doing so, they work around institutionalized citational practices to document how their white WGS colleagues perform disciplinary boundary maintenance by contrasting positive associations with white women's solidarity with suspicions of Black women's friendships. Lewis says, "Yes, we have to hide, like enslaved women going down to the river under the new moon to make ceremony and community away from the prying eyes of the master! If two faculty of color are friends, particularly Black women, then white folks feel like it's a slave rebellion! We meet off campus. It's ironic, first the white folks on campus can't tell us apart and call us by the wrong names, but if we are known to have friendships with other Back faculty [laughs], there is a backlash" (p. 86). They also speak of how white women simply deny race as a factor in their experiences of the discipline: "It happens every time I go into a room." They say, "'I don't think that's about race, it's about gender, because I experienced the same thing as a white woman chair'" (p. 81). These same senior white WGS practitioners seek to temper Lewis's and Miller's respective quests for power and influence with reminders that they need to "be the chair for everyone" (pp. 81–82), a sanctioning move that speaks to white fears of Black power to create decolonial spaces in the university. Lewis and Miller's testimony diverges from the dominant disciplinary narrative about "progress" and "diversity" in contemporary WGS by systematically linking historical eras to create meaningful alignments for understanding white women's behavior. Specifically, their margin talk takes up plantation politics' use of "allochronism"(*allo-*, "another," and *–chrono*, "time") as a framework that describes how "white people think of Black people as slaves, as inhuman, as lesser than" (Squire et al., 2018, p. 5), while also providing a complementary framing that exposes the

Future Thinking and Freedom Making | 159

disconnect from reality that characterizes how white people misperceive themselves and their own power to "oversee." In narrating their experiences as university administrators, Lewis and Miller resist white women's attempts to "commodify" their presence in the contemporary university generally and WGS as a discipline specifically.

Understanding the potential of how the framework of plantation politics can be utilized to decenter whiteness within our respective disciplinary knowledge projects means that, at some point, the question must be asked within every discipline: why reproduce narratives that perpetuate the mindsets embedded in anti-Blackness in the first place? And a likely answer is a collective investment in disciplinary innocence, or "attempts to protect the solidarity of the system from outside change" (Squire et al., 2018, p. 8). But what happens when we forgo our willingness to protect such systems? What might it look like to invest instead in the creativity of truth telling about our disciplinary histories?

At our institution, it wasn't until WGS made a deliberate move away from the "women's and gender studies" label to that of "critical identity studies" that assumptions about requisite curriculum, learning goals, and key texts/authors/terms to be passed on to our students could be questioned in fundamental ways. Critical identity studies has been our attempt to produce the *disciplinary* terrain for "antidiversity work." Until CRIS, there was an absence of curricular space specifically designated to take up race, dis/ability, indigeneity, and trans identities. As such, we hoped CRIS could become the long overdue response to the perennial call for Black/ethnic studies (a recurring and yet unmet student demand since 1969). But we wanted more than an add-on, single-identity program such as Black studies *or* disability studies *or* indigenous *or* trans studies—which too often becomes a replication—albeit rearranged—that merely privileges of different set of dominant identities (masculinity, cis-ness, ableism, settler logics, etc.).

With CRIS, more than diversifying "content" or checking off a series of monikers (gender, race, class, sexuality, etc.), we are trying to figure out how to tell a story of the various ways that institutions invest in anti-Blackness and actually make the discipline fulfill our undertheorized college-wide pledge of "aspiring to become an antiracist institution" (still a pro forma statement in all of the college's job ads). For example, we now require all CRIS students—from the intro level to the capstone—to put their knowledge into practice with projects aimed at exposing the anti-Blackness and decentering the whiteness that pervades college structures, processes, or narratives. Rather than center "women" or "gender" or any other singular axis of identity, CRIS attempts to understand how such categories are mutually constitutive and how they intersect as modes of power to produce structures of oppression *at the college itself.* In this way, CRIS has doubled down on the deep meanings that inhere in the concept of intersectionality as its institutional work.

Interestingly, as the shift from WGS to CRIS progressed at our institution, and the Decolonizing Pedagogies Project (described in detail below) took hold, new ways of thinking about how power was raced and gendered in the college came into view. We noticed that white women, as a group, were often among the most resistant, defensive, and hostile to our work. Their hostility was typically framed around a stubborn insistence that their own marginalization *as women* meant that they had insufficient power or influence to enact meaningful change (and that they could not possibly be complicit in the marginalization of others). In a time when discussions of "toxic masculinity," #MeToo, and #Timesup circulate in popular culture, we came to understand that our institution suffers from a less-analyzed practice of *toxic white femininity*. Because white women dominate our professoriate as well as our administration, many became the primary structural hindrances to the work of institutionalizing decolonization because of their investments in both personal and disciplinary performances of whiteness (or as they read it, "goodness"). Following the ways in which allochronism can expose how white people think about themselves, we watched as white women were among those tapped as the new overseers—the ones who self-select through their investments in whiteness to surveil and direct the work of people of color generally, and specifically women of color. They do this all while claiming they lack "real" power to enact change. Given this, it seems important to mark whiteness and its auxiliaries—class, sexuality, gender, and so on—as problematic sites for decolonial interventions.

Of course, there are no guarantees when it comes to how disciplines or administrative projects function as sites of plantation politics. This work of decolonization that comes from taking seriously the ways in which academic knowledge production echoes racialized relations of previous historical eras is never a point of arrival. But the work must begin.

From CRIS to the Whole Institution

In 2013 coauthors Catherine M. Orr and Lisa Anderson-Levy began a small Mellon-funded project focused on social identities, and coauthor

Nicole Truesdell became the college's new director of the McNair Scholars program. While Orr and Anderson-Levy were thinking about how to decenter whiteness in disciplinary/academic spaces, Truesdell was beginning to theorize a framework that pushed back against the deficit-based approaches embedded in how institutions engage with first-generation, low-income and/or minority students. Collectively, they began to talk, dream, and reimagine what it would look and feel like to create a campus environment where we (people who sit at the margins) did not try fit into a box that did not want or understand us. Instead, we thought about what it would look like to see our marginalized locations within our institution as an asset. The advantage of being at the margins of an institution is that, because many times people are not paying attention to you, these locations can and should become spaces of creativity and innovation—*if* you can disinvest from the overseer role and decenter whiteness and the white gaze in relation to your work.

That is what we each realized we were thinking about and starting to do in our specific institutional locations. From transitioning our women and gender studies department into critical identity studies to actively calling out whiteness within disciplinary locations to demanding students at the margins be centered in our work around student development, each of us was tinkering with what it would look like to decenter whiteness and bring a Black feminist lens to the decolonization of academic affairs writ large. In doing so we moved away from white crisis mode as an orienting lens and toward new spaces of possibility that are both exciting and challenging.

THE DECOLONIZING PEDAGOGIES PROJECT

In practice—for better and for worse—"decolonizing pedagogies" at a predominantly white institution means teaching white folk and their allies to recognize *and challenge* the operation of whiteness across multiple dimensions of college life. Part of the plane that we are building as we fly involves developing a specific pedagogy to achieve these difficult ends, of getting white people and their allies to perceive and reject whiteness—what took "generations, and a vast amount of coercion" to create in the first place (Baldwin, 1984).

To this end, the Decolonizing Pedagogies Project uses a developmental model, starting with basic self-reflection, and leading toward deeper and more complex work tied to concrete actions; concrete action is paired with continued reflection, making "antidiversity" an iterative project rather than a box to be checked off by attending a single workshop or training. We begin with a foundational seminar in which faculty, teaching staff, and administrators work together over the course of a semester to critically reflect on what it means to decenter whiteness in classrooms, in work areas, in programming, in advising relationships, in bureaucratic protocols—in fact, to decenter whiteness across all institutional domains. In this iteration of the grant, we have been less interested in making folks comfortable and more interested in pushing participants to think critically about their disciplinary legacies and their personal investments in whiteness, and to identify how these investments affect their practice, broadly defined. We have moved away from a workshop model offering "tips and tricks" for working with this or that population. Instead we imagine ourselves to be in the business of paradigm shifting, where the aim is to have participants integrate and sustain antiracist and decolonial praxis in their own location.

Once participants have completed the initial reading series and engaged in significant reflection and discussion of these topics, they become eligible to participate in the next steps in this tiered development program: the curriculum workshop, the peer coaching program, and the research and action teams. The curriculum workshop allows a participant to completely overhaul a course, program, office, or some other major part of their work, putting into practice the concepts they learn in the foundation reading series. They then implement these changes with the support of the facilitation team and structured peer coaching, as well as having access to an outside consultant. The research and action teams allow participants to propose and conduct further research into equitable practices that can then be put into practice down the line. The purpose of this is to support the kind of long-term, in-depth engagement that is required for the commitment to "antiracism" to be made real. Rather than reproducing the exploitative labor dynamic of the plantation economy, in which mostly people of color and LGBTQ+ "diversity workers" must create value for the institution even while being a dumping ground for all "diversity-related" problems, the goal of this model is to put other people—white people—on the hook for doing this work and for creating equitable, antiracist spaces (even when people of color are not pushing them to do so).

So far, this approach has revealed itself to have a number of advantages, opening up possibilities for more rapid change than we could ever accomplish from our disparate locations. If the outcome of plantation economies is to concentrate wealth and resources in relatively few hands, the success of antidiversity work can partly be measured by how well it serves to decentralize the work of decolonization, so that both the labor is being performed by everyone (including majority bodies) and the benefits are being shared by everyone (especially minoritized bodies). By making the program cut across typical domains of institutional power (tenured or tenure track versus adjunct, staff versus faculty versus administrators, and so on), we have seen broader departmental and institutional buy-in, and more rapid spread of new ideas and practices. And with the decentralization of the work comes as well an increased difficulty for institutional suppression. It is no longer the same old voices speaking up in email threads, committee meetings, faculty governance, and so on. Adjuncts, visitors, and junior faculty need not wait for tenured faculty or department chairs to take the lead; staff and administrators, from the ground up, are empowered into a "if you see something, say something!" attitude toward whiteness. This in turn is leading to the more long-term effects that come from an actual paradigm shift (as opposed to short-term or nonexistential effects that come from sitting through a "sensitivity training"). Participants are incorporating ideas from the series into their departmental reviews, their hiring process, their work with students, and their syllabi. Such changes touch on issues of structure, policy, and personnel that can affect institutional climate for years to come.

Perhaps most encouraging, despite numerous conflicts with individual participants who had what we now call "white fragility meltdowns," our programs have had big numbers for five semesters running (significant given our institution's small size). At time of publication we have had 85 faculty, staff, and administrators go through our foundation pedagogies series. The participants represent the divisions of college administration;[4] cocurricular or academic support programs;[5] and 16 departments.[6]

But let us also acknowledge that there are challenges and downsides to this work. In Vincent Harding's seminal article "Vocation of the Black Scholar," he was laying a framework that focused on the ways being a Black scholar/intellectual/academic was about truth telling and being possessed by that truth. In doing so, many of us then occupy positions and orientations that fall outside disciplinary boundaries as we are called to speak about and on the truth of our communities, and others, at the margins. Yet we know this orientation sits outside the sensibilities and legibility of whiteness, and this is okay. But when you push back against the dominant power structure, there will be consequences. In our foundation pedagogy series, the facilitators—particularly Truesdell and Anderson-Levy as Black women—have been subjected to white rage, white women's tears and disrespect, mansplaining, and fragility. These reactions have been consistent across every reading series, every semester, in part because whiteness and its allies use a system of uninspired and unimaginative reproduction and replication, pulled repeatedly from the same playbook. But recognizing it for what it is does not necessarily make it easier to swallow; and for people whose institutional existence might already feel precarious, engaging in this kind of work can put you even further "out on a limb." While the aforementioned advantage of decentralization might make it more likely that other people are out there with you, it's not an easy position to maintain over the long haul.

Another disadvantage—predictable, yet infuriating—is that, in its typical colonizing way, whiteness tends to steal work that has value, even as it denigrates the laboring bodies that produced that value. We have seen this occur as concepts and formats we developed through this project and in other specific locations are coopted by administrators and faculty who then water down the content and forget about the origins. Indeed, we've seen certain terminology—"asset based," "decolonize," and "antiracist"—show up in more and more places and institutional documents without the requisite commitment to deep interrogation and concrete structural change. Although the proliferation of subversive terminology and thinking is exciting and hopeful, the entailing loss of control opens the work to a dangerous cooptation. This is particularly frustrating when our offices are looked to as a muling source to "fix" institutional messes that result from the ongoing marginalization and mistreatment of minority bodies. In short, the work takes a toll on our bodies, minds, and souls, as we seek to walk a fine line of spreading our message without blunting the force of its critique.

Even among the four of us, we still grapple with the fact that our end goals are different. Some of us, at times, have hope that the institution can transform, becoming a place that is capable of acknowledging the ways whiteness underpins the university plantation economy, and then actively working to dismantle those systems. Indeed, Jesse Carr holds that it is the responsibility of white people such as himself to push for this kind of institutional change, to not let the institution get away with complacency, smugness, or self-satisfaction. Yet others of us do not hold out hope for systematic change of an institution that sits on stolen land and replicates plantation politic ways of knowing and being. For Truesdell in particular, she is interested in decolonization as a practice of space making, where people at the margins create liberatory spaces within an oppressive system. These spaces are both a means and an end in themselves: within these spaces, people who sit at the margins are both cared for and politicized. It is the act of space making in and of itself that serves as an engine for revolutionary change. Toward this goal, Truesdell is interested in developing future "scyborgs" (la paperson), those who can and will take their decolonial learnings and put them into practice in the world. This work does not require marginalized folks to try and "fix" rigid institutional structures that will take their labor, but rather it redirects attention and focus to those most in need and asks them to take the time and space to discover what they want the world to be.

But the funny thing is, even when our end goals are different, that does not stop us from working together, since the tools and methods of getting to these possible futures are the same. In order for institutions to transform, liberatory spaces must be created within oppressive systems. Whether or not these liberatory spaces "succeed" in transforming the institution, they play a crucial role in maintaining the wellspring of decolonial possibility, where the lessons of the past and the potential of the future coexist in the present moment. Even if attempts at institutional transformation fail, the work of decolonization means that the possibility of future transformation is never off the table. In other words, institutionalization can never become a goal in and of itself. Rather, the question is: What forms of institutionalization will be most (or least) useful in the ongoing project of decolonization? What combination of resources, and access to levers of power, will offer the most capacious opportunities for change?

By design, the work we've accomplished already will take on a life of its own and be self-sustaining past the end of our funding. Our project was designed to decenter whiteness and challenge dominant modes of "doing diversity," and part of that has been to challenge the ways in which this work tends to be "siloed" into one or two locations. The projects that have been completed through the various tiers of our program will have afterlives of their own: course syllabi that have been overhauled to decenter whiteness, assignments and classroom practices developed to recenter the needs of underrepresented students, divisional self-studies where antiracism and equity are prioritized, and so on. Most importantly, those who deepened their politicization or experienced paradigm shifts during the project will move through and with the institution differently than they did before. The presence of people in the institution who see its whiteness and are emboldened to seek out opportunities to dismantle existing structures of power is possibly one of our most important outcomes. We hope these "free floating radicals" will foment some modern-day plantation rebellions, rebellions that are not easily predicted or contained by plantation administrators.

So long as the underlying conditions of exploitation and dispossession remain in place, we predict new iterations of decolonization work will recur. The Department of Critical Identity Studies will also remain a key site out of which politicized students and faculty shift the terrain of knowledge production. Yet just as it's important not to reify institutionalization, it's important as well not to glamorize precarity. If the institution does not absorb some or all of our project into its own budget, or if the current project leaders cannot secure new sources of funding, important aspects of the work will cease or stall out over time. When resurgences of the work take place under new auspices, some resources will be wasted due to the loss of institutional memory and lack of continuity. In this context of shifting possibility and precarity, it is worthwhile to remember the words of Audre Lorde: "It is better to speak / remembering / we were never meant to survive" (Lorde, 1975). In other words, although survival (in the form of institutional funding and continuity) is important, it's not a goal in and of itself. Institutional survival is merely one (of several) possible means of achieving the larger goal of decolonization. This work will continue, at our institution and elsewhere, regardless of what form it takes.

We leave you with some final questions to think through as you carry our experience into your own locations and contexts. If all this makes you uneasy, what are you afraid of and why, in thinking about decolonizing your institutions, departments, or units? What can you do when you finish reading this to effect a shift in your thoughts and actions? As we have argued here, the only way to start the process of decolonization is by decentering whiteness. Ask yourself—as we ask participants in our foundation series—what is your attachment to whiteness, and what do you fear you are "giving up" if you sever the tie? In being honest and telling the truth we just might be able to imagine new worlds and ways of knowing and can bring (or introduce for the first time) the humane back into humanity. From this space of possibility we can imagine and enact our decolonizing desires. The proposition of antidiversity is what gives structure to enacting the decolonial within the plantation economy of higher education—we do not have to wait, because it already exists. If we lift the veils we can see the spaces that the past carved out for the present to future-make new worlds. So we say, pick up those tools that have been stolen, repurpose them, and use them to make the world anew.

Notes

1. Coulthard borrows the phrase from Marx. But Marx suggests that accumulation by dispossession is primitive and precapitalist, while Indigenous theorists such as Coulthard point to how it is central to capitalism, particularly in relation to imperial and settler-colonial economies.
2. The term itself should not be fetishized. Undoubtedly, whiteness—as a colonizing force—will seek to extract and co-opt the value of any new language we devise. If and when "antidiversity" loses its critical force, new terms can and should be created to subvert new patterns of marginalization.
3. At the time of writing and submission, all four authors worked at the same institution. However, at the time of publication, the authors collaborate from separate institutions. We must note, however, that the more institutions we collectively work for, the more iterations we encounter of these same patterns.
4. Institutional Research, Assessment, and Planning; The President's Office; Student Affairs; Academic Affairs; Health and Wellness; Human Resources; IT; Admissions; Alumni Relations; and Athletics.
5. Library; Disability Services; Liberal Arts in Practice Center; the Sustainability Office; Student Engagement and Community Based Learning; the Office of International Education; McNair; and SEL.
6. Anthropology, Biology, Chemistry, Cognitive Science, Computer Science, Critical Identity Studies, Economics, Geology, Mathematics, Modern Languages (French, German, and Spanish), Music, Philosophy, Physics, Psychology, Sociology, and Theatre/Dance/Media Studies.

References

Ahmed, S. (2012). *On being included: Racism and diversity in institutional life.* Duke University Press.
Ahmed, S. (2015, June 25). Against students [Web log post]. https://feministkilljoys.com/2015/06/25/against-students/
American Council on Education. (2017). *American college president study.* http://www.aceacps.org/summary-profile/
Austin, S. D. W. (2006). *Transformation of plantation politics: Black politics, concentrated poverty, and social change.* SUNY Press.
Baldwin, J. (1984, January). On being white and other lies. *Essence Magazine 14*(12), 90.

Banks-Santilli, L. (2014). First-generation college students and their pursuit of the American Dream. *Journal of Case Studies in Education, 5,* 1–32.

Bauman, D. (2017, December 10). Private colleges had 58 millionaire presidents in 2015. *Chronicle of Higher Education.* https://www.chronicle.com/article/Private-Colleges-Had-58/242013

Baxandall, R. (2001). Re-visioning the women's liberation movement's narrative: Early second wave African American feminists. *Feminist Studies, 27*(1), 225–45.

Bierria, A. (2017). Pursuing a radical anti-violence agenda inside/outside a nonprofit structure. In INCITE! Women of Color Against Violence (Ed.), *The revolution will not be funded: Beyond the nonprofit industrial complex* (pp. 151–64). Duke University Press.

Bonilla-Silva, E. (2009). *Racism without racists: Color-blind racism and the persistence of racial inequality in America.* Rowman & Littlefield.

Braithwaite, A., and C. M. Orr. (2013). Feminism's attachments. *Feminist Studies, 39*(2), 512–16.

Brandzel, A. (2012). Haunted by citizenship: Whitenormative citizen—subjects and the uses of history in women's studies. *Feminist Studies, 37*(3), 503–33. http://www.jstor.org/stable/23069920

Caplan, P. J., & Ford, J. C. (2014). The voices of diversity: What students of diverse races/ethnicities and both sexes tell us about their college experiences and their perceptions about their institutions' progress toward diversity. *Aporia, 6*(3), 30–69.

Castagno, A. E. (2014). *Educated in whiteness: Good intentions and diversity in schools.* University of Minnesota Press.

Clycq, N., Nouwen, M. A., & Vandenbroucke, A. (2013). Meritocracy, deficit thinking and the invisibility of the system: Discourses on educational success and failure. *British Educational Research Journal, 40*(5), 796–819.

Coulthard, G. (2014). From wards of the state to subjects of recognition? Marx, indigenous peoples, and the politics of dispossession in Denendeh. In A. Simpson & A. Smith (Eds.), *Theorizing native studies.* Duke University Press. https://www.dukeupress.edu/theorizing-native-studies

DiAngelo, R. (2012). *What does it mean to be white? Developing white racial literacy.* Lang.

DiversityInc. (2016, April 11). Diversity crisis communications: What to do when scandals erupt. *DiversityInc.* http://www.diversityinc.com/diversity-management/diversity-crisis-communications-what-to-do-when-scandals-erupt/

Frum, D. (2016, September 8). Whose interests do college diversity officers serve? *The Atlantic.* https://www.theatlantic.com/education/archive/2016/09/americas-college-diversity-officers/499022/

Ginsberg, B. (2011). *The fall of the faculty: The rise of the all-administrative university and why it matters.* Oxford University Press.

Gluck, S. B., M. Blackwell, S. Cotrell, and K. Harper. (1997). Whose feminism, whose history? Reflections on excavating the history of (the) U.S. women's movement(s). In N. Naples (Ed.), *Community activism and feminist politics: organizing across race, class, and gender* (pp. 31–56). Routledge.

Growe, R., & Montgomery, P. S. (2003, Spring). Educational equity in America: Is education the great equalizer? (2nd ed., Vol. 25). *The Professional Educator.*

Hartwell, E. E., Cole, K., Donovan, S. K., Greene, R. L., Burrell Storms, S. L., & Williams, T. (2017). Breaking down silos: Teaching for equity, diversity, and inclusion across disciplines. *Humboldt Journal of Social Relations, 39,* 143–62.

Iverson, S. V. (2007). Camouflaging power and privilege: A critical race analysis of university diversity policies. *Educational Administration Quarterly, 43*(5), 586–611.

Jascik, S. (2017, May 3). Race, safety, anger: Issues of race and security inflame two campuses. *Inside Higher Education.* www.insidehighered.com/news/2017/05/03/issues-race-and-security-inflame-two-campuses.

Jones-Rogers, S. E. (2019). *They were her property: White women as slave owners in the American South.* Yale.

Journal of Blacks in Higher Education (JBHE) staff. (2017). Many instances of racial hate on college campuses. *The Journal of Blacks in Higher Education.* https://www.jbhe.com/2017/09/many-instances-of-racial-hate-on-college-campuses/

Kessler, Z., & McDonald, M. (2016, December 4). The college president millionaires club. *Bloomberg.* https://www.bloomberg.com/news/articles/2016-12-04/the-college-president-millionaires-club

la paperson. (2017). *A third university is possible.* University of Minnesota Press.

Lewis, M. M., & S. J. Miller. (2018). How does it feel to be a problem? A conversation between two feminist Black queer femme chairs. *Feminist Formations, 30*(3), 79–90. DOI: https://doi.org/10.1353/ff.2018.0039

Lorde, A. (1983). *Sister/Outsider.* Crossing Press.

Lorde, A. (1975). *The Black unicorn.* W. W. Norton.

McKenzie, K. B., & Phillips, G. A. (2016). Equity traps then and now: Deficit thinking, racial erasure, and naïve acceptance of meritocracy. *Whiteness and Education, 1*(1), 26–38. DOI: 10.1080/23793406.2016.1159600

Newman, L. (1999). *White women's rights: The racial origins of feminism in the United States.* Oxford University Press.

Pelfrey, W. V., S. Keener, and M. Perkins. (April 2016). Examining the role of demographics in campus crime alerts. *Race and Justice.* DOI: 10.1177/2153368716675475

Sandoval, C. (2000). *Methodology of the oppressed.* University of Minnesota Press.

Schmidt, P. (2014, December 28). Tasked to protect all on campus, but accused of racial bias. *The New York Times.* https:www.nytimes.com/2014/12/29/us/tasked-to-protect-all-on-campus-but-accused-of-racial-bias.html

Sharma, M. (2016). Seeping deficit thinking assumptions maintain the neoliberal education agenda: Exploring three conceptual frameworks of deficit thinking in inner-city schools. *Education and Urban Society*. DOI: 10.1177/0013124516682301

Smith, L. T. (2012). *Decolonizing methodologies: Research and indigenous peoples* (2nd ed.). Zed.

Squire, D., Williams, B., & Tuitt, F. (2018). Plantation politics and neoliberal racism in higher education: A framework for reconstructing anti-racist institutions. *Teachers College Record, 120*(14), 1–20.

Stewart, D. L. (2017, March 30). Language of appeasement. *Inside Higher Ed.* https://www.insidehighered.com/views/2017/03/30/colleges-need-language-shift-not-one-you-think-essay

Stulberg, L. M., & Weinberg, S. L. (2011). *Diversity in American higher education: Toward a more comprehensive approach*. Routledge.

Squire, D. (2016, December 1). Reframing racial justice: A discussion on plantation politics, neoracism, and critical race tempered radicalism [Speech presented at Reframing Racial Justice: A Discussion on Plantation Politics, Neoracism, and Critical Race Tempered Radicalism in University of Illinois-Champaign, Champaign]. https://education.illinois.edu/about/news-events/events/event/2016/12/01/default-calendar/reframing-racial-justice-a-discussion-on-plantation-politics-neoracism-and-critical-race-tempered-radicalism

Thompson, B. (2002). Multiracial feminism: Recasting the chronology of second wave feminism. *Feminist Studies, 28*(2), 336. DOI: 10.2307/3178747

Truesdell, N., Carr, J., & Orr, C. (2018, January). The role of Combahee in anti-diversity work. *Souls, 19*(3), 359–76.

Wagner, V. (1995). In the name of feminism. In D. Elam and R. Wiegman (Eds.), *Feminism beside itself* (pp. 119–30). Routledge.

Wang, L. (2016, November 15). Personal correspondence with author J. Carr.

Wilder, C. S. (2013). *Ebony and ivy: Race, slavery, and the troubled history of America's universities*. St. Martin's Press.

Wilkinson, S. M. (2014, December 5). Diversity and corporate America's reputation #crisis. *Reputation Communications.* https://reputation-communications.com/you-online/diversity-corporate-americas-reputation-crisis

Wong, G., Derthick, A. O., David, E. R., Saw, A., & Okazaki, S. (2014). The what, the why, and the how: A review of racial microaggressions research in psychology. *Race and Social Problems, 6*(2), 181–200. DOI: 10.1007/s12552-013-9107-9

Chapter 7

The Contemporary Chief Diversity Officer and the Plantation Driver

The Reincarnation of a Diversity Management Position

FRANK A. TUITT

In recent years, many higher education institutions have witnessed a significant increase in campus activism regarding the range of experiences and conditions facing racially and ethnically minoritized communities in higher education. Specifically, minoritized students, faculty, and staff (and their allies) at some of the United States' finest traditionally white institutions (TWIs) have been speaking out in resistance to their daily encounters with microaggressions, macro-invalidations, and other not-so-subtle acts of racial discrimination (Tuitt, 2016). Consider that shortly after the election of the forty-fifth president of the United States in November 2016, there were reports of "at least 700 cases of hateful harassment or intimidation" (Evans, 2016). More recently, there has been a resurgence of white supremacy poorly disguised under the banner of white nationalism seeking to reclaim and strengthen the power and privilege of white people and their allies as they strive to make America great again. Furthermore, there has been a reinforcement of institutional commitment to free speech resulting in the sanctioning of racial violence and the maintenance of an oppressive campus environment in which the privileges of a small majority are prioritized over the humanity of the marginalized minoritized. Lastly, the persistence of racially hostile learning environments in which instructors default to doing what they have the right to do instead of striving to do what is right suggests that campus unrest is not going to subside anytime soon (hooks, 1994).

The unfortunate reality is that in spite of their best intentions, TWIs have not been successful in their efforts to close the gap between their espoused inclusive excellence (IE) values and aspirations and their ability to create inclusive, affirming, and equitable campus environments for *all* students.[1] The range of student demands that has emerged across these institutions has served as a wakeup call for campus leaders.[2] Not surprisingly, one of the more frequent student demands has been the call to add chief diversity officer (CDO) positions, resulting in a sharp increase in the number of these types of roles on college campuses throughout the United States.

According to Archie Ervin, president of the National Association of Diversity Officers in Higher Education,[3] CDO positions have been appointed at over 250 universities and colleges across the United States (Borruto, 2016). Moreover, the rapid growth in the number of institutions implementing CDO positions has garnered attention in national higher education media outlets. For example, several articles have appeared in *Diverse Issues in Higher Education*, such as "Hire a Chief Diversity Officer, Check!" (Parker, 2015); "The Role of Chief Diversity Officer Expanding" (Tomlin, 2016); and "More Community Colleges Are Hiring Chief Diversity Officers" (Pennamon, 2018). Likewise, in 2017, the *Chronicle of Higher Education* featured an article titled "College Diversity Officers Face a Demanding Job" (Brown, 2017); and that same year *Campaign* magazine featured a story titled "As Sensitivities Rise, the Diversity Officer's Role Expands" (Sherwood, 2017). A consistent theme that cuts across all of these articles is the tendency of TWIs to implement CDO roles as a common response to student protests in higher education. These CDOs are often expected to assume the lead role of architects of diversity and inclusion. Having served as a CDO for five years, I have to admit I was a little skeptical of this growing tendency because I had witnessed all too often that when TWIs create a position or office with "diversity" in the title, there was a frequent propensity to see IE work as belonging only to the individuals who have "IE" and "diversity" in their titles (Tuitt, 2016).

Having visited numerous TWIs as a consultant or trainer, I quickly learned that when TWIs isolate diversity work to a specific person or unit on campus, it sends a message that unless diversity, equity, and inclusion work is in an individual's job description, it is someone else's problem (Tuitt, 2016). It was in this context that I began to question whether or not the emergence of CDO positions as a common response to student protest was actually a good thing. More importantly, a growing concern of mine was that the very position I had taken on could actually work against its stated goals to advance diversity, equity, and inclusion and instead be complicit in the creation of exclusive campus environments. In search of critical answers, I began to think about what some of the preemancipation antecedents of the CDO role might have been, and with the help of the character Cato Powell from the acclaimed WGN television show *Underground* turned my attention to the role of the plantation driver.[4] Accordingly, in this chapter, I explore the eerie similarities between the contemporary chief diversity officer and the plantation driver during slavery, and highlight the roles these two positions have played in the management of Black people in traditionally white-owned spaces. More specifically, I focus on how these two roles have been and potentially continue to be complicit in the systematic oppressive and often violent dehumanization of Black and Brown people in TWIs. To accomplish these goals, I anchor my analysis by featuring a daydream scenario in the form of a short allegorical story.

In his seminal book *Faces at the Bottom of the Well*, Derrick Bell (1992) describes his use of stories "that offer an allegorical perspective on old dreams, long-held fears, and current conditions" (p. 12). Specifically, Bell states that the provocative format of an allegorical story, which he sees as a product of experience and imagination, allows him to discern racial themes that are seldom revealed. In my writing of this chapter I hope to highlight what Bell (1992) describes as the fictional coincidence of the similarities between the plantation driver and the contemporary CDO. Bell reminds us that the past and the present are always connected because lurking in the shadow of the current moment is the likelihood that the unexpected coincidence of something that occurred in the past will be used to justify an action that is believed to be a benefit for all but in reality ends up serving the interests of whites. Therein rests my focus for this chapter. Specifically, I consider the possibility that the CDO position, which is gaining popularity throughout higher education in this country and more and more across the globe, might just be the reincarnation of a previous mechanism of control for managing racially minoritized people in white-owned spaces. This may be especially true in the current context in which adding CDO positions has been utilized by some TWIs as a quick fix of their diversity problems (Parker, 2015). Moreover, I am increasingly concerned with the possibility that numerous professionals—mostly academic and administrators of color like me—may apply for these positions believing that we can make a difference without giving critical consideration to the embedded current and historical racial realities of how these positions might not be designed to serve the purposes we hope they will. As for Bell, it is my desire that readers—particularly current CDOs and diversity workers—will embrace the tension that this chapter presents for them and remain open to the possibility that even though divided by time and space, vestiges of plantation culture and life still influence modern university culture, climate, and structures of power (Squire et al., 2018). Most importantly, I hope to exemplify how the contemporary CDO, like its predecessor, the plantation driver, is inherently contaminated by the permanence of racism in American life (Bell, 1992).

Accordingly, this chapter begins with a brief overview of the role of the chief diversity officer and then moves on to an analysis of the role of the plantation driver, which I refer to as the chief driver officer, aka "plantation CDO." This analysis is then brought to life in the form of an allegorical story in which I imagine what a job posting for a plantation CDO might have looked like if the position had been recruited in a similar manner to the common approach taken to find CDOs in higher education today.[5] This chapter ends with a brief discussion of the benefits of viewing the contemporary CDO position through the lens of plantation politics (Squire et al., 2018) and how TWIs can work to enhance the transformative potential of these roles.

The Emergence of Chief Diversity Officer

Although the position of chief diversity officer has received a great deal of attention recently, diversity leadership positions have been in existence for over 40 years. Initially, these roles emerged during the civil rights movement and nationalist social movements (Ogbar, 2005). In its earlier form, the CDO position often included responsibilities related to affirmative action and equal opportunity, multicultural affairs, and student development. These duties were prioritized when the first wave of Black students were allowed to enroll in TWIs in large numbers (Williams & Wade-Golden, 2007). According to J. Goosby Smith (2009), the duties and responsibilities of a CDO are rooted in historical and recent higher educational events. These include (1) access and success of underrepresented student populations; (2) campus climate and intergroup relations; (3) education and scholarship; and (4) institutional viability and vitality. Damon A. Williams and Katrina C. Wade-Golden (2007) suggest that what separates the current CDO from its historical predecessors is the shift in TWIs' understanding of diversity as a resource that can be used to enhance the educational experience of all students. They contend that this functional approach requires that CDOs be at the center of leading the formal diversity competences of the institution in an effort to build sustainable capacity to achieve an environment that is inclusive and excellent for all (Williams & Wade-Golden, 2007). Specifically, in its current manifestation, the primary role of the CDO is to help TWIs utilize diversity as an asset in improving all higher education students' intellectual and social skills (Gurin et al., 2002).

SYMBOLIC OR TRANSFORMATIONAL ROLE?

While there is no denying the ascendancy and current prominence of the CDO (especially in the context of the current trend of CDOs becoming college presidents[6]), the question is whether or not the growth in positions will result in transformative progress for TWIs in their efforts to advance diversity, equity, and inclusion. Unfortunately, while the hiring of CDOs might promote diversity within TWIs, the research is unclear as to whether or not the position will be effective toward implementing diversity initiatives (Wilson, 2013). According to Damon Williams, founder of the Center for Strategic Diversity Leadership and Social Innovation, even though CDO positions are being created at colleges across the country in increasing numbers, many of them are not at the cabinet level and often don't have the full support of the administrative leadership or trustees of TWIs (Valbron, 2018). Williams and Wade-Golden (2007) contend that CDOs generally have very little formal authority to hold other campus administrators and faculty accountable, and as a result their influence is often based in status, persuasion, and symbols. Moreover, when TWIs fail to make diversity, equity, and inclusion everybody's business—not just a peripheral issue relegated to the CDO, it can significantly stifle institutional efforts to build momentum and sustain efforts for change (Tuitt, 2016). I agree with Eugene T. Parker (2015) in that the recent tendency to hire a CDO has to be more than a predictable reaction by TWI leaders to demonstrate their commitment to diversity and/ or to respond to single contentious campus incident of racism. For CDO positions to have any chance at true transformation, TWIs must ensure that the position is not just a symbolic one by allocating the resources that support its potential for success (Tuitt, 2016; Williams & Wade-Golden, 2007; Parker, 2015).

While the debate over whether or not appointing a CDO will result in deep meaningful institutional transformation will continue in the near future, what is not up for debate is how the CDO role has been positioned to not only manage diversity efforts but also ultimately to control Black people desegregating TWIs. According to Parker (2015), although the increase in appointments of chief diversity officers is a relatively recent trend at TWIs in the past few decades, early and mid-career administrators of color have always served as the de facto CDOs since mid to late 1960s, when they were hired to take care of the increasing number of racially minoritized students enrolling at colleges and universities across the nation.

The practice of appointing administrators of color has been well highlighted in the literature as well as in popular culture. Walter M. Kimbrough, president of Dillard University, noted in a recent interview that when TWI senior leaders realize they have a diversity problem, they often look for the easy way out by opting to hire a CDO and delegate responsibility to some Black or Brown person.[7] For example, as Black student enrollment grew on TWI campuses, students often had to navigate socially and culturally isolating campus environments filled with the insensitive attitudes of white faculty, staff, and students (Sutton, 1998). These hostile campus environments, coupled with a lack of institutional support, gave rise to Black student campus demonstrations. Michael E. Sutton (1998) posits that it was an effort to squash campus rebellions and provide a vehicle through which Black students could express their grievances and acquire access for support for their integration into TWIs that led to the creation of offices of minority affairs. These offices and their midlevel professionals served as the formal liaison between Black students and the university administration (Sutton, 1998; Williams & Wade-Golden, 2007). Thus, even though some TWIs may justify their decision to add CDO positions as an authentic response to help their institutions become more inclusive, arguably at the center of their action is the historical pattern of appointing primarily people of color in roles designed to manage the increased number of racially minoritized people attending TWIs. Not surprisingly, the notion of appointing Black people in a management role over their own people dates back to even before the early formations of the director of minority affairs positions of the 1960s and 1970s.

Earliest Antecedents of the CDO: The Rice Plantation Driver

According to James M. Clifton (1981), slave codes required that overseers be white. Some owners, however, ignored the law and placed enslaved Black men as overseers, allowing for a few of them to move into the highest level of plantation management (Clifton, 1981). Correspondingly, the role of greatest significance and responsibility available to most enslaved men was that of driver, in which they were allowed to serve as both foreman of the labor gangs and supervisor of the decorum of the slave quarters (Clifton, 1982). Drivers were appointed by plantation owners, not other enslaved Blacks (Kolchin, 1983), and quickly assumed the role as most important African of the enslaved people on the plantation (Clifton, 1981). Louis J. Stewart (2010) remarked that owners relied on plantation drivers to assign daily chores to the field hands and monitor their performance (p. 91). Drivers' responsibilities included inspecting production output to make sure that each of the enslaved met their daily quotas (Stewart, 2010) and slave watch to prevent runaways (Clifton, 1981). Additional duties of the plantation driver included (1) in the absence of the overseer, managing the day-to-day activities of the enslaved as well as maintaining order (Clifton, 1985); (2) occasionally accompanying groups of the enslaved whenever they left the plantation to ensure their safety and safe return (Clifton, 1981); and (3) serving as the pivotal link and buffer between Black independence and white authority as they negotiated the need, to keep the enslaved "working and minimally content with everyday plantation life" (Chaplin, 1992, p. 57). Overall, the primary work activities of the plantation driver focused on managing the other enslaved peoples that were under their supervision (Stewart, 2010).

Symbolic Status or Real Power of the Plantation Driver

Historical accounts of plantation drivers describe them as possessing a considerable amount of power and influence in the slave management business. For example, when overseers traveled for official business, in their absence, the driver assumed responsibility for management of the plantation (Clifton, 1985). According to Louis J. Stewart (2010), "The drivers' job conveyed considerable status and power. The drivers were often invested with their powers publicly amid great pomp and circumstance by their masters" (p. 111). Stewart contends that many overseers delegated "considerable supervisory authority to the drivers in order to control the plantation's agricultural and supporting activities" (p. 116–17). Drew Gilpin Faust (1980) denotes that some plantation drivers had the authority to bypass the overseer and go directly to the master with suggestions or concerns regarding plantation management or the overseer's behavior. Apparently, this arrangement allowed plantation owners to have in place a system of checks and balances that would serve to limit the power of either the driver or the overseer (Faust, 1980). Ultimately, plantation masters wanted to ensure that drivers had enough authority to convince the enslaved to accept drivers as their official leaders (Faust, 1980).

According to James Lockley and David Doddington (2012), plantation drivers "occupied contentious positions of power that could be used to abuse or protect other slaves" (p. 135). For example, some drivers learned how to control a whip "with marvelous dexterity and precision, throwing the lash within a hair's breadth of the back, the ear, the nose, without, however, touching either of them" (Kolchin, 1993, p. 595). This skill allowed drivers to mitigate how harshly the enslaved Africans would experience their discipline. Correspondingly, drivers had to be extremely careful as they negotiated the protection of their peers without relinquishing their power and not betraying the trust of their masters (Clifton, 1981). Additionally, some of the plantation drivers were often required to check in with their masters on a regular basis when it came to discipline (Faust, 1980), especially in a context in which many of the enslaved viewed drivers not as protectors but as cruel oppressors (Kolchin, 1983). This notion of the oppressive plantation driver was confirmed by Dan Josiah Lockhart, a fugitive who escaped to Canada who admitted, "I was harder on the servants than [my master] wanted I should be" (Wyatt-Brown 1988, p. 1249). Thus, while drivers may have been Black like the enslaved Africans and were in a position to communicate their interests to the overseer and owner, and, where possible, shielded the slaves from abusive whites (Clifton, 1985), neither the enslaved peers nor the masters viewed them as a representative of the slave community (Kolchin, 1983). Consequently, plantation drivers were forced to live a life of isolation in the slave quarters, where other enslaved Africans "regarded the driver as the white man's man, not to be trusted and one who would quickly betray them to owner or overseer" (Clifton, 1981, p. 350).

Compensation and Other Benefits

According to Clifton (1981), "The greatest thorn in the driver's flesh was a sense of frustration in that there was no further chance for advancement"

(p. 349). Nevertheless, because good plantation drivers were hot commodities, they received decent benefits and were well taken care of in terms of their health and wellness (Clifton, 1981). Phillip D. Morgan (1982) shares an account of an ex-enslaved man who "recalled that 'drivers had the privilege of planting two or three acres of rice and some corn and having it worked by the slaves'" (p. 584). Additionally, plantation drivers were well dressed, often wearing a blue uniform, a greatcoat, and whip, which was displayed with great pride (Clifton, 1981). So even though plantation drivers did not have the privilege of career advancement, they benefited in other ways (Morgan, 1982). For example, some of the enslaved viewed plantation drivers as living just as well as the white man except for his color, because he was almost like a free man who could have credit and property (Morgan, 1982). Clearly, the driver played a pivotal role in the realm of plantation politics (Squire et al., 2018), which set him apart from the other enslaved and allowed him to occupy a space of privilege that reached just short of freedom. In that regard the driver became an essential component of the oppressive plantation politics that allowed him as well as the masters he served to benefit from the control and exploitation of enslaved Black people. In the next section I attempt to draw connections between contemporary chief diversity officer and its earlier antecedent, the plantation driver, by way of an allegorical story.

Daydream Scenario or Nightmare: The Chief Driver Officer Allegorical Short Story

In chapter 1 of this volume, Dian Squire notes, "That is to say that Black people are seen, understood, and treated by others as existing in a space that is not contemporary but rather situated in material and nonmaterial realities of time and place as originally defined by their captors centuries ago." Accordingly, in a manner similar to Derrick Bell's (1992) "Space Traders" chapter in *Faces at the Bottom of the Well*, what follows is a short allegorical story, depicted in the form of a daydream scenario in which I engage in interaction with a recruiting firm representative and discuss a position profile that describes what the position I currently hold as chief diversity officer might look like if it was in existence on the plantation. To frame this imaginary job posting, I draw from James M. Clifton's (1981) article "The Rice Driver: His Role in Slave Management," in which he describes the role that the head driver assumed as a part of plantation management and politics. To construct this job posting, I integrate the description of the head driver with my understanding of the role of the contemporary CDO. As a result, the daydream scenario or nightmare (depending on how you view it) is written in style that exemplifies the convergence of the past and the present. Specifically, the intention here is to create a temporal anomaly—in which the past and present collide—that allows the reader to join me on a journey in which I travel through time by way of wormhole to experience the uncanny and not-so-coincidental similarities between the CDO and the plantation driver.[8] In some cases James Clifton's original understanding of the role of the plantation driver is left intact. In other places the past and present are fused together. This short allegorical story in the form of a daydream scenario consist of five elements: the characters, the setting, the plot, the conflict, and the resolution.

∽

Earlier this year, while listening to a keynote address during a national conference for chief diversity officers, my imagination shifted for a moment and I began to daydream about what it would have been like to have been at national conferences or association meetings for plantation drivers during slavery. And as my creativity continued to get the better of me, I imagined walking up to a table hosted by a search firm and meeting a white woman named Charlotte Virginia. Charlotte noticed me eyeing the various materials on her table and politely asked me in a deep Southern drawl, "Might you be interested in taking a look at some of the plantation CDO vacancies that my firm is assisting with their hiring process?" I hesitated for a moment before picking up a job posting for a vacant chief driver officer position at the James Monroe Plantation owned by a group of wealthy white men who belong to the Thomas Jefferson Trust.[9] Here is that job posting:

CDO Job Posting:

Wanted! Qualified Chief Driver Officer with diligence who will be responsible for managing a vast number of enslaved workers.

Specific Responsibilities:

1. Daily direction of the plantation workforce

2. Assessment of daily production of workers. We seek a CDO who is capable of extracting the optimum amount of labor from the workers

3. Management of the day-to-day operations, which also includes ensuring that all equipment is in good working condition

4. Beyond the daily directions of the workers, the CDO's main function is to maintain the discipline among the workers. This includes:

   a. Mediation of both intrafamily and interfamily disputes before serious trouble develops

   b. Keeping crime and violence to absolute minimum

   c. Setting a good moral example for the workers and reprimanding those who do not follow suit

   d. Running occasional interference to prevent workers from defecting

   e. Neutralizing as quickly as possible any challenges on the part of workers to the authority of the white members of the plantation

   f. Reprimanding or punishing any of the workers who step out of line

   g. Managing quiet hours and enforcing curfew

   h. Periodically representing or testifying on behalf of the plantation in any potential legal disputes

5. CDOs are expected to pay attention to the climate and conditions under which the workers work and provide shelter in the case of potential dangerous circumstances. The CDO is expected to do what they can to prevent undue or cruel treatment of the workers by whites

6. Every now and then the CDO will be expected to accompany groups of workers whenever they travel away from the plantation

7. By maintaining a foot in both worlds, the CDO will be expected to represent the interest of fellow workers and occasionally provide information concerning the overseer to the master

8. Additional duties as assigned by the plantation owner or overseer

Candidate Required Qualifications:[10]

Critical Thinking Ability: Candidates for the CDO position must have the ability to make quick and correct decisions. Must be knowledgeable of the complex organization of plantation operations.

Technical Mastery: The CDO should have an excellent command of all aspects of rice plantation's agricultural and supporting activities.

Political Savviness: The CDO must be particularly astute at navigating the plantation's political landscape; CDOs occupy contentious positions of power that could be used to abuse or protect the enslaved.

Ability to Cultivate a Common Vision: The CDO has to be able to direct the daily tasks of labor on the plantation as well as supervise the decorum of the enslaved quarters.

Sophisticated Relational Abilities: Using a high degree of emotional intelligence, CDOs have to be able to represent the interest of the enslaved to the owner and where possible protect the enslaved.

Understanding of Plantation Culture: The CDO should possess in-depth knowledge and experience regarding the culture of the plantation.

Results Oriented: Although not singularly responsible for results, the CDO must be results oriented and committed to encouraging the enslaved to reach their daily output quotas.

Preferred Qualifications:

We especially seek CDOs who possess maturity, physical size and strength, intelligence, and knowledge of the plantation industry.

Special consideration will be given to CDOs who are mixed-blood/ multiracial, and/or of Noble African descent between the ages of 35 and 55. As well as candidates who have exceptional communication (oral and verbal) skills.

Because we hope to hire a CDO who has demonstrated that they possess the talents essential to the position, candidate must indicate on their application whether or not they have previous experience as a deputy or assistant CDO.

CDOs who are successful (aka earn tenure) will be able to retain their position until poor health, old age, or death.

The CDO will be provided with a blue suit/uniform, which includes a great coat, pea jacket, shirt, trousers, and tie.

Compensation includes the following:

1. A salary commensurate with experience and just enough to seduce you into falsely believing your role is an important one
2. More and better rations than what the workers get
3. CDOs who excel at their duties will be eligible for bonus pay
4. Additional benefits include:
    a. Meal plan and premium housing
    b. Access to plantation resources
    c. Workers to tend to personal and professional needs
    d. Not having to work in the field
    e. Medical/health services

Screening of applications for this CDO position will begin immediately and remain open until filled. Members from minority groups are especially encouraged to apply.

As I finished reading the job posting, Charlotte noticed the perplexed look on my face. In wanting to appease any concerns that I might have, she reiterated that this was a unique opportunity that only the most talented individuals, such as me, could dream of. She referenced the extremely generous compensation package, and the great health benefits that came with the job. She also mentioned that the Thomas Jefferson trustees and overseers were some of the most progressive leaders in the region. As I looked at the position profile one more time, I contemplated whether or not to indulge Charlotte with a couple of questions, such as, Will this job result in my eventual freedom or the freedom of my Black brothers and sisters? Or will this job eventually allow me to become a trustee? Or will this job provide free tuition for my grandchildren so that they will be able to attend the University that will be built on James Monroe's plantation land several decades from now? As I started to say something to Charlotte, I noticed an elderly African man observing my interaction from a distance. As we made eye contact, he waved me over and introduced himself with a firm handshake as N'Jadaka and asked if I was considering becoming a plantation CDO.[11] With a bit of hesitation, I started to mumbled the words "I'm not sure," but before I could finish he revealed that he had been CDO for 20 years and that I should think long and hard before applying for the role. Specifically, he offered several points:

> The CDO position relies heavily on the exploitation of Black people to maximize profit and maintain a system of control; you will be required to assist in the acquisition of new slaves, the retention of current slaves, and the recapture of runaway slaves.
>
> You will have no real power: As CDO you will have to rely on symbolic power to facilitate change while at the same time not becoming seduced by the illusion of privileges, status, and authority.
>
> It's not easy being a chief driver officer. If you assume the role, you will be subject to having insults hurled at you, such as "pimp," "Uncle Tom," and "sellout" "window dressing." Thus

having a thick skin and a healthy dose of perspective will be essential to the role.

Access to "whiteness as property" will be a tempting source of conflict for CDOs, with the racial reality that their very existence in their position means that they have now become complicit in the maintenance of a system of white supremacy.

This position requires long hours and is a dead-end role in that there is little opportunity for career advancement. Additionally, assuming this role can lead to higher levels of stress and social isolation, as you will no longer be viewed as a member of your people and more as the masters' man or as a part of the White Elite. Navigating the space between liberator and oppressor will be hazardous to your health, resulting in high blood pressure, depression, and weight gain; early greying; and an occasional addiction to brown liquor.

Most importantly, plantation CDOs will be required to be complicit in institutional forms of violence that use intimidation, coercion, and fear to reach daily production quotas. Also, you will occasionally be called upon to keep enslaved Africans in line by using a physical and verbal whip.

Additionally, please keep in mind that CDOs are chosen by plantation owners and trustees, and not by other enslaved Africans; although some in these positions desire to protect individual slaves, you will owe your power to the trust of your masters, not to your fellow enslaved people. As a result, you will be asked to protect the interests of the plantation over the humanity of the enslaved Africans you manage.

Finally, in my experience, plantation CDO positions are subject to punishment and dismissal, especially if you challenge the status quo too much.

N'Jadaka revealed to me that although he had lived a good life while enjoying the many benefits that came with the role, if he had to do it all over again, he wouldn't. Sensing that I was going to ask why, he stated that he would rather be buried in the ocean with his "ancestors who jumped from the ships, because they knew death was better than bondage."[12] In that very moment I came to understand that N'Jadaka was extremely conflicted about his decision to become a plantation CDO. For him, the racial reality of his complicity in continued oppression of enslaved Africans was a price too significant to pay, regardless of benefits the job afforded him. Before I could ask N'Jadaka a follow-up question, loud applause for the keynote speaker snapped me out of my daydream, and I quickly joined in. As I got up to head to the next session, I couldn't help but notice that my heart was pounding and that I needed to wipe the sweat off my forehead. I quickly attempted to pull myself together and tried to forget my quick journey into that sunken place and back, dismissing it as just the remnants of racial battle fatigue messing with my imagination.

Similarities between the Chief Diversity Officers and the Plantation Driver

In the above short allegorical story of a plantation chief driver officer position profile, I attempted to illuminate a system of plantation politics embedded in the parallel organizational systems used to manage Black people between contemporary TWIs and slave plantations (Squire et al., 2018). Specifically, my goal was to expose what some might conveniently view as fictional coincidence by illustrating how an old tool (plantation driver) previously used to marginalize and oppress Black people is directly connected to the contemporary strategy of hiring chief diversity officers (Squire et al., 2018). This is just one example of how TWIs engage in plantation politics. Not wanting to leave my analysis to chance here, I now offer a few clarifying points of connection to further discern the range of ways in which the similarities between the plantation driver and CDO represent an example of the epistemological vestiges of slavery that persist in the programs and practices of US higher education today (Squire et al., 2018).

In their article "The Chief Diversity Officer," Williams and Wade-Golden (2007) outline six key attributes that a chief diversity officer should possess in order to be successful. These are technical mastery, political savviness, the ability to cultivate a common vision, sophisticated relatable abilities, an understanding of culture and context, and a results orientation.

Table 7.1. Framework for Understanding the Connections between the CDO and Plantation Driver. Adapted from *The Chief Diversity Officer* by Damon Williams and Katrina Wade-Golden, 2007. CUPA-HR Journal.

CHIEF DIVERSITY OFFICER	CHIEF DRIVER OFFICER
TECHNICAL Mastery of Diversity Issues: The CDO should have an excellent command of all aspects of diversity issues in higher education.	TECHINICAL Mastery: The CDO should have an excellent command of all aspects of rice plantation's agricultural and supporting activities.
POLITICAL Savviness: The CDO must be particularly astute at navigating an institution's political landscape, responding well to politically charged or politically sensitive situations.	POLITICAL Savviness: The CDO must be particularly astute at navigating the plantation's political landscape; CDOs occupy contentious positions of power that could be used to abuse or protect the enslaved.
CULTIVATE a Common Vision: The CDO must be able to develop and cultivate a collaborative vision of diversity on campus	CULTIVATE a Common Vision: The CDO has to be able to direct the daily tasks of labor on the plantation as well as supervise the decorum of the enslaved quarters.
SOPHISTICATED Relatable Abilities: The CDO must possess a high degree of emotional intelligence, charisma, and communication abilities	SOPHISTICATED Relational Abilities: Using a high degree of emotional intelligence, CDOs have to be able to represent the interests of the enslaved to the owner and, where possible, protect the enslaved.
UNDERSTANDING the Culture of Higher Education: The CDO should possess in-depth knowledge and experience regarding the culture of the academy.	UNDERSTANDING of Plantation Culture: The CDO should possess in-depth knowledge and experience regarding the culture of the plantation.
RESULTS Oriented: Although not singularly responsible for results, the CDO must be results oriented and committed to encouraging the change agenda along to achieve significant results.	RESULTS Oriented: Although not singularly responsible for results, the CDO must be results oriented and committed to encouraging the enslaved to reach their daily output quotas.

These six attributes provide a useful framework for understanding the connections between the CDO and the plantation driver. In terms of technical mastery both the CDO and the driver should have an excellent expert command of all aspects of the organizational enterprise. For the CDO this involves an understanding of the business of diversity in higher education, including best practices for recruiting and retaining minoritized faculty, students, and staff and paying attention to aspects of institutional climate that hinder or promote their overall success. Similarly, plantation drivers were expected to have a mastery of the plantations' agricultural and supporting activities (Stewart, 2010), as they were responsible for ensuring that the enslaved reached their daily production quotas.

In addition to technical mastery, both the CDO and the driver must be particularly astute at navigating the political landscape and responding well to politically charged or politically sensitive situations. According to Williams and Wade-Golden (2007), the CDO must have the capability and willingness to secure win-win solutions when contentious situations emerge. Additionally, the CDO must know how to facilitate consensus building and buy-in in order to work through competing interests (Williams & Wade-Golden, 2007). Likewise, the driver had to be able to navigate politically sensitive plantation matters as the buffer between whites and the Black enslaved labor-force (Chaplin, 1992). Moreover, both the CDO and the driver must be able to create and cultivate a collective vision to maintain a high level of production and functionality (Williams & Wade-Golden, 2007). For example, the plantation driver had the responsibility to get "the hands fields each morning, organize the gangs for the day and assign, and excuse them after the day's labor" (Clifton, 1985, p. 58). Correspondingly, CDOs need to build authentic relationships with students, faculty, staff, and administrators so that they can work collaboratively to design strategic initiatives that affect campus diversity (Williams & Wade-Golden, 2007). Navigating politically sensitive environments and cultivating a collective vision requires that both the plantation driver and the CDO have a high degree of emotional intelligence and charisma, as well as good communication skills (Williams & Wade-Golden, 2007). Both roles require representing the needs and interests of Black people to the leadership of their respective institutions by adapting to different audiences as they traverse various institutional stakeholders and boundaries (Williams & Wade-Golden, 2007).

Successfully navigating various institutional stakeholders and boundaries requires that both the CDO and the plantation driver acquire an in-depth understanding of the culture and context of their respective organizations. While the CDO must understand the politics of an organizational culture that involves shared governance, tenure and promotion, and decentralized academic units with competing goals (Williams & Wade-Golden, 2007), plantation owners relied heavily on drivers in their absence, as they viewed them as having the most knowledge about rice planting (Chaplin, 1992), which occasionally resulted in the driver having the responsibility for managing the plantation when the overseer was absent (Clifton, 1985). Overall, although not solely responsible for results, both the CDO and the driver had to be goal oriented and dedicated to achieving institutional objectives (Williams & Wade-Golden, 2007). Whether making sure those under their supervision were productive (reaching daily quotas) or working hard to prevent plantation or campus rebellion, both the CDO and the driver were central to the business operations of their respective institutions.

In the next section I conclude the chapter with some personal reflections that capture some of my inner conflicts about the nature of the contemporary CDO role and its connections to the plantation driver as I navigate my current position as a chief diversity officer in a TWI that, like its peers around the country, has experienced a significant number of campus rebellions. By deconstructing the potential for CDOs (myself included) to be complicit in the use of plantation politics, I hope to provide some insight as to how those of us in these roles can activate our emancipatory imaginations to increase the likelihood that our presence will facilitate and not impede the transformation of our institutions into antiracist campus environments.

Implications for Emancipatory Imaginations and the Elusive Search for Antiracist Campus Environments

According to Derrick Bell (1992), "Slavery is, as an example of what white America has done, a constant reminder of what white America might do. We must see this country's history of slavery, not as an insuperable racial barrier to blacks, but as a legacy of enlightenment from our enslaved forebears reminding us that if they survived the ultimate form of racism, we and those whites who stand with us can at least view racial oppression in its many contemporary forms without underestimating its critical importance and likely permanent status in this country" (p. 12).

By juxtaposing the role of the contemporary CDO with what I argue was its earlier antecedent, the plantation driver, I hope to forefront Bell's warning that Black people may never be fully emancipated, may never be fully equal, unless we recognize that often what "we hail as successful will produce no more than temporary 'peaks of progress,' short-lived victories that slide into irrelevance as racial patterns adapt in ways that maintain white dominance" (p. 12). My fear is that the TWIs who have appointed CDOs and the people who accept these complicated and challenging roles have and will continue to look past the ways in which our very existence in these positions has the potential to render us complicit in our own and others' oppression. As someone who has fully embraced Debra Meyerson and Maureen Scully's (1995) notion of the tempered radical,[13] I attempt to work from inside, and in collaboration with my TWI, attempting to transform it into a more inclusive and equitable campus environment for racially minoritized people. This decision to work for racial justice as a CDO inside the very institution that is a frequent collaborator in the oppression of racially minoritized peoples often requires that CDOs are positioned to represent institutional policies and practices that can result in the further marginalization of Black people, especially when we are called on to intervene in campus rebellions.

According to Squire (2017), CDOs can wield a significant amount of power as it relates to diversity, equity, and justice that others in TWIs do not. Specifically, he contends that CDOs can leverage institutional resources to respond to community concerns when they emerge. Alternatively, Monica L. Nixon (2013) reminds us that although the CDO role offers the potential for the exercising of agency, it also by design carries the potential for cooptation. Likewise, Mechthild Nagel (2016) argues that "despite best intentions, the diversity officer's key role, in this hyperreal world of diversity management, is to shield the president and other power brokers from liability and to provide maximum damage control. Because they are 'management confidential' or otherwise worry about job retention, these diversity officers are unlikely to go to bat for a Black student(s)" (p. 66). Chaunda Myretta Allen (2013) provides some support for Nagle's position that suggests that, like the plantation driver, the CDO position can be used to represent the interest of TWIs to the detriment of racially minoritized populations on campus. In their dissertation study *"Feels Like Racial Battle Fatigue": Managing Diversity Crisis Moments in Higher Education*, Allen (2013) shares participant' accounts of times when CDOs were asked to manage and control the behavior of protesting students. Specifically, Allen (2013) wrote, from the interview and observations it was clear that Mike communicated a larger message about the behavior of students of color that had been expressed by the campus Chief Diversity Officer (CDO), who was also his supervisor and someone with whom he had a close relationship. While Mike acknowledged that the space existed for potential diversity crisis moments to occur around sensitive issues related to diversity, this message seemed problematic as it prescribed a mode of behavior for students that might be at odds with how they chose to express themselves. This tension between the perceptions of how the CDO believed students should conduct themselves and how students thought they should express themselves created a perfect environment for a potential diversity crisis moment to occur on Mike's campus. p. 75

The situation described above is one I am quite familiar with, as I have been called on by senior colleagues at my institution to respond to student demands and protests with the expectation that I will persuade campus activists to be patient and not do anything that is going to create bad press for the institution. Ironically, in those situations in which I was sitting across the table as a representative of the institution, reaffirming to student leaders its commitment to diversity, equity, and inclusion, in most cases I tasked with putting out fires I helped to start, meaning that the issues being raised and the strategies that students were using often emerged out seeds I had planted and directed their way. In this regard, I see my role as CDO in a similar manner to Sara Ahmed (2012), who states, "We might need to be the cause of obstruction. We might need to get in the way if we are to get anywhere. We might need to become the blockage points by pointing out the blockage points" (p. 187). Unfortunately, my sense is that not all CDOs possess the critical racial consciousness that is necessary for limiting cooptation and their complicities in plantation politics. As result, they end up reinforcing a plantation politics form of diversity management in which CDOs who have become accustomed to using diffuse resistant practices are no longer reliable to the racially minoritized populations they were hired to serve (Nagel, 2016).

In cases in which CDOs are called to intervene in campus rebellions, they often face the ethical dilemma of figuring out how to navigate the interests and concerns of racially minoritized people who are advocating for the creation of antiracist campus environments against the interests and fears of primarily white administrators. Allen (2013) refers to this tension as the "interest convergence dilemma" in which the CDO becomes responsible for ensuring that "students' concerns might be heard but only in a manner that was palatable for whites" (p. 76). Thus CDOs, like their predecessors, plantation drivers, inhabit precarious positions of power that can be wielded to support or oppress Black people (Lockley & Doddington, 2012). Seeking to find a convergence of interests can result in a destructive form of plantation politics in which the suppression of campus rebellions limits the potential for real transformation, contributing to incremental change at best. Herein exists my own personal dilemma with my role as a CDO. The reality is that I have spent more than half of my years on this planet working from within TWIs ivory towers to experience incremental progress at best. And while I am not ready to advocate for the complete destruction of contemporary higher education as we know it, I cannot continue to justify the acritical adoption of current trendy responses to the permanence of racial inequities and just hope for better results.

As you might have figured out, I am conflicted about the conclusions I draw here in this chapter. On the one hand, I absolutely believe that it is important to have positions that have as a central component of its responsibilities an explicit commitment to advancing racial diversity, equity, and inclusion. On the other, I have argued elsewhere that every leader in a TWI should see themselves as a CDO and take responsibility for creating an antiracist campus environment in the domains that fall within their spheres of influence (Tuitt, 2016). Accepting that we are nowhere close to that being a reality, arguably, like the plantation driver, the CDO becomes a necessary evil. That being the case, TWIs should ensure that when they add a CDO to their institution, they are committed to a change process that has at its center an explicit goal of creating an antiracist campus environment and move away from the happy talk of diversity (Ahmed, 2012). Adding a CDO position without making changes to institutional systems and structures that drive day-to-day operations is like putting a Band-Aid on a cut without removing the sharp instrument that created the cut in the first place (Tuitt, 2016). Holding everyone accountable for the creation of an antiracist campus environment is not just a peripheral issue relegated to the newly hired CDO but has to be a priority shared by all campus leaders. Furthermore, TWIs must stop believing the myth of the magical CDO who will be a quick fix to their campus racism and white supremacy problems. The next T'Challa and Shuri are not going to be in the pool of finalists, and even if by chance they were, they alone would not be able to easily transform a campus with more than 100 years of practice being a traditionally white and inherently racist higher education institution.[14]

Finally, TWIs seeking to add a CDO must choose carefully. In my experience, TWIs, like plantation owners seeking drivers, are often looking for candidates who will not be too radical in their approach. I get that this role requires someone who is sensitive to the institution's readiness and capacity to change, but all too often this gets translated into hiring someone who is easily coopted and invested in not getting fired. TWIs must make it a priority to hire highly skilled candidates who have a successful track record of race-conscious leadership. Hiring a diversity specialist no longer guarantees that you can appoint someone who can boldly lead a collaborative effort to create antiracist campus environments. TWIs must prioritize the hiring of CDO candidates who (1) are aware of the history, pervasiveness, and salience of race and racism in US society in general, and higher education in particular, and understand the pitfalls associated with race-neutral or colorblind ideologies, policies, and practices (Horsford, 2014); (2) demonstrate their understanding of what race is, why it is, and how it is used to reproduce inequality and oppression in higher education (Horsford, 2014); (3) can critically analyze the institutional environment and recognize how racism operates within campus systems/structures (Cerezo et al., 2013); and (4) are able to centralize the potential impact of race and the probability of racism embedded in campus policy creation, enactment, and enforcement (Cooper et al., 2017). Hiring CDOs with high levels of critical race-conscious leadership abilities improves the odds that they will be able to successfully navigate and disrupt the racial realities of plantation politics' business as usual. Ultimately, even though the connections between the contemporary CDO and its predecessor on the plantation maybe a hard reality to accept as fact, I strongly believe that if we are going to have any chance of true emancipation, "we must acknowledge it, not as a sign of submission, but as an act of ultimate defiance" (Bell, 1992, p. 12).

Notes

1. "Making Excellence Inclusive," American Association of Colleges and Universities, https://aacu.org/making-excellence-inclusive

2. H. Chessman & L. Wayt (2016, January 13), "What Are Students Demanding?," *Higher Education Today* (Blog), http://higheredtoday.org/2016/01/13/what-are-students-demanding/

3. "Standards of Professional Practice for Chief Diversity Officers in Higher Education 2.0," National Association of Diversity Officers in Higher Education, https://www.nadohe.org/

4. Underground Wiki, "Cato Powell," http://underground-tv.wikia.com/wiki/Cato_Powell http://underground-tv.wikia.com/wiki/Cato_Powell; Wikipedia, "*Underground* (TV series)," https://en.wikipedia.org/wiki/Underground_(TV_series)

5. According to Garcia (2012), allegorical stories are designed to illustrate or teach a truth.

6. See M. Valbrun (2018, May 7), "From Diversity Chief to College President," *Inside Higher Ed*, https://www.insidehighered.com/news/2018/05/07/chief-diversity-officer-position-new-path-presidency#

7. See B. McMurtrie (2016), "How Do You Create a Diversity Agenda?," *The Chronicle of Higher Education*, https://searchproquestcom.du.idm.oclc.org/docview/1790790370?accountid=14608

8. See "Wormhole for description," Wikipedia, https://en.wikipedia.org/wiki/Wormhole_for_description

9. M. Hill (2015, November 6), Wikipedia, https://en.wikipedia.org/wiki/Monroe_Hill; Brendan Wolfe, "Unearthing Slavery at the University of Virginia," (n.d.), *Virginia*, http://uvamagazine.org/articles/unearthing_slavery_at_the_university_of_virginia

10. Adapted from Williams & Wade-Golden (2007).

11. N'Jadaka is the Wakandan name of the young boy who would eventually evolved into Erik Kilmonger, one of the main characters in the Marvel film *Black Panther*.

12. S. Vasta (2018, February 25), Wakanda and world-building, *Flashing Paleley in the Margins*, https://www.inthemargins.ca/wakanda-reading

13. "Tempered radicals are individuals who identify with and are committed to a cause, community, or ideology that is fundamentally different from, and possibly at odds with the dominant culture of their organization" (Meyerson & Scully, 1995, p. 586).

14. "T'challa, Black Panther," Marvel, http://marvel.com/characters/5/black_panther; http://marvelcinematicuniverse.wikia.com/wiki/Shuri; T'Challa and Shuri are Marvel characters in the film *Black Panther* who figured out how to use modern technologies to promote racial equity.

References

Allen, C. M. (2013). *"Feels like racial battle fatigue": Managing diversity crisis moments in higher education* [Doctoral dissertation]. Louisiana State University.

Ahmed, S. (2012). *On being included: Racism and diversity in institutional life.* Duke University Press.

Bell, D. (1992). *Faces at the bottom of the well: The permanence of racism*. Basic Books.
Borruto, A. (2016, May 20). Ithaca College reconsiders chief diversity officer position. *The Ithacan*. https://theithacan.org/news/ithaca-college-reconsiders-chief-diversity-officer-position/
Brown, S. (2017, August 8). College diversity officers face a demanding job and scarce resources. *Chronicles of Higher Education*. https://www.chronicle.com/article/College-Diversity-Officers/240875
Cerezo, A., McWhirter, B. T., Peña, D., Bustos, C., & Valdez, M. (2013). "Giving voice": Utilizing critical race theory to facilitate consciousness of racial identity for Latina/o college students. *Journal for Social Action in Counseling and Psychology, 5*(3), 1.
Chaplin, J. E. (1992). Tidal rice cultivation and the problem of slavery in South Carolina and Georgia, 1760–815. *The William and Mary Quarterly, 49*(1), 29–61.
Clifton, J. M. (1981). The rice driver: His role in slave management. *The South Carolina Historical Magazine, 82*(4), 331–53.
Clifton, J. M. (1982). Hopeton, model plantation of the antebellum South. *The Georgia Historical Quarterly, 66*(4), 429–49.
Clifton, J. M. (1985). Jehossee Island: The antebellum South's largest rice plantation. *Agricultural History, 59*(1), 56–65.
Cooper, J. N., Nwadike, A., & Macaulay, C. (2017). A critical race theory analysis of big-time college sports: Implications for culturally responsive and race-conscious sport leadership. *Journal of Issues in Intercollegiate Athletics, 10*, 204–33.
Evans, C. (2016, November 19). Hate, harassment incidents spike since Trump election. *CBS News*. https://www.cbsnews.com/news/hate-harassment-incidents-spike-since-donald-trump-election/
Faust, D. G. (1980). Culture, conflict, and community: The meaning of power on an ante-bellum plantation. *Journal of Social History, 14*(1), 83–97.
Garcia, L. (2012). Making cultura count inside and out of the classroom: Public art and critical pedagogy in South Central Los Angeles. *Journal of Curriculum and Pedagogy, 9*(2), 104–14.
Gurin, P., Dey, E., Hurtado, S., & Gurin, G. (2002). Diversity and higher education: Theory and impact on educational outcomes. *Harvard Educational Review, 72*(3), 330–66.
Horsford, S. (2014). When race enters the room: Improving leadership and learning through racial literacy. *Theory into Practice, 53*(2), 123–30.
hooks, b. (1994). *Teaching to transgress*. Routledge.
Kolchin, P. (1983). Reevaluating the antebellum slave community: A comparative perspective. *The Journal of American History, 70*(3), 579–601.
Lockley, T., & Doddington, D. (2012). Maroon and slave communities in South Carolina before 1865. *The South Carolina Historical Magazine, 113*(2), 125–45.

Meyerson, D. E., & Scully, M. A. (1995). Crossroads tempered radicalism and the politics of ambivalence and change. *Organization Science, 6*(5), 585–600.

Morgan, P. D. (1982). Work and culture: The task system and the world of low-country Blacks, 1700 to 1880. *The William and Mary Quarterly,* 564–99.

Nagel, M. (2016). Pitfalls of diversity management within the academy. *Wagadu: A Journal of Transnational Women's & Gender Studies, 16*.

Nixon, M. (2013). *Women of color chief diversity officers: Their positionality and agency in higher education institutions* [Doctoral dissertation].

Ogbar, J. (2005). *Black power: Radical politics and African American identity.* The John Hopkins University Press.

Parker, E. T. (2015, December 9). Hire a chief diversity officer, check! *Diverse Issues in Higher Education.* http://diverseeducation.com/article/79300/

Pennamon, T. (2018, January 4). More community colleges are higher chief diversity officers. *Diverse Issues in Higher Education.* https://diverseeducation.com/article/107862/

Sherwood, I. (2017, May 8). As sensitivities rise, the diversity officer's role expands. *Campaign US.* https://www.campaignlive.com/article/sensitivities-rise-diversity-officers-role-expands/1432685

Smith, J. (2009). Twenty questions for chief diversity officers. *Diversity Factor (Online), 17*(4), 1–8.

Squire, D. (2017). The vacuous rhetoric of diversity: Exploring how institutional responses to national racial incidences effect faculty of color perceptions of university commitment to diversity. *International Journal of Qualitative Studies in Education, 30*(8), 728–45.

Squire, D., Williams, B, & Tuitt, F. (2018). Plantation politics and neoliberal racism in higher education: A framework for reconstructing anti-racist institutions. *Teachers College Record, 120*(14), 1–20.

Stewart, L. J. (2010). A contingency theory perspective on management control system design among US ante-bellum slave plantations. *The Accounting Historians Journal, 37*(1), 91–120.

Sutton, E. M. (1998). The role of the office of minority affairs in fostering cultural diversity. *College Student Affairs Journal, 18*(1), 33–39.

Tomlin, O. (2016, October 27). The role of chief diversity officers expanding on college campuses. *Diverse Issues in Higher Education.* https://diverseeducation.com/article/88638/

Tuitt, F. (2016, Spring). Making excellence inclusive in challenging times. *Liberal Education, 102*(2), 64–68.

Valbron, M. (2018, May 7). Chief diversity officer position is new path to presidency. *Inside Higher Ed.* https://www.insidehighered.com/news/2018/05/07/chief-diversity-officer-position-new-path-presidency#.WyxQzxQcmmc.link

Wilson, J. L. (2013). Emerging trend: The chief diversity officer phenomenon within higher education. *The Journal of Negro Education, 82*(4), 433–45. DOI: 10.7709/jnegroeducation.82.4.0433

Williams, D. A., & Clowney, C. (2007). Strategic planning for diversity and organizational change: A primer for higher education leadership. *Effective Practices for Academic Leaders* 2(3), 1–16.

Williams, D., & Wade-Golden, K. (2007). The chief diversity officer. *CUPA-HR Journal,* 58(1), 38–48. http://du.idm.oclc.org/login?url=https://search-proquest-com.du.idm.oclc.org/docview/61925123?accountid=14608

Wyatt-Brown, B. (1988). The mask of obedience: Male slave psychology in the old South. *The American Historical.* 93(5), 1228–52.

Chapter 8

The Campus Underground Railroad

Strategies of Resistance, Care, and Courage within University Cultural Centers

Toby S. Jenkins, Rosalind Conerly, Liane I. Hypolite, and Lori D. Patton

> I was the conductor of the Underground Railroad for eight years, and I can say what most conductors can't say; I never ran my train off the track and I never lost a passenger.
>
> —Harriet Tubman, PBS Black Culture Connection

This volume is grounded in the understanding of plantation politics as intricate systems of policies, practices, and ideologies that universities use to oppress and exploit Black campus community members (faculty, staff, and students) (Squire et al., 2018). Historically, strategy existed on both sides—strategies of oppression and strategies of liberation. In this chapter, we focus on the side of resistance and draw parallels between the spirit of liberatory action taken through the Underground Railroad and the spirit of liberatory action taken in contemporary higher education settings. Being engaged in the complex network of student leaders, faculty, staff, and community members who discretely and strategically work to change the very institutions to which they belong is risky business. In many ways, it is reminiscent of the experience during slavery of the

Underground Railroad—an intricate system of allies and supporters who offered refuge, resources, and information to reach freedom. They met in secret. They met late at night. They organized and strategized among unidentified comrades in the struggle. This type of strategic resistance and networking happens today on our college campuses and most often within the culturally safe confines of university cultural centers. Today, the idea of "freedom" means something drastically different from what it meant to enslaved Africans and African Americans who were living under intense terrorist conditions. While undoubtedly many students at all levels of education continue to enter schools, colleges and universities where their lives are literally at risk (death threats, gun violence, sexual violence, and hate crimes), we do not compare this contemporary threat to the legally sanctioned life sentence of servitude, terrorism, and the subjugation of slavery. However, the spirit of freedom seeking today continues to concern successfully navigating oppressive environments. It continues to be about seeking and reaching goals to help advance one's self, one's family, and one's community by walking what can be an incredibly tough path. But more importantly, it is about reaching that goal safely—with one's person intact. The dedicated professionals of university cultural centers are more than administrators; they are activists, modern-day conductors of a campus-based underground railroad that helps students travel safely and successfully to and through college.

While a rich body of scholarship has helped to tell the story of activism and protest *by* college students, not much attention has been given to the support networks that have operated *for* students from within the administrative departments of the university. From the early days of student protest, there have always been university faculty and staff exhibiting ethics of both care and courage to work with and for students to help them navigate the culture and politics of the college campus. These staff members often work to leverage and align resources (fiscal, physical, and human) to ensure student success and to inspire a desire among students not only to do well in college but also to contribute to campus in meaningful ways. In other words, visionary university staff members provide students with a type of liberatory education that often results in change to both the student and the campus. While these activist-minded university personnel come from all over the college campus—academic departments, upper administration, residence halls, and advising centers—overwhelmingly this role is generally being assumed by university cultural center staff is rooted in the role of university cultural center staff.

Similar to the Underground Railroad's infamous conductor, Harriet Tubman, these staff members repeatedly do the brave, bold, and loving work of leading students to educational freedom through access to significant and critical learning experiences, personal development opportunities, career opportunities, and leadership development. They do this while often putting their job security and reputations of institutional loyalty at risk. Cultural center staff often do the important work of combating issues of exclusion, access, justice, and equity within their own institutions because they are ambitious beyond their careers. They are dedicated to a sort of modern-day community uplift. They use the resources and power of their positions to transform the lives of students and the structures of campus. In the chapter that follows, we analyze the ways that cultural centers orchestrate strategies to resist the subjugation of ethnically diverse communities. Just as plantation society informs and teaches the higher education system how to organize oppression, the activist work of abolitionists, civil rights activists, and freedom workers instructs university cultural centers on how to navigate and confront these systems (Squire et al., 2018).

Strategic Activism

In the recent years of Black Lives Matter protests, "Not My President" walkouts, anti–police violence die-ins, and "Carry That Weight" mattress walks to protest sexual assault, student activism has once again surfaced as a critical issue (Skovos, 2014; Daily Tarheel, 2017; Foley, 2014). While many administrative leaders are legitimately trying to determine the best way to support students, address student needs, and keep the campus safe, there are still many institutions that are scrambling to figure out ways to quickly dismantle campus protests (Jenkins, 2016; Linder, 2017). This is what makes the work of university cultural centers so incredibly complicated. Cultural center staff must balance expectations of institutional loyalty and job requirements that direct them to help maintain campus order and safety while also working to meet student expectations for them to be the campus champions of justice. For many students, the staff of the cultural center belong to them—not the institution. Students expect these staff members to have a strong presence among their administrative colleagues and to speak truth to power in campus meetings. And they also expect cultural center staff to educate and guide student leaders as the students push for campus change. The staff often play both roles willingly and brilliantly. They know exactly what paths to walk, what doors on which to knock, and what code words to use. They know when to sit quiet, when to whisper words of advice, and when to talk firmly to a student who won't listen. These were the requirements of the Underground Railroad conductors. You needed not only the courage to do the job but the wisdom to do it well.

The strategic activism demonstrated by university cultural centers offers us a new vision of what activism can also look like on a college campus. Most cultural centers leaders firmly reject the creation of learning environments that fail to directly confront and address sensitive issues of race, sexism, gender discrimination, class discrimination, and the many other forms of oppression (Patton Davis, 2008; Conerly, 2017; Patton, 2010; Jenkins, 2008). Difficult dialogues must be had. Conscious administrative leaders understand that inclusion is not simply about being "allowed" to be present; rather, it is about being treated as an equal member of a community. And so many students, faculty, and staff continue to fight for greater and more nuanced approaches to campus inclusion. They fight by standing up on campus, speaking out in meetings, marching on the university lawn, or lying down with their students at a "die-in" in the student union. And sometimes they fight by providing an important space to organize strategic resistance. As has been the case historically, the allies and supporters who use their knowledge, experience, resources, or influence to help the cause often cross-racial lines. The politics of any group of people working to strategically assist others outside of their own privileged community is complicated. On our campuses, sometimes calls are made to move a need along that was ignored when minoritized colleagues made the same call. Other times it takes the shape of well-resourced departments sharing fiscal and even human resources with underresourced units. But this also brings into play the continued issue with unfair policies that allocate resources differently or the lack of importance or priority often attributed to ethnically diverse units. Finally, there is a sense of safety that has been historically present for allies. Historically, in parts of the South a white person could and would lose their life for helping an enslaved person escape. But there was also a culture of reprimand and warning not afforded to African American freedom fighters. Bold acts such as standing alongside students might present serious risk to any professional, regardless of color. However, strategic but less visible acts can be enacted with minimal risk. Of course, both acts are needed, important, and appreciated. But there is a privilege in the very ability to take action that must also be acknowledged. More research needs to be done exploring activism among faculty and staff and determining what if any differences exist in risk taking and job threat across racial groups.

Regardless of the existence or lack of existence of institutional power (concerning executive decision making and policy development) within units such as the university cultural center, place is paramount in any struggle for freedom. Many enslaved Africans would not have escaped without the warm and supportive homes where they could rest, refuel, and map out a plan. Cultural centers provide this type of refuge for student leaders and activists. Most marginalized communities need space to organize, strategize, think, and sometimes just breathe. Expanding the campus from solely being a center of knowledge production to also becoming an incubator for strategic action on social justice is important. Historically, within the larger society, cultural centers and cultural clubs were those community spaces that taught leaders to be activists when schools did not (Asante, 2005; Foster-Pegg, 1971; Patton, 2010; Jenkins, 2013).

On Being an Abolitionist

Anyone who favors the abolishment of an oppressive practice or institution can be considered an abolitionist. The National Underground Railroad Freedom Center contends that "Abolitionists stand up to demand an end to the enslavement of their fellow humans wherever and whenever they see it . . . we tell the story of abolitionists then and now, to empower each of us with the knowledge that we can end slavery" (Freedom Center, n.d.).

This notion can be extended beyond issues of historic or modern slavery, and include a dedication to abolishing oppression, exclusion, or marginalization of any kind. Undoubtedly, university staff and faculty who choose to take an active role in college access, inclusion, and transformation are abolitionists of sorts.

Modern-day abolitionist movements on college campuses look different from facilitating escape—they are actually about efforts to create the opposite—retention and belonging. By using strategies that essentially embody culturally conscious frameworks, university cultural center staff members in particular help to keep students in college by making them feel at home there. In the article "The Impact of Culturally Engaging Campus Environments on Sense of Belonging," Samuel D. Museus et al.

(2017) underscore the importance of understanding the impact of culturally conscious frameworks by connecting these approaches to psychological dimensions of success, such as a sense of belonging:

> Another concept that has helped shift discourse to focus more on culturally conscious frameworks and psychological dimensions of success is sense of belonging, which typically refers to students' psychological sense of connection to their campus community. . . . In contrast to Tinto's concept of academic and social integration, studies that examine the sense of belonging are based on the notion that students from different backgrounds can perceive and experience environments and their interactions with those environments in distinctive ways. (p. 190)

To continue with our metaphor of the underground railroad, something as simple as a woodland can feel very different depending on your situation. To a couple in love, the woods are a romantic experience; to an athlete the woods are an exciting challenge; but to an escaped slave the woods were a frightening space of both fear and possibility. For the enslaved, the woods were both the physical path to freedom and an intimidating and scary environment filled with the danger of animals, unstable ground that could lead to serious injury, and of course the risk of being caught, hope and opportunity riddled with fear and anxiety. While our beautiful college campuses are not nearly as fear-inducing as the deep and thick woods of the South, the environment still presents a dual reality for some students—hope and opportunity riddled with intimidation and anxiety. It was important for travelers along the Underground Railroad to have places along the path that warmed the spirit and helped them to remember the goal. Sometimes there were just cold empty hiding places, but at other stations there was a warm basement and food. And there were comrades who gave you instruction and direction. These were spaces of affirmative action, not inactive existence.

Museus's (2014) campus environment framework identifies nine elements of a culturally engaging campus environment, four of which are particularly concerned with issues of cultural responsiveness: collectivist cultural orientations (values of community versus individualism); humanized educational environments ("environs in which institutional agents care about, are committed to, and develop meaningful relationships with students"; p. 192); proactive philosophies (going beyond making information and support available to ensuring the effective and productive use of such opportunities); and holistic support (having faculty or staff that students genuinely trust to provide them with support and to act on their behalf). This research captures the type of approach to student service required to abolish systems of oppression and to create culturally engaging campus environments.

Hearing Harriet's Voice: Cultural Center Directors and the Intersectional Politics of Leadership on the Plantation

> God's time [Emancipation] is always near. He set the North Star in the heavens; He gave me the strength in my limbs; He meant I should be free.
>
> —Erica Armstrong Dunbar, *She Came to Slay: The Life and Times of Harriet Tubman*

Any discussion of cultural centers as underground railroads is incomplete without first taking account of the numerous conductors or cultural center leaders who usher racially minoritized students to and through college. This section is inspired by the life, labor, and legacy of Harriet Tubman, best known for her role as "conductor" of the Underground Railroad. Tubman, whose birth name was Araminta Ross, was born into slavery in Dorchester, Maryland, in the 1820s. Nicknamed "Minty," she spent her childhood doing both house and field labor. In 1849 she escaped due to concerns of being sold. She repeatedly returned (nineteen times between 1849 and 1860) to the South to usher family members and other enslaved persons to freedom (Public Broadcasting Service, n.d.). In an 1868 letter to Tubman, Frederick Douglass wrote, "Excepting John Brown—of sacred memory—I know of no one who has willingly encountered more perils and hardships to serve our enslaved people than you have" (Bradford, 1901, p. 157). Tubman also served the Union as a cook, nurse, and spy.

Although Tubman died in 1913, her legacy in many ways can be used to inform an understanding of cultural centers and those who lead them. Tubman bore no children, but she most certainly has daughters. Tubman's daughters are Black women and women of color, many of whom lead cultural centers across the country. As they lead with strength and an unwavering commitment to serving students and ensuring their graduation, these women leaders are rarely rewarded for their efforts, and their significant labor is oftentimes overlooked and disregarded. The same was true for Tubman. As explained by the African American Policy Forum,

> What many people don't realize is that despite her unparalleled achievements, she spent her final years in dire economic straits, working in white families' homes to support herself and her family. Although she served as a spy for the Union Army, she was not able to get a pension in her own right for her service to her country. After years of agitation, Tubman at last received a pension—not as Harriet Tubman, Moses, the Conductor of the Underground Railroad, the General, or an army medic, but as the wife of Private Nelson, a soldier in the Union Army. A century after her death, what we can learn from Harriet Tubman's refusal to adhere to the limits placed on her race and gender by society? How has her legacy inspired and informed Black women who came after her . . . ? In what ways do women and girls of color continue to be erased from contemporary racial and gender justice agendas? (AAPF, n.d.)

This excerpt from Tubman's life not only calls attention to the centuries-long struggle that women of color have endured but also prompts a need to consider how the work of women of color leaders in cultural centers rests at the nexus of intersectional politics within postsecondary plantations.

Few studies focusing on cultural centers exist, and even fewer grapple with the intersectional politics that shape the lives and labors of directors. However, a few examples are worth noting in terms of identifying the political landscape of culture centers and how they are situated on college campuses. Jessica Harris and Lori D. Patton (2017) conducted a study to examine how Black culture center leaders address Black student's intersectional identities. More specifically, the authors explored how directors maintained a "race-salient agenda" along with efforts to incorporate other salient aspects of identity. They found that center directors faced significant macrolevel challenges, mainly the *post racial rhetoric* that imbued campus politics and led to questions of relevance for Black cultural centers (BCCs) and the *lack of funding*. With these two challenges, the directors were caught in a vicious cycle in which they fought against postracial rhetoric and the threat it posed to their centers, yet operated on limited budgets and resources, which made it much more difficult to customize programming for the diverse students they served. Harris and Patton (2017) stated, "Just as BCC directors struggled to assert the relevance of the BCC in a post racial society, they also struggled to fund and carry out their missions. The macrolevel systems of domination influence the ways in which BCC directors can, or rather, cannot negotiate intersectionality at the microlevel, impacting students' identity-specific experiences" (p. 341–42).

In addition to funding and postracial rhetoric, cultural center directors must also deal with issues related to status. Plantation politics highlight the structural elements of slavery and how such elements are reflected in higher education. One structural element focuses on status and decision making power (Squire et al., 2018). Cultural center directors may make decisions within their respective unit, but such decisions can be stifled due to funding, as mentioned previously. Decision making power can also be limited given the organizational structure in higher education that prohibits cultural center directors from access to larger administrative conversations that ultimately affect the center. The phenomenon of limiting cultural center directors' status is an example of career typecasting. Typecasting refers to instances "when an employee is perceived as able to perform only the job for which he or she was hired or does the job so well that it would be a major loss to the campus should the staff member decide to move on, so promotional opportunities are not provided" (Sutton & McCluskey-Titus, 2010, p. 160). The mere act of serving as a cultural center professional may result in individuals being viewed as "diversity workers only." This designation presumes that cultural center professionals are incapable of advancing as leaders beyond the confines of the cultural center. Moreover, it presumes that they are capable only of working within the cultural center environment.

Michael Sutton and Phyllis McCluskey-Titus (2010) explained the numerous benefits and skills that accrue through professional experiences in cultural centers, such as developing relationships with students and mentoring them, promoting student recruitment and retention, and sustaining the institutional commitment to academic excellence. Yet cultural center directors, when typecast, often face a career plateau in which there are too few opportunities for career advancement. The plateau is even more pronounced given that most directors do not possess advanced degrees. As a result, these directors may be either viewed as less credible or altogether excluded from institutional decisions that adversely affect the viability of the center itself.

Career typecasting is also rooted in white supremacy. The perception that cultural center directors are pigeonholed dismisses the dynamic work in which they are engaged, much of which reflects performance as an abolitionist. Often, cultural centers operate as mini student affairs divisions, in which directors serve as academic advisor, ombudsperson, conflict mediator, financial aid counselor, programmer, and student organization advisor. Even as these multiple roles are significant for serving students, the fact that culture center directors juggle such tasks is an indication that the campus departments or functional areas charged with these responsibilities, often led by white people, are absolved from any accountability at the institutional level.

Grasping the plantation politics that influences cultural centers is critical when considering that the vast majority of directors are women of color. Dian Squire et al. (2018) noted, "People of color, and particularly Black people, are exploited in various ways for economic gain at the sake of their humanity" (p. 3). Where center directors are concerned, this exploitation often sits at the nexus of race, gender, and institutional status and it is unsurprising that center directors deal with significantly heavy workloads that require them to assume multiple roles. Equally unsurprising is the fact that their work is rarely rewarded with limited opportunities for advancement. The status of women of color as cultural center directors closely mirrors the status of women of color in society. From an intersectional standpoint that recognizes the existence of plantation politics on campuses, women of color who serve as cultural center directors occupy a peculiar position at best. They are expected "to serve as vehicles for the achievement of a liberation that functions to perpetuate their own subordination" (Crenshaw, 1991, p. 1293). In other words, they are more than successful in providing support and resources to usher students through college (e.g., the plantation), but in doing so, they remain in roles that may yield intrinsic rewards but few extrinsic rewards (e.g., pay, acknowledgment, career advancement). Herein lies the precarious positioning of cultural center directors. They, like Tubman, are the "conductors" who guide cohorts of students to graduation (i.e., freedom). Graduation in a neoliberal system positions college as the pathway to "freedom" and recycles the master narrative that success can be experienced only through attending college. This same master narrative suggests that a college degree brings greater validation of one's worth, humanity, and capacity to contribute to society. Yet a plantation politics lens illuminates the reality that while a college degree is certainly an accomplishment, it is not enough to save Black students and other racially marginalized groups in a society that is structured, by design, to exploit and devalue them. Although cultural center directors use creative strategies with inequitably distributed resources and work tirelessly to construct "safe houses" for smoother passage through an otherwise tumultuous terrain of college going, they, like Tubman, must labor within a system that insidiously operates to ensure their subordination, as well as the subordination of the students with whom they work and guide.

The Way through the Woods: Strategic Allies and Collaborators

> Slavery can only be abolished by raising the character of the people who compose the nation; and that can be done only by showing them a higher one.
>
> —Maria Weston Chapman, *How Can I Help to Abolish Slavery?*

It might be accurate to assume that for cultural center staff, navigating the hostile and confining terrain of the college campus might often feel as rough, rugged, and dangerous as making your way through the dark woods toward freedom. But similar to abolitionists of the past, who held steady and continued to organize, continued to protest, continued to build coalitions, so do modern-day abolitionists on our college campuses. For cultural center staff as modern-day abolitionists, their primary role is to fight for the survival and academic success of their students on campuses while also working with allies across campus to address the embedded systems of racism that are perpetuated through programs, policies, and the hiring and promotion of problematic white people in positions of power. They are also fighting to ensure that students have a safe space to explore and develop their racial identity while also providing them with opportunities to connect this exploration to their disciplines of study. The consequences of this work by modern-day abolitionists include racial battle and compassion fatigue, along with the duality of balancing the promotion of sometimes contradictory messaging from the university. In 2015, during the height of the Black Lives Matter movement at the University of Missouri at Columbia (Mizzou), Black students as modern-day abolitionists risked their safety and enrollment at the institution to respond to the anti-Black racial climate on their campus. This led to Black football players refusing to practice or play until the president announced his resignation (Inside Higher Education, 2018). In the plantation politics framework, Black athletes are seen as a source of profit through labor; once this was threatened at Mizzou, there was an immediate shift in the dynamics of upper administration that led to the resignation of the president. Cultural centers continue to emerge on college campuses in the present day primarily through student protest and other forms of activism. Though there are some universities that are now proactive in creating these spaces, ethnic-specific, multicultural, and cross-cultural center models have been established through the physical and emotional labor of racially minoritized students exposing challenges related to the lack of support and connection to their campus. The primary role of these spaces is to assist with retention efforts of specific underrepresented populations and also to attract students to enroll at these institutions (Patton, 2010; Stewart, 2011). Once these centers have established an identity on their campuses, they evolve into spaces that provide a sense of safety and affirmation, as well as opportunities for minoritized students to connect around shared experiences inside and outside of the classroom.

Conductors, Stationmasters, and Stockholders

Cultural centers are by nature of their emergence safe houses by being places of refuge for underrepresented students. They are also utilized to identify other safe houses throughout a given institution that may not outwardly appear as a place of support for racially minoritized students. Conductors, stationmasters, and stockholders were instrumental to the Underground Railroad (National Park Service, n.d.). As referenced earlier, conductors were the individuals who guided slaves to safe houses where they could find food and shelter. The abolitionists who opened their homes as a place of refuge were called "stationmasters." Stationmasters also assisted freed slaves with securing work, gaining some form of basic education, and transition into life as a "free" person where they were expected to provide for themselves (Rodgers, 1997). In some cities stationmasters also paid conductors based on the number of trips made to funnel slaves to safety. Those allies in the struggle who donated money and goods to help the cause were known as "stockholders." We see many of these roles still working to guide and assist those in need on college campuses today.

The leadership in cultural centers serve as *conductors*, establishing relationships with entities across campus to funnel students to the appropriate resource (stationmaster). Some departments align naturally with the mission of cultural centers. In other departments, individuals are identified as the representative—dedicating their personal time, expertise, and assistance (stockholder)—while their department in general may not typically be considered an ally. Often, those identified are racially minoritized administrators in entry-level or middle management roles. This can lead to constant negotiation between wanting to go the extra mile to assist students or risking losing one's jobs. This can also decrease chances of institutional incentives such as merit pay and other forms of recognition. This is especially salient at institutions where specific classifications of roles are not unionized. This logic also applies to faculty that may be pursuing tenure or other research and grant opportunities, limiting their productivity and negatively impacting their chances of advancement. Again, the work comes with risks.

Safe Houses

Campus entities that naturally align with providing support for racially minoritized student populations will be discussed below. These individuals and departments are prevalent on many college campuses and often play an integral role in assisting students persist through the university. They are also important in that they help identify areas of opportunity for students, such as connections to internships, fellowships, and mentorship.

Themed/Special Interest Housing Communities

At many institutions themed or special interest housing (floors or buildings) for underrepresented racial groups serve as an inherent safe space for students to live with peers with a shared cultural background. Similar to cultural centers, such housing creates opportunities for these students to connect with others from different disciplines that may share similar experiences navigating the academic and social spaces of campus.

Cultural centers partner with residential education to increase awareness of these living communities as well as collaborate on programming and other forms of education. Though there are ongoing incidents of racially minoritized students experiencing microaggressions and blatant forms of racism from their roommates (Harwood et al., 2012), the students that live in these communities are able to adjust to life on their campus and know they are able to come "home" to their peers and a community of supporters. One example of these racially charged experiences was a Black student at San Jose State University who was being harassed by his white roommates, they hung pictures of Hitler and a confederate flag in their room, referred to the Black student as "3/5" in reference to the US Constitution that counted slaves as three-fifths of a person, and hung a bicycle lock around the Black student's neck (Inside Higher Education, 2013). Though the harassment eventually led to the suspension and battery (no hate crime) conviction of the white students involved, special interest housing can alleviate the need for students of color to have to endure this type of experience in their living space on campus.

Ethnic Studies Departments

On many college campuses, cultural centers and ethnic studies departments are sibling entities, since many emerged during or following the civil rights movement as a result of student protest and demands. This connection is not always recognized, since the two often live in different worlds at institutions, ethnic studies being attached to an academic discipline, and cultural centers being connected to student affairs or a general diversity and inclusion department. Cultural centers are able to partner with faculty and administrators from ethnic studies to amplify the challenges and opportunities geared toward racially minoritized students. This can aid in advocacy efforts since ethnic studies departments often occupy spaces on campus not privy to cultural centers.

Counseling and Psychological Services

Cultural centers and counseling services are tightly connected in that some racially minoritized students in distress often seek solace in these spaces first. Most cultural center administrators are not trained counselors or psychologists, so they often lean heavily on their colleagues in Counseling and Psychological Services (CAPS) to provide specialized services for their students. On some campuses CAPS representatives hold office hours in cultural centers so that students can access these individuals in a comfortable and familiar environment. This also reduces the stigma of students being seen visiting the counseling center. On many campuses, there are a limited number of trained counselors and psychologists of color; partnerships with cultural centers allows these individuals to engage with students, since many students of color choose not to take advantage of counseling sessions or other services provided by these departments.

First-Generation College Student Programs

First-generation college student programs are emerging on many college campuses and provide support to any student that is considered the first in their family to attend college. Many racially minoritized students, especially at Ivy League and other elite universities, are not first-time degree seekers. Some racially minoritized students that may be the second or third generation in their family to attend college may still encounter similar challenges on campus as their first-generation peers. Therefore, there is often an allyship between first generation programs and cultural centers, since this identity still intersects with being a student of color. Cultural centers often funnel students to this department so that they can have access to additional resources specific to their needs.

Racial/Ethnic Specific Alumni Associations

Alumni associations focused on racially minoritized populations exist on many campuses in different ways. Some are folded into cultural centers, others are volunteer based, and some are stand-alone entities at institutions. Alumni associations are able to provide many tangible benefits to students of color, such as scholarships, connections to alumni mentors, and career opportunities. This is also a natural alignment with centers, because associations can leverage the power and voice of alumni to address inequities in racially minoritized student populations. They can also be positioned to amplify the voice of cultural centers when the centers are unable to speak fully on behalf of their students due to the politicized nature of their roles on campus.

Gender and Sexuality Centers

Gender and sexuality centers at times align with cultural centers since they are focused on the empowerment of individuals that identify across the gender and sexuality spectrum. The alignment of these centers with ethnic-specific cultural centers can vary depending on the composition of professional leadership in the spaces. Since these centers are primarily focused on identities other than race and ethnicity, a concerted effort has to be made to address the intersections of gender and sexuality with race and ethnicity through programs, services, and the overall feel of the space. Though the physical center may not appear to be a safe house, there are typically student and professional staff that are seen as resources for racially minoritized students.

The entities discussed in this section can be positioned to work in unison with cultural centers in their efforts to assist racially minoritized students with navigating the campus and preparing for success when they graduate. Though these safe houses are spread out across the campus and may not be easily accessible to students, cultural centers serve as the connector, and often the entry point, to access these resources.

Toward the North Star: Cultural Centers as Guides to College Completion

> Knowledge unfits a child to be a slave.
>
> —Frederick Douglass, in Henderson, 2006

Though their ancestors were not allowed to learn how to read and write, let alone access formal education, many Black students dream of attending college and earning a degree despite how elusive this dream was for enslaved people just a few hundred years ago. In fact, studies have found that in the 1960s as well as today, Black students have expressed greater college aspirations than their white peers (Schneider & Saw, 2016). Yet institutional barriers persist in limiting access to such pathways. These roadblocks have widespread consequences in the current economic climate, especially since earning a college degree is increasingly fundamental to attaining financial freedom and social stability. Institutions of higher education continue to be gatekeepers to opportunities for survival in multiple ways. University systems are incentivized to reduce admission rates to move up in rankings, admit wealthier students who can afford their growing price tags, and implement discriminatory policies that shape their exclusionary cultures.

These are just a few of the many reasons that universities continue to be precarious environments for marginalized students.

These factors have a direct bearing on college outcomes for racially minoritized students, who must not only contend with campuses imbued with histories of exclusion but also with policies that continue to offer insufficient support at inhospitable institutions. Data shows that racially minoritized students continue to lag behind their peers. A 2017 report from the National Student Clearinghouse Research Center determined that only 38 percent of Black students and 45.8 percent of Latinx students completed a degree or certificate within six years of entering a postsecondary institution. This can be compared to white and Asian students, who completed their programs at similar rates to one another—62 percent and 63.2 percent, respectively. This comparison cannot be made in absolute terms given that data about Asian students is rarely disaggregated, often shadowing smaller, marginalized Asian subpopulations. So while universities have made a more public commitment to opening access to their institutions in some ways, retention and completion remain goals deferred for racially minoritized students (Norlin & Morris, 2000).

Cultural centers offer physical spaces and programs of support for racially minoritized students to help address this gap in completion. Many cultural centers share a mission to support the retention and college completion of these students (Patton, 2010; Pittman, 1994). Campus climate literature suggests that racially minoritized students often experience the extremities of isolation and hypervisibility in academic and social contexts (Harper & Hurtado, 2007; Hurtado & Carter, 1997). Cultural centers are positioned to combat these issues of alienation by offering welcoming spaces at historically and predominantly white institutions. This function becomes particularly important as racially minoritized students transition from their home to university contexts. By assisting with their adaptation to the complexities of academia, cultural centers contribute greatly to students' retention and completion (Norlin & Morris, 2000). Cultural centers function as a "home away from home," as students often refer to them, by guiding students toward college completion through the support of their staff and the content of their programmatic offerings. Just as the North Star was part of a constellation that enslaved peoples looked to for a path to freedom, cultural centers offer multiple supports to guide racially minoritized students in their journey to college completion, given its importance to financial independence and social prosperity.

A Constellation of Supports: Staff as Family

Professional staff serve as the backbone of cultural centers. Not only do they manage the day-to-day activities and logistical functions of the center, but they also provide students who use the space with guidance and support that they may struggle to find elsewhere on campus (Conerly, 2017; Patton, 2006). Staff help students adjust to their campus environments. As one Asian American student shared in the Museus (2011b) study about the staff from the Asian American cultural center, "I would always go in there and they were kind of like my unofficial mentors in a sense just because I would come in with a lot of questions about how to adjust from high school to college. They've been helping me throughout the process" (p. 9). This example is indicative of the immense value that administrators and staff contribute to their campuses by offering support to students from matriculation through graduation.

Lori D. Patton (2006) uncovered similar findings in a study of a Black cultural center where students associated the staff and the space with home. Due to the positive, welcoming, and relaxing environment fostered by the center staff, "home was the sense of community and familial ties that the students felt when they visited the BCC" (Patton, 2006, p. 644). Rosalind Conerly (2017) also found that cultural center staff reciprocate these feelings, given that they often extend their services beyond typical professional office hours, leading to students who also feel like family from the staff's perspectives in return. These familial relationships between cultural center staff and students are deeply connected to the programming they offer and the impact of their initiatives, but they also require center staff to extend themselves beyond typical job expectations. This exploitation of their labor benefits the students and the institution. Simultaneously, such efforts also occur at the expense of center staff's time and emotional energy.

A Constellation of Supports: Programs to Develop Self and Skills

Cultural centers offer a variety of student programming intended to support students' identity development and social connections to others, as well as providing them with academic and professional skills to prepare them for their future careers. Given their explicit frame of "culture," these centers understand student identity development in the context of race and ethnicity, and they value how a student's connection to their culture's history informs how they think about themselves today.

Cultural centers can provide these opportunities through individual programs related to heritage celebrations via the arts, invited speakers, and workshops that inspire students to reflect on their identity and culture (Liu et al., 2010). Others establish more formal partnerships with race and ethnic studies departments. For example, in Patton's (2010) analysis of two Black cultural centers identified as exemplars, the author described one center at a public research university that housed the institution's Black studies minor program. Students shared that these interdisciplinary courses allowed them to learn about themselves, the African diaspora, and potential solutions to modern-day dilemmas in Black communities.

Cultural centers also help foster social connections as a strategy to improve students' sense of belonging to the campus and increase their likelihood of retention. Some cultural centers combine social connections and academic supports. For example, Latina/o cultural centers can offer programming such as "peer mentoring, peer tutoring, faculty-student mentoring, and alumni-student mentoring" (Lozano, 2010, p. 14). While they range in levels of formality, Latina/o cultural centers aim to establish connections between peers, staff, faculty, and alumni (Lozano, 2010). These partnerships can also extend to other departments, as with the career center at the University of Illinois at Urbana-Champaign, which offers drop-in hours to provide career-related advice in the La Casa Cultural Latina space (Lozano, 2010). These are just a few examples of the ways that cultural centers act as guides that collaborate with entities across the university campus to meet the particular needs of racially minoritized students and support their college retention and completion.

Ultimately, cultural centers and their professional staff serve as intermediaries between racially minoritized students and other campus spaces, many of which feel inaccessible and, at times, hostile to racially minoritized students. Beyond creating an initial protective, familial environment, center staff act as advocates and guides who help students navigate and access other campus resources, such as academic and career supports. Despite the fact that marginalized students of color often describe these centers as "a home away from home," external entities continue to ask why colleges need affinity spaces. The answer is simple: cultural centers have the capacity to help students better understand who they are and where they are going. As the metaphorical North Star of a college campus, cultural centers must remain a constant shining bright light that helps students navigate their journey to graduation so that they can meet their aspirations and have opportunities that were not afforded to their ancestors.

Cultural Centers as Pathways to Freedom

I am not interested in picking up crumbs of compassion thrown from the table of someone who considers himself my master. I want the full menu of rights.

—Archbishop Desmond Tutu, BBC News

While it is contested whether or not Harriet Tubman actually said, "I freed a thousand slaves. I could have freed a thousand more if only they knew they were slaves," what has been verified is that there were two reasons that Tubman carried a small pistol—for protection from slave catchers and to motivate anyone who became scared on the journey and wanted to turn back (KCTS Resource Bank, n.d.). In many ways, when you are working to transform people's lives, you are also doing some psychological work to change mindsets—not just of the oppressor but also of the oppressed. You are helping the oppressed to understand who they are and what they deserve. The Underground Railroad did not just free bodies it also freed minds. Ultimately, the real goal is not simply to get free but also to critically value that freedom and to understand that it was always rightfully yours.

And so it is critical to understand that while cultural centers absolutely accomplish the important work mentioned above—creating networks of support on campus and guiding students toward college completion, they also serve a much larger purpose of affecting not only what students are able to achieve but also who they eventually become. The work of university cultural centers is concerned with both professional development and human development. Speaking love and appreciation to students who often meet with disregard and resistance in higher education is important. Having someone within the university to help student leaders to know that their work is valuable and important to the institution is a critical form of freedom seeking. These leaders are helping students to free themselves from the pressures to conform, comply, and be quiet. It is important to understand this work as a critical form of resistance. Through fully embracing and supporting students, privileging historically marginalized cultures, and helping to develop strong cultural efficacy among students, cultural centers are ultimately taking action that critiques and denounces larger institutional cultures of exclusion. The reality is that though cultural center leaders might not hold the positions that create policy, they all play a part in shaping the institutional culture, either through silence that sustains it or strong voices that critique it. From the expectations of compliant student conduct to the obligation of university staff to monitor student behavior—there is a rule of law to sustain institutional culture and order. As referenced earlier in this volume, the concept of "sanctions" was a core structural component of the system of slavery that manifests in different ways on college campuses (see Squire in chapter 1). Then and now there are structures to punish disobedience and to reward quiet compliance. Loud, angry students screaming for change are often seen as a disruption to the calm tradition of college. Faculty and staff who strategically work to support these students also risk the possibility of being targeted as noncompliant. Many institutions create an environment where the very people hired to change issues of inclusion, such as chief diversity officers and cultural center directors, have limited agency and are silenced by fear of losing their job (Jenkins, 2010; Jenkins, 2016). Critical to the concept of oppression is pressure—pressing an entity in order to force it down. Fear is often a central force used to put pressure on communities. On college campuses, a fear among faculty or staff to speak, question, or critique the institutions for fear of retaliation often serves as one form of pressure that sustains oppressive practices and policies.

Establishing a truly authentic and loving cultural environment on our campuses requires an ethic of genuine care—to care enough to do the difficult and challenging work of creating strategies, spaces, and networks of resistance. But how do we push back on the plantation politics that establish cultures of fear and conformity? First, we continue to push the conversation. We talk about it and name it when we see it. We confront the use of resource allocation as a tool to disenfranchise departments such as cultural centers. We challenge the plantation politic that creates citizenship classes among campus departments. Classes of citizenship occur when units such as student activities is well resourced and not allowed to fail, while the multicultural affairs office is understaffed, unable to produce much work, and no institutional leader truly cares if the office is underperforming. We address microaggressions when they occur. We confront postracial rhetoric and dissect it as a false strategy of oppression. We continue to build networks. But we also use those networks to not only move students through college but also move our comrades up into positions that yield more power. Toby Jenkins, one of the authors of this chapter, uses the strategy of being seen to secure her place on campus. The first thing she does when she starts a new job is prioritize meeting folks—folks in other academic colleges, folks in research centers, folks in student affairs, folks with large budgets, folks truly connected to students. The goal is not just to build friends on campus but also to let everyone know she is there in case she goes missing. Make noise. Be seen. And typically, it is that same network of voices all across campus that pushes the university to take notice and reward her work. Those campus voices push for her participation, inclusion, opportunities, and promotions. This idea of being seen is also about controlling the image—forcing the campus to see and acknowledge our contemporary embodied presence. Pushing to be seen as a real person, not a concept ("the diversity representative"). Owning one's presence and making it seen directly confronts allochronism. It is difficult to treat someone through an imaginative lens that romanticizes bondage when you are constantly forced to witness them exercising their freedom. Speak. Move. Act.

A strategy that Rosalind Conerly, another author of this chapter, uses is counsel and affirmation from a professional organization that has been instrumental in her development as a cultural center scholar practitioner. The California Council of Cultural Centers in Higher Education is composed of individuals that govern cultural centers at two- and four-year public and private institutions in California and surrounding states. Having access to colleagues that have been in the field from one to more than 30 years gives her the opportunity to receive feedback about the best ways to approach and navigate highly politicized situations that may arise on her campus. These colleagues also offer an affirming space when at times cultural centers can feel like they are operating on an island at their institution.

Finally, Liane Hypolite, a graduate student author of this chapter, views mentorship as not just service but also an opportunity for rejuvenation. It is yet another strategy that can be employed to push back against plantation politics. Within institutional structures where egos and a focus on self often take precedence, a process that centers the needs of others is needed to counter the individualistic push of academia. By spending time in spaces of community, such as cultural centers and affinity spaces, Liane is reminded of the purpose of educational research as a means for collective understanding and genuine connection.

These are our politics. At its very core, a politic is a very good thing. A politic is actually a set of strategies that a group uses to advance themselves (Jenkins, 2013). Minoritized communities have always created their own politics of survival to help them navigate racism, sexism, classism, and oppression (Jenkins, 2013). We need to claim and control the political strategy on campus, or in other words we need to take the institution (its physical, fiscal, and human resources) and start a revolution. We must do this by creating our own set of resistance politics. This requires courage. It demands resilience, boldness, and audaciousness to map out a path to freedom that transforms both the lives of students and the culture of our institutions.

References

African American Policy Forum (AAPF). (n.d.). Harriet's daughters: An evening of conversation and celebration. http://www.aapf.org/harrietsdaughters/

Asante, M. (2005). Challenging orthodoxies: The case for the Black cultural center. In F. Hord (Ed.) *Black culture centers: Politics of Survival and Identity* (pp. 37–40). Third World Press.

Bradford, S. H. (1901). *Harriet: The Moses of her people.* J. J. Little & Company.

Chapman, M. W. (n.d.). How can I help to abolish slavery? Office of the American Antislavery Society. http://nationalhumanitiescenter.org/ows/seminarsflvs/Abolish%20Slavery.pdf

Conerly, R. D. (2017, May). Campus change agents: Examining the experiences of cultural center scholar practitioners at a predominantly white institution (PhD dissertation) (T. Tambascia, Ed.). University of Southern California. ProQuest. http://search.proquest.com/openview/1df17c611bc6ff46691693e8c795146c/1?pq-origsite=gscholar&cbl=18750&diss=y

Crenshaw, K. W. (1991). Mapping the margins: Intersectionality, identity politics and violence against women of color. *Stanford Law Review, 43*(6), 1241–99.

Daily Tarheel. (2017). Students lead "not my president" walkout in protest of the inauguration of president Donald Trump. https://www.dailytarheel.com/gallery/students-lead-not-my-president-walkout-in-protest-of-the-inauguration-of-president-donald-trump

Dunbar, E. A. (2019). She came to slay: The life and times of Harriet Tubman. New York: Simon & Schuster.

Foley, A. (2014). Penn State students stage "die-in" to protest Ferguson decision. *StateCollege.com.* http://www.statecollege.com/news/local-news/penn-state-students-stage-diein-to-protest-ferguson-decision,1461930/

Foster-Pegg, P. (1971, October 21). Inaugural of culture center emphasizes Black awareness. *Daily Collegian* (Penn State University), 4.

Freedom Center (n.d.). Abolitio. http://freedomcenter.org/enabling-freedom/modern abolition

Harper, S. R., & Hurtado, S. (2007). Nine themes in campus racial climates and implications for institutional transformation. *New Directions for Student Services, 2007*(120), 7–24.

Harriet Tubman Historical Society (n.d.). Harriet Tubman Underground Railroad. http://www.harriet-tubman.org/moses-underground-railroad/

Harris, J. H., & Patton, L. D. (2017). The challenges and triumphs in addressing students' multiple identities for Black culture centers. *Journal of Diversity in Higher Education, 10*(4), 334–49.

Harwood, S. A., Huntt, M. B., Mendenhall, R., & Lewis, J. A. (2012). Racial microaggressions in the residence halls: Experiences of students of color at a predominantly white university. *Journal of Diversity in Higher Education, 5*(3), 159–73.

Henderson, D. M. (2006, February 17). Knowledge unfits a child to be a slave. *EIR History, 33*(7).

Hine, D., & Thompson, K. (1999). *A shining thread of hope.* Broadway Books.

Hurtado, S., & Carter, D. F. (1997). Effects of college transition and perceptions of the campus racial climate on Latino college students' sense of belonging. *Sociology of Education, 70*(4), 324–45.

Inside Higher Education. (2013). Outrage at San Jose State. https://www.insidehighered.com/news/2013/11/22/3-white-students-san-jose-state-charged-tormenting-black-roommate

Inside Higher Education. (2018). Missouri 3 years later: Lessons learned, protests still resonate. https://www.insidehighered.com/news/2018/09/12/administrators-students-and-activists-take-stock-three-years-after-2015-missouri

Jenkins, T. (2008). The five-point plan: A practical framework for university cultural practice. *About Campus Magazine, College Student Educators International 13*(2), 25–28.

Jenkins, T. (2010). Patriotism: A love story. *Journal of Black Masculinities, 1*(1), 12–21.

Jenkins, T. (2013). *My color, my culture, my self: Heritage, resilience, and community in the lives of young adults.* Temple University Press.

Jenkins, T. (2016a, Fall). Budgets are moral documents: Resource allocation as a function of social justice. Special issue, *The Chronicle of Higher Education,* September 18, 2016.

Jenkins, T. (2016b). Kaepernick's patriotism: A lesson in love. *Huffington Post.* https://www.huffingtonpost.com/entry/kaepernicks-patriotism-a-lesson-in-love_us_57dc2e70e4b0d5920b5b2a8a

KCTS Resource Bank. (n.d.). Harriet Tubman, c. 1820–1913. https://www.pbs.org/wgbh/aia/part4/4p1535.html

Linder, C. Myers, J. (2017). Institutional betrayal as a motivator for campus sexual assault activism. *NASPA Journal about Women in Higher Education, 11*(1) 1-16. DOI: 10.1080/19407882.2017.1385489

Liu, W. M., Cuyjet, M. J., & Lee, S. (2010). Asian American student involvement in Asian American culture centers. In L. D. Patton (Ed.), *Culture centers in higher education: Perspectives on identity, theory, and practice* (pp. 26-45). Stylus Publishing.

Lorde, Audre. (2007). "The master's tools will never dismantle the master's house." In *Sister outsider: Essays and Speeches* (pp. 110-14). Crossing Press.

Lozano, A. (2010). Latina/o culture centers: Providing a sense of belonging and promoting student success. In L. D. Patton (Ed.), *Culture centers in higher education: Perspectives on identity, theory, and practice* (pp. 3-25). Stylus Publishing.

Moffic, E. (n.d.). 20 things you can learn about leadership from Moses. http://www.yfc.net/images/uploads/general/20-tips-from-moses.pdf

Museus, S. D. (2011a). Using cultural perspectives to understand the role of ethnic student organizations in Black students' progress to the end of the pipeline. In D. E. Evensen and C. D. Pratt (Eds.), *The end of the pipeline: A journey of recognition for African Americans entering the legal profession* (pp. 162-72). Carolina Academic Press.

Museus, S. D. (2011b). Generating ethnic minority student success (GEMS): A qualitative analysis of high-performing institutions. *Journal of Diversity in Higher Education, 4*(3), 147.

Museus, S. D. (2014). The culturally engaging campus environments (CECE) model: A new theory of college success among racially diverse student populations. In M. B. Paulsen (Ed.), *Higher education: Handbook of theory and Research*. Springer.

Museus, D., Yi, V., & Saelua, N. (2017). The impact of culturally engaging campus environments on sense of belonging. *The Review of Higher Education*, Winter 2017, *40*(2), 187-215.

National Park Service. (n.d.). The language of slavery. https://www.nps.gov/subjects/ugrr/discover_history/terminology.htm

Norlin, E., & Morris, P. (2000). Developing proactive partnerships: Minority cultural centers. *The Reference Librarian, 32*(67-68), 147-60.

Patton, L. D. (2006). The voice of reason: A qualitative examination of Black student perceptions of Black culture centers. *Journal of College Student Development, 47*(6), 628-46.

Patton, L. D. (2010). *Culture centers in higher education: Perspectives on identity, theory, and practice*. Stylus Publishing.

Patton, L. D., & Alcaraz, J. (Forthcoming). *A trend analysis of culture centers in higher education*.

Patton, L. D. (2008, January–February). Learning through crisis: The educator's role. *About Campus, 12*(6), 10–15.

Pittman, E. (1994). Cultural centers on predominantly white campuses: Campus, cultural and social comfort equals retention. *Diverse Issues in Higher Education, 11*(16), 104.

Public Broadcasting Service. (n.d.). Harriet Tubman. http://www.pbs.org/wgbh/aia/part4/4p1535.html

Rodgers, L. R. (1997). *Canaan bound: The African-American great migration novel.* University of Illinois Press.

Schneider, B., & Saw, G. (2016). Racial and ethnic gaps in postsecondary aspirations and enrollment. *RSF: The Russell Sage Foundation Journal of the Social Sciences, 2*(5), 58–82.

Shapiro, D., Dundar, A., Huie, F., Wakhungu, P., Yuan, X., Nathan, A. & Hwang, Y. (2017, April). *A national view of student attainment rates by race and ethnicity—Fall 2010 cohort* [Signature report no. 12b]. National Student Clearinghouse Research Center.

Skovos, A. (2014). Students bring out mattresses in huge "carry that weight" protest against sexual assault. *Huffington Post.* https://www.huffpost.com/entry/carry-that-weight-columbia-sexual-assault_n_6069344

Squire, D., Williams, B, & Tuitt, F. (2018). Plantation politics and neoliberal racism in higher education: A framework for reconstructing anti-racist institutions. *Teachers College Record, 120*(14), 1–20.

Stewart, D. L. (2011). *Multicultural student services on campus: Building bridges, re-visioning community.* Stylus.

Stovall, D. (2005). The school a community built. *Educational Leadership, 62*(6), 34–37.

Sutton, M., & McCluskey-Titus, P. (2010). Campus culture center directors' perspectives on advancement, current issues, and future directions. In L. Patton (Ed.), *Culture centers in higher education: Perspectives on identity, theory, and practice* (pp. 157–77). Stylus.

Tubman, H. (2019). PBS Black Culture Connection. https://www.pbs.org/black-culture/explore/harriet-tubman/

Tutu, D. (2010, July 22). BBC News. https://www.bbc.com/news/world-africa-10734471

Part 3

Resistance and Repression:
Campus Politics and Legislative Acts
of Anti-Blackness

Chapter 9

Resistance In and Out of the University
*Student Activist Political Subjectivity
and the Liberal Institution*

KRISTI CAREY

> I don't think [student protest] would happen again. . . . I think there's lessons learned from that. I doubt there'd be approval to allow overnight camping again on campus.
>
> —Alan Burdziak, "University of Missouri Expected to No Longer Allow Protest Camps"

Universities learn quickly how to quell student rebellion, a University of Missouri police officer suggests. Where students are actively claiming public and digital spaces as sites of resistance against the historically present weight of oppression, institutional responses are rapidly emerging. Contemporary student movements are not without historical recourse, as they draw from 1960s organizing and also observe that the absorption of these movements into university structures—the institutionalization of what Roderick Ferguson (2012) terms the "interdisciplines" (e.g., Black Studies, Women's Studies, Ethnic Studies)—serves to contain their radical possibility. In the post–welfare state university, flooded with discourses of "diversity," the interdisciplines assert the university's moral structure of liberal inclusion that in fact *relies* upon their adoption—the university's own showcase of intersectional lived experience. The institutionalization of the interdisciplines, through such performativity, reliance, and containment, is an exacting example of how plantation politics both materially and metaphorically haunts university campuses. That is, if we understand plantation politics to be about the historical basis of the university as founded within empire, coloniality, and racial and sexual economies of power (Wilder, 2013; Spillers, 1987), *and also* through its control of Black bodies and bodies of color within its space, institutionalization as moral structure is an investment of those bodies, and their political/ emotional labor, as a marker of the university's liberalism.

This chapter engages conversations of antiracist student activist mobilization over the past 10 years, how universities are responding to Black students and students of color, and what the university's logics are now, with and beyond institutionalization. As part of a collection on plantation politics, this work attends to how the historical basis of universities necessitates our understanding of the continual exploitation of Black students' labor within a colonial and imperial space. I understand Craig Steven Wilder's (2013) analysis of coloniality as the founding basis for the space of the university and its enactment on institutional bodies, and Piya Chatterjee and Sunaina Maira's (2014) work as primary to understanding its imperializing effects. I interrogate the space of the public university in the contemporary United States through the lens of student protest, and work to understand the limits to university protest, and the demand to know its effects and affects within formations such as neoliberal capitalism (Brown, 2015), the carceral state (Davis, 1983; Shakur, 2005), and as "somewhere in advance of nowhere" (Cortez, cited in Kelley, 2002, p. xii). As part of a larger project that speaks to historical institutionalization of the interdisciplines and the containment of radical potential,[1] I provide different leverage to this complex terrain, considering the production of student political subjectivity, constituted in relation to capitalist subjectivity (Guattari & Rolnik, 2008) as process and product. I interrogate student activism as both in and of the university, both forceful resistance and also entangled within its desires.[2]

Introduction

In the fall of 2015, the University of Missouri (Mizzou) was one of over 100 universities involved in demonstrations against institutionalized racism, during the third year of the #BlackLivesMatter Movement for Black Lives. The demonstrations, detailed in this paper, provide an important analytic for studying political power and university/community response. Using Mizzou as case study, this project will investigate the formation of the student-activist as political subject. Following Michel Foucault (1989), we must understand how it is that humans are made into subjects, and as subjects that signify the state, being subject to another's control and obtaining an identity position. If we are, as Foucault (1989) intimates, to understand the development of the modern state—and the modern educational institution—we must look to the "antagonism of strategies" against power relations (p. 329). Put differently, resistance betrays the power of institutions. Following Fred Moten and Stefano Harney's (2004, 2013) suggestion that "governance is the management of self-management" (p. 55), I am interested in how that resistance is (self-)managed on the individual level. Considering that institutions of higher education in the United States operate in an environment imbued with values legitimated by our economic system (Readings, 1996; Tuchman, 2009; Washburn, 2005), in order to conduct this analysis, I will first historicize the emergence of the university as directly affected by national and global political and economic structural violence—namely, neoliberalism and empire. These two industrial systems are both seeped into and informed by the university's operations, and we can read them as manifestations of how plantation politics act as a foundational cornerstone of university campuses in the United States.

The genesis of this project has much to do with my experience as a queer student activist of color, organizing at my undergraduate university in the fall of 2014, and also trending commentary on student activism. Gaining traction are perspectives on student activism from everyone except those involved in the movements themselves. While productive critique is a powerful way to disrupt ideological certainty, I question the intention of critique without providing space for understanding and respecting these movements with relationship to the university terrain on which they are enacted. With demands for students to be more resilient, questions are hardly asked about what they are expected to be resilient from. For example, the critique that name changes to buildings are unproductive rejects highly strategic and legible tactics of university change, even while students might know that plantation politics runs deeply. This points to a critical juncture in current analyses of student-led protest movements on university campuses.

Politics and the Public University

In his work *Unmaking the Public University*, Christopher Newfield (2008) outlines how the rise of neoliberalism with Ronald Reagan and Margaret Thatcher shaped public universities and, more specifically, their responses to campus protest. While political response to student activism allowed for crucial change in the early 1960s, the Reagan administration articulated that the university had turned into "a haven of protesters and sex deviants," and therefore served as a political threat to the "good" nation shaped by free market capitalism (Newfield, 2008, p. 52). Reagan's political (and economic) movement was indeed responsible for defining the "deserving American as white, middle-class Christian conservative without taint of conscious contact with the social state" (Newfield, 2008, p. 53). This offers important context for a seemingly minimal historical account of student activism from the late 1960s until the early 2000s. While, as Ferguson (2012) suggests, student movements from the sixties pointed to "an academic moment that helped rearticulate the nature of state and capital," creating the academy as "a training ground for state and capital's engagement with minority difference as a site of representation and meaning" (p. 11), the Reagan administration directly targeted liberal and multicultural humanism. In other words, neoliberalism not only birthed economic policy and cultural codes but also "attacks on downwardly redistributive social movements" (Duggan, 2003, p. xii) in working toward a probusiness climate in and out of the university.

With lead from political theorists such as Tayyab Mahmud (2012) and Wendy Brown (2015), I understand neoliberalism to name an economic and historical moment that genders social and political conditions of being. This naming suggests not only configurations of the nation-state but also the ways in which economic terms come to inform individuals' own thinking, feeling, relations among and interactions with one another. Neoliberalism is characterized by the drive for corporate profit through individualism, holding values of accountability, individual rationality, and efficiency. As an economic/political project and process of subjectivation, neoliberalism names a material relationship, a force that constructs our physical surroundings and the intangible conditions moderating how subjects are recognized as thinking and feeling beings. Following Ferguson (2012), minority difference within neoliberalism functions as a kind of "fetishization"—a rendering of both object and aberration *outside of* the productive neoliberal subject that is able to pass through systems of power in order to both survive and thrive, both individualizing and totalizing at the same time (Foucault, 1989, 1991). In this way, neoliberalism as both system and ideological foundation is directly tied to the exploitation of Black and Brown bodies as they exist in spaces such as the university—a continuous thread from/to historical recourse of the plantation. As for neoliberalism's effects on universities, Reagan's era made palpable the idea of bashing political correctness, giving birth to the culture wars (the idea that addressing topics such as feminism or gun politics *engendered* polarization), which attempted to destabilize student statements of oppression and discrimination. Effectively, the result was a hostile political climate that foreclosed possibilities of student protest.

The kinds of political strategy articulated above were exemplified during the Clinton administration at the end of the twentieth century. Because of Reagan's culture wars, concepts of race and civil equality had been underhandedly slandered, reducing the population's acumen of historically reparative steps such as affirmative action. The Clinton administration further eviscerated the welfare state with policies such as the Violent Crime Control and Law Enforcement Act, which allocated ten million dollars to prison construction, the death penalty, and reduced funding for prisoner education, as well as increased racial profiling and police surveillance. Further, the Personal Responsibility and Work Opportunity Reconciliation Act pressured states to reduce welfare rolls, causing state governments to strategize ways to deter people from applying for welfare. The result was a degrading application process to weed out the "criminal element," which assumed all those applying for welfare were potential criminals (Judt, 2010; Nadasen, 2016). This punitive approach to eliminate poverty invoked fear of racialized street crime and the breakdown of families, in addition to threatening the drain of public funding. Resulting from the inculcated neoliberal state of the 1980s and driven by concepts of self-reliance, the crises of affirmative action and creation of the "New Economy" inspired advocates for racial justice to organize around a new term that would be recognizable to sentiments of the American dream and the white middle class: diversity.

Fast-forward to a convincing win in the Supreme Court in 2003, when diversity and decisions around the use of affirmative action returned to political discourse. That is, the Supreme Court's reauthorization of affirmative action confirmed this practice as a market standard in businesses and other sectors of social and political life, including universities. Denise Ferreira da Silva (2016) illuminates the ways in which affirmative action's founding proposal as a route for reparations was then folded into what she terms a "social inclusion agenda" (p. 195). Diversity, in this sense, had nothing to do with racial equality or "cultural agency" as Newfield (2008) describes, but rather, it was an input into military and economic security—another mode by which bodies were made legible to institutions. The case marked affirmative action's purpose as not to necessarily address historical wrongs but rather to benefit the state by making individuals and institutions more prepared to operate in a global economy. Materially, and within higher education, despite the incorporation of the discursive incorporation of diversity, the number of full-time professors who are people of color and women are decreasing, while the sectors of higher education most like service work see increased integration (US Department of Education, 2015). In other words, diversity becomes implemented and managed through stratification rather than social and political structure rehaul—what political Marxists such as David Harvey (2003) and Jamie Peck (2010) might term "flexible labor," increasingly racialized and thus disposable. Read as interwoven and as legacy to plantation politics, disposable bodies and labor are also invisibilized work in the university, while whiteness and codes of power remain unchanged. Thus, though diversity is framed as "progress," little tangible effect of justice is felt by communities of color.[3]

The historical foundations regarding the politics of diversity come to bear on our contemporary understandings of its both discursive and material effects within higher education. University politics of inclusion and exclusion have been critiqued as insufficient to address the weight of oppression on campuses (e.g., Alexander, 2005; Anzaldúa, 1999; Applebaum, 2010, among others). Amalia Dache-Gerbino and Julie White (2016), in conversation with George Lipsitz (2011), helps us to understand whiteness as process and social field, which offers leverage to "higher education *progress* doubly constrained by the spatialization of race and the racialization of space" (p. 50). That is, when diversity is employed as a marker of progress and is yet merely a shift of the rhetorical plan, it is a tool furthering white supremacy, upholding the ideological fallacy of whiteness as superior. Furthermore, as diversity is palatably incorporated into institutions, "diversity management" (Ahmed, 2012, p. 13) becomes a mode of regulatory power by which the institution regulates dissent (e.g., Alexander, 2005; Mohanty, 2003; Urciuoli, 2016). People of color then become a site to *withstand* and *navigate* that power—an intentional molding of ourselves into this carefully crafted institution in order to gain spatial and organizational access. One of the structural elements of plantations was precisely organizing certain governing factors in order to control behavior by using the Black body as a site of power—a representational arrangement of hierarchy, violence dispossession, and, importantly, an illusion of autonomy in a system that was created and sustained to disenfranchise and strip the body, mind, and soul of worth. In a legacy ensconced in violence, the racialized body is trapped within a performative, ornamental arrangement and, further, methodical "administrative calculus" of diversity (Mitchell, 2011, p. 139) that, first and foremost, benefits the institution responsible.

The student movements analyzed in this chapter are just some articulations of continued dispossession/displacement within institutions of higher education, expressed by students prepared to think critically about their own experiences as college students in this post–affirmative action/diversity moment. Their momentum and ability to hold space and enable traction is, too, interpellated by our contemporary political moment. The next section will consider how specific demonstrations at the University of Missouri came into being in relation with epistemic and political violence. Questions of efficacy are not my primary mode of analysis. For a protest to be "effective" (a situated term) one need look at multiple realms: effective for students engineering a mode of survival, effective for material changes in the institution, effective for public understanding of lived experience, and so forth. My analysis is more concerned with the ways in which institutional and interpersonal memory come together to shape the dynamism of a university's ecology. I argue that we must direct our attention into understanding its radical potential and limitations, hope and despair, aspirations and negotiations.

"It Is Not Working, and We Have Been Telling You": Mizzou's Concerned Student 1950

"1839 was built on my B(L)ACK," about forty tee shirts are aligned in a row, their backs visible as the students stood silently in a blockade around their encampment. Each of their right fists are raised, they look out onto passers-by that seem disinterested, or even annoyed. On their horizon, tents and sleeping arrangements lie stagnant in central campus, their place of rest when not on spectacle, gazed upon by ungenerous and affect-less bodies. They've been protesting for days now, the only documents of their feeling coming in their self-published Twitter account—most other sources that have covered their story portray them as outrageous, whining, and yet.

Black students link arms, some look down at the brief shuffle in their feet as they come together. The microphone is passed back and forth, hands linked onto neighbors' hips, eyes closed, mouths open. And the camera catches the eye of one of the students, his face looking up while those to his left and right solemnly gaze downwards. Eyes through foggy glasses, fingers gripped tightly, he is tired. "And we are not tolerating it any longer; we are resisting, continually," a voice of young Black woman rings through the grounds. "It is not working, and we have been telling you."[4]

—Concerned Student, 2015

In the fall of 2015, over 100 university campuses in the United States were home to student movements, all of which pointed to campus climate and university structure as their object of change. Reporting varying manifestations of institutionalized oppression, university administration neglect of the issue of sexual violence, and asking universities to divest from the prison industrial complex and the state of Israel, students were demanding something different. The University of Missouri (Mizzou), located in Columbia, Missouri, and home to over 30,000 students, was/ is but one site of protest. The university is just a two-hour drive from Ferguson, Missouri, where 18-year-old Michael Brown was murdered the previous year, and is also home to continual resistance as part of the Movement for Black Lives. Organizing students called themselves Concerned Student 1950, so named because 1950 was the year in which Black students were first admitted to the university and brought attention to institutional problems related to race, workplace benefits, and lack of representational leadership. Five years prior, the university commenced a "diversity initiative" titled One Mizzou, which began after two racially charged events. In 2010, two white students spread cotton balls outside the university's Black Culture Center, and the following year a student wrote racist graffiti in a student residence hall. The university's response, One Mizzou, led by the chancellor, was discontinued in 2015, the reason cited being that it had "lost its meaning" (Wynn, 2015).

In September 2015, when racial slurs were yelled at student government president Payton Head while he was walking down the street, the university refused responsibility. Head's reporting on social media resulted in Black students and students of color on campus galvanizing to form the first set of student protests, "Racism Lives Here." Students responded to Head on Twitter after the university chancellor, Richard Bowen Loftin, refused to act: "#LoftinCantExplain the trauma it takes for @HeadthePrez to tell his story and not have support from his own University."[5] Students escalated this momentum to form a more sustained movement in late October, Concerned Student 1950. After yet another incident in which the Legion of Black Collegians were called the N-word by a white student, the group provided both digital and physical spaces where students of color could come together to talk about steps of action. Jonathan Butler, a Black graduate student at the university, watched these events closely and in concert with a number of other moves made by the university, including the elimination of health care for graduate students. Students were recognizing that institutionalized oppression was echoing across campus. At the end of October, Butler started a hunger strike that he vowed would not end until the president stepped down. Meanwhile, Concerned Student 1950 pressed onward, holding mock tours on campus that informed the public of the institution's history of racism. Action was not taken until early November, when the Black football players on Mizzou's team refused to practice or play until the president stepped down—a move that would cost the university over one million dollars and cause the president's resignation[6]—all the while denying the direct labor that had led up to said resignation, invisibilizing the students' demonstrations and work before this moment. Campus culture was further affected by this series of events, as Black students were then subject to death threats and immense insecurity in their campus community.

Concerned Student 1950 submitted a list of demands that asked for the university to meet the demands of the Legion of Black Collegians protests from 1969, antioppressive curricula, hiring and retention of Black faculty and staff, and an increase of funding for social justice centers on campus—all of which, of note, were echoed in other institutions across the nation. They also drew connections to Mizzou's roots in slave labor, stolen land, and the continued exploitation of Black labor. The demands set by students were pushed further through Concerned Student 1950's encampment, where protesters lived on the main academic quad. It was here that one of the biggest controversies was unleashed into public discourse: the rhetoric of safe spaces. As expressed by the protesters, they wanted to keep their living areas free of reporters in order to protect themselves from specific kinds of vitriol that come with the coverage of student protest. What resulted, however, was national attention that students were demanding safe spaces and violating free speech—a discourse that has now taken hold as main criticism of student movements and what conservatives have called "militant political correctness" (Meadors, 2015). The false dichotomy of safe space versus free speech was posited as the only intention of student protesters, despite their attempts to articulate otherwise.

I point to the University of Missouri as case study precisely because of outside commentary and generalizability of student protest as student complaint. Despite the fact that students were voicing very real experiences of physical, spiritual, and mental threat and toll, the protests at Mizzou were used to denounce the aims of almost all other student movements of similar kind. Imbricated within conservative attempts to ostensibly "protect" free speech on college campuses is the complete disavowal of hostile learning environments, student threat, and racism that foreground the histories of institutions of higher education. Greg Lukianoff and Johnathan Haidt (2015), for example, claim that students are "catastrophizing" situations of identity-invalidation, and point to a need for resilience rather than claims of "oversensitivity."

In conversation with these critiques, Gene Demby (2015) conveys that "there's a very thin line between telling students that they have to learn to navigate a racist world and telling them that racism is a thing they should have to tolerate," the latter a refrain seeped into the university conversation. With a more than triple increase in enrollment of Black and Latinx students since the 1990s, as well as the creation of both difference as political branding (Clough, n.d.) and tolerance as political branding, it remains in the university's best interests to "make space" for Black and Brown students (and, of course, their labor). Moreover, the United States is a settler-colonial state—that is, its existence depends upon the active domination, dislocation, and eradication of indigenous populations in order to exist. Thus, the United States, both in settlement and through its development by way of slavery, is built upon the exploitation and reliance on Black and Brown bodies and labor, while also, and simultaneously, holds the *fear* of more Black and Brown labor (see Sakai, 1989).[7] That is, referring to the structural element of "sentiment" in plantation politics, during enslavement, the paternalistic hold that enslavers forced upon enslaved persons transposes itself onto higher education through the overregulation of Black and Brown bodies and the increase of bureaucracy for said regulation, all while maintaining goals of profit through utilizing these persons as bodies of representation, performance, and other forms of capital. Furthermore, "Boundary Maintenance" as a processual element of plantation politics also provides language for how the fear of an increase of Black and Brown labor is actualized. During enslavement, in order to preserve the system and status quo, enslavers held tightly to a sense of business as usual, vigilant to protect the system they had built. In contemporary university spaces, we might understand this as a fear of those who deviate or are considered deviant—and the further categorization of persons into bodies who were *let in* to these spaces rather than ostensibly entitled to them. "Diversity management" then becomes a tool to address this fear, to ensure that Black students and students of color become neither too powerful nor too essential—what Leigh Patel (2015) points to as a "conflicted desire for diversity" (p. 658), where diversity is simultaneously wanted, rejected, and "works to elide a larger framework of white supremacy and settler rights" (p. 666). As students are being "made space" for in this rhetorical plane, while historically and continuously disabused of their own abuse in the material plane, they are still here, and making clear that more structural changes must be made—the demands called for by students such as those at Mizzou.

Mizzou's protests also occurred at the heels of the Supreme Court's hearing of *Fisher v. University of Texas*, a case that was first heard in 2012 under the Fifth Circuit, and again in 2015. The court heard from Abigail Fisher and Rachel Michalewicz, both white and both denied admission to the University of Texas in 2008, who alleged that they were discriminated against on the basis of race. Affirmative action in public university institutions was up for national negotiation. While the 2015 decision did uphold affirmative action, the rhetoric used during court discussion made claims about the inability of Black students to thrive at "rigorous" universities, and Justice Scalia pushed this further to state that Black college students needed to attend remedial schools. The vitriolic invocation of correlating race and intelligence draws from US histories and colonial vestiges of eugenics, enslavement, and systemic racism. Thus, the presence of Black students and students of color necessitates their own speaking back to the hostile conditions out of which they must create thriving conditions to merely survive. The next section will outline how university responses have further capitalized on student labor while simultaneously working to dismiss and invisibilize their experiences, continuing a legacy of plantation politics even as students attempt to move beyond its grasp.

The Political Subject(ivity) of the Student

In the years following the protests at the University of Missouri, searching for data on the movements themselves comes in the form of student uploaded YouTube videos and media accounts. On the schools' websites, few records are found. This section introduces the simultaneous erasure of student movements from institutional memory and their tokenization. I think alongside critical geographers who have theorized urban gentrification in terms of cleaning, containment, and control—how universities similarly *clean themselves* (Carey, 2016). Put differently, in order to maintain itself within its own historically developed model of "business as usual," the university cleans and sanitizes (read: erases and/or turns productive) the modes of student resistance within its hold. While adopting some of their strategies for change, university administrations often create these additives to campus life as something the university had strived to achieve in the first place—using Black students' and students' of color labor without acknowledgment or appreciation of their struggle and presence.

Part of that institutional cleaning comes with the creation of a uniform identity across the institution. With recourse to the whiteness of institutions as politics of the plantation, and their roles in upholding white supremacy, certain bodies are made to feel as though they belong, while deviancy is eliminated. Performativities of whiteness allow for ontological complicity, whereas other bodies are what Nirmal Puwar (2004) might name "trespassers . . . politically, historically, conceptually circumscribed as being out of place" (p. 9). In other words, as haunted by colonial illusions, both material and psychological effects of a legacy of plantation politic, the university profits off of certain bodies' presence and performance— Ferguson's concept of fetishization—without deeming their subjectivities legitimate. This production of student political subjectivity is important to understanding how universities validate some and erase others.

The production of students' political subjectivity is constituted in relation to what Félix Guattari and Suely Rolnik (2008) term capitalist subjectivity—"manufactured, modeled, received, and consumed." They argue that the production of capitalist subjectivity is a mode of capitalist profit, reducing individuals to "a value that responds to the . . . market. They are like solitary, anguished robots, increasingly absorbing the drugs that power offers them" (p. 54). The production of subjectivity is not just that (product), but further indicates *processes* of subjectivation—how people are made into beings (Foucault, 1995). While my argument focuses on how two industrial systems of neoliberalism and empire have produced subjectivities in the university, much of my work remains on tightening our analyses on how a particular, perhaps alternate, kind of student (activist) political subject(ivity) emerges in/out of confrontation with the university's normative student subjectivity, but nonetheless constituted *in relation to it*. To produce the conditions for collective life *outside* of capitalist production, in addition for the embodiment for life of oneself—of singularity—is what Guattari and Rolnik (2008) propagate as "a willingness to love, in a willingness simply to live or survive, in the multiplicity of these willingnesses" (p. 63), which, is, we cannot overlook, echoing a strong Black/Indigenous/of color genealogy regarding the power of loving our way through moments of struggle—these are also the refrains that students express in their movements.

Student protesters, especially those of the past ten years, have articulated their political subjectivities as different—a rejection of the normative capitalist subjectivity produced within the university. Students of color have both been pronounced and also pronounce themselves within marginality and minority, an active claim to subject and society, that concerns the life of the collective.

Many of these student protesters are trained within the interdisciplines, equipped with acute analyses of the university and state, and already radically existing within spaces that are *contained for them*. That is, while the interdisciplines offer space for revolutionary work, their institutional legibility must remain inside Guattari and Rolnik's (2008) capitalist subjectivity—institutionally reproducing the university's psychic agencies, remaining the resting place for its desires of tolerance: their tactics must remain legible to the politic of the plantation. They are embedded in what Nick Mitchell (2011) terms the "integrative logic of administrative capitalism" (p. 161). Student activist movements, in their origination *outside of* disciplinary formation and politics of the institutions, offer a different site of analysis. What we might interpret within student movements is an outward pronunciation of interiority—alternate subjectivity—prior to university regulation and the quelling of dissent. Within neoliberal capitalism, we might interpret this emphasis of the self and structural violence against the self as a route of legibility: a way for the university to understand, hear, and respond to student voices. Unlike how the formation of the interdisciplines has required the rendering of social reality as disciplinary object (see Gordon, 1997; Mitchell, 2011; Wiegman, 2012), student activism doesn't require the institution to create them *into* object—indeed, their previously unregulated political subjectivity (articulated interiority as construction of self) gives way to different kinds of regulation. Guattari and Rolnik (2008) offer, "So there are processes of social marginalization as society becomes more totalitarian, and that is in order to define a certain kind of dominant subjectivity to which everyone must conform" (p. 173). And it is this that brings us to the particular ways in which the university cleans itself of student statements of political subjectivity that might crumble its own capitalist subjectivity: erasure from institutional memory and the pathologization of the students themselves.

Strategy, Regulation, and Dis-ease

Tony Judt (2010) speaks to neoliberalism as focused on the efficiency of categorization and need for legibility as a mode of disciplinary knowledge. In order to maintain institutional containment, university administrations place the problem within the individual student rather than implicating the structure of the university: subjectivity becomes demonized and in need of cleansing.[8] In accounts from both the university and outside voices of criticism, students from the movements at Mizzou were deemed depressed, crazy,[9] and individually responsible for their own "discomfort" within the institution.

Much of the rhetoric of the responses from the University of Missouri administration is reliant on making students "feel comfortable" rather than addressing more structural histories of the plantation and dispossession. This framework takes up the difference between what Sara Ahmed (2012, 2013), Ann Cvetkovich (2012), and Jackie Orr (2006) call "disease versus dis-ease": *disease* represents the kinds of medical knowledges that position illness as a biological, ontological, and thus individual diagnosis, while *dis-ease* calls out the way historical, political, cultural, and social forces have called into being certain affective conditions. Offering services such as counseling, while perhaps productive for the individual, neglects to understand the magnitude of what students are looking to address. Administrative approaches to these symptoms is a new kind of soap used to clean the university of traces of dissent. The lives and bodies of the university community are legible based upon the ways in which they are productive to the institution. Power becomes productive in that not only does the institution enact power and regulation to discipline its community, but also it creates the desire within its population to also be part of that community—to be disciplined by. Therefore, when deviant identities or resistant imaginaries arise, they are often read as threat. In a time when progress is heavily related to cleanliness, to pathologize student political subjectivity draws heavy recourse to the university as a corporate (preserving image), imperial (individuation and medicalization), and colonial (elimination of deviancy) space.

Within the legibility of student political subjectivity might also lie strategy in the face of a calculated university. That is, I do not think that students are unaware that if they individuate their experiences of racism, in times of neoliberal individualism and customer satisfaction, the university will respond. While the enunciation of one's interior—to speak to feelings—is not necessarily lacking any measure of radicality, one might ask what the expense of speaking at this individual level might be? What kinds of radicality are sacrificed; what kinds of futures are precluded with this pronunciation? To reference Robin Kelley's recent theorizing on student activism, while the emphasis on interiority seems to elevate levels of sympathy rather than visions of social justice, and while it may be seen that "where words such as *trauma, PTSD, micro-aggression,* and *triggers* have virtually replaced *oppression, repression,* and *subjugation*" (Kelley, 2016; emphasis in original), I argue that student political subjectivity is pronounced *only ever in relation* to the subjectivity produced by the university—their legibility and thus success of their movement depends on an understanding of how the university had been handling questions of difference and tolerance *prior to* their pronunciation. Put differently, if students know the university's discourses of diversity trainings, individual responsibility, depoliticized discussions of social conflict, then their pronunciation must, too, be in strategic conversation with the university's language. If they know that the university is always already ensconced in logics that their ancestors were made to perform in, on land that is stolen, on land that is often literally atop the bones of their kin, student activists of color make these alternate subjectivities so that they might attempt to survive in systems made to exploit them. Student movement platforms that are seemingly "misdirected" might also emanate from fear that they (or their demands of structural rehaul) may be illegible (and, rejected) if not framed by way of feeling, pain, and tolerance.

Histories of social movements within universities, too, dictate the normative limits of legibility for the demands of student activists, as the interdisciplines were institutionalized because of student protest (e.g., Ferguson, 2012; Mitchell, 2011). Mitchell (2011) argues that there are multiple ways to tell these histories, and that the interdisciplines often tell romanticized versions of revolutionary turnover rather than legible acceptance, which, while politically important, may also foreclose a certain amount of reflexivity. So, while students are indeed equipped with sharp analyses of the neoliberal university and the logics of capital, they and we are also entangled in and by the desires of the institution. In other words, they may know they can't dismantle the master's house with the master's tools, and yet their investment in attempting to do so remains high, as the ecological space in which students find themselves inherently gives shape to their sociality—how they move and exist, resist within and protest against.

Conclusion

As students from Mizzou have commented, how do universities expect them to bring more Black students and students of color to campus when their current conditions of existence are unbearable? Student activists look to remake their political and social realities in ways that will not only ensure the longevity of student of color survival but will also take up Moten and Harney's (2004) dictum that "in the face of these conditions one can only sneak into the university and steal what one can" (p. 101). If asking for change of campus culture allows for students of color to further their academic and critical work, if inclusion offers space for chipping away at institutional bias and tolerance gives way for a crack in the hostility that impedes their ability to do well, might we consider this as taking something back from the university, from a place of historically and presently exploited bodies, labor, and land? Of course, we remain in a double bind where this taking back can be easily coopted—the strategic gain made because of university interest is easily cleaned away. How do students and how do we theorize this double bind of legibility, of necessarily supporting students of color while realizing subjective and institutional limitations? While our social justice work clearly lies beyond inclusion, and does this in more secluded radical basements—spaces that might, too, "sneak and steal what one can"—I think that student activists are both strategizing for limited university change and nourishing their radicalism to create and sustain what Jalil Bishop Mustaffa (2017) calls "life-affirming movements."

Thus, the questions "Are students radical enough?" and "Did it work?" are not my main interest, for we are neither fully transparent nor self-determined beings that could know the answer. We are, and must be, more than our subjectivities. It is not that we must choose between supporting student activism and offering critical analyses of their work. Rather, if we are made as subjects by these institutions, we make strategic choices about how to present our critiques *because* of the double-bind of legibility *and also* because we are entangled in and by the desires of the institution (as nested within capital and the state, neoliberalism and imperialism, the grasp of the plantation).

As we look for ways out of the tensely bound logics of plantation politics, to imagine a university that might be different, what Ashon Crawley (2015) might term "otherwise," what la paperson (2017) might call a "third university," I wonder if one way out must be a way in—to do the work of radical community building and intimate kinship, and have faith in student radicalism, and also know that it is not enough, to accept that it might never be enough. To look elsewhere, we must first name the very processes that so often refuse us the liberty of calling them by name. If current conceptions of alternate student political subjectivity are always already in relation to capitalist subjectivity, then to say that we might know a world *without* plantation politics is not yet able to be determinably imagined. Tangibly, I think we can continue to support student activists of color in the ways that they already do build community and hold each other accountable; try to protect them and each other from the ways that the university abuses them/us; and find ways to show solidarity while also recognizing our own precarity. We can use other levers and grammars, and encourage creativity and different methodologies of engagement processing in the small enclaves that we are located. We can support the archiving and translation of student activist histories, both nationally and globally, to create a map for future work. This chapter offers context to student of color activism to honor the complexity of their and our humanity, as surviving in, made by, and resisting institutions marked by the hauntings of colonial fantasies and realities. And it is within that honoring, naming, supporting, and listening that we might build toward something that we cannot possibly yet know but must yearn for regardless.

Acknowledgments

I would like to thank Denise Ferreira da Silva, Renisa Mawani, and Sunera Thobani for their critical and generous insight on this project in the Social Justice Institute at the University of British Columbia. Thank you to Mark

Stern and Sharon Stein for their insight, generous feedback, and friendship. And to Madison Paulk, Alexandria Dyer, and Kiran Sunar for their patience and acute skillsets. To Abha Apte, for everything. The majority of this chapter was written on the traditional, unceded, ancestral, and occupied territories of the xʷməθkʷəy̓əm (Musqueam), Skwxwú7mesh (Squamish), and Tsleil-Waututh peoples. Echoing plantation politics, histories of racialized violence live and multiply through us, informing our engagement with our work and each other. I owe an insurmountable debt. Thank you for hosting me.

Notes

1. I understand institutional responses not only in the framework of sanitization and absorption into university structure but also those that are perhaps not completely insignificant for violence-reduced causes, such as greater funding toward survivor-centered sexual assault resources, and the opening of more cultural centers. The above argument is not to dismiss what are hard-fought contributions to making campus climates more livable for students and faculty of color, queer students, and other minoritized identities. Rather, this acknowledgment is to take up that conversation critically, in tension, and recognize its absorption in ways that are still legible within certain structures of power (Stern and Carey, 2019).

2. This project was originally part of my master's thesis at the University of British Columbia, located on the traditional, ancestral, unceded, and occupied territory of the Musqueam people—what is recognized as Vancouver, British Columbia, Canada. I regret that I did not have the time or means during this program to seek out interviews with students, staff, or faculty at the University of Missouri, as ethnographic research would enrich not only my own impression of the events at Mizzou but also data sources on student activism in general. Future projects might conduct ethnographic interviews about student activism to contribute to what is currently a very slim (and active) archive of its resurgence.

3. Denise Ferreira da Silva (2016) writes exactly on this. In arguing that because communities of color are "governed by necessity—that is, by violence," she articulates two logics of racial subjugation as exclusion and obliteration. When policies are formed to address the former but not the latter, there are limits to justice in that it works to disenfranchise and harm communities of color and serve institutions of power. In relationship to the shifting of the terrain of the university, to mobilize only a "thesis of discrimination" rather than a more nuanced analysis of the state's collusion in colonial violence and white supremacy, "raciality works from within the liberal text, checking the ethical claims and the

juridical strategies available to those demanding remedies to address the effects of racial subjugation" (p. 190). According to da Silva (2016), the state-centered/institutionally structured approach to governing (as opposed to an historical redress) "reproduces the *occlusion* of colonial expropriation and *oblivion* to injuries to racial subaltern collectives"—though a material shift in some ways, still pronounces and emulates an adherence to the state that governs by/through violence (p. 190; emphasis in original).

    4. In this creative description, I analyze a series of videos and photographs posted by Concerned Student, the YouTube account of the Association of Black Collegians et al. at the University of Missouri. The video described here is titled "1893 Built on Our Black Homecoming Parade Demonstration."

    5. #LoftinCantExplain was a trending hashtag on Twitter during the protests at Mizzou. This quotation was originally sourced from these threads, during the preliminary research for this work in 2016. Since then, many of the tweets in this thread have been scrubbed. Some mentions are still available through searching this hashtag on the site.

    6. Featured in a *New York Times* article titled "Black Football Players Lend Heft to Protests at Missouri" (Tracy and Southall, 2015), this sequence of events offers an example of what Tuchman (2009) names as what is often the route of change in the corporate space of universities: negative publicity due to rising costs of both money and power—a direct hit to university branding.

    7. J. Sakai (1989) speaks to this historical argument as one of the negotiated terms upon which the slave trade was ended. Because of white reliance on the labor of enslaved persons, "simply by stopping work, they could threaten the Confederacy with starvation. By walking into the Federal camps, they showed to doubting Northerners the easy possibilities of using them as workers and as servants, as farmers, and as spies, and finally, as fighting soldiers" (p. 38). Thus, the fear of this collapse and thus end of the slave trade was indeed a tool to *protect* white supremacy and empire, not any ostensible shift of ethics.

    8. I emphasize the subjectivity of the student rather than the subject itself in that the subjectivity has the capacity to be formed and molded by the university as its own production.

    9. Andrea Nicki (2001) speaks to the complexity and gendered and ableist nature of using the term "crazy" as a pejorative, namely as it "feeds on and expresses . . . that strong or intense emotion is devoid of meaningful, directive cognitive content; that people with mental illness are irrational; that they are cognitively impaired; and that they are frightening. The label of 'craziness' directed at people who are simply nonconformist or who challenge the status quo, without serious inquiry into their mental health, derives its power from prejudiced views of those genuinely suffering from mental illness as irrational, disordered, cognitively impaired, and frightening" (pp. 86–87).

References

Ahmed, S. (2012). *On being included*. Duke University Press.

Ahmed, S. (2013, March). Institutional habits. *feministkilljoys*. http://feministkilljoys.com/

Alexander, M. J. (2005). *Pedagogies of crossing: Meditations on feminism, sexual politics, memory, and the sacred*. Duke University Press.

Anzaldúa, G. (1999). *Borderlands/La frontera: The new mestiza* (2nd ed.). Aunt Lute Books.

Applebaum, B. (2010). *Being white, being good*. Lexington Books.

Brown, W. (2015). *Undoing the demos*. MIT Press.

Burdziak, A. (2016, May 16). University of Missouri expected to no longer allow protest camps. *Columbia Daily Tribune*. http://www.columbiatribune.com/76a16e09-1d5d-5c67-80a7-6b6ca6398c19.html

Carey, K. (2016). On cleaning: Student activism in the corporate and imperial university. *Open Library of Humanities*, 2(2), e4, pp. 1–30. DOI: http://dx.doi.org/10.16995/olh.92

Concerned Student. (2015, October 13). *1839 Built on my Black homecoming parade* [Video]. Demonstration. YouTube. https://www.youtube.com/watch?time_continue=2&v=u6zwnmlzZSQ&feature=emb_title

Chatterjee, P., & Sunaina, Maira (Eds.). (2014). *The imperial university: Academic repression and scholarly dissent*. University of Minnesota Press.

Clough, P. (n.d.). Remarks on Roderick Ferguson's reorder of things [Unpublished paper]. *Academia.edu*. http://www.academia.edu/4170255/Remarks_on_Rod_Fergusons_Reordering_of_Things

Crawley, A. (2015, January 19). Otherwise movements. *The New Inquiry*. http://thenewinquiry.com/essays/otherwise-movements/

Cvetkovich, A. (2012). *Depression: A public feeling*. Duke University Press.

Dache-Gerbino, A., & White, J. A. (2016). College students or criminals? A postcolonial geographic analysis of the social field of whiteness at an urban community college branch campus and suburban Main Campus. *Community College Review*, 44(1), 49–69.

Davis, A. (1983). *Women, race, and class*. Random House Books.

Demby, G. (2015, December 17). The long, necessary history of "whiny" Black protesters at college. *NPR*. http://www.npr.org/sections/codeswitch/2015/12/17/459211924/the-long-necessary-history-of-whiny-Black-protestors-at-college

Duggan, Lisa. (2003). *The twilight of equality?: Neoliberalism, cultural politics, and the attack on democracy*. Beacon Press.

Ferguson, R. (2012). *The reorder of things: The university and its pedagogies of minority difference*. University of Minnesota Press.

Ferreira da Silva, D. (2016). The racial limits of social justice: The ruse of equality of opportunity and the global affirmative action mandate. *Critical Ethnic Studies* 2(2), 184–209.

Foucault, M. (1979). *Society must be defended: Lectures at the Collège de France, 1978-1979*. Picador.
Foucault, M. (1989). The subject and power. In H. L. Dreyfus and P. Rabinow (Eds.), *Michel Foucault: Beyond structuralism and hermeneutics* (pp. 208-28). University of Chicago Press.
Foucault, M. (1991). Governmentality. In *The Foucault effect: Studies in governmentality* (pp. 87-104). University of Chicago Press.
Foucault, M. (1995). *The history of sexuality: The use of pleasure* (Vol. 2). Random House.
Gordon, A. (1997). *Ghostly matters: Haunting and the sociological imagination*. University of Minnesota Press.
Guattari, F., & Rolnik, S. (2008). Subjectivity and History. In *Molecular revolution in Brazil* (pp. 35-178). Semiotext(e).
Harvey, D. (2003). *The new imperialism*. Oxford University Press.
Judt, T. (2010). *Ill fares the land*. Penguin Group.
Kelley, R. (2002). *Freedom dreams: The Black radical imagination*. Beacon Press.
Kelley, R. (2016, March 7). Black study, Black struggle. *Boston Review*. http://bostonreview.net/forum/robin-d-g-kelley-Black-study-Black-struggle
la paperson. (2017). *A third university is possible*. University of Minnesota Press.
Lipsitz, G. (2011). *How racism takes place*. Temple University Press.
Lukianoff, G., & Haidt, J. (2015, September). The coddling of the American mind. *The Atlantic*. http://www.theatlantic.com/magazine/archive/2015/09/the-coddling-of-the-american-mind/399356/
Mahmud, T. (2012). Debt and discipline. *American Quarterly 63*(3), 469-94.
Meadors, M. (2015, August 26). Is political correctness really "killing America"? *The Huffington Post*. http://www.huffingtonpost.com/marvin-meadors/is-political-correctness-_b_8026152.html
Mitchell, N. (2011). *Disciplinary matters: Black studies and the politics of institutionalization* [Doctoral dissertation]. University of California at Santa Cruz. [Currently being prepared as a book monograph under the title *Disciplinary matters: Black studies, women's studies, and the neoliberal university*.]
Mohanty, C. (2003). *Feminism without borders: Decolonizing theory, practicing solidarity*. Duke University Press.
Moten, F., & Harney, S. (2004). The university and the undercommons: Seven theses. *Social Text, 22*, 101-15.
Moten, F., & Harney, S. (2013). *The undercommons: Fugitive planning and Black study*. Minor Compositions.
Mustaffa, J. B. (2017). Mapping violence, naming life: A history of anti-Black oppression in the higher education system. *International Journal of Qualitative Studies in Education 30*(8), 711-27.
Nadasen, P. (2016, February). How a Democrat killed welfare. *Jacobin*. https://www.jacobinmag.com/2016/02/welfare-reform-bill-hillary-clinton-tanf-poverty-dlc/

Newfield, C. (2008). *Unmaking the public university: The forty-year assault on the middle class* Harvard University Press.

Nicki, A. (2001). The abused mind: Feminist theory, psychiatric disability, and trauma. *Hypatia, 16*(4), 80–104.

Orr, J. (2006). *Panic diaries: A genealogy of panic disorder.* Duke University Press.

Patel, L. (2015). Desiring diversity and backlash: White property rights in higher education. *The Urban Review, 47*(4), 657–75.

Peck, J. (2010). *Constructions of neoliberal reason.* Oxford University Press.

Puwar, N. (2004). *Space invaders: Race, gender, and bodies out of place.* Berg.

Readings, B. (1996). *The university in ruins.* Harvard University Press.

Sakai, J. (1989). *Settlers: The mythology of the white proletariat.* Morningstar Press.

Shakur, A. (2005). Women in prison: How we are. In Joy James (Ed.), *The new abolitionists: (Neo)slave narratives and the contemporary prison writing* (79–90). SUNY Press.

Spillers, H. J. (1987). Mama's baby, papa's maybe: An American grammar book. *Diacritics 17*(2), 65–81.

Stern, M., & Carey, K. (2019). Good students and bad activists: The moral economy of campus unrest. *Journal of Curriculum and Pedagogy*, DOI: 10.1080/15505170.2019.1649768

Torres, E. (2003). Wisdom and weakness: Freire and Education. In *Chicana without apology: The new Chicana cultural studies* (pp. 73–97). Routledge.

Tracy, M., & Southall, A. (2015, November 8). Black football players lend heft to protests at Missouri. *The New York Times.* https://www.nytimes.com/2015/11/09/us/missouri-football-players-boycott-in-protest-of-university-president.html

Tuchman, G. (2009). *Wannabe U: Inside the corporate university.* University of Chicago Press.

Urciuoli, B. (2016). The comprised pragmatics of diversity. *Language and Communication, 51,* 30–39.

US Department of Education, National Center for Education Statistics. (2015). The Condition of Education 2015 (NCES 2015-144), Characteristics of Postsecondary Faculty.

Washburn, J. (2005). *University Inc.: The corporate corruption of higher education.* Basic Books.

Wiegman, R. (2012). *Object lessons.* Duke University Press.

Wilder, C. S. (2013). *Ebony and ivy: Race, slavery, and the troubled history of American University.* Bloomsbury Publishing.

Wynn, S. (2015). Administrators discontinue One Mizzou, developing new marketing campaign this summer. *The Maneater.* http://www.themaneater.com/stories/2015/6/3/administrators-developing-new-marketing-campaign-s/

Chapter 10

Repurposing the Confederacy

Understanding Issues Surrounding the Removal and Contextualization of Lost Cause Iconography at Southern Colleges and Universities

R. Eric Platt, Holly A. Foster, and Lauren Yarnell Bradshaw

In the fall of 2015, on Sunday afternoons, protesters gathered in front of the University of Southern Mississippi (USM) to wave the former Mississippi state flag with its symbolic "Lost Cause" representation of the Confederacy—the rebel "stars and bars." This symbol has historically represented the Confederate States of America secessionist government founded in 1861 to maintain antebellum plantation heritage, racially and socioeconomically oppressive caste systems, and agricultural fortitude built on the backs of enslaved Black people. Protesters, angered by the flag's removal from the campus in 2015 due to its connection with racial oppression, gathered with signs that read "no state flag, no state funds" (Magee, 2015; Varon, 2008). Despite the flag's continued absence, protestors have maintained their Sunday-afternoon campus presence despite the ongoing COVID-19 pandemic (Cloud, 2020). Regardless of the "stars and bars" 2020 state-legislative removal as Mississippi's official flag (Rojas, 2020), dissenters decry the emblem's absence and deny that Confederate "Lost Cause" icons, including statues, plaques, building names, mascots, songs, student organization titles, and so on, represent and enhance modern racial discord capitalized by an era of oppressive plantation political and economic dominance. The phrase "Lost Cause" represents a politicized "historic" movement, as explained by Gaines Foster (1988), that canonized the Confederacy as "heroic" rather than antipatriotic and secessionist. Regardless, modern Confederate iconography supporters champion a message of "heritage, not hate" that ignores the reality that many Southern images are based on a history of antebellum plantation enslavement and racial prejudice. Sadly, these images have been woven into the corporeal fabric of American higher education and, as a result, have become institutionalized as a part of the Southern college and university landscape. Many, however, disagree with and oppose their presence.

After two years of watching flag-bearing protestors, USM alumnae Elizabeth Cobbins stated, "They try so hard to 'preserve' their heritage, but what they are really doing is harboring hate and racism. When has the Confederate flag or Mississippi state flag ever represented all people equally? The state flag reeks of injustice, oppression, and inequality, yet they still wave it proudly. Mississippi has its flaws . . . [, but] we've lived far past what the state flag represents" (Word Wire, 2017, para. 2–3). As expressed by members of the Southern Poverty Law Center (2018), "To many white Southerners, the flag is an emblem of regional heritage and pride. But to others, it has a starkly different meaning—representing racism, slavery, and the country's long history of oppression of African Americans" (p. 6). For some college students, Confederate images foster a dominant, racialized narrative in which higher education spaces are overshadowed by past and present racism. As such, racially minoritized students, supportive faculty and administrators, and some external stakeholders have called for the removal of Lost Cause iconography from college and university campuses, while Confederate heritage supporters want said symbols to remain as testimonies to regional history.

The Mississippi flag joins a growing list of antebellum, Civil War era–associated icons excised from campus communities. While cities such as New Orleans, Louisiana; San Antonio, Texas; Memphis, Tennessee; and Gainesville, Florida have removed monuments to the Lost Cause, other cities, such as Charlottesville, Virginia, and Stone Mountain, Georgia, struggle with white supremacist rallies and hindering legislation surrounding the removal of Confederate icons (Bidgood et al., 2017; Park, 2017). Even so, several colleges and universities, encouraged by vocal employees and students, have either removed monuments or are contending with how to do so. While some higher education leaders want to appease students and employees by purging Confederate memorabilia, others are concerned about possible legislative and external stakeholder backlash. This administrative struggle illustrates the palpable concern of displeasing wealthy white alumni and influential political figures, which would result in the loss of their social and financial support (Harris, 1993). This phenomenon is yet another nod to the lingering effects of plantation politics in modern higher education—particularly in the American South.

Indeed, most of these Lost Cause symbols, representative of an era of enslavement and the numerous Civil War military battles to maintain it, were erected during the Jim Crow era of the late nineteenth and early twentieth century (a period capitalized by de jure racial disenfranchisement) or the mid-twentieth-century civil rights movement in efforts to remind African Americans of "their place" under the boot of white supremacy, despite legislative enfranchisement attempts such as the Thirteenth, Fourteenth, and Fifteenth Amendments (Svrluga, 2017). Absolutely, these Lost Cause images, as several leading scholars contend, perpetuate plantation politics (notions concerning the superiority of whites, the subjugation of African Americans, and the continued investiture of Southern higher education in its antebellum roots) in our regional societies and learning environments (Foner, 2017; Hesse, 2016). As such, the continued presence of such symbols on college campuses normalizes a message of race-based hierarchical acceptance and does much to illustrate that the "long arm" of plantation-era ethos stretched through the nineteenth and twentieth centuries, and continues to influence twenty-first-century higher education.

During the late nineteenth, twentieth, and twenty-first centuries, songs such as "From Dixie with Love" could be heard at University of Mississippi football games in Oxford, Mississippi, and stained glass windows were installed in academic halls to commemorate students and faculty who fought for the South. All the while, statues of bronze and granite were placed on campuses to commemorate Confederate "heroes" such as Robert E. Lee and Jefferson Davis. Today, however, discussions and associated actions, often spurred by students in attempts to reclaim their campuses as accessible spaces free from racially normalized histories, are occurring as to what to do with these symbols that no longer reflect the educational desires, personal cultures, and intellectual pursuits of a majority of the modern college population. Already we have seen changes to campuses, such as the renaming of Raphael Semmes Road (Semmes was a celebrated Confederate admiral) at Louisiana State University to

Veterans Drive (Ballard, 2017), the removal of a statue of Confederate soldier and Randolph College founder George Morgan Jones (Carmel, 2017), ousting of the University of Mississippi's former mascot "Colonel Reb" (an embodiment of an aged Confederate military officer), and attempts to add explanatory, contextualizing information to existing campus monuments (Cleveland, 2003; Hale, 2016). Though there has been some success at removing or contextualizing Lost Cause icons, not all institutions have divorced themselves from the physical presence of Confederate legacies. For example, administrators at the University of Georgia have not addressed campus discussions regarding the renaming of Candler Hall—named for Confederate colonel Allen Candler (Scott, 2015). Likewise, institutional leaders at Tulane University of Louisiana have yet to acknowledge student complaints concerning a campus facility named for Confederate general Randall Lee Gibson—Gibson Hall (Pierre, 2017). Even so, student, faculty, and administrative groups at other institutions are taking steps to better understand why these icons are in their midst, what to do with them, and how to integrate them into the larger college teaching environment.

In light of the aforementioned, and to better understand the discourse, action, and reactions surrounding the removal and/or contextualization of Confederate symbols from Southern campuses, this chapter examines the historic placement, institutionalization, and reasoning behind the establishment of Lost Cause icons on Southern college campuses, how they have been used to venerate the memory of plantation control as a glorified phenomenon, how stakeholders (including students, administrators, and alumni) are influencing the understanding and/or removal of said images, and how higher education authorities are choosing to deal with these memorializations of African American oppression to reclaim the higher education landscape as one of total inclusion and acceptance. In part, this chapter attempts to address Derek Alderman's (2000) comment, "Although largely neglected by scholars, the names attached to schools, businesses, streets, and other features have an important place in the symbolic changes and struggles occurring within the American South" (p. 672).

Establishing Campus Memorials to the Lost Cause

As Southern plantation control fell away during Reconstruction (1865–77), a new form of racial tyranny took hold: sharecropping, antebellum reverence, Lost Cause celebration, and intense legalized racial oppression.

As Jim Crow law grew in power, it became essential for white citizens to remind Southern society of the import of remembering plantation control, Confederate militancy, white supremacy, and the celebration of what, in the minds of the former wealthy and political elite, could have been the Confederate States of America. Memorializing the Lost Cause in both townships and educational spaces was a powerful and politically rife discursive movement that, in essence, trumpeted a dominant account of white power in the face of slowly evolving African American rights. Though Reconstruction saw enhanced rights for formerly enslaved persons, the end of Reconstruction and the return of Southern Democratic control played host to movements that repealed basic human rights for freedmen and their children. These include, for example, the 1896 "separate but equal" legislation put forward by *Plessy v. Ferguson* (1896) and harsher white outcry against African Americans in political office (Medley, 2003; Perman, 1984).

When Jim Crow gave way to the civil rights movement (1954–68) and the school desegregation decision of *Brown v. Board of Education of Topeka* (1954), political and memorializing groups, such as the Dixiecrats (a political party founded in 1948 to champion segregationist legislation) (Frederickson, 2001), handed out Confederate flags to be waved at University of Mississippi sporting events to acknowledge and reinforce the institution's ties to the Old South. The tradition took hold en masse and remained part of football games, along with singing the tune "Dixie," until the twentieth-first century (American Civil War Forums, n.d.). Further, women's organizations such as the United Daughters of the Confederacy (a women's heritage organization established in 1894 to commemorate Confederate soldiers via the erection of monuments) (Mills & Simpson, 2003), funded the creation and establishment of statues and other icons on college campuses, such as the University of North Carolina's untitled bronze statue of a Confederate soldier (known regionally as *Silent Sam*) (Lees & Gaske, 2014). The effigy stood atop a stone plinth inscribed with the words "To the sons of the university who entered the war of 1861–65 in answer to the call of their country and whose lives taught the lesson of their great commander that duty is the sublimest word in the English language."

Despite misconceptions that these statues, icons, and so on were placed on college campuses during or directly after the Civil War, they were, in actuality, erected just prior to or during the twentieth century (Hale, 2016). Indeed, "as white Southerners resisted efforts to dismantle

Jim Crow segregation ... it [the Confederate flag] began to fly over the state capitols and city halls across the region. Elements of it were also incorporated into several state flags. Worst of all, it became a mainstay at Ku Klux Klan rallies" (Southern Poverty Law Center, 2018 p. 33). All such icons were fabricated and "placed" as romanticized symbols (Newman, 2007) that characterized the antebellum South as a "grand and lordly life" (Follett, 2005, p. 235) of plantation rule and the "brave" fight to maintain the South's zenith as a bastion for racial purity and hegemonic order undergirded by skin color and eugenics (Winfield, 2007). At the same time, these Lost Cause images and white student activities (such as Confederate memorializing music, organization titles, etc.) were purposefully incorporated into college life to punctuate an unwelcoming message: that Southern higher education was the sole privilege of white citizens and, for those campuses not founded as historically black colleges and universities, closed to African Americans (Newman, 2007). This message conveyed via Lost Cause iconography represents the institutionalization of plantation politics on Southern college campuses by means of pseudoimmortalized images, statues of Confederate soldiers crafted from stone and metal, and engraved Civil War phrases that reinforce the very idea that African Americans, socially, are positioned beneath white people.

These symbols, as has been mentioned, were crafted to "laud a breakaway republic which idealized and waged war to perpetuate black slavery" (Tsesis, 2002, p. 543), and not purely to aggrandize the individual lives of military leaders or to memorialize lives lost due to Civil War battles. These persistent symbols attached to their larger institutions teach lessons of reverence to a bygone era that was exemplified by and reinforced the desire to maintain chattel servitude (Squire et al., 2018). As Joshua Newman (2007) elucidates, by their presence, these monuments "enact an antihuman polity and ideology that to this day maps privilege and works to oppress the marginalized peoples of the region" (p. 316). For college campuses, which are educational sites meant to encourage learning, enhance personal freedoms, and provide a safe space for liberating discourse, Lost Cause visualizations decrease the academic access potential for marginalized persons, particularly those directly affected by the long-standing lineage of plantation enslavement, to voice their concerns or develop true "connectedness" with their academic communities (Arnett, 2017; Pettus, 2014). To rectify this issue, Vanderbilt University administrators, for example, went so far as to return an 83-year-old donation in current value in order to remove the title "Confederate Memorial

Hall" from a residence facility, as the label was, according to chancellor Nicholas Zeppos, a "symbol of exclusion" (Koren, 2016, para. 2) and a reminder of enduring racism (Durkee, 2016).

As students, faculty, staff, administrators, and external stakeholders consider and debate the presence of Lost Cause iconography on Southern campuses, it is important to understand why they were put there in the first place, what overt messages they were meant to convey, and what realities they continue to impress on students who are desirous of a learning environment free of the trappings of negative yesteryears. As the presence of such symbols conveys a message that what happened prior to, during, and after the Civil War was acceptable, we highlight a select few college Confederate monuments, icons, and symbols that represent a sampling of campuses across the American South.

These symbols were selected due to their prevalence in media, state representation, and/or historiographic relevance. In all cases, the chosen iconography exemplify the entrenchment and institutionalization of said symbols into the physical campus environment, the conveyed lessons of Confederate memorialization meant to socialize the viewer into an understanding of racialized hierarchy on the college campus, and reflect vestigial plantation politic underpinnings as illustrated by Dian Squire et al. (2018) in their article "Plantation Politics and Neoliberal Racism in Higher Education: A Framework for Reconstructing Anti-Racist Institutions." These selected icons do not, however, exhaust the numerous Confederate representations on college and university campuses across the American South. With this in mind, it is important to acknowledge that while some Southern colleges and universities have experienced significant controversies related to Confederate memorabilia, others have experienced little rebuttal for a variety of reasons (explored in the subsequent case examples). Below we provide a series of related "placement" and "message" histories to better detail the normalization of long-standing plantation power, white supremacy, and Lost Cause veneration in Southern higher education, as well as the responses from students, employees, and campus leaders. In the vignettes that follow, brief histories regarding each selected icon and its placement is discussed. In addition, student and employee responses have been recorded to situate the existence and, for some, removal of said symbols from campus communities. The meaning behind each icon and the discourse surrounding its existence, purpose, and future as part of a larger set of learning environments are essential to consider. These aspects become paramount as colleges and universities choose either to reclaim their campuses as liberated spaces of learning free from the remnants of plantation politics or continue to cling to an era marked by racial subjugation and intense secessionist tension.

Robert E. Lee's Monument and Institutional Namesake at Washington and Lee University

Not long after the conclusion of the Civil War (1865), Robert E. Lee assumed the college presidency at Washington College in Lexington, Virginia—named for US president George Washington ("About W&L," 2017). Recruited for the position by the institution's board of directors due to his military background, Lee initially hesitated to take the position, fearful that his presence as a defamed Confederate general might damage the academy's reputation. After further persuasion, he accepted the post and revitalized academic programs by introducing modern curricula. Additionally, he sought to unite Southern and Northern students through higher education in hopes that they would become dutiful, honorable citizens (Shapiro, 2014; Roll, 2017; Toscano, 2017). Following Lee's death in 1870, communities across the South publicly mourned the lead military strategist of what might have become the Confederate States of America ("Very Small Indeed," 1870). Later that same year, Washington College was renamed Washington and Lee University in honor of Lee's academic and administrative service to the institution. In addition to the university's name, three buildings bore Lee's name—two academic buildings and Lee Chapel. Lee commissioned the chapel while serving as president. After Lee's death, university officials built an addition to the chapel that houses a life-sized marble statue of the Confederate general resting on a military camp bed. Lee and members of his immediate family were interred in a crypt beneath the building and remain there today. Formerly, the chapel housed Lee's office in the basement level, where it is preserved for visitors to view when they visit the Chapel Museum (Shapiro, 2014; "History of Lee Chapel Museum," 2017).

It has been noted on the Lee Chapel website that the structure serves as the "gathering place for the University's most important academic events." It plays host to invited speakers and other academic ceremonies throughout the year. Until 2014, the chapel also housed reproductions of historic Confederate flags that hung on the walls, framing the statue of Lee. In that year a group of African American students, referred to as "the committee," petitioned the university's board of trustees to have the flags removed, as they "felt uncomfortable attending school events in the chapel where Confederate flags were clearly visible" (Shapiro, 2014, para. 12). Soon thereafter, the flags were taken down. University president Kenneth Ruscio responded to further complaints about the need to publicly acknowledge the fact that the institution, as a cooperation, once enslaved approximately eighty Black women and men. Ruscio complied and made a public apology on behalf of the university and its governing board. Still, memorials to Confederate military figures, including Lee, remain on the campus. Pasquale Toscano, a Washington and Lee University alumnus, asserts that without further contextualization, these images "don't present a candid or nuanced account of history. They signal that these men are heroic and worthy of honor. Period" (Toscano, 2017, para. 16). This message does little to convey a complete institutional narrative inclusive of the college's racial desegregation in 1969 and modern attempts to increase campus diversity ("Minority Recruitment at Washington and Lee," n.d.). Still, in 2018, efforts were put forth by the institution's administration to rename several buildings named for Confederate leaders and regional planters who engaged in antebellum enslavement practices (Svrluga, 2018).

Silent Sam Statue at the University of North Carolina at Chapel Hill

On June 2, 1913, a Confederate monument was unveiled at the University of North Carolina at Chapel Hill (UNC). The monument, known at first as the "Soldier's Monument," then "The Confederate Memorial," has been colloquially referred to as *Silent Sam* since the campus newspaper, the *Daily Tar Heel*, titled it as such in a 1954 issue (Warren-Hicks, 2017). The United Daughters of the Confederacy commissioned Canadian sculptor John Wilson to design a statue that would memorialize "the young men who left college to go to war" ("Minutes," 1913) at a price of $7,500 (Svrluga, 2017). In 1913, North Carolina governor Locke Craig and University of North Carolina alumnus and former Confederate soldier Julian Carr spoke at the statue's dedication (Warren-Hicks, 2017). Carr's speech referenced Lost Cause sentimentality including statements of white supremacy and support of violence against African Americans (Carr, 1913). Carr proclaimed that "no nobler young men ever lived; no braver soldiers ever answered the bugle call nor marched under a battle flag" than the students who left the University of North Carolina to join the Confederate Army. Carr speculated that UNC was second only to the University of Virginia in the number of students that served in the Confederate armies. Carr thanked all former Confederate soldiers (living and deceased) for their efforts to "save the very life of the Anglo-Saxon race in the South." The former Confederate soldier further attested that "the purest strain of the Anglo-Saxon is to be found in the 13 Southern States." Continuing his dedication speech, Carr boasted of a time when he "horse-whipped a negro wench until her skirts hung in shreds" for insulting a "Southern [white] lady," which, in his purview, was evidence of his overwhelming support of Southern honor and the noble white women of the Confederacy (Carr, 1913, n.p.).

All of this was spoken in front of the *Silent Sam* statue to a large group of white onlookers. Due to its history, the statue has been the focal point of protests, vandalism, and media attention since the 1950s. Beginning in the 1960s, challenges to *Silent Sam* arose. A letter to the editors of the *Daily Tar Heel* in 1965 stated that "although . . . Silent Sam has become a part of the UNC tradition: it certainly cannot be argued that traditions should be maintained for tradition's sake" (Ribak, 1965). In the twenty-first century, *Silent Sam* has often been defaced and shunned by various student groups who want the statue removed. In 2017, the mayor of Chapel Hill, Pam Hemminger, asked that university officials remove the statue "in the interest of public safety" due to protests centered on the icon's continued campus presence. Despite this official call, campus leaders failed to act (Webster, 2017).

However, on August 20, 2018, an estimated 250 UNC students and activists gathered around the statue to protest its existence as part of the university community. That evening, protestors tore down the bronze upper half of the statue. After local police secured the scene, a dump truck was used to transport the statue away (Farzan, 2018; Kosnitzky, 2018). That same year, UNC administrators proposed to build a $5.3 million museum that would house the statue and contextualize its history, but various student groups opposed the construction plan. The museum proposal was ultimately denied by the UNC governing board, citing high construction costs and concerns centered on future student unrest connected with the building project that, ultimately, would have housed *Silent Sam* ("UNC Board of Governors," 2018). In January of 2019, UNC chancellor Carol Folt ordered the removal of the remainder of the statue—its marble pedestal inclusive of tablets bearing the names of UNC students who served in the Confederate Army (Wall, 2019).

Lawrence Sullivan ("Sully") Ross Statue at Texas A&M University

Centrally located on the College Station campus of Texas Agricultural and Mechanical University (Texas A&M) stands a bronze likeness of Lawrence Sullivan Ross—known to students, alumni, faculty, and administrators as "Sully." Texas ranger, Confederate general, governor of Texas, president of the Texas Division of the United Confederate Veterans, and former president of Texas A&M, Ross had a career in higher education administration that lasted until his death in 1898 (McGaughy, 2017). Ross enlisted in the Confederate Army at the onset of the Civil War and rose to the rank of brigadier general. After the war, he served as the state governor of Texas and supervised the Redeemer Constitutional Convention of 1875 that resulted in the repeal of the 1869 Texas Constitution (Calvert, 1984; Moneyhon, 2004). Subsequent to his career as a public official, Ross was selected to become president of Texas A&M and held a celebrated tenure as a fierce supporter of the institution and promoter of modern curricula. Due in large part to his administrative efforts, student enrollment increased, new buildings were constructed, and the local community rallied to support the college. Because of Ross's success, the institution chose to commemorate his role not only as a successful university administrator but also as a state leader and Confederate general (McGaughy, 2017).

Local Texas newspapers, such as the *Bryan Daily Eagle*, reported in 1917 on a proposed statue to be placed on the college campus honoring Ross. Newspapers commented that Ross was "modest, quiet, gentle, and brave, he was [as] gallant a knight as ever flashed a falchion or faced a foe" ("Proposed Monument to Sul Ross," 1917). The bronze statue, sculpted by Italian artist Pompeo Coppini, was installed in 1918 (Thomas, 2017). However, as Patrick Slattery (2006) explains, in recent years, students and professors have criticized the presence of Ross's statue due not only to the bygone president's Confederate connection but also to suspicions that the statue's plaque, which refers to Ross as a "knightly gentleman," serves as a possible allusion to his affiliation with the Ku Klux Klan. Proposals to erect a statue of Matthew Gaines, a former enslaved man who became the first African American Texas legislator in 1869, near the "Sully" statue have been active for approximately two decades. As Gaines worked to support the Federal Land Grant College Act, and arguably played an equally significant role in the development and history of Texas A&M, advocates attest that a statue to honor him would help cultivate a more diverse "visual culture" on the university campus (Slattery, 2006).

However, the Gaines statue project was halted due to the 1999 "bonfire tragedy" that killed twelve students and left many more injured when the massive bonfire structure collapsed. Efforts to create the Gaines statue were immediately curtailed to create a memorial to honor the deceased students (Slattery, 2006). Despite years of opposition to the "Sully" statue, Texas A&M's administration has been slow to act. Currently, university president Michael Young has assembled a task force to consider removing the statue given increased US racial tensions and student response. "Following the death of George Floyd while in police custody in Minneapolis, tensions surrounding the ["Sully"] statue . . . reached new heights. . . . Students at Texas A&M's College Station flagship have zeroed in on it as the campus' most flagrant reminder of systemic racism" (Justin, 2020, par. 2).

The University of Alabama's "Lost Cause" Tiffany Window

On October 22, 1925, the United Daughters of the Confederacy presented a Tiffany stained glass window to the University of Alabama "as a memorial to the gallant University cadets who defended Tuscaloosa during the Civil War" ("Memorial Window Dedicated," 1925, p. 1). The Alabama division of the United Daughters of the Confederacy paid Tiffany Studios in New York $5,000 to design and create the window, which pictures a romanticized "Christian Knight" in polished amour, brandishing a helmet, sword, and cross-laden shield. The window was crafted out of costly painted glass, drapery glass, mottled glass, and confetti glass. Surrounding the central knightly image are the Alabama state flag, the Confederate battle flag, and the flag of the Confederate States of America. Captioned with phrases such as "As the crusaders of old they fought for their heritage to save" and the Latin transcription "Dulce et decorum est pro patria moi," which is translated as "It is sweet and proper to die for the fatherland," the window serves as a mythical emblem of the perceived heroism behind the secessionist movement, Southern involvement in the Civil War, Confederate patriotism and Alabama's lost youth, and an idealization of the postwar Lost

Cause. Gifted to the university sixty years after the institution was burned during the Civil War, the stained glass window was originally installed in Amelia Gayle Gorgas Library (today known as Carmichael Hall). In 1993, the window was taken down and relocated to the William Stanley Hoole Special Collections Library located in Mary Harmon Bryant Hall. This was not done due to protests against the icon and its Confederate, Lost Cause iconography, but to better preserve it as a work of art created by a long-standing and well-known stained glass company (Mellown, 1993).

Students, politicians, faculty, community members, representatives of the United Daughters of the Confederacy, and Confederate student alumni attended the window's 1925 installation. The festivities included the singing of Confederate songs and a speech by former state governor Braxton Bragg Comer, who reminisced on the "righteous discipline" of the University of Alabama's student cadets (Green, 2017a). As well, comments were made by university president George Denny, who lauded the "gallant band of men who heaped glory not merely on themselves, but for thousands of Alabamians" ("Memorial Window Dedicated," 1925, p. 1). The university glee club sang renditions of the Civil War–era song "We're tenting tonight on the Old Campground," as well as Confederate favorites such as "The Bonny Blue Flag" and "Dixie." Marketed as a Lost Cause celebration in the college newspaper *Crimson White*, a student staff writer noted that the window would serve as a "brave . . . challenge to time that made the students . . . know that here was something real—something more than vaunting bravado and vain show. Here was the unconquerable spirit of the South" ("Memorial Window Dedicated," 1925, p. 1).

As Robert Mellown (1993) explains, "The dedication of the [window and its] 'Christian Knight' represented the climax of the 'Lost Cause' in Alabama" (n.p.)—a noble, patriotic, and divine cause that would, had it been successful, perpetuated plantation dominance and chattel servitude. Even though the Tiffany window has received little anti–Lost Cause attention, University of Alabama leaders have made efforts to remove other pro-Confederate campus iconography. On June 6, 2020, an announcement was made concerning the removal of three plaques honoring Confederate soldiers. Additionally, the university's board of trustees created a committee "to study the names of campus buildings named after slave owners and proponents of white supremacy" (Taylor, 2020, par. 5). Despite the attention garnered by University of Alabama campus Confederate symbols, the Tiffany stained glass has failed to attract significant attention, due, presumably, to its current placement in a rather discreet locale withdrawn from general public view. Though housed in the university's archives, the window and its visual symbolism display the institution's connection with Lost Cause sentimentality tied to antebellum hegemony.

The University of North Georgia's "Blue Ridge Rifles"

The University of North Georgia's (UNG) Blue Ridge Rifles (a student military cadet organization), founded in 1950 as a branch of the institution's Reserve Officer's Training Corps (ROTC) and named to memorialize the Civil War company, the Blue Ridge Rifles of the Confederate States of America, has been a high-ranking military drill team for a significant portion of its existence (Coffman, 1982). The University of North Georgia has had a strong military program since the institution's inception; thus, military life is an integral part of the campus community. The Blue Ridge Rifles have traveled throughout the United States to march in parades, perform in opening ceremonies, and participate in military competitions. UNG's student military organization was the first US drill team to affix bayonets to their rifles in 1968, and are the only drill team to use ten-inch bayoneted weapons while performing ("NGC First over Citadel," n.d.).

In addition to their Confederate commemorative name, modern Blue Ridge Rifle cadets wear insignia based on patches and other symbols first worn by the original Civil War military company. The current student organization's patch is based on the flag of Phillip's Legion of the Confederacy. The fabric patch is square and consists of one blue diagonal bar set against a red background. The diagonal bar contains seven white stars. The seven stars originally represented the first seven states to join the Confederacy (South Carolina, Mississippi, Florida, Alabama, Louisiana, Texas, and Georgia), but current Blue Ridge Rifle cadets express that the seven stars represent the seven Confederate Blue Ridge Rifle members buried in Mount Hope Cemetery adjacent to the university grounds. While most of the historic lore surrounding the Blue Ridge Rifles is recorded as being positive, the archived documents tell a different story. The original Blue Ridge Rifles were one of nine companies mustered from residents of Lumpkin County, and one of several Confederate companies that went by the same name. While regional accounts elicit that the Civil War–era Blue Ridge Rifles' fame was due to the volunteers enlisting early and fighting throughout the war, several members of the company deserted. Similarly, when some company members were issued war furloughs, they did not return. Yet their Civil War story is remembered as one of "honor" against all odds. The same veneration is applied to modern-day UNG Blue Ridge Rifle cadets ("Blue Ridge Rifle Manual," n.d.).

While presently known as the Blue Ridge Rifles, the drill team has had a long history of renaming and reinventing itself. The institution's first official drill team was formed in 1936 but disbanded during World War II as drilling was not the college's priority given the need to enlist able-bodied soldiers. Reinstated in the latter half of the 1950s and simply known as "Drill Platoon," the student military organization's commanding officer solicited alternative titles from UNG faculty and students. Responding to the call, Dorothy Brown, an English professor at the university, suggested the historic "Blue Ridge Rifles" title due to the "previous unit in the vicinity and the applicability to the college" ("Blue Ridge Rifle Manual," n.d., p. 1). The timing and context of the organization's name change may have been related to the fact that preparations were underway in 1958 to reactivate the Blue Ridge Rifles in Dahlonega, Georgia. The Dahlonega-based military reactivation was meant to commemorate the upcoming one hundredth anniversary of the Civil War. As such, it has been suggested that Brown's promotion of the Confederate moniker might have been an attempt to connect the veneration of a well-known Civil War company to the University of North Georgia and its ROTC unit (*Cyclops 1958*, 1958). Like the University of Alabama's Tiffany window, the modern-day Blue Ridge Rifles have experienced little protest, which may be indicative of the normalization process that has occurred with respect to such symbols on other campuses.

Modern Response to Confederate Symbols on College Campuses

Each of the previously discussed icons have become or were normalized as part of their respective campuses. The idea of Confederate icon memorialization as physical norms in educational spaces require that students, faculty, administrators, and external stakeholders become socialized into a campus community where such symbols exist and are perpetuated. Further, those who oppose these icons may face challenges associated with their removal, which further illustrates the significance of such symbols in the Southern higher education community. Even so, opposition in the form of anti-Confederate symbol protest and related actions have occurred and, in several instances, have resulted in the removal of or contextualization of Lost Cause iconography.

As explained in this chapter's introduction and detailed in the Southern campus icon examples described above, "Confederate symbols certainly commemorate history, but it's not the history of the Confederacy. Rather they commemorate the history of how Confederate symbols have been mobilized as white backlash against the attainment of black civil liberties throughout this country's post–Civil War era" (Oliver, 2017, para. 7). As a result, Southern higher education leaders have responded in various ways to deal with present-day reactions to Lost Cause symbols. One reason for administrative action is the fear of protestor violence. For example, at the University of Texas in Austin, the call for monument removal was a "preemptive strike against . . . emotional and physical violence" (Lloyd, 2017, para. 2). This is especially significant as Confederate symbols on college campuses or in cities and townships have become "lightning rods for protestors" (Mazza, 2017, para. 1). In a similar vein, Duke University's administration removed a campus monument to Robert E. Lee, citing violent incidents in Charlottesville concerning protestors and vandalism of the Lee statue itself. Duke president Vincent Price ordered the statue's removal and stated that it is the administration's duty to encourage students, faculty, and staff "to come together as a community to determine how we can respond to this unrest in a way that demonstrates our firm commitment to justice, not discrimination; to civil protest, not violence; to authentic dialogue, not rhetoric; and to empathy, not hatred" (Neuman, 2017, para. 4). Duke University students expressed approval at how campus administration handled the situation, and in particular, the university's creation of the Truth, Racial Healing, and Transformation Center designed to "help eliminate societal structures that perpetuate racism" (Kadis, 2017, para. 4). In 2018 Florida State University's administration removed a campus statue of Frances Eppes—FSU's mythologized founder, plantation owner, and enslaver. However, in 2019 the statue was returned to campus along with a plague that details Eppes's "dark past as a slave owner" (Dobson, 2019, par. 12).

In an effort to make Confederate, Lost Cause monuments focal points for student discourse, several colleges and universities throughout the South have used the existence of these symbols as means to discuss issues related to diversity, inclusiveness, and historical preservation/contextualization. A University of Alabama professor uses the dedication speech of the Tiffany stained glass window as an example of Lost Cause mythology in her course "Black History in the Nineteenth Century" (Green, 2017b). Similarly, faculty at the University of North Georgia have held panel discussions to address "the nuances, complexities, and challenges regarding the current political and cultural debate" surrounding modern-day racism and Confederate imagery (Kemling, 2017, para. 3). Roundtable discussions included "the layered nature of power in and around the image; how public monuments and their locations reflect and facilitate cultural values; situating monuments in a broader cultural and historical context; issues of the changing meaning of the monuments; and social responsibility and sensitivity" (Kemling, 2017, par. 1).

As the debate intensifies over "what to do" with these icons of white supremacy, Southern antebellum moralization, and Lost Cause celebration, some Southern colleges and universities are taking action. In certain cases statues and other images are being relocated to museums where they can be further contextualized, while other solutions, though not as educative, include removing statues, plaques, and the like to cemeteries where Confederate soldiers are buried (Grinberg, 2017).

Whatever the solution, bringing these icons into a historically accurate context is essential, particularly if institutions of higher education want to retain them in pedagogical spaces dedicated to critical inquiry. As Sheffield Hale (2016) states, "If we keep them, we cannot maintain the status quo. We must transform them from objects of veneration into historical artifacts that tell the story of why so many of them were erected" (par. 9). Going beyond Hale, college and university leaders must permit analytic conversation that delves deep to further explore, understand, and make modern meaning of these Lost Cause images and their connection to the Southern higher education scene. Moreover, college administrators and faculty must acknowledge that Civil War– and plantation-era-linked symbols serve to mute discourse regarding racial uplift and educational access, as their presence normalizes the myth of the Lost Cause and the presence of white supremacy within the academic sphere. As Alexander Tsesis (2002) illustrates, "They [Confederate images] are laden with combustible social and political messages which 'like long buried ammunition, can go off without warning'" (p. 599). When state, community, and academic leaders allow these symbols to remain without context, they "give them an air of respectability. . . . By maintaining and paying for upkeep of Confederate symbols, states reinvigorate hurdles still facing blacks [and other minorities] living in the United States" (Tsesis, 2002, p. 606). As a result, these icons, if left in place, will, as Newman (2007) proffers, continue to demark portions of educational spaces or whole higher education institutions as "territories representative of ideologies and identities of the dominant faction" (p. 316).

In that vein, some Southern institutions are opting to leave monuments and images in their physical place and add additional context via new plaques with inscriptions that better explain who funded and erected them as well as their motivation for having done so. For some, however, this option does not carry enough transformative weight, as these symbols construct a worldview that negatively affects students—particularly if icons do not directly contribute to educational access, freedom of speech, freedom of expression without worry of harmful repercussions (physical or otherwise), and racial equality (Tsesis, 2002). The continued existence of Lost Cause images on Southern college campuses fosters an academic community in which these icons exist as the norm. As Liza Oliver (2017) explains, "The myth of the Lost Cause in perpetuating historical amnesia has been a particularly powerful and insidious one" (para. 9). Consequently, colleges and university leaders must eliminate the romanticism associated with these symbols through their removal and/or placement within heavily contextualized and explanatory environments such as museums, archives, or educational centers (Newman, 2007). This, in effect, has the potential to help sever Southern colleges and universities from the lasting influence of plantation politics by presenting these icons alongside historically accurate narratives that explain why they were crafted, what they meant when originally erected, and how they influence modern higher education.

This suggested iconographic transformation holds to the essential tenet of emancipatory learning, which is "to develop understanding and knowledge about the nature and root causes of unsatisfactory circumstances in order to develop real strategies to change them" (Thompson, 2000, para. 2). As a result, higher education scholars, administrators, students, and alumni must be intentional in working together to analytically deconstruct and, if necessary, physically deconstruct and relocate icons and symbols that fetter institutions from creating truly equitable spaces where all can learn without the shadow of past oppressive ideologies burdening the pedagogical process. This change must come in the form of open, reciprocal dialogue opportunities in which students have a chance to express their perceptions of and concerns with existing Confederate icons. Likewise, students and university employees should be given the opportunity to explore and further understand the meaning behind Lost Cause symbols on college campuses. By placing these images in contextualized spaces (archives, museums, learning centers, etc.), they can be better studied, ideologically deconstructed, and analyzed to reveal further truths regarding higher education's connection to historic and ongoing plantation politics. As a result, Lost Cause statues, plaques, flags, and the like have the potential to become part of the educative process. Through the critical examination of said symbols, colleges and universities have the ability to transform historical icons from objects that normalize racism and venerate the Confederacy to artifacts that lend themselves to the academic investigation of a bygone era typified by enslavement, succession, and persistent racial oppression. Further, these actions promote the liberation of higher education environments from racial tyranny through an enhanced understanding of the antebellum South, the Civil War, and its lasting impact on American society.

References

About W&L. (2017) *Washington and Lee University.* www.wlu.edu/about.

Alderman, D. H. (2000). A street fit for a king: Naming places and commemoration in the American South. *The Professional Geographer, 52*(4), 672–84. DOI: 10.1111/0033-0124.00256

American Civil War Forums. (n.d.). *Civil War Talk.* https://www.civilwartalk.com/

Arnett, A. A. (2017, July 10). As campuses begin to tear down Confederate symbols, leaders weigh donor, student interests. *Education Dive.* https://www.educationdive.com/news/campuses-grapple-with-student-donor-debate-over-confederate-monuments/446669/

Ballard, M. (2017, November 27). LSU renamed well-known campus street named after Confederate admiral as part of modernization plan. *The Advocate.* https://www.theadvocate.com/baton_rouge/news/education/article_88019a04-d398-11e7-8323-730f74dc7d02.html

Bidgood, J., Bloch, M., McCarthy, M., Stack, L., & Andrews, W. (2017). Confederate monuments are coming down across the United States. Here's a list. *The New York Times.* https://www.nytimes.com/interactive/2017/08/16/us/Confederate-monuments-removed.html

Blue Ridge Rifle manual: History of the Blue Ridge Rifles. (n.d.). *Blue Ridge Rifles Collection,* University of North Georgia Archives, Dahlonega, GA.

Calvert, R. (1984). "Review of Judith Ann Benner's *Sul Ross: Soldier, statesman, educator* (Texas A&M University Press: College Station, TX, 1983)." *The American Historical Review, 89*(4), 1162.

Carmel, M. (2017, August 25). Update: Randolph president: Jones statue in storage until school can display it with "proper context." *The News & Advance.* http://www.newsadvance.com/news/local/update-randolph-president-jones-statue-in-storage-until-school-can/article_3b60f020-8990-11e7-9ffd-1f4ebf823043.html

Carr, J. (1913, June 2). "Unveiling of confederate monument at university. Julian Shakespeare Carr papers #141, Southern Historical Collection. The Wilson Library, University of North Carolina at Chapel Hill.

Cleveland, R. (2003, June 19). Colonel not exactly a longtime tradition. *The Clarion-Ledger*, 19.

Cloud, J. D. (2020, June 15). Black lives matter, flag protests held Sunday at Southern Miss. *Pine Belt News*. https://www.hubcityspokes.com/news-hattiesburg-southern-miss/black-lives-matter-flag-protests-held-sunday-southern-miss

Coffman, R. M. (1982, January). A vital unit: Being a brief and true history of 10,000 volunteers, Phillips' legion. *Civil War Times Illustrated, 20*, 40–45.

Cyclops 1958. (1958). University of North Georgia Archives, Dahlonega, GA.

Dobson, B. (2019, May 13). Mixture of surprise and anger as controversial Eppes statue returns to FSU. *Tallahassee Democrat*. https://www.tallahassee.com/story/news/2019/05/13/francis-eppes-statue-finds-news-home-north-westcott-building/1187335001/

Durkee, T. (2016). Ole Miss to stop performing Confederate anthem "Dixie." *Sporting News*. http://www.sportingnews.com/ncaa-football/news/ole-miss-dixie-marching-band-confederacy/1wvx8xy8w9c3r1503rbagqs4z7

Farzan, A. N. (2018). "Silent Sam": A racist Jim Crow–era speech inspired UNC students to toppled Confederate monument on campus. *The Washington Post*. https://www.washingtonpost.com/news/morning-mix/wp/2018/08/21/silent-sam-a-racist-jim-crow-era-speech-inspired-unc-students-to-topple-a-confederate-monument-on-campus/

Follett, R. J. (2005). *The sugar masters: Plantations and slaves in Louisiana's cane world, 1820–1860*. Louisiana State University Press.

Foner, E. (2017, August 20). Confederate statues and "our" history. *The New York Times*. https://www.nytimes.com/2017/08/20/opinion/confederate-statues-american-history.html

Foster, G. M. (1988). *Ghosts of the Confederacy: Defeat, the lost cause, and the emergence of the New South, 1865–1913*. Oxford University Press.

Frederickson, K. (2001). *The Dixiecrat revolt and the end of the solid South, 1932–1968*. University of North Carolina Press.

Green, H. N. (2017a). Memorial window dedicated to all old bama cadets. http://hgreen.people.ua.edu/transcription-udc-stain-glass.html

Green, H. (2017b, December 4). Personal communication.

Grinberg E. (2017). What can communities do with Confederate monuments? Here are 3 options. *CNN*. http://www.cnn.com/2017/06/30/us/what-to-do-with-Confederate-monuments/index.html

Hale, F. S. (2016). Finding meaning in monuments: Atlanta History Center enters dialogue on Confederate symbols. *Atlanta History Center*. http://www.atlantahistorycenter.com/research/confederate-monuments/press

Harris, C. I. (1993). Whiteness as property. *Harvard Law Review, 106*(8), 1707–91. DOI: 10.2307/1341787

Hesse, M. (2016). The South's Confederate monument problem is not going away. *The Washington Post.* https://www.washingtonpost.com/lifestyle/style/the-souths-Confederate-monument-problem-is-not-going-away/2016/05/08/b0258e4a-05af-11e6-a12f-ea5aed7958dc_story.html?utm_term=.addae2b402f4

History of Lee Chapel Museum. (2017). *Washington and Lee University.* https://www.wlu.edu/lee-chapel-and-museum/about-the-chapel/history

Justin, R. (2020, June 17). Texas A&M announces task force to weigh removing statue of Sul Ross, Confederate general and former governor. *The Texas Tribune.* https://www.texastribune.org/2020/06/17/sul-ross-statue-texas-am-task-force/

Kadis, L. (2017, August 29). "Right move": Students react to Robert E. Lee statue being removed. *The Chronicle.* http://www.dukechronicle.com/article/2017/08/right-move-students-react-to-robert-e-lee-statue-being-removed

Kemling, M. (2017). *The power of the image: Placing the debate over Confederate monuments in context* [Pamphlet]. University of North Georgia.

Koren, M. (2016). Vanderbilt Confederate Hall. *The Atlantic.* https://www.theatlantic.com/news/archive/2016/08/vanderbilt-Confederate-hall/495941/

Kosnitzky, Z. (2018). When rioters tore down UNC's Confederate monument Silent Sam, I saw mob rule triumph. *USA Today.* http://www.usatoday.com/story/opinion/voices/2018/09/04/silent-sam-confederate-statue-protest-unc-chapel-hill-column/1072535002/

Lees, W., & Gaske, F. (2014). *Recalling deeds immortal: Florida monuments to the Civil War.* University Press of Florida.

Lloyd, A. B. (2017, September 18). Tearing down a statue is one thing. What do you do about a campus with a deep Confederate legacy? *The Weekly Standard.* http://www.weeklystandard.com/tearing-down-a-statue-is-one-thing.-what-do-you-do-about-a-campus-with-a-deep-confederate-legacy/article/2009707

Magee, P. (2015). Southern Miss removes Mississippi flag from all campuses. *The Sun Herald.* http://www.sunherald.com/news/article41689311.html

Mazza, E. (2017, August 28). New memorial in Alabama honors Confederate soldiers. *The Huffington Post.* https://www.huffingtonpost.com/entry/brantley-alabama-cofederate-statue_us_59a3a142e4b0821444c45402

McGaughy, L. (2017). Amid debate over Confederate monuments, Texas A&M will not remove Sul Ross statue. *Dallas Daily Morning News.* https://www.dallasnews.com/news/education/2017/08/21/amid-debate-over-confederate-monuments-texas-am-will-not-remove-sul-ross-statue/

Medley, K. W. (2003). *We as freemen: Plessy v. Ferguson.* Pelican Publishing.

Mellown, R. O. (1993). Everything you ever wanted to know about Hoole's incredible Tiffany Window. *Alabama Heritage,* 27. http://www.alabamaheritage.com

Memorial window dedicated to all old 'bama cadets. (1925, October 29). *Crimson White,* 1.

Mills C., & Simpson, P. H. (2003). *Monuments to the lost cause: Women, arts, and the landscapes of Southern memory*. University of Tennessee Press.

Minority recruitment at Washington and Lee. (n.d.). *The American Century*. https://omeka.wlu.edu/americancentury/exhibits/show/desegregation-at-private-unive/minority-recruitment-at-washin

Minutes of the Annual Convention of the United Daughters of the Confederacy: North Carolina Division." (1913–1919). The Collection of the North Carolina, Library of the University of North Carolina.

Moneyhon, C. H. (2004). *Texas after the Civil War: The struggle of reconstruction*. Texas A&M University Press.

Neuman, S. (2017, August 19). Duke University removes Robert E. Lee statue from chapel entrance. *NPR*. https://www.npr.org/sections/thetwo-way/2017/08/19/544678037/duke-university-removes-robert-e-lee-statue-from-chapel-entrance

Newman, J. I. (2007). Army of whiteness? Colonel Reb and the sporting South's cultural and corporate symbolic. *Journal of Sport and Social Issues, 31*(4), 315–339. DOI: 10.1177/0193723507307814

NGC first over citadel. (n.d.) Blue ridge rifles collection, University of North Georgia Archives, Dahlonega, GA.

Oliver, L. (2017, August 24). What Confederate monuments do [Blog post]. *Wellesley College*. https://www.wellesley.edu/albright/about/blog/3536-what-confederate-monuments-do

Park, M. (2017). Removal of Confederate monuments stirs backlash in statehouses. *CNN*. http://www.cnn.com/2017/05/12/us/Confederate-monument-state-bills/index.html

Perman, M. (1984). *The road to redemption: Southern politics, 1869–1879*. University of North Carolina Press.

Pettus, E. W. (2014, October 24). As Rebs win, Ole Miss balances Dixie and diversity. *Clarion Ledger*. http://www.clarionledger.com/story/news/2014/10/24/rebs-win-ole-miss-balances-dixie-diversity/17863701/

Pierre, N. (2017, April 6). Tulane Confederate monuments remind students of past, present oppression. *Tulane Hullabaloo*. https://tulanehullabaloo.com/23673/intersections/reminders-oppresion-students-consider-tulanes-confederate-monuments/

The proposed monument to Sul Ross. (1917, February 22). *Bryan Daily Eagle*. https://chroniclingamerica.loc.gov/lccn/sn86088651/1917-02-22/ed-1/seq-2/#date1=1917&index=0&rows=20&words=MONUMENT+PROPOSED+ROSS+SUL&searchType=basic&sequence=0&state=&date2=1917&proxtext=The+proposed+monument+to+Sul+Ross&y=15&x=17&dateFilterType=yearRange&page=1

Ribak, A. (1965, March 17). "Silent Sam" should leave. *The Daily Tar Heel*. http://newspapers.digitalnc.org/lccn/sn92073228/1965-03-17/ed-1/seq-2/

Rojas, R. (2020, June 30). Mississippi governor signs law to remove flag with Confederate emblem. *The New York Times*. https://www.nytimes.com/2020/06/30/us/mississippi-flag.html

Roll, N. (2017). At Washington and Lee, complicated debate about Robert E. Lee. *Inside Higher Ed.* https://www.insidehighered.com/news/2017/08/23/washington-and-lee-complicated-debate-about-robert-e-lee

Scott, E. (2015, December 22). Stars and barred: The sanitization of Confederate history on college campuses overlooks UGA. *Georgia Political Review.* http://georgiapoliticalreview.com/stars-and-barred-the-sanitization-of-confederate-history-on-college-campuses-overlooks-uga/

Shapiro, T. R. (2014, July 8). Washington and Lee University to remove confederate flags following protests. *The Washington Post.* https://www.washingtonpost.com/local/education/washington-and-lee-university-to-remove-confederate-flags-following-protests/2014/07/08/e219e580-06bb-11e4-8a6a-19355c7e870a_story.html?utm_term=.f637e05ebdf4

Slattery, P. (2006). Deconstructing racism one state at time: Visual culture wars at Texas A&M University and the University of Texas at Austin. *Visual Arts Research, 32*(2), 28–31.

Southern Poverty Law Center. (2018). The Confederate flag remains a racist symbol. In A. Cunningham (Ed.), *The Confederate flag* (pp. 24–27). Greenhaven Publishing.

Squire, D., Williams, B. C., & Tuitt, F. (2018). Plantation politics and neoliberal racism in higher education: A framework for reconstructing anti-racist institutions. *Teachers College Record, 120*(14), 1–20.

Svrluga, S. (2017). Students demand that Confederate statue be removed from UNC campus saying it violates federal laws. *The Washington Post.* https://mooresvilletribune.com/news/u_s/students-demand-that-confederate-statue-be-removed-from-unc-campus/article_c0128a6a-799b-522a-8803-20befb271875.html

Svrluga, S. (2018, October 11). Washington and Lee renames buildings, replaced military portraits of its namesakes. *The Washington Post.* https://www.washingtonpost.com/education/2018/10/11/washington-lee-renames-buildings-replaces-military-portraits-its-namesakes/

Taylor, Stephanie. (2020, June 9). University of Alabama removes Confederate monument. *Tuscaloosa News.* https://www.tuscaloosanews.com/news/20200609/university-of-alabama-removes-confederate-monument

Thomas, D. (2017). Texas A&M says it will not remove campus statue of Lawrence Sullivan Ross. *The Statesman.* www.statesman.com/news/local/texas-says-will-not-remove-campus-statue-lawrence-sullivane-ross/1oJhS14oi9zpTDp7K0s1VK/amp.html

Thompson J. (2000). *Emancipatory learning* [NIACE Briefing Sheet 11]. National Institute of Adult Continuing Education.

Toscano, S. P. (2017). My university is named for Robert E. Lee. What now? *The New York Times*. https://www.nytimes.com/2017/08/22/opinion/washington-lee-university-trump-nationalism.html

Tsesis, A. (2002). The problem of Confederate symbols: A Thirteenth Amendment approach. *Temple Law Review, 539*, 539–612. http://lawecommons.luc.edu/facpubs

UNC Board of Governors "cannot support" $5.3M plan to house Silent Sam statue on UNC campus. (2018, December 15). *ABC 11 Eyewitness News*. http://abc11.com/politics/unc-board-of-governors-cannot-support-trustees-silent-sam-plan/4897075/

Varon, E. R. (2008). *Disunion!: The coming of the American Civil War, 1789–1859* (9th ed.). University of North Carolina Press.

Very small indeed. (1870, October 14). *The New York Herald Times*. https://chroniclingamerica.loc.gov/lccn/sn83030313/1870-10-14/ed-1/seq-6/#date1=1870&index=2&rows=20&words=E+Lee+Robert&searchType=basic&sequence=0&state=New+York&date2=1870&proxtext=Robert+E+Lee+&y=17&x=5&dateFilterType=yearRange&page=1

Wall, J. (2019, January 15). UNC chancellor pushed out early after "Silent Sam" Confederate statue's remnants removed. *NBC News*. https://www.nbcnews.com/news/us-news/unc-chancellor-pushed-out-early-after-silent-sam-confederate-statue-n959141

Warren-Hicks, C. (2017, August 23). A look at the long and controversial life of Silent Sam. *News and Observer*.

Webster, H. (2017). Chapel Hill mayor asks for Silent Sam to be removed from UNC campus. *WRAL.com*. www.wral.com/chapel-hill-mayor-asks-for-the-removal-of-silent-sam-from-unc-campus/16890333/

Whose heritage? Public symbols of the Confederacy. (n.d.). *Southern Poverty Law Center*. https://www.splcenter.org/20160421/whose-heritage-public-symbols-confederacy

Winfield, A. G. (2007). *Eugenics and education in America: Institutionalized racism and the implications of history, ideology, and memory*. Peter Lang.

Word Wire. (2017). What do you have to say to the Mississippi state flag protesters? *Deep South Daily*. http://deepsouthdaily.com/2017/04/18/say-mississippi-state-flag-protesters/

Chapter 11

Codes of Silence

Campus and State Responses to Student Protest

Kevin J. Bazner and Andrea Button

Many of the early "slave codes" established a legal framework of social control in order to stave off protest and rebellion within early American society. Oftentimes, one of the mechanisms was to attempt to control language to prevent controversy or an uprising (Goodell, 1853; Ingersoll, 1995). More recently, college and university administrators have been attacked for their inability to control student activists' behaviors, protest speech, and means of resistance on their respective campuses. This has garnered the attention of political leaders, policymakers, and the public making calls for reform and action on the growing presence of student resistance on campuses. While student resistance within colleges and universities is not a new phenomenon, this time college and university administrators are seemingly more attentive to the concerns of lawmakers and their governing bodies regarding the response to student activism. Moreover, increased attention on student activism cannot be divorced from growing skepticism and public distrust directed toward the value of higher education nationwide (Fingerhut, 2017). Institutional leaders have become more attentive to the relationship between the university, economic, political, and other social forces. Policymakers and institutional leaders, specifically, are increasingly cautious of politics they must navigate to maintain good relations with institutional constituencies and, most importantly, their funders.

One of the more recent manifestations of the interplay between campus protest and economic and political power began with the students at the University of Missouri when forming Concerned Student 1950, named for the year the first Black student was admitted to the university (Schmich, 2015). Revealing the deeply embedded structural racism within the university, Black student activists organized in response to ongoing racist incidents and issued a set of demands that they wanted the university administration to begin addressing (Concerned Student 1950, 2015). After months of protests and an undesirable attempt on behalf of the university administration to meet the demands, graduate student Jonathan Butler began a hunger strike until the university president resigned from his position (Miller, 2015). One week later, thirty-two members of the university football team announced that they would not play until the president was removed or resigned. The action of the nationally recognized Mizzou football team marked the first time student athletes had engaged in a protest that also posed a real economic threat to the institution. The university stood to lose millions of dollars if they had to cancel their upcoming game (Green, 2015). While the university president eventually resigned and student protesters engaged in a more substantial dialogue, a response from the state legislature seemed warranted. In an attempt to silence the collective and individual voices of student-athletes, Republican state representative Rick Brattin introduced legislation revoking scholarships and jeopardizing the athletic future of any student-athlete refusing to play for a reason unrelated to health (Zirin, 2015). While later withdrawn, this piece of legislation has marked a new era of contemptuous relationships between student protesters, university administrators, and state lawmakers.

Throughout this chapter, we highlight means of social control and dominance that have been maintained or reinforced through institutional practices of oppression and that problematize the (in)action taken by state and university leaders. We begin by providing an account of the institution's use of education as a system of hegemonic socialization and control (Bourdieu & Passeron, 1990; Harney & Moten, 2013), followed by an overview of Brazilian educational philosopher Paulo Freire's (2008) assessment of education-as-resistance, illustrating the role educational institutions have in maintaining social control, including examples of student movements that have resisted this power. We then provide an overview of recent state legislative and university policy aimed at maintaining social control over student protest movements, and illustrate their ties to the political and economic interests of those outside of the university. We illuminate the parallels to practices of plantation pedagogy (Bristol, 2010) and the plantation society (Durant, 1999) that are deeply rooted in a systematic structure that maintains power and control. We finally express the belief that student activism not be reduced to a level of inconvenience but rather utilized as a reminder of the increased corporatization and power imbalance taking over academic and political interests, and consider how educators should reimagine the future of student resistance.

Institutionalized Dominance and Student Resistance

Student activism and resistance to structures of oppression in the United States have been mainstays on college campuses nationwide (Broadhurst, 2014; Thelin, 2011). From the "freedom schools" organized by college students in the 1950s, the Columbia divestment protests, the various waves of the women's movement, and the sustained student participation in antiwar and human rights campaigns (Goodwin & Jasper, 2014), the history of social movement protests has often placed students at the center of many of these pivotal processes. However, it would be inaccurate to characterize the university environment as "welcoming" this student activism, as it often results in further (at times fatal) violence against students. It is also important to address how the climate of the university has changed as historically oppressed and minoritized student populations have increased in size.

Centered in this context is the importance of knowledge: the knowledge of how to organize, how to resist, how to communicate one's resistance, and how to recognize oppression (Freire, 2008). Where this knowledge comes from and how it is applied is most commonly a reflection of the student-teacher dynamic, in part because the power of the university over both the faculty and the students is a mirror of the relationships of the student to all individuals and institutions capable to wielding control over them. Applying Freire's work to the Freedom Summer and freedom schools movements of the past (McAdam, 1990), as well as to current student antiracism activism, allows for a nuanced approach to understanding how the policing of both the institution of the university and the activism of educators and students is central to maintaining the structure of power of the dominant culture. Prior to that application, however, we must understand the "purpose" of the institution of education.

Through Freire's (2008) work, the complicated relationship between the student-teacher and the teacher-student is posited within the institution of education. This institution, while reflecting the taken-for-granted and enforced relationships of power between the oppressed and the oppressor, serves as a dynamic location to analyze the agency of multiple social actors: students, teachers, administrators, and politicians. The dialectical relationship between the educational process as both a liberating experience and a system of control over thought and identity has been an area of inquiry and discussion in several disciplines in academia. Early theorists in sociology Emile Durkheim (1956) and Max Weber (1946/2009) focused on issues relating to social control, establishing how educational systems produced complicit and competent citizens, reinforced dominant ideologies, and provided status markers for individuals operating within the dominant cultures. More recently, scholars have pointed toward early manifestations of the American university as a means of white colonial propaganda directed at civilizing indigenous populations and as a form of social control of enslaved and free Black people (Calloway, 2010; Wilder, 2013; Wright, 1988).

Durkheim's insight into the crucial role of education in societies reflected his sociological approach, which is similar to Freire's pedagogical analysis (Saha, 1997). According to Durkheim's (1956) theory, education was central to the continuation of a society through the transmission of dominant cultural values, language, ideologies, and technology. Durkheim's writings centered on the factors that gave rise to social control—an order defined by those in power rather than those within—and the social consequences that result from the deterioration of that order. Durkheim promoted a functionalist view of education that was expected to create local citizens for a more structured society.

Building on the foundations of traditional theorists such as Weber and Durkheim, Pierre Bourdieu and Jean-Claude Passeron (1990) studied education as an institution. They note that the education system is not socially neutral, as Durkheim posits, in that schools adopt the habitus of the dominant class as the "natural" habitus and expect all students, regardless of their social milieu, to have access to it. Students enter the educational system with different social cues, represented by their varying identities and status, and are disenfranchised or advantaged according to their lack of familiarity with the dominant class habitus adopted by the educational institution (Bourdieu & Passeron, 1990). Those individuals who can assimilate to a number of the dominant social cues are less likely to be academically penalized and are rewarded for their educational investments (Freire, 2008). These students then replicate the social cues, reifying the status and power of both the institution and their teachers, which are recognized by the system as their own, and internalize and strengthen the mechanism of social exclusion. Therefore, different groups stand in different relationships to their schools, depending on their trajectory and objectified use in relation to the dominant group (Mahar et al., 1990).

Traditionally, some groups have been able to use the school system to reproduce their class position, while others have not (Mahar et al., 1990). For example, the practice of "legacy" students at Ivy League institutions and predominately white institutions enables the reproduction of class- and race-based privilege. As education becomes increasingly widespread among all groups, white elites design other means to maintain social differentiation and to modify the value of the educational "deposits" (Mahar et al., 1990; Freire 2008). Dian Squire, Bianca Williams, and Frank Tuitt (2018) direct attention to the manner in which colleges utilize differential terminology to describe Students of Color as "at-risk, unprepared, and remedial" (p. 12) and thus viewed through disempowered and deficit lenses. As a means of social control, the institution requires students to perceive themselves as being "inadequate" (Harney & Moten, 2013) and internalize this oppression. Students' internalization of their individual and social identity as "problematic" emphasizes the ability of a university to police students and thus render them "dangerous." For the majority of white people in the university who serve as administrators and faculty, students are seen not for their intellectual ability but rather as a threat to the educational milieu that also demands being labeled inadequate and deserving of control.

In line with earlier scholars' critique of the university, Stefano Harney and Fred Moten (2013) are correct in locating the intended purpose of the university as one dedicated to the reproduction of dominant ideologies and internal identities that operate as integrated systems of oppression. In this sense, Squire et al. (2018) make the assertion that universities create an *involuntariness of membership* in which the simple expectations of society and the collective "purpose" of the institution of education require a degree of conformity and create social deviants of anyone who resists. Freire (2008) illuminates this relationship by stating, "The dominant elites consider the remedy to be more domination and repression, carried out in the name of freedom, order, and social peace . . . [and] call upon the state in the same breath to use violence in putting down the strike"

(p. 78). It is at this intersection that a conversation about the modern university as both an institution of social control and one of resistance and change must be situated.

Slave Codes and the Modern University

Slave plantations, much like institutions of higher education, were complex organizations that had to relate to both the internal demands of the plantation and the environmental factors existing within society. Moreover, they operated in an environment utilizing both an open and a closed system of control factors to advance their goals, minimize disruptions to operations, and direct the behavior of the enslaved on the plantation (Yates, 1999). Reliance on an open system of social control to exercise greater control over the enslaved in Southern plantation society is not terribly different from the neoliberal university's use of societal expectations of students, particularly Students of Color. Squire et al. (2018) referred to this practice as "boundary maintenance," and it reinforces the social reproduction of the dominant class habitus (Bourdieu & Passeron, 1990).

While to maintain social control the slave plantation relied mostly on internal mechanisms such as torture, social hierarchies, and incentive systems, it was a commitment to maximizing profits and *relationships* with the larger society that created an interdependent function within the larger economic, political, and cultural environments. These open systems of organizational behavior positioned the slave plantation as an important player in the larger economic, political, and social systems of the time (Maurer, 1971). Regular interaction between the plantation and society created systematic linkages that were mutually beneficial yet required mechanisms to maintain social control and a level of order and consistency. Slave codes, sometimes referred to as "Black Codes," or "Code Noir" in Louisiana, controlled or limited enslaved and free Black populations' access to social institutions and privileges reserved for whites (Goodell, 1853; Yates, 1999). Slave codes were one of the most prevalent means of societal control, and sanctioned enslavers' justification of their continued exploitation of the labor of the enslaved (Durant, 1999). These laws were born from a fear of rebellion and provided a mechanism of social control to prevent controversy.

The plantation society maintained order through the use of slave codes, further reinforcing societal norms of a racial hierarchy and white supremacy (Durant, 1999), in which whites constructed meanings, possessed the highest value, and maintained control. By not being regarded as a member of society, Blacks were largely forbidden from gaining access to education (Goodell, 1853), which was withheld to prevent enlightenment and rebellion. A member of the Virginia House of Delegates in 1832 stated, "We have, as far as possible, closed every avenue by which light might enter their [slave's] minds. If we could extinguish the capacity to see the light, our work would be completed; they would then be on a level with the beasts of the field, and we should be safe!" (as cited in Goodell, 1853, p. 301). Slave codes required the enslaved and, to a greater extent, freed Blacks to maintain a level of passivity toward whites, and withheld from them ways of exercising the right of self-defense. A Louisiana statute stated, "Free people of colour ought never to insult or strike white people, nor presume to conceive themselves equal to the whites; but, on the contrary, they ought to yield to them on every occasion, and never speak or answer them but with respect, but under penalty *of imprisonment*, according to the nature of the offence" (as cited in Goodell, 1853, p. 335). Thomas Durant (1999) also pointed out the plantation society's reliance on Southern racial and cultural hegemonic traditions as a means of social control. Like the cultural and racial stratification that took the place of white supremacy and Black subordination, the modern university maintains its own ethos of white-framed foundation (Wilder, 2013) and modern symbols and practices of white institutional space (Gusa, 2010; Moore, 2008). Such foundational ideology and broad adoption of societal practices informed the views that enslaved Blacks could be treated as property, and is the same ideology that informs the adoption of social control mechanisms against those speaking out, which often results in their silencing.

In a closed system, boundary maintenance preserved the inner workings of the slave plantation, ensuring a continued smooth operation. Donald Yates (1999) points to the slave plantation's reliance on "white patrols" (p. 36) to keep the enslaved on the plantations and to maintain social control, and on "demotions and humiliations" (p. 38), with penalties or outright public humiliation, in order to preserve the system. While intended for the security of the campus, the campus police often take on this role of patrolling Black and Brown students, and demonstrate an increased presence at events and within spaces populated by those students (McCabe, 2009). The increased police presence, and the pattern of overpolicing, has a long history. Early examples, from the response to the 1924 Fisk University marching protest to the fatal response to the

1972 Southern University protests, show little difference from protocol used in modern times, in particular the use of the tools of war (tanks and soldiers) to police the voices and bodies of Students of Color. More recently, faculty and student protests against the addition of a private police force at Johns Hopkins University demonstrate a continued resistance to boundary maintenance mechanisms targeting historically minoritized student populations at universities.

State and Campus Response

In the recent wave of campus activism, university administrators and public officials have been embroiled in a debate about exactly how to respond to student protesters and the methods they have used to protest (Adams, 2017). While some have empathized with and advocated for the right of students to voice their frustration and engage in activism, others have called for the curbing of students *interfering* with the free speech and expression rights of those being protested. In early 2017, the Goldwater Institute, a conservative think tank and policy center, developed a legislative proposal aimed at encouraging states to adopt language that would curb protesters' interfering with another's right to free speech, limit the ability of institutions to engage in discourse on issues of public controversy, and require institutions to adopt policies sanctioning students' engaging in protests that interfere with the free speech rights of others (Kurtz et al., 2017). At least twelve states have introduced or adopted legislative language requiring public institutions to adopt broad statements of support for free speech, forbid campuses from taking positions on speech-related issues, and even going as far as sanctioning students for *infringing* on the expressive rights of others (Quintana & Thomason, 2017). Those states include California, Colorado, Illinois, Louisiana, Michigan, New Hampshire, North Carolina, Tennessee, Texas, Utah, Virginia, and Wisconsin. While this chapter focuses on legislation and policies directly affecting colleges and universities, there are other states with similar legislation extending beyond college campuses and limiting the ability of protesters to occupy public roadways or interfere with individuals' rights within any public space (Ingraham, 2017; Quintana & Thomason, 2017). Of these twelve states, all have language reinforcing protections outlined in the First Amendment or similar language in state constitutions. Eight states denied the ability of campuses to designate certain public outside areas as "free-speech zones," and six require universities to remain neutral on matters of public controversy. Most concerning, however, are the five states (Illinois, Louisiana, North Carolina, Texas, and Wisconsin) requiring public colleges and universities to develop sanctions punishing student activists for exercising their constitutionally protected right to protest if they re found to have interfered with the rights of others. Specifically, institutions would be required to sanction students, in some cases involving expulsion from the institution, for engaging in speech that "disrupts" the rights of others.

As recently as January 2018, the Texas Senate convened a hearing to discuss the issue of free speech on campus. The hearing occurred after white supremacist flyers had been posted on several campuses, and "alt-right" speaker Richard Spencer had visited Texas A&M University for a hosted presentation. This hearing indicates an important connection between contested spaces on college campuses and the ability of the state to push policy. Specifically, the interim changes presented by the Texas Senate are to "ascertain any restrictions on Freedom of Speech rights that Texas students face in expressing their views on campus along with freedoms of the press, religion, and assembly. Recommend [are] policy changes that protect First Amendment rights and enhance the free speech environment on campus" (Texas Senate Committee on State Affairs, 2018).

While these statements have the appearance of neutrality, it should be noted that this hearing convened after a student-led newspaper called attention to the lack of denouncement of hate speech by individuals in positions of power, as well as the vocal protests of students at Texas Southern University to a speech by a senator with a history of campaign support from alt-right and anti-LGBTQ organizations. Despite students' expressed concern about feeling unsafe on campuses with white supremacist flyers, the response by university and state leaders was to reaffirm the very structure that enables such oppression. By enabling hate speech—either by granting speaking privileges to alt-right/white supremacists or by not addressing the posting of white supremacist literature on campus, universities are, at best, reaffirming the systems of oppression. At worst, universities are creating the necessary conditions in which their most vulnerable populations experience violence, and are limiting educational freedoms aimed at maintaining a level of social control.

The University of Wisconsin system preemptively adopted a policy on freedom of expression that would "require suspension for a student who has twice been found responsible and expulsion for a student who [has] thrice been found responsible for disruption of freedom of expression"

(University of Wisconsin System, 2017), mirroring legislation at the state level. This policy was lauded as a measure to protect individuals' freedom of speech, though it went even further by preventing discourse and threatening students with sanctions in an attempt to prevent students from voicing their opinions or positions on societal issues. It is extremely important, however, that these policies and legislative actions grossly underestimate the role of white supremacy and systemic racism embedded within American colleges and Universities.

Durant (1999) notes that laws of race and slavery were intertwined in the plantation society. Landowning and nonslaveholding whites were frequently governed by one set of laws, and enslaved and freed Black, by another. By the nature of the enslaved being Black, and landowners and their nonslaveholding counterparts being white, these laws were further codified into laws of race. These laws helped inform the racial hierarchy of white superiority and Black subordination still in existence today (Durant, 1999). White racial domination occurred during the plantation society by institutionalizing laws that were largely based on race and positioned power over the minoritized group.

To be sure, these proposed pieces of legislation affecting campus resistance movements are not that different. While race-neutral on the surface, the current speech legislation working its way through the legislative halls disproportionately targets the voices of racially minoritized students, faculty, and staff speaking out against acts of racism and constant threats to their existence. Wisconsin's proposed Campus Free Speech Act states in part "that it is not the proper role of an institution to shield individuals from speech protected by the First Amendment of the US Constitution, including ideas and opinions they find unwelcome, disagreeable, or even deeply offensive. . . . That each institution shall strive to remain neutral, as an institution, on the public policy controversies of the day, and may not take action, as an institution, on the public policy controversies of the day in such a way as to require students or faculty to publicly express a given view of social policy" (A. B. 299, 2017). A crucial discursive component of this legislation is its color-blind approach and attempt to minimize the effects of racism (Bonilla-Silva, 2010) by drawing attention away from racist practices and institutional structures. Being codified into legislation, it adds considerable weight to the balance of power between the state and the institution. For racially minoritized students, it serves as a state strategy (Harney & Moten, 2013) of social control to eliminate or reduce deviancy from those who resist (Squire et al., 2018) and a reinforcement of white institutional space (Gusa, 2010; Moore, 2008).

From a mechanical perspective, policies may not appear to be racist on the surface yet can still function as a vehicle to reproduce racism and economic, political, and cultural power (Gillborn, 2005; van Dijk, 1993). In fact, when the University of Wisconsin adopted its system-wide policy mirroring the state's proposed legislation, the president of the board of regents stated that adopting the policy "shows a responsiveness to what's going on in the Capitol, which helps build relationships" (Richmond, 2017). This illustrates the political power relationship between the board of the university and the state legislature's control of funding allocations for the public institutions.

Social Control as Plantation Pedagogy

In his focus on the dialectical relationship between teacher-student and student-teacher identities, Freire (2008) asserts the necessity and practicality of protest within systems of oppression. However, in the context of white supremacy, the rules for acceptable discourse are not mutually agreed upon, and an exertion of control and power creates an imbalance placing minoritized communities at a disadvantage. Students who do not conform or who resist or subvert the university are thus clearly rejecting the internalization of white supremacy, and thus re a *threat* to the order and social control power of the institution (Bristol, 2010).

University leaders, heavily influenced by the desire to keep funding entities content, are quick to implement policy or *remain silent* on legislative matters that may affect the bottom line of the institution. This is clearly evident in the comment by the University of Wisconsin system president about a desire "to build relationships" with state lawmakers by preemptively implementing a policy prior to proposed state legislation being passed. It reinforces a systematic linkage between the university and social policy. These linkages often get masked under the neoliberal imperatives of *professionalism* and *civility*, yet the plantation parallel is that the agency of anyone who resists is threatened with removal (Squire et al., 2018) and deemed a subversion to the established dominant class habitus of education (Bourdieu & Passeron, 1990).

Education often carries an assumption of freedom, democratic participation, and economic progress within the larger society. Yet, as Laurette Bristol (2010) asserts, the educational practice of a plantation pedagogy maintains a "patriarchal understanding of the transfer of knowledge" (p. 173). It is rooted in a relationship between the educational institution and society, organized along the lines of a plantation economy through mutually supportive linkages to maintain public harmony or allow limited leeway for Students of Color to feel a sense of humanity (Squire et al., 2018). These linkages are illuminated in the relationships between university programs and policy, and interests established outside the institution.

A distinct characteristic of slave codes was their ability to empower any white person to reinforce their dominance over any Black person on a whim (Durant, 1999; Squire et al., 2018). In Texas, for example, Senate Bill 18 was signed into law in June 2019, requiring universities to "establish disciplinary sanctions for students, student organizations, or faculty who unduly interfere with the expressive activities of others on campus" (S. B. 18, 2019). While the law reinforces principles of free speech, without defining "interference," it deters insurrection by those who may disagree with oppressive or racist speech acts. States and the institutions adopting this type of language empower any (white) person to discipline students for actions deemed as interference—a broad declaration.

State actions aimed at further controlling behaviors of students limit full participation in society by completely ignoring their voices or threatening their organization altogether. White and cultural hegemony within Southern society very much favored and justified the behaviors of social control in order to maintain this dominance. As Craig Steven Wilder (2013) asserts, higher education institutions were founded not to advance educational freedom and inquiry but rather to expand colonialist control, and to support a religious orthodoxy and a cultural ethos that have maintained their existence in higher education institutions to this day. As noted earlier, further manifestations are being seen at Johns Hopkins University, where Black student activists decried the university's plan to add a private police force to an overpoliced Baltimore (Richman, 2019). This is also evident in university administrators' quicker responses condemning the methods of activism than acts of racism and white supremacy themselves (see Bauer-Wolf, 2017; Flaherty, 2017; Morse, 2017).

Freire (2008) offers his concept of "false charity" (p. 45) to describe the actions of the oppressor class (whites) to bestow generosity to the oppressed, doing little to disrupt or destroy the causes of the oppression. For example, during the civil rights movement of the 1950s and 1960s, white students and Students of Color protested segregated learning environments and unequal resources. This Freedom Summer movement, and the Freedom School movement, in parallel to the larger civil rights movement, was a turning point of student activism because it directly engaged privileged students, faculty, and administrators, as well as minoritized Students of Color (McAdam, 1990). While these coalitions resulted in some educational progress, they also met with their share of opponents. Many white educational administrators and state leaders delivered a backlash against student and community protesters out of fear of losing control of their student population or fear of losing economic or societal status (McAdam, 1990). To quell these protests by introducing and enacting policies and legislation that reinforce a sense of power, superiority, and paternalistic control over students' ability to protest or to resist in the face of oppression instead regulates it to the margins of campus, where it can be more easily ignored.

This pedagogical messaging reinforces the false charity and reifies an assumed hegemonic structure of control in which the (white) educator is bestowing the gift of education upon a presumed "unworthy" population. Bristol's (2010) challenge to the white colonizing narrative subverts the process of educating for compliance by focusing on the manner in which Students of Color already possess the skills for activism and agency through collective behavior and recognition of their own ability to establish a narrative of liberation.

Envisioning the Future

In order to remake our college and university campuses into just places where white supremacy is abolished and economic, political, and social power is equalized, emancipatory praxis must be at the forefront of education. Educators need to reimagine what campus and state policy, as well as authority, might look like.

In 1894, Frederick Douglass delivered a speech at the Manassas Industrial School in which he stated, "Education . . . means emancipation. . . . It means the uplifting [of] the soul of man in to the glorious light of truth, the light by which men can only be made free" (Douglass, 1894). Douglass was speaking at a time when nonwhite persons were forbidden to assemble for the purpose of education, however, his quote can also provide a critique to modern campus policy and state legislation attempting to silence student voices or to simply dismiss any wave of student activism as a disturbance. In his historical analysis of American colleges and universities, Wilder (2013) documents how institutions were not established to deliver emancipatory outcomes; rather, they were set up as a means of white colonial propaganda directed at civilizing indigenous populations with the goal of preventing or controlling violence directed toward the colonial population. Much like the historic period during the Freedom Summer, and on a national rather than predominantly regional scale, colleges and universities are once again the focal point of many within society that feel that the curriculum is far too liberal, and that the students, faculty, and administrators of many universities are becoming too radical and should be removed or significantly quelled. Campus politics are heavily influenced and controlled by individuals with significant power and influence over the institution's resources. It is precisely this type of power and control over financial resources and academic freedom, exerted over college faculty, administrators, and students, that has slowed the progress of racial and social justice, and has been a continued force to reckon with throughout the history of American higher education. The historical ties of power within the American university system have been previously documented yet seldom addressed from a systemic perspective.

As the educational and political landscape in the country continues to evolve, educators, scholars, and even policymakers must not look to the student as a voiceless receptacle into which learning is simply deposited (Freire, 2008). Scholars have previously documented the role student activism can play in student development (Astin, 1975; Kezar, 2010), transforming civil society (McAdam, 1990), and civic engagement (Jacoby, 2017; Rhoads, 1998). Institutional leaders must see students as individuals with all their possessed knowledge, lived experiences, and solutions to some of the more complex issues plaguing our campuses and societies. Students must be provided with the opportunities to develop their voices, defend their opinions, and actively engage with others as a part of their activism. Anything less should be viewed as an act limiting the educational attainment of students and a detriment to the future of civil discourse.

The resurgence of resistance to the systemic issues of racism and acts of white supremacy being seen on campuses do not always begin with the "shouting down" of campus leaders or with the more physical forms of resistance. In fact, minoritized students quite regularly attempt to address campus leaders through "proper" channels only to be met with empty promises or ignored altogether (Hoffman & Mitchell, 2016; Kezar & Maxey, 2014). These silenced students instead become institutional scapegoats who disrupt the cultural traditions and practices of the institution. They are provided with pedagogical messages of neglect and passivity. Campus leaders and policymakers ignore the "knowledge and skills fostered through oppositional behavior that challenges inequality" (Yosso, 2005, p. 80). Oppressed students regularly receive messages that their struggle is not recognized or does not warrant consideration by the university (Suoranta & FitzSimmons, 2017). Therefore, we challenge institutional leaders and those engaged in this work to interrogate more deeply the institution's history, the messages being sent to students with marginalized identities, and the institution's role in maintaining that oppression.

Institutional leaders, researchers, and policymakers need to "explicitly discuss the role of racism/white supremacy in the academy" (Patton, 2016, p. 335). They must begin to grapple with the idea of how policies, legislation, and (in)action affect those students and institutional community members who constantly struggle to see themselves within an institutional structure that was built not *for* them but *by* them. As pointed out by Barbara Jacoby (2017) and Adrianna Kezar (2010), institutional leaders must begin to support student activists in their developmental journey as students and as societal change agents. If institutional leaders and state policymakers followed those closest to the pain and considered the voices of student activists as an exercise of leadership and a form of cultural wealth (Yosso, 2005), they might respond differently. Present-day student activists point to the university classroom as a pedagogical site for Black liberation, call upon institutional leaders to *teach* and *do* interrogations of whiteness, and collectively push beyond the institutional bondage of white supremacy (Haynes & Bazner, 2019). Instead of writing neutral and objective papers that minimize the effects of racism and white supremacy (Harper, 2012), students and researchers should expose schools as masks of systemic dominance and privilege.

Moving forward, it is imperative for university and political leaders alike to engage in reflection and interrogation of our collective history and envisioned future. The reality is that most institutional leaders seemingly desire to condemn overt acts of racism and its effects. Yet when confronted with entrenched white supremacy, leaders retreat into the comfort of their current privileges and position themselves above the messy implications of rebellious struggle. To be sure, the management of universities has never been an easy task for the leaders of these institutions, who must balance the needs of multiple constituent groups and power relationships, as illustrated throughout this chapter and as seen in the historical works of Hubert Park Beck (1947), Frederick Rudolph (2011), and Wilder (2013). Students, especially Black students, should never feel that they have to maintain a level of conformity, or be afraid to question contemporary means of institutional social control. In fact, they should be rewarded with gratification when calling attention to these tensions and processual elements of the modern university.

In the eyes of those with power and social dominance, there will never be such a thing as a perfect protest. As institutions of higher education face a deeper entrenched neoliberal agenda, it becomes increasingly important to envision the university as a constant arena of struggle and develop a level of critical consciousness (Freire, 2008) that allows an examination of the association of white supremacy, institutionalization, and calls for social control. And it is increasingly important to engage in *action* disrupting their preservation.

References

A. B. 299, 2017 Biennium, 2017 Reg. Sess. (Wis. 2017).

Adams, L. (2017, October 19). Heckling is a staple of controversial campus speeches. Should colleges intervene? *The Chronicle of Higher Education*. https://www.chronicle.com/article/Heckling-Is-a-Staple-of/241504

Astin, A. W. (1975). *The power of protest: A national study of student and faculty disruptions with implications for the future.* Jossey-Bass.

Bauer-Wolf, J. (2017, December 1). Column starts a culture war. *Inside Higher Ed.* https://www.insidehighered.com/news/2017/12/01/texas-state-president-blasts-racist-student-column

Beck, H. P. (1947). *Men who control our universities: The economic and social composition of governing boards of thirty leading American universities.* King's Crown Press.

Bonilla-Silva, E. (2010). *Racism without racists: Color-blind racism and the persistence of racial inequality in the United States.* Rowman & Littlefield.

Bourdieu, P., & Passeron, J. C. (1990). *Reproduction in education, society, and culture* (Vol. 4). Sage.

Bristol, L. (2010). Practising in betwixt oppression and subversion: plantation pedagogy as a legacy of plantation economy in Trinidad and Tobago. *Power and education, 2*(2), 167–82.

Broadhurst, C. J. (2014). Campus activism in the 21st century: A historical framing. *New Directions for Higher Education, 2014*(167), 3–15.

Calloway, C. G. (2010). *The Indian history of an American institution: Native Americans and Dartmouth.* University Press of New England.

Concerned Student 1950. (2015, October 20). List of demands to the University of Missouri. *The Demands.* http://www.thedemands.org/

Douglass, F. (1894, September 3). Speech at the dedication of the Manassas VA. Industrial School. [Manuscript/mixed material]. Library of Congress. https://www.loc.gov/item/mfd.26011/

Durant Jr., T. J. (1999). The slave plantation revisited: A sociological perspective. In T. J. Durant & J. D. Knottnerus (Eds.). *Plantation society and race relations: The origins of inequality* (pp. 3–15). Praeger.

Durkheim, E. (1956). Education and Sociology: Glencoe. *The Free Press*, 27(87), 124–26.

Fingerhut, H. (2017, July 20). Republicans skeptical of colleges' impact on U.S., but most see benefits for workforce preparation. *Pew Research Center*. http://www.pewresearch.org/fact-tank/2017/07/20/republicans-skeptical-of-colleges-impact-on-u-s-but-most-see-benefits-for-workforce-preparation/

Flaherty, C. (2017, June 26). Professors are often political lightning rods but now are facing new threats over views, particularly on race. *Inside Higher Ed*. https://www.insidehighered.com/news/2017/06/26/professors-are-often-political-lightning-rods-now-are-facing-new-threats-over-their

Freire, P. (2008). *Pedagogy of the oppressed*. Bloomsbury Publishing.

Gillborn, D. (2005). Education policy as an act of white supremacy: Whiteness, critical race theory and education reform. *Journal of Education Policy*, 20(4), 485–505.

Goodell, W. (1853). *The American slave code in theory and practice its distinctive features shown by its statutes, judicial decisions, and illustrative facts*. 3rd ed. American and Foreign Anti-Slavery Society.

Goodwin, J., & Jasper, J. M. (Eds.). (2014). *The social movements reader: Cases and concepts*. John Wiley & Sons.

Green, A. (2015, November 09). The financial calculations: Why Tim Wolfe had to resign. *The Atlantic*. https://www.theatlantic.com/business/archive/2015/11/mizzou-tim-wolfe-resignation/414987

Gusa, D. L. (2010). White institutional presence: The impact of whiteness of campus climate. *Harvard Educational Review*, 80, 464–90.

Harney, S., & Moten, F. (2013). *The undercommons: Fugitive planning and Black study*. Minor Compositions.

Harper, S. R. (2012). Race without racism: How higher education researchers minimize racist institutional norms. *The Review of Higher Education*, 36(1), 9–29.

Haynes, C., & Bazner, K. J. (2019). A message for faculty from the present-day movement for Black lives. *International Journal of Qualitative Studies in Education*. Advance online publication. DOI: 10.1080/09518398.2019.1645909

Hoffman, G. D., & Mitchell, T. D. (2016). Making diversity "everyone's business": A discourse analysis of institutional responses to student activism for equity and inclusion. *Journal of Diversity in Higher Education*, 9(3), 277.

Ingersoll, T. N. (1995). Slave codes and judicial practice in New Orleans, 1718–1807. *Law and History Review, 13*(1), 23–62.

Ingraham, C. (2017, February 24). Republican lawmakers introduce bills to curb protesting in at least 18 states. *The Washington Post*. https://www.washingtonpost.com/news/wonk/wp/2017/02/24/republican-lawmakers-introduce-bills-to-curb-protesting-in-at-least-17-states/?utm_term=.5703d6f263ca

Jacoby, B. (2017). The new student activism: Supporting students as agents of social change. *Journal of College and Character, 18*(1), 1–8.

Kezar, A. (2010). Faculty and staff partnering with student activists: Unexplored terrains of interaction and development. *Journal of College Student Development, 51*(5), 451–80.

Kezar, A., & Maxey, D. (2014). Collective action on campus toward student development and democratic engagement. *New Directions for Higher Education, 2014*(167), 31–41.

Kurtz, S., Manley, J., & Butcher, J. (2017). *Campus free speech: A legislative proposal*. Goldwater Institute.

Mahar, C., Wilkes, C., & Harker, R. K. (Eds.). (1990). *An introduction to the work of Pierre Bourdieu: The practice of theory*. St. Martin's Press.

Maurer, J. G. (1971). *Readings in organization theory: Open-system approaches*. Random House.

McAdam, D. (1990). *Freedom summer*. Oxford University Press.

McCabe, J. (2009). Racial and gender microaggressions on a predominantly-white campus: Experiences of Black, Latina/o and white undergraduates. *Race, Gender & Class, 16*(1–2), 133–51.

Miller, M. E. (2015, November 6). Black grad student on hunger strike in Mo. after swastika drawn with human feces. *The Washington Post*. https://www.washingtonpost.com/news/morning-mix/wp/2015/11/06/black-grad-student-on-hunger-strike-in-mo-after-swastika-drawn-with-human-feces/?utm_term=.af19c69ab19e

Moore, W. L. (2008). *Reproducing racism: White space, elite law schools, and racial inequality*. Rowman & Littlefield.

Morse, B. (2017, May 10). President Young responds to controversial comments made by A&M professor Tommy Curry. *The Battalion*. http://www.thebatt.com/news/president-young-responds-to-controversial-comments-made-by-a-m/article_36b06da6-35ff-11e7-96ff-137c02893705.html

National Conference on State Legislatures (NCSL). (2017, August 1). State partisan composition. http://www.ncsl.org/research/about-state-legislatures/partisan-composition.aspx

Patton, L. D. (2016). Disrupting postsecondary prose: Toward a critical race theory of higher education. *Urban Education, 51*(3), 315–42.

Quintana, C., & Thomason, A. (2017, May 15). The states where campus free-speech bills are being born: A rundown. *The Chronicle of Higher Education*. https://www.chronicle.com/article/The-States-Where-Campus/240073

Reilly, K. (2017, May 24). Middlebury has sanction students for shutting down Charles Murray's lecture. *Time Magazine*. time.com/4792694/middlebury-college-discipline-charles-murray-protest/

Rhoads, R. A. (1998). *Freedom's web: Student activism in an age of cultural diversity*. The Johns Hopkins University Press.

Richman, T. (2019, April 22). What's next for the Johns Hopkins police force? University prepares for rollout as protests continue. *The Baltimore Sun*. https://www.baltimoresun.com/education/bs-md-ci-hopkins-police-next-steps-20190418-story.html

Richmond, T. (2017, October 6). University of Wisconsin approves free speech policy that punishes student protesters. *The Chicago Tribune*. http://www.chicagotribune.com/news/nationworld/midwest/ct-university-of-wisconsin-protest-punishment-20171006-story.html

Rudolph, F. (2011). *The American college and university: A history*. University of Georgia Press.

Saha, L. J. (1997). *International encyclopedia of the sociology of education*. Pergamon Pr.

S. B. 18, 86(R) Session, 2019. (Tex. 2019).

Schmich, M. (2015, November 10). University of Missouri student protesters' missteps part of their college education. *The Chicago Tribune*. http://www.chicagotribune.com/news/columnists/schmich/ct-university-of-missouri-mary-schmich-1111-20151110-column.html

Squire, D., Williams, B. C., & Tuitt, F. (2018). Plantation politics and neoliberal racism in higher education: A framework for reconstructing anti-racist institutions. *Teachers College Record*, *120*(14), 1–20.

Suoranta, J., & FitzSimmons, R. (2017). The silenced students: Student resistance in a corporatized university. *Cultural Studies ↔ Critical Methodologies*, *17*(3), 277–85.

Texas Senate Committee on State Affairs. (2018, January 31). The Texas State Senate [Cong. Doc. from 85th Session Interim Cong.]. http://www.senate.texas.gov/cmte.php?c=570

Thelin, J. R. (2011). *A history of American higher education*. The Johns Hopkins University Press.

University of Wisconsin System. (2017, October 6). UW Regents approve new policy on freedom of expression on campus (day 2 news summary). *News*. https://www.wisconsin.edu/news/archive/uw-regents-approve-new-policy-on-freedom-of-expression-on-campus-day-2-news-summary/

van Dijk, T. A. (1993). *Analyzing racism through discourse analysis: Some methodological reflections*. Sage Publications.

Weber, M. (2009). *The theory of social and economic organization*. Simon & Schuster. (Original work published 1947)

Wilder, C. S. (2013). *Ebony and ivy: Race, slavery, and the troubled history of America's universities*. Bloomsbury Publishing.

Wright, B. (1988). "For the children of the infidels"? American Indian education in the colonial colleges. *American Indian Culture and Research Journal, 12*(3), 1–14.

Yates, D. L. (1999). Plantation-style social control: Oppressive social structures in the slave plantation system. In T. Durant & J. D. Knottnerus (Eds.), *Plantation society and race relations: The origins of inequity* (pp. 29–40). Praeger.

Yosso, T. J. (2005). Whose culture has capital? A critical race theory discussion of community cultural wealth. *Race ethnicity and education, 8*(1), 69–91.

Zirin, D. (2015, December 15). "Plantation politics": Racist legislation stalks the Mizzou football team. *The Nation.* https://www.thenation.com/article/plantation-politics-racist-legislation-stalks-the-mizzou-football-team/

Chapter 12

"When Lions Have Historians"
Black Political Literacy in the Carceral University

Orisanmi Burton

It is well known that the prohibition of slave literacy was central to the maintenance of the plantation system in the antebellum South. Following the Stono Rebellion of 1739 and intensifying after the Nat Turner Rebellion of 1831, the planter bloc in various slaveholding states passed legislation prohibiting people to teach enslaved Africans to read and write (Genovese 1976, 1992). Adopting the voice of his enslaver, Frederick Douglass (2003) explained compulsory Black illiteracy as a strategy of plantation management:

> A nigger should know nothing but to obey his master—to do as he is told to do. Learning would *spoil* the best nigger in the world. "Now," said he "if you teach that nigger (speaking of myself) how to read there would be no keeping him. It would forever unfit him to be a slave. He would at once become unmanageable, and of no value to his master." (p. 64)

According to Douglass, the planter bloc understood that a literate enslaved population could more easily enact subversive politics. They could forge passes or freedom papers, produce abolitionist propaganda, access cartographic data, and circulate insurrectionary plans. According to historian

Ed Baptist, "Compulsory illiteracy was necessary to restrict access to ideas about freedom," and thus secure reproduction of the slave system (Baptist, 2014, p. 209).

The framework of this volume—that US universities and slave plantations are enjoined by "parallel organizational and cultural norms" (Squire et al., 2018, p. 2)—obliges us to consider how the impetus for the historical prohibition on slave literacy continues to animate contemporary Black education. I argue that while formal prohibitions of Black literacy are no longer codified in law, a de facto proscription of what I am calling Black political literacy remains firmly in place. According to Damien Sojoyner (2016, p. xi), education is the "linchpin" of the US nation-state's reactionary assault on Black social mobilization. It is a *preemptive* assault upon the very possibility of Black mobilization, an assault achieved through a series of ideological, cultural, and intellectual enclosures that often remain undetected. However, following Eli Meyerhoff (2019), I argue that education is but one among many different modes of study. There are other configurations, ethical foundations, and sites of knowledge production and transmission. These alternative modes of study can summon alternative worlds that are not so entwined with white supremacist, colonial, patriarchal, and capitalist logics.

By "Black political literacy" I mean the capacity to "read" between, beyond, and against the hegemony of the education-based mode of study and its authorized texts. I also mean the capacity to "write" alternative scripts that imagine, recover, and enact Black liberationist futures through praxis. In order to obtain this form of literacy, the subjects of study must come to see education as a site of ideological struggle rather than one of transcendental freedom and equality.

Moreover, as important as it is, formal literacy—the technical ability to read and write—is not sufficient for Black political literacy, as it commonly results in what singer Curtis Mayfield called "educated fools from uneducated schools" (Mayfield 1970).

This chapter focuses on my attempts to generate Black political literacy by introducing Black and Latinx undergraduate students enrolled in a criminal justice program to the self-directed mode of study generated via Black radical prison movements. In the first section, I elaborate the structural, ideological, and practical continuities between universities, prisons, and slave plantations. I then draw on the thought and praxis of imprisoned members of the Black Panther Party (BPP) and the Black Liberation Army (BLA) to demonstrate how the historical orientation of formalized education in prisons and universities regulates Black political literacy in an effort to maintain a manageable Black population. In the final section, I discuss my own attempts to engender Black political literacy within, against, and beyond the education-based mode of study. In particular, I focus on how I introduced my students to the concept of ideology and hegemony, and engaged them in discussions around the National Strike Against Prison Slavery of 2016, which unfolded throughout the semester. I resist the temptation to present my pedagogical practice as a success because it would play into the seductive tendency to present education as a transcendental force for progress. At best, my efforts in the classroom helped students situate what they were learning (and what they were not) within the context of a broader political struggle over ideas about freedom. However, the fact remains that we are still ensnared within a plantation regime.

Universities and Prisons as Sites of Plantation Politics

Universities and prisons are key nodes in a contemporary plantation system. The contemporary plantation is distinct from those of the antebellum South insofar as it is not a discrete geographical terrain; rather, the neoplantation is a geographically dispersed network of institutions, ideologies, and social practices that bolster racial capitalism—the prevailing political economic system in which a minority elite accumulates wealth and power at the expense of a racialized and increasingly disposable majority. While the prison and the university are both sites of labor exploitation, I argue that their primary role with regard to plantation politics is to secure a *generalized condition of exploitability* for those that lie *beyond* their (diffuse) institutional boundaries.

It is by now well established that with 2.3 million people behind bars, the United States is the world's foremost carceral state and that the targets of this massive carceral project are overwhelmingly economically poor Black people and other people of color (Alexander, 2012; Gottschalk, 2014). There is a massive corpus of literature detailing the intimate relationship between US prisons and slave plantations (Childs, 2015; A. Y. Davis, 1998; James, 2005; McKittrick, 2011). Much of this scholarship orbits around the exception in the Thirteenth Amendment to the US Constitution, which reformed chattel slavery into a potential punishment for a crime. Following the demise of radical reconstruction, the imbrication of prisons and chattel slavery ensured that formerly enslaved people remained available as unfree labor via systems of convict leasing. These systems, which in the words of Angela Y. Davis (1998, p. 75) "transferred symbolically significant numbers of Black people from the prison of slavery to the slavery of prison," persisted throughout the first half of the twentieth century (Blackmon, 2009).

Within the walls of contemporary prisons, plantation politics are enacted via the near total subjection of captive populations to the will of the "master-state" (James, 2005). Indeed, roughly 700,000 prison captives are put to work, performing the various forms of labor required to keep prisons running (Gilmore & Kilgore, 2019; Schwartzapfel, 2016; Stein, 2017). Thousands more work for prison industries for which they produce material goods such as office furniture, equipment, and uniforms, which by law must be sold to other state institutions, including universities, via monopoly contracts (Heiner, 2015). The average remuneration for captive laborers in state prisons ranges from $0 per hour to $1.41 per hour, figures that are indeed tantamount to "slave wages" (Sawyer, 2017). Responding to this condition, imprisoned people have long described themselves as slaves (Berger, 2014; Jackson, 1994/1970; James, 2005; Shakur, 2001).

However, the very real conditions of labor exploitation within US prisons are often misrecognized as the prison's raison d'être, obscuring the broader dynamic at play. Prisons are primarily concerned neither with labor exploitation nor with generating profit for corporations. This explains why *the majority of incarcerated people do not work at all*, and why, of those who do, just over 5,000 of them work for private corporations (C. Gilmore, 2019; R. W. Gilmore, 2007; Gilmore & Kilgore, 2019). In her book *Golden Gulag*, Marxist geographer Ruth Wilson Gilmore explains that beginning in the early 1970s, California's elite class fractions mobilized prison expansion as a strategy for absorbing surplus land, labor, finance capital, and state capacity, thereby (temporarily) resolving a crisis capital overaccumulation that appeared in the post-Keynesian state (R. W. Gilmore, 2007). From this perspective, the massive expansion of human caging that exploded in the 1970s was not a conspiracy to extract slave labor from captives inside the walls (although this did take place on a limited scale) but rather a mechanism for removing surplus populations from circulation, neutralizing their labor power, and thus for securing the conditions of generalized exploitability for workers *outside the prison walls*. Consider the fact that while 2.3 million people are currently imprisoned in the United States, at least 65 million have a criminal record and can therefore legally be excluded from various forms of work. In the words of Ruth Wilson Gilmore, this means that "half of the US labor force is documented not to work" (Gilmore & Kilgore, 2019).

Like prisons, US universities also have historical linkages and contemporary parallels to slave plantations. As Craig Steven Wilder (2013) has shown, elite universities established during the antebellum period were constructed on stolen indigenous land using enslaved Black labor. University benefactors, many of whom amassed their wealth from the plantation economy, mobilized their economic influence to shape the production and circulation of knowledge in ways that naturalized Native genocide, Black enslavement, and white supremacy. Khalil Gibran Muhammad (2010) has shown how university-based scholars mobilized the burgeoning fields of statistics, sociology, and criminology to establish a spurious yet enduring association between Blackness and criminality as a means of legitimating Black subjugation.

The contemporary university is increasingly organized through plantation and carceral logics (Ferguson, 2012; Meyerhoff, 2019). Universities employ exploitative labor practices resulting in the generalized disposability of university staff and faculty, producing especially brutal effects for the "adjunct-majority," some of whom have been pushed into the informal economy (Gee, 2017). Like the techniques of agricultural productivity developed on antebellum slave plantations, metrics of scholarly "productivity" are strictly enforced under the threat of punitive measures (Baptist, 2014; Ferguson, 2012). Curricular priorities authorize the circulation of particular kinds of narratives while silencing others. Universities have progressively succumbed to neoliberal regimes of management that prioritize the monetization of knowledge. They have underfunded and shuttered critical and potentially radical programs that fail to "add value" to the university's bottom line (Giroux, 2002). University administrators are increasingly capitulating to pressure from right-wing and white supremacist organizations seeking to systematically silence leftist professors through public smear campaigns (Eltagouri, 2017; Kolowich, 2017). Campus security patrol and surveil university campuses in racially targeted ways, a point that was driven home to me in ironic fashion when, while sitting in my campus office over the winter holiday, at work on this very essay, an armed campus police officer appeared at my door and compelled me to produce identification (freedom papers?) proving that I was faculty. Had I refused I may have been detained. Had I resisted I may have been shot.

The primary commodity of the university-cum-plantation is the exploitable worker. For perhaps the majority of young people, university education does not present itself as a "choice," or as simply one path among many leading to their ability to economically support themselves and their families. Rather, the omnipresent lash of late capitalism has rendered university education a compulsory regime. To meet the colossal financial obligations of university education, undergraduate students in the United States have collectively amassed nearly one and a half trillion dollars in student loan debt (Bloomberg, 2018). This debt is a form of unfreedom that channels its bearer, under the threat of imprisonment, toward the pursuit of "marketable" degrees that are more likely to yield financial returns, shackling them to the wage economy for the foreseeable future. This is the way of the contemporary plantation.

US Political Prisoners and the Regulation of Black Political Literacy

As Frederick Douglass's observation in this chapter's introduction makes clear, the survival of the plantation system necessitated the intellectual stultification of enslaved populations. Literacy, according to Douglass would make enslaved people "unmanageable" and would divest them of the "value" so maniacally sought by the planter bloc. But it was not simply the ability to read that was the threat, rather it was the possibility that literacy would enable new forms of insurrectionary study, strategy, planning, and action. Understanding this, Douglass and countless other enslaved people embarked upon the dangerous task of surreptitiously obtaining that which would make them unmanageable for the planter bloc.

In her *Autobiography*, written more than a century after Douglass's *Narrative*, Assata Shakur, the Black revolutionary activist and self-proclaimed "20th century escaped slave" (Shakur, 2014), explained the repressive function of formal education on Black populations in the following way:

> The schools we go to are a reflection of the society that created them. Nobody is going to give you the education you need to overthrow them. Nobody is going to teach you your true history, teach you your true heroes, if they know that that knowledge will help set you free. Schools in amerika are interested in

brainwashing people with amerikanism, giving them a little bit of education, and training them in skills needed to fill the positions the capitalist system requires. (Shakur, 2001, p. 181)

Shakur's analysis highlights the oft-obscured fact that formal education takes place within a broader context of political struggle. For Shakur, the function of education is not to liberate but rather to produce subjects that are available for exploitation. As such, certain formations of knowledge, particularly Black political literacies, which seeks to maintain connections between Black pupils and their intellectual and political inheritances, is seen as inherently threatening to the manageability and value of Black populations.

Shakur's evolution as an activist while enrolled in Manhattan Community College during the late 1960s is illustrative of how university education alone is not sufficient for the development of Black political literacy. Shakur supplemented her formal education by joining a student organization called the Golden Drums, which sought to infuse the university with knowledge "to help us free our people" (2001, p. 186). Like other formations in the burgeoning student movement on the 1960s, the Golden Drums asserted demands for a Black studies program and for more Black faculty on campus. They invited members from radical organizations such as the Young Lords and the Black Panthers to speak and they also launched a program to teach reading, writing, math, and Black history to young children. This campus activism developed in dialogue with community-based movements beyond the campus. Golden Drum members also belonged to a variety of Black organizations, such as the Nation of Islam, the Organization of Afro-American Unity, and the National Association for the Advancement of Colored People. Campus activism taught Shakur (2001) that "theory without practice is just as incomplete as practice without theory. The two have to go together. I was determined to do both" (p. 180). While still a student at Manhattan Community College, she joined the Black Panther Party.

Shakur's aboveground and underground activities with the BPP and later with the clandestine BLA ranged from administering the Free Breakfast for Children program to engaging in expropriations and armed struggle. These activities brought Shakur in direct confrontation with the forces of organized state violence, including FBI counterintelligence programs (COINTELPROs), often-illegal US government initiatives designed to "expose, disrupt, misdirect, discredit, or otherwise neutralize" Black radical organizations, and the BPP in particular (Churchill & Vander Wall, 2002b, p. 92). One of the imperatives of these COINTELPROs was to "prevent the long-range growth of militant black nationalist organizations, especially among youth" (p. 111). In other words, in the late 1960s, the forces of organized state violence became increasingly preoccupied not only with "neutralizing" extant revolutionary activists such as Assata Shakur but also with impeding the generational transmission of Black radical knowledge formations, thereby stunting the development of future activists. This is why the FBI also launched COINTELPROs against Black-owned bookstores and Black writers, and placed spies in university Black student unions throughout the United States (Churchill & Vander Wall, 2002a; Corson, 1970; J. C. Davis, 2018).

Shakur and her comrade Sundiata Acoli were arrested on May 3, 1973, following a shootout with New Jersey state troopers, which resulted in the deaths of Zayd Malik Shakur, another BPP/BLA member, and Werner Foerster, a trooper. Death and imprisonment were two of the government's primary modes of "neutralization," and yet imprisonment failed to contain the dissemination of Black political literacy. Instead, imprisoned intellectuals in the 1970s, like the insurgent enslaved Africans of the seventeenth, eighteenth, and nineteenth centuries, formed illicit study groups in which they continued to disseminate Black political literacy, thereby advancing broader efforts to achieve liberation within and beyond the prison. As Sundiata Acoli explained, "The jails are Universities of the Revolutionaries and the finishing schools of the Black Liberation Army. Come, brothers and sisters, meet Assata Shakur. She is here holding seminars in 'Getting Down,' 'Taming the Paper Tiger,' and 'The Selected Works of Zayd Malik Shakur.' So brothers and sisters do not fear jail. Many of you will go anyway—ignorance will be your crime. Others will come—awareness their only crime" (1973, p. 6). Taken together, Shakur and Acoli's reflections invert the dominant narratives about schools and prisons. They present the school—ostensibly a site of freedom, upward mobility, and transcendence—as a space of ideological incarceration and intellectual repression, while offering the prison—a space of overt repression, bodily captivity, and generalized dishonor—as the privileged site of intellectual and political development. In this way, they saw schools as more effective than the prisons in regulating Black political literacy. The repressive function of schools was more effectively mystified via discourses of transcendence, while the explicitly dehumanizing rituals of prisons acted as an accelerant to the captives' struggle to obtain Black political literacy through the unsanctioned archives of Black liberationist praxis (Rodríguez,

2006, 2010). Aided by the pedagogy of state repression, captive populations were compelled to analyze the material conditions of Black unfreedom and develop diverse methodologies of collective resistance. The forms of Black political literacy that circulated within prisons in the 1970s gave rise to forms of political rebellion that heralded the possibility of the prison's abolition. One national study identified 5 prison riots in 1967, 15 in 1968, 27 in 1970, 37 in 1971, and 48 in 1972 (Useem & Kimball, 1991), indicating an intensifying crisis of unmanageability among captive populations.

Assata Shakur escaped from prison in 1979. However, imprisoned intellectuals such as Acoli and Jalil Muntaqim, also a former BPP/BLA member, remain in prison after decades. Muntaqim has been in prison for more than 45 years and has been denied parole eleven times (Gross, 2019). In their most recent decision denying his parole, the New York State Parole Board claimed that Muntaqim's release "would be incompatible with the welfare of society," despite citing no evidence that the elderly teacher is a social threat.[1]

Although the FBI officially discontinued COINTELPRO operations in 1974, the forces of organized state violence continue to prioritize containing the spread of Black political literacy. In December 2016, Muntaqim was punished for teaching an administratively sanctioned Black history class in Attica, the New York State prison made famous by a massive rebellion in 1971. Muntaqim's lecture focused on the organization and ethics of the Black Panther Party, including its 10-Point Program, Codes of Conduct, and Eight Points of Attention. At one point during the lesson, which was video recorded, Muntaqim stated that the Bloods gang "could be the biggest army across this country if they were to organize themselves."[2] For this, Attica's administration charged Jalil with disciplinary violations, including "an inmate shall not engage in or encourage others in gang activities," "an inmate shall not engage in any violent conduct," and "an inmate shall not lead, organize, participate, or urge other inmates to participate, in a work-stoppage, sit-in, lock-in or other actions which may be detrimental to the order of facility."[3] Jalil was transferred to the supermax prison Southport Correctional Facility, where he was held in solitary confinement for nearly four months despite the fact that the United Nations, the Center for Constitutional Rights, and other agencies consider solitary confinement a form of torture (Boyd, 2018).

Muntaqim filed a lawsuit against the New York State Department of Corrections and Community Supervision in which it was argued that he had been unjustly punished for teaching a legitimate history lesson. The judges of the New York Supreme Court agreed, writing in their opinion,

"A review of the videotape of the class clearly reveals that petitioner made the statements at issue while discussing African-American organizations from a historical, cultural and political perspective and that such statements were consistent with the approved subject matter of the class." They continued, "[The] petitioner engaged in a detailed discussion of various historical events during the 1½-hour class and recited facts regarding these organizations that he thought were relevant in an effort to engage the class participants."[4] The very conveyance of particular facts within the institutional context of the prison was enough to be interpreted as a threat to the manageability and value of the captive population and thus the order of the prison itself.

"When Lions Have Historians"

Whereas the naked repression of prison captivity, like that of the slave plantation, facilitates incarcerated peoples' recognition of themselves as unfree and activates their desire to obtain illicit knowledge, the university effectively mystifies its role as an instrument of domination. The university presents itself as a pristine site of "freedom," "opportunity," "diversity," and "upward mobility." This mystification is one of the chief reasons the university is so effective at maintaining the contemporary plantation system. "The university is not grounded into the needs of any community in struggle," opines Joy James, a philosopher of race, democracy, slavery, and incarceration. While organizing a conference on US political prisoners at Brown University, James encountered several subtle and overt obstacles: "I found that if you treated the history of liberation movements not as an abstraction, but as a living testimony to the will and desire of people to be freed from repression but also to not succumb to state terror and that would include, to quote Malcolm 'by any means necessary,' that in fact was a taboo" (Steele, 2019). As the conference came together, James was called into office of the president and told that she could study and write about whatever she wanted but that her "advocacy" needed to stop. As it relates to Black political struggle, merely to pursue certain lines of inquiry is seen as synonymous with advocacy. James refers to this as a "prohibition on critical thinking" (Steele, 2019). I call it compulsory political illiteracy.

In the fall of 2016, while still completing my dissertation in social anthropology, I began teaching in a criminal justice program. My dissertation traced a tradition revolutionary Black organizing within New York State prisons from 1970 to the present. It also examined how, in response to a series of rebellions in the 1970s, prison authorities innovated new penal techniques as a means of maintaining order. I had been hard at work developing a methodological approach, a mode of study, and a narrative style that challenged criminological common sense. In fact, a core part of my argument was that discourses of "criminal justice" and "law enforcement"—even in their progressive, reform-oriented iterations—obscure the essential function of the criminal legal system as an instrument of domestic warfare. I approached my role as a criminal justice professor as a way to promote Black political literacy by destabilizing hegemonic criminological ways of seeing and by introducing my students to alternative sources of knowledge production, particularly the Black radical thought emanating from the prison itself.

I knew that teaching in a standard criminal justice program would be difficult. While universities do not employ violence to police political discourse in the same way that prisons do, universities are not the pristine spaces of intellectual freedom many believe them to be. Few disciplines reveal the university's deep "structural complicities" with the armed apparatus of the state and its plantation legacies more clearly than university criminology programs (Schept et al., 2015). The discipline of criminology proliferated in tandem with the FBI's counterintelligence operations. In 1968, as part of the "war on crime," the federal government established the Law Enforcement Assistance Administration (LEAA) a federal funding agency tasked with enhancing the state's repressive and seductive capacity. Through its repressive side, the LEAA supplied new weapons, surveillance technologies, training, and technical expertise to local and state law police, courts, and prison systems throughout the country (Murakawa, 2014). Through its seductive side it distributed millions of dollars so that universities could establish criminology programs and more effectively circulate law-enforcement ideology throughout the population. It also funded the implementation, by police agencies, of "diversity and inclusion" initiatives seeking to enlist greater numbers of Black police officers and prison guards (Center for Research on Criminal Justice, 1977; Forman, 2017). These and other efforts were an attempt to pacify restive Black populations by channeling Black protest into avenues that preserved the stability of the contemporary plantation system (Schept et al., 2015). This process typifies education's role in what Sojoyner (2016) calls "strategic incorporation," through which "radical social movements and actions pertaining to communal, educational, and gendered marginalization [are] willingly or forcefully subsumed into the state process" (p. xv).

During my first week on the job it became immediately apparent that my students were learning a very narrow, state-sanctioned version of the function of "criminal justice" in society, and that they were being actively groomed for positions as enforcers of the contemporary plantation system. They were learning contested concepts as though they were value-free, naturally occurring phenomena. As one example among many, virtually all of my students had been taught in a previous class that the "broken windows theory," the right-wing doctrine that serves as the frail intellectual justification for racist policing practices across the world (Parenti, 1999), was an effective public safety strategy.

Yet throughout the year, my students, who were overwhelmingly Black and Latinx, revealed that they were not the uncritical automatons they were being trained to be. Many of them expressed deep resentment toward law enforcement based on personal experience. A formerly incarcerated Black male student regularly spoke in class about the "dehumanization" and "abuse" he experienced while confined in a local jail. Two Black female students shared separate experiences of being harassed and neglected by police during the course of their response to an alleged crime committed by someone else. Several first- and second-generation immigrant students were pursuing degrees while in the midst of maddening struggles with the bureaucracy of US Immigration and Customs Enforcement. Yet despite these experiences, they aspired to become police and parole officers, court clerks, and homeland security analysts, because few other degrees held out the promise of gainful employment in this severe employment landscape. The structural conditions of the contemporary plantation complex are so constrained that they aspired to become functionaries in the very system that oppresses them.

At the top of my syllabus for my survey course on criminological thought, I included an oft-cited African Proverb: "Only when lions have historians will hunters cease being heroes." During the customary review of the syllabus on our first meeting, I asked students what they thought this proverb meant. My question was met with total silence. I could see from the looks on their faces that the students were thinking, but no one ventured an answer. I tried to prompt them further by rephrasing the question. "If you're a hunter and you go out and kill a lion and bring it home to feed your family, what story do you tell them about the hunt over dinner?" I asked.

"You gonna talk about how big and scary the lion was and how brave you were," came the voice of a young man with long dreadlocks sitting in the back of the class.

"Right," I replied, relieved that we were getting somewhere. Pushing further, I added, "Now if those same lions were able to tell their own stories, how might their version be different?"

Shana, a visibly pregnant student in the front of the class matter-of-factly said, "We was in our house minding our own business when a man with a gun broke into our house and killed Simba." The whole class broke out into laugher at her reference to the Lion King.

"Exactly," I said as the laughter subsided. "So, what is this proverb about?"

"There's different sides to every story," Shana replied.

Confident that they understood, I explained that much of what they were going to learn from me would contradict what they were learning in their other classes. I explained that this is because I teach based on a theory of history that privileges the hunted rather than the hunter. I displayed the proverb on at the beginning of each subsequent lecture. It turned out to be a very effective framing device, even a mantra of sorts. Over the course of the semester, it was not uncommon for students to express dismay and incredulity at never having learned a particular historical fact, only to have one of their classmates respond by reciting some version of the proverb.

Early in the semester, I added analytical heft to the proverb by introducing students to the Marxist concepts of ideology and hegemony. Many were familiar with ideology and knew that it had something to do with deeply held ideas and belief systems. One student had discussed it in her class on counterterrorism and understood it essentially as a distortion of Truth and a catalyst for violent extremism against the Western world.

I pointed out that the students were correct in recognizing that ideology was largely about ideas, but that everyone, ourselves included, inhabited and reproduced an ideology. We collectively analyzed Stuart Hall's (1996) useful conceptualization, which defines ideology as "the mental frameworks—the languages, the concepts, categories, imagery of thought, and the system of representation—which different classes and social groups deploy in order to make sense of, define, figure out and render intelligible the way society works" (p. 26). Hall's definition reveals a critical and underacknowledged aspect of ideology, namely that "different classes and social groups deploy" it, often to achieve particular political objectives. In other words, ideology is a terrain of struggle. I explained that ideology was less a set of beliefs than a set of assumptions that structure what and how one believes. We discussed the ways in which "language" and "systems of representation" served as the foundation for ideas—they made certain ideas possible, while obscuring alternative possibilities. I told them that standard criminology provided a particular language for describing and making sense of the world, but that it wasn't the only one.

I facilitated an activity designed to illustrate the importance of language and representation as a key domain of struggle. I asked students to collectively do word associations with a set of images I displayed on the board. The first image depicted a Black man with cornrows wearing an orange jumpsuit peering ominously at the camera through prison bars. I asked them to call out as many different terms as they could think of to describe the image. The first three words were rattled off immediately: "prisoner," "convict," and "criminal." I wrote them on the on the board, disheartened but not surprised at the extent to which these working-class students of color had so thoroughly internalized the punitive and racialized language of the state. I asked them to keep going, provoking them to "think outside the box."

"Detainee, gangsta, thug," they continued hesitantly.

Then one student, visibly thinking, intoned, "Wait, just because he's in prison and he has cornrows doesn't mean he's a thug. Maybe he's innocent." A few students nodded in agreement. I wrote "innocent" on the board with a question mark. (This observation was, of course, correct. People languish in prisons and jails for crimes they did not commit. But there are also people who commit heinous acts yet continue to live in the free world, because those acts are not labeled criminal. Consider that no one was convicted of crimes stemming from the 2010 BP oil spill despite the fact that 11 workers died, and millions of gallons of oil poured into the Gulf of Mexico, causing catastrophic damage to the natural environment, public health, and the local economy. By interpreting the image as depicting either the "criminal" subject deserving of punishment or the "innocent" subject deserving of rights, we remain ensnared within the language of criminological hegemony and affirm the authority of the racial-capitalist state's hierarchical ordering of the body politic.) Finally, Carl, the student who earlier disclosed that he spent time in jail, made the comment that challenged hegemonic language. Shaking his head at where the discussion was going, he said, "It really don't matter whether he did it or not. He's still a human being."

I wrote "human being" on the board.

"Yeah, my uncle is locked up," someone else said. I wrote "uncle" on the board. I asked how many of them had family members that were currently or formerly incarcerated. The majority of the class, including myself, raised our hands. These were people we loved and had close bonds with. We discussed why it was that despite so many of us having incarcerated family members, when we see images like this, we use language that negates peoples' humanity. They had no answers.

We segued into a discussion of "hegemony," which we defined as a period in which a particular group has achieved ideological dominance (Hall et al., 1978). I explained that we construct the world using the language that is available to us, and that the language we use appears natural but is actually the outcome of struggle. We examined this point by reading "An Open Letter to Our Friends on the Question of Language," commonly referred to as the "Language Letter," written by Eddie Ellis, a former Black Panther. Ellis wrote the letter in the early 1990s after spending 25 years in New York State prisons. "We habitually underestimate the power of language," Ellis writes. He demands a shift away from criminological terms that are "devoid of humanness" and toward terms that "simply refer to us a PEOPLE. People currently or formerly incarcerated, PEOPLE on parole, PEOPLE recently released from prison, PEOPLE in prison, PEOPLE with criminal convictions, but PEOPLE" (Ellis, n.d.).

The letter, circulated widely within universities, think tanks, and prisons, was a key impetus behind the widespread replacement of terms such as "ex-convict" with the term "formerly incarcerated person," as is commonly used today. The students appreciated the letter and began to make connections between language, hegemony, and social action. Yet everyone was not impressed. Shana, the pregnant student in the front of the class, made an important point: "This doesn't matter. Regardless of what we call him, he's still locked up. This is stupid," she said.

While I disagreed with Shana's assertion that language didn't matter, the substance of her critique—that my efforts to destabilize hegemonic criminological language did not change the fact that millions of people remain "locked up"—was absolutely correct. Shana's comment was in fact a protoabolitionist framing of the problem that implied that the goal of education should not be to change people's minds but, more radically, to change material conditions. By calling the exercise "stupid," she called attention to the structural limitations of my classroom-based pedagogical practice, which, while purportedly radical, remained confined within the boundaries of the university. She called out the essential contradiction of my attempts to cultivate Black political literacy without connecting concepts we were learning about to concrete movements emerging beyond the university.

The semester coincided with the launch of nationally coordinated strikes within US prisons, which provided an opportunity for me to further clarify the notions of history, power, language, and hegemony that were central to the course. Initiated by the Free Alabama Movement (FAM), an organization of incarcerated activists in the Alabama and Mississippi State prison systems, the National Strike Against Prison Slavery was an effort to "finally end slavery in 2016" (Free Alabama Movement, 2016).

FAM organized the strike to start on September 9 in order to coincide with the 45th anniversary of the Attica prison rebellion. On that day in 1971, a Black-led, multiracial coalition of nearly 1,300 state captives seized control of New York's Attica Prison and articulated a series of demands for basic human rights. Because of the brutal siege that brought the rebellion to an end, Attica is most commonly remembered as an exemplary case of state repression (Burton, 2017). Yet for FAM, Attica and the numerous prison uprisings of the era represented a historical moment in which "people were standing up, fighting and taking ownership of their lives and bodies back from the plantation prisons" (Free Alabama Movement, 2016).

On of FAM's key objectives for the strike was to illuminate the ways in those of us who reside in the "free world" are ensnared within the same planation and carceral logics as those within the prisons:

> Our protest against prison slavery is a protest against the school to prison pipeline, a protest against police terror, a protest against post-release controls. When we abolish slavery, they'll lose much of their incentive to lock up our children, they'll stop building traps to pull back those who they've released. When we remove the economic motive and grease of our forced labor from the US prison system, the entire structure of courts and police, of control and slave-catching must shift to accommodate us as humans, rather than slaves. (Free Alabama Movement, 2016)

FAM's protest was not focused on the 2.3 million people currently incarcerated. It broadly targeted carceral practices within the public education system, policing practices in Black communities, and distended forms of carceral supervision. It targeted a broader plantation system that treated economically poor people of color as subjects of domination. FAM's discourse places a heavy emphasis on "forced labor [in] the US prison system," playing into the dominant leftist misinterpretation of the prison as primarily a site of profit generation through labor exploitation. However, the fact that labor exploitation is not a major driver of mass criminalization and human caging does not detract from the fact that labor exploitation does take place and that such exploitation is experienced as slavery. It is also worth noting that the strike originated in Alabama, Mississippi, Texas, and Florida, states that employ some of the most draconian and exploitative prison labor practices. Moreover, in recognition of the unevenness of carceral labor practices throughout the country, the second round of national prison strikes, which emerged in 2018, deemphasized the role of labor exploitation in prison.

In the word-association exercise, I encouraged my students to think critically about how state-sanctioned language shapes our perception of reality. Now, using the literature of the national prison strike, I was able to expose them to the power of self-organization and to the notion that the university is simply one among many spaces of study and learning. To contextualize the connection between the prison and putatively past forms of racial slavery articulated by FAM, our class read and discussed Angela Y. Davis's essay "From the Prison of Slavery to the Slavery of Prison: Frederick Douglass and the Convict Lease System," which explains how the ultimate demise of reconstruction in 1877 was accompanied by the proliferation of "Black codes," legitimizing the generalized policing, criminalization, and incarceration of Black existence. We discussed how prisons perform ideological work on the captured and "free" alike, particularly in the way that they, in Davis's words, "relieve us of the responsibility of seriously engaging with the problems of our society, especially those produced by racism and, increasingly, global capitalism" (A. Y. Davis, 1998, p. 16).

As part of the national prison strike of 2016, captive men and women caused "disturbances" in as many as 50 prisons in Florida, Michigan, Alabama, Texas, California, and elsewhere. They led labor strikes, hunger strikes, acts of civil disobedience, and rebellions. Administrative reprisals were swift and severe. Although we will likely never know the full extent of these reprisals, we do know that organizers were tortured through solitary confinement and that affected facilities were placed on "lockdown" and captives confined to cages 24-7.

The strike did not achieve its ultimate objective of decisively abolishing slavery, yet it succeeded in educating the broader public about the "present tense" of this putatively bygone form of racial domination (Rodríguez, 2006). By bringing the pedagogy of this movement into a criminal justice classroom, and by taking it seriously as intellectual labor, I was able to destabilize the university's hegemony over the concept of "education." By studying this movement—its historical development and demands, and the repression its leaders faced—my students were able to apprehend the existence of an alternative modes of study that now appeared as conspicuously absent from their formal education. By providing them with the tools to understand the central role of ideology and hegemony in contemporary political struggle, and by showing them that unbroken traditions of struggle are taking place around them, I invited them to cultivate the Black political literacy necessary to "read" and "write" this living archive.

Conclusion

In this chapter I have shown how universities and prisons enact plantation politics insofar as both institutional formations are centrally concerned with the production of exploitable subjects for capitalism. One of the chief means by which this is achieved is by regulating Black political literacy, that is, by ensuring that deep histories and contemporary resonances of Black radical struggle and self-emancipation are not comprehensively engaged with. However, by making these claims, I am not asserting that the contemporary university should be abandoned as a site of political struggle. Rather, I am suggesting that, as a small but important political act, university educators who aspire to achieve progressive, transformative, and/or liberatory social justice objectives should work within and against education by helping their students recognize that by virtue of their status as students, they are immersed in an ongoing ideological and political struggle and that they should not treat their formal classroom education as their sole or even their primary source of knowledge acquisition. I also suggest that university educators strive to expose their students to alternative modes of study and organization that exceed the university. Such an orientation will provide students with a repertoire of effective strategies for how one might work "within and against" the forms of surveillance, control, and punishment that keep the contemporary plantation system alive.

Notes

1. The Plaid Dragon Collective. (n.d.). NYS Parole Board's 2016 Decision. Retrieved July 18, 2020. http://freejalil.com/2016decision.html

2. Anthony Bottom v. Anthony J. Annucci (2018), WL 2139105 Supreme Court Appellate Division, Third Department, New York.

3. "Official Compilation of Codes, Rules and Regulations of the State of New York Title 7. Department of Corrections and Community Supervision Chapter V. Procedures for Implementing Standards of Inmate Behavior and for Granting Good Behavior Time Allowances Subchapter C. Standards of Inmate Behavior in All Facilities Part 270. Standards of Inmate Behavior—Behavior Prohibited in All Facilities and the Classification of Each Infraction." 7 Nycrr 270.2[B].

4. Anthony Bottom v. Anthony J. Annucci (2018), WL 2139105 Supreme Court Appellate Division, Third Department, New York.

References

Acoli, S. (1973). Break de chains [Pamphlet in author's possession].
Alexander, M. (2012). *The New Jim Crow: Mass incarceration in the age of colorblindness.* New Press.
Baptist, E. E. (2014). *The half has never been told: Slavery and the making of American capitalism.* Basic Books.
Berger, D. (2014). *Captive nation: Black prison organizing in the civil rights era.* UNC Press Books.
Blackmon, D. A. (2009). *Slavery by another name: The re-enslavement of Black Americans from the Civil War to World War II.* Anchor.
Bloomberg. (2018, December 17, 2018). Why record $1.465 trillion student debt could test U.S. economy. *Fortune.*
Boyd, J. W. (2018). Solitary confinement: Torture, pure and simple. *Psychology Today.* https://www.psychologytoday.com/us/blog/almost-addicted/201801/solitary-confinement-torture-pure-and-simple
Burton, O. (2017). Diluting radical history: Blood in the water and the politics of erasure. *Abolition Journal* [Blog]. https://abolitionjournal.org/diluting-radical-history-blood-in-the-water-and-the-politics-of-erasure
Center for Research on Criminal Justice. (1977). *The iron fist and the velvet glove: An analysis of the U.S. police.* Crime and Social Justice Associates.

Childs, D. (2015). *Slaves of the state*. University of Minnesota Press.

Churchill, W., & Vander Wall, J. (2002a). *Agents of repression: The FBI's secret wars against the Black Panther Party and the American Indian movement* (2nd ed.). South End Press.

Churchill, W., & Vander Wall, J. (2002b). *The Cointelpro Papers: Documents from the FBI's secret wars against dissent in the United States* (Vol. 8). South End Press.

Corson, W. R. (1970). *Promise or peril: The Black college student in America*. W. W. Norton & Company.

Davis, A. Y. (1998). From the prison of slavery to the slavery of prison: Frederick Douglass and the convict lease system. In Joy James (Ed.), *The Angela Y. Davis Reader* (pp. 74–95). Blackwell.

Davis, J. C. (2018). The FBI's war on Black-owned bookstores. *The Atlantic*.

Douglass, F. (2003). *Narrative of the Life of Frederick Douglass, an American slave, written by himself* (2nd ed.). Bedford/St. Martin's.

Ellis, E. (n.d.). *An open letter to our friends on the question of language*. The Center for NuLeadership on Urban Solutions.

Eltagouri, M. (2017, December 29). Professor who tweeted, "All I want for Christmas is white genocide," resigns after year of threats. *The Washington Post*. https://www.washingtonpost.com/news/grade-point/wp/2017/12/29/professor-who-tweeted-all-i-want-for-christmas-is-white-genocide-resigns-after-year-of-threats/

Ferguson, R. A. (2012). *The reorder of things: The university and its pedagogies of minority difference*. University of Minnesota Press.

Forman, J. (2017). *Locking up our own: Crime and punishment in Black America* (1st hardcover ed.). Farrar, Straus and Giroux.

Free Alabama Movement. (2016). Announcement of nationally coordinated prisoner workstoppage for Sept. 9, 2016. *Industrial Workers of the World*. https://www.iww.org/content/announcement-nationally-coordinated-prisoner-workstoppage-sept-9-2016

Gee, A. (2017, September 28). Facing poverty, academics turn to sex work and sleeping in cars. *The Guardian*. https://www.theguardian.com/us-news/2017/sep/28/adjunct-professors-homeless-sex-work-academia-poverty

Genovese, E. D. (1976). *Roll, Jordan, roll: The world the slaves made*. Vintage Books.

Genovese, E. D. (1992). *From rebellion to revolution: Afro-American slave revolts in the making of the modern world*. Louisiana State University Press.

Gilmore, C. (2019, July 12). On the business of incarceration. *Commune*. https://communemag.com/on-the-business-of-incarceration/

Gilmore, R. W. (2007). *Golden gulag: Prisons, surplus, crisis, and opposition in globalizing California* (Vol. 21). University of California Press.

Gilmore, R. W., & Kilgore, J. (2019). Some reflections on prison labor. https://brooklynrail.org/2019/06/field-notes/Some-Reflections-on-Prison-Labor

Giroux, H. (2002). Neoliberalism, corporate culture, and the promise of higher education: The university as a democratic public sphere. *Harvard Educational Review, 72*(4), 425–64. DOI: 10.17763/haer.72.4.0515nr62324n71p1

Gottschalk, M. (2014). *Caught: The prison state and the lockdown of American politics.* Princeton University Press.

Gross, D. A. (2019, January 25). The eleventh parole hearing of Jalil Abdul Muntaqim. *The New Yorker.* https://www.newyorker.com/news/dispatch/the-eleventh-parole-hearing-of-jalil-abdul-muntaqim

Hall, S. (1996). The problem of ideology: Marxism without guarantees. In S. Hall, D. Morley, & K.-H. Chen (Eds.), *Stuart Hall: Critical dialogues in cultural studies* (pp. 24–45). Routledge.

Hall, S., Critcher, C., Jefferson, T., Clarke, J., & Roberts, B. (1978). *Policing the crisis: Mugging, the state, and law and order.* Macmillan London.

Heiner, B. (2015). Excavating the sedimentations of slavery: The unfinished project of American abolition. In *Death and other penalties: Philosophy in a time of mass incarceration.* New York: Fordham University Press.

Jackson, G. (1994). *Soledad brother: The prison letters of George Jackson.* Lawrence Hill Books. (Original work published 1970)

James, J. (2005). *The new abolitionists: (Neo)slave narratives and contemporary prison writings.* SUNY Press.

Kolowich, S. (2017, August 3). What is a Black professor in America allowed to say? *The Guardian.*

Mayfield, C. (1970). (Don't worry) if there's hell below we're all going to go [Song]. *Curtis.* Warner Strategic Marketing.

McKittrick, K. (2011). On plantations, prisons, and a Black sense of place. *Social & Cultural Geography, 12*(8), 947–63. DOI: 10.1080/14649365.2011.624280

Meyerhoff, E. (2019). *Beyond education: Radical studying for another world.* University of Minnesota Press.

Muhammad, K. G. (2010). *The condemnation of Blackness: Race, crime, and the making of modern urban America.* Harvard University Press.

Murakawa, N. (2014). *The first civil right: How liberals built prison America.* Oxford University Press.

Parenti, C. (1999). *Lockdown America: Police and prisons in the age of crisis.* Verso Books.

The Plaid Dragon Collective. (n.d.). NYS Parole Board's 2016 Decision. Retrieved July 18, 2020. http://freejalil.com/2016decision.html

Rodríguez, D. (2006). *Forced passages: Imprisoned radical intellectuals and the US prison regime.* University of Minnesota Press.

Rodríguez, D. (2010). The disorientation of the teaching act: Abolition as pedagogical position. *Radical Teacher* (88), 7–19, 80.

Sawyer, W. (2017). How much do incarcerated people earn in each state? [Blog post] *Prison Policy Initiative*. https://www.prisonpolicy.org/blog/2017/04/10/wages/

Schept, J., Wall, T., & Brisman, A. (2015). Building, staffing, and insulating: An architecture of criminological complicity in the school-to-prison pipeline. *Social Justice, 41*(4), 96–115.

Schwartzapfel, B. (2016). A primer on the nationwide prisoners' strike. *The Marshall Project*. https://www.themarshallproject.org

Shakur, A. (2001). *Assata: An autobiography*. L. Hill Books.

Shakur, A. (2014, December 30). I am a 20th century escaped slave. *CounterPunch*. https://www.counterpunch.org/2014/12/30/an-open-letter-to-the-media/

Sojoyner, D. M. (2016). *First strike: Educational enclosures in Black Los Angeles*. University of Minnesota Press.

Squire, D., Williams, B. C., & Tuitt, F. (2018). Plantation politics and neoliberal racism in higher education: A framework for reconstructing anti-racist institutions. *Teachers College Record, 120*(14), 1–20.

Steele, C. T. (Producer). (2019, June 30). Time talks: History, politics, music, and art [Podcast]. *Stitcher*. https://www.stitcher.com/podcast/chris-time-steele/time-talks-history-politics-music-and-art/e/62262797

Stein, D. (2017). Trumpism and the magnitude of mass incarceration. *Black Perspectives*. https://www.aaihs.org/trumpism-and-the-magnitude-of-mass-incarceration/

Useem, B., & Kimball, P. (1991). *States of siege*. Oxford University Press.

Wilder, C. S. (2013). *Ebony & ivy: Race, slavery, and the troubled history of America's universities* (Paperback ed.). Bloomsbury Press.

Afterword

Against Higher Education: Instruments of Insurrection

D-L STEWART

In *Plantation Politics and Campus Rebellions: Power, Diversity, and the Emancipatory Struggle in Higher Education*, Bianca C. Williams, Dian D. Squire, and Frank Tuitt have curated a collection of incisive, provocative, and compelling treatises on the condition of higher education, its effects on Black and other racially minoritized bodies, and how resistance is enacted. Upon reading this volume, two questions came to my mind: Is higher education necessary, and for what? If it is necessary, then is it sufficient, and for what? Considering these questions led me to consider what it means to be(come) an instrument of insurrection.

The Oppressive Necessity of Higher Education

Sara Ahmed (2012) has described higher education institutions as having brick walls against which diversity workers consistently bruise themselves as they attempt to shift institutions away from policies of exclusion toward those of inclusion and equity. These workers—perhaps we can think of them as plantation drivers, as Tuitt analogizes in chapter 7—serve the dual roles of both driving minoritized bodies to continue to offer their labor as well as (sometimes) attempting to soften the violence of the plantation system. The permanence and intractability of violence is experienced as a brick wall that does not yield to pushing. It is obstinate.

There is another way in which higher education acts as a brick wall. In the oft-told parable of the three little pigs, one pig builds a house of straw, and another builds a house of sticks. These houses stand until a wolf comes along and blows them down and eats the pigs hiding inside. The third pig, however, who is portrayed as wiser and more diligent, uses bricks to build the walls of his house. When the wolf comes to blow down his house, he is able to stay secure inside, the walls of his house not yielding to the gale-force of the predatory wolf. In a similar way, higher education can be thought of as a house made of brick by settlers who intended to preserve a way of life that relied on violence against Indigenous and enslaved African peoples. These builders used obstinate materials—systems, policies, and practices—that could withstand any forces that would rise up to resist them. Higher education is a brick house in the project of settler colonial white supremacy.

Neoliberal capitalist investment in increased labor production, particularly in service industries, is another brick house. Some within higher education decry what they see as a turn away from the liberal arts toward mechanistic, utilitarian outcomes such as employment and job placement (Lemann, 2016); others see a way to combine the two (Freeland, 2004).[1] Ultimately, however, employment and job placement are not questioned as desirable outcomes of higher education.

Indeed, higher education in the United States has always worked to make people fit for work. All that has changed over time is merely the type of occupation. Initially, colonial colleges sought to prepare ministers and politicians—who were necessary to legitimate and secure the theft of land and bodies—from among the sons of the landed gentry that settled the territory later incorporated as the United States (Thelin, 2011; Wilder, 2013). As with growth in industry and technology, collegians have made up an ever-broader swath of the populace. Concurrently, the types of jobs for which industries have expected colleges to prepare future laborers have also diversified.

These expectations have been segregated along intersected lines of gender, race, and class. Certain jobs have been feminized, and to restrict access along gender lines, colleges and departments presumed to be related to women's natural place as nurturers and servants were formed, including teaching, secretarial, and home economics departments (Eisenmann, 2002; Zschoche, 1989). Other jobs were racialized. Indian boarding schools and the developing historically Black colleges and universities (HBCUs) were expected to give their students the industrial education that was considered fit for those considered to be naturally subservient to whites (Anderson, 1988; Wright & Tierney, 1991). Such industrial (or vocational) educations also had the effect of cementing the relationship between racial minoritization and social class immobility. Higher education has therefore proved necessary to maintaining the US social order informed by racial, gender, and class hierarchies.

As Armond Towns demonstrates in chapter 5, people of color have always already been included in the project of US higher education through the practice of "necessary violence," as I have noted above. Also, as Williams and Tuitt write in the introduction to this volume, central to the "inner workings of higher education" is an essential underlying structure of Indigenous physical and cultural genocide, as well as Black oppression and dehumanization. Higher education is a technology of power essential to maintaining the permanence of settler colonialism and white supremacy.

The Questionable Sufficiency of Higher Education

Necessity does not inherently logically indicate sufficiency. To achieve a certain result, something may be necessary but prove itself to be insufficient. In contrast, something may be sufficient to achieve a certain goal but not wholly necessary for the same. What is higher education sufficient for? The authors in this volume argue that higher education is sufficient to be turned against itself for emancipatory ends. As Toby Jenkins, Rosalind Conerly, Liane Hypolite, and Lori D. Patton enjoin readers in chapter 8, "We need to take the institution . . . and start a revolution." Relatedly, as R. Eric Platt, Holly A. Foster, and Lauren Yarnell Bradshaw assert in chapter 10 (citing Thompson, 2000), a tenet of emancipatory learning is an "understanding and knowledge about the nature and root causes of unsatisfactory circumstances in order to develop real strategies to change them" (para. 2). Interventions such as ethnic studies courses and identity-based centers can work within higher education to equip students with the knowledge necessary to do the work of complaint (Ahmed, 2017) and insist on pointing out what is wrong as praxis.

Doing this work makes an investment in the institution—an investment that does not always have a return. As Ahmed (2019) has written elsewhere and as I have asserted above, institutions are skilled at refuting complaints, seemingly saying "Yes" as a means of simply putting off the complaint. This "language of appeasement" (Stewart, 2017) contests the sufficiency of orchestrating "strategies of resistance" (see chapter 8 of this volume) *if the goal is to transform the institution.* Questioning the sufficiency of the work then becomes questioning the sufficiency of the goal the work is meant to achieve.

Becoming Instruments of Insurrection

When will we who engage complaint as diversity work know when we have succeeded? What is success, and who defines it? We cannot make higher education sufficient for recognizing success of our efforts. Again, we must offer up the goals of our efforts for interrogation while refusing to accept "ongoing domination" as inevitable. Instruments of insurrection are not formed in view of higher education's mechanisms of surveillance. Rather, as Wilson Kwamogi Okello argues in chapter 4, we must "take up the work of escape" using fugitivity to enact culpability with institutional systems as a form of resistance. The false binary of culpability and resistance does not work to do the work. The strategic activism of cultural center workers (discussed in chapter 8 of this volume) may need to perform cooperation with(in) institutional structures in order to perform insurrection.

Throughout this volume, insurrections are presented as daily and mundane, as well as spectacular and episodic. Both kinds of insurrection are necessary to "defy the murder of selfhood" (Bell, 1992, p. 197, as cited by Williams and Tuitt in the introduction) that is the necessary violence of higher education. Daily mundane insurrections include using critical pedagogies and curriculum; hosting space for minoritized groups to gather, support, and plot; and even greeting one another in passing on campus—seeing one another's humanity in a space where to be human is an act of defiance.

Spectacular and episodic acts of insurrection are assumed to represent only spontaneous flash points of frustration and anger rather than the careful planning and strategizing brought about by those daily mundane rebellious acts. A hunger strike, administrative occupation, or die-in as a protest of yet another Black life lost to state-sanctioned police violence makes spectacular national news but is treated as a one-off—not persistent, not strategic. Ashon Crawley (2015) refuted such interpretations, arguing instead of "otherwise movements" that "perhaps the organizing that is taking place—an otherwise than strategy—is operating out of a different set of concerns altogether, fundamentally about not assenting to current configurations of power and authority, but about creating new lines of flight, of force, for operation, for action" (para. 13). I am brought back to the question, what is success and who defines it? Adopting the same old "set of concerns" keeps rebellion within the legible framework of oppressive systems and structures, making it vulnerable to cooptation and dispersal.

Insurrection—whether mundane or spectacular—may not change the institution, but it does change those who surrender to become its instruments. Insurrection, the emancipatory struggle in the midst of higher education, takes back the right to selfhood. As Derrick Bell (1992) asserted, their bodies may indeed be subjected to dehumanization, but their minds are set free to imagine otherwise.

Notes

1. For an early statement in these debates, see "The Yale Report of 1828" (1961).

References

Ahmed, S. N. (2012). *On being included: Diversity and institutional life*. Duke University Press.

Ahmed, S. N. (2017, November 10). Complaint as diversity work [Blog post]. *feministkilljoys*. https://feministkilljoys.com/2017/11/10/complaint-as-diversity-work/

Ahmed, S. N. (2019, April 29). Nodding as a non-performative [Blog post]. *feministkilljoys*. https://feministkilljoys.com/2019/04/29/nodding-as-a-non-performative/

Anderson, J. D. (1988). *The education of Blacks in the South, 1860–1935*. University of North Carolina Press.

Bell, D. (1992). *Faces at the bottom of the well: The permanence of racism*. Basic Books.

Crawley, A. (2019, January 15). Otherwise movements. *The New Inquiry*. https://thenewinquiry.com/otherwise-movements/

Eisenmann, L. (2002). Educating the female citizen in a post-war world: Competing ideologies for American women, 1945–1965. *Educational Review, 54*, 133–41.

Freeland, R. M. (2004, October). The third way. *The Atlantic*. http://www.theatlantic.com/magazine/archive/2004/10/the-third-way/303512/

Lemann, N. (2016, January 8). What should graduates know? *The Chronicle of Higher Education*. https://www.chronicle.com/article/What-Should-Graduates-Know-/234824

Stewart, D.-L. (2017, March 30). The language of appeasement. *Inside Higher Ed.* https://www.insidehighered.com/views/2017/03/30/colleges-need-language-shift-not-one-you-think-essay

Thelin, J. R. (2011). *A history of American higher education* (2nd ed.). Johns Hopkins University.

Thompson, J. (2000). *Emancipatory learning* (NIACE Briefing Sheet 11). National Institute of Adult Continuing Education.

Wilder, C. S. (2013). *Ebony and ivy: Race, slavery, and the troubled history of American universities.* Bloomsbury Press.

Wright, B., & Tierney, W. G. (1991). American Indians in higher education: A history of cultural conflict. *Change, 23*(2), 11–18.

The Yale Report of 1828. (1961). In R. Hofstadter & W. Smith (Eds.), *American higher education: A documentary history* (Vol. 1, pp. 275–91). University of Chicago.

Zschoche, S. (1989). Dr. Clarke revisited: Science, true womanhood, and female collegiate education. *History of Education Quarterly, 29*, 545–69.

About the Editors

Dr. Bianca C. Williams (she/her) is an associate professor of anthropology, women and gender studies, and critical psychology at the Graduate Center, CUNY. Her research interests focus on Black women and emotional wellness; race, gender, and equity in higher education; and Black feminist pedagogical and organizing practices. In her award-winning book *The Pursuit of Happiness: Black Women, Diasporic Dreams, and the Politics of Emotional Transnationalism* (2018), Williams argues that pursuing happiness is a political project for Black women, while examining how African American women use travel to Jamaica and the Internet as tools for escaping US racism and sexism. Additionally, she has written about "radical honesty" as feminist pedagogy in the volume *Race, Equity, and the Learning Environment,* and published on Black Lives Matter, anthropological writing, and tourism in the journals *Souls, Cultural Anthropology,* and *Teachers College Record*, and on the blogs Anthrodendum and Anthropoliteia. Williams earned her PhD in cultural anthropology from Duke University, and is a recipient of the American Anthropological Association and Oxford University Press Award for Excellence in Undergraduate Teaching of Anthropology. Williams is a cofounder and former colead of Black Lives Matter 5280 (the Denver chapter of the global network).

Dr. Dian D. Squire is an assistant professor of counseling-student affairs at Northern Arizona University. He was previously a visiting assistant professor in the student affairs program at Iowa State University. Prior to starting at Iowa State University, Dian was a postdoctoral fellow in the University of Denver's Interdisciplinary Research Institute for the Study of (In)Equality. Dian's research focuses on issues of diversity, equity, and justice in higher education. He particularly focuses on access to graduate education and the experiences of diverse graduate students. He utilizes organizational perspectives to help explain individual behavior and experience in order to transform organizational structures to support equity and justice. He also writes on student activism, racial justice, campus institutional change, and critical praxis in student affairs. He has published multiple peer-reviewed manuscripts, book chapters, and periodical pieces. He was the cofounder and first editor in chief of the *Journal of Critical Scholarship on Higher Education and Student Affairs* housed at Loyola University Chicago. Prior to pursuing his doctorate, Dian was the assistant director of orientation and new student programs at the University of Maryland, College Park.

Dr. Frank A. Tuitt is the vice president and chief diversity officer at the University of Connecticut, and professor in the Neag School of Education. His research explores topics related to access and equity in higher education, teaching and learning in racially diverse college classrooms, and diversity and organizational transformation. Dr. Tuitt is a coeditor and contributing author of the books *Race and Higher Education: Rethinking Pedagogy in Diverse College Classrooms; Black Faculty in the Academy: Narratives for Negotiating Identity and Achieving Career Success; Contesting the Myth of a Post-Racial Era: The Continued Significance of Race in U.S. Education;* and *Race, Equity, and the Learning Environment: The Global Relevance of Critical and Inclusive Pedagogies in Higher Education.* Dr. Tuitt received his doctorate from the Harvard Graduate School of Education and his BA in human relations from Connecticut College.

Contributors

Dr. Lisa Anderson-Levy is an associate professor of anthropology at Beloit College in Beloit, Wisconsin, and co-principal investigator of the Mellon-funded Decolonizing Pedagogies Project. Her training and expertise center on feminist anthropology, critical race studies, transnational whiteness, and gender and sexuality studies, and her research is situated in the Caribbean. Her scholarship has appeared in *Transforming Anthropology* and *New Directions in Anthropological Kinship*.

Kevin J. Bazner is a PhD candidate in higher education administration at Texas A&M University. Prior to entering his doctoral program, Kevin spent almost a decade as a student affairs practitioner in various functional areas. His research focuses on the intersection of social equity work and student affairs / higher education administration. Kevin further incorporates his knowledge of student affairs administration and organizational behavior to examine issues of race and racism in student affairs leadership, whiteness in higher education, and the application of critical scholarship to higher education practice.

Dr. Lauren Yarnell Bradshaw is an assistant professor at the University of North Georgia. She graduated from Georgia State University with a PhD in social studies teaching and learning. She has published on topics related to educational biography, the history of education in the American South, and social studies curriculum.

Dr. Orisanmi Burton is an assistant professor of anthropology at American University who studies Black radical politics and state repression in the United States. His research has been published in *Cultural Anthropology*,

North American Dialog, and *The Black Scholar*, and he has forthcoming work in *American Anthropologist*. Dr. Burton is an active member of the Critical Prison Studies Caucus of the American Studies Association and the Abolition Collective and is working on a book manuscript titled *The Tip of the Spear: Revolutionary Organizing and Prison Pacification in the Empire State* that analyzes the prison as a domain of domestic warfare.

Dr. Andrea Button is an assistant professor of practice in sociology at Texas Tech University at Waco. She specializes in social movements, political sociology, and criminology. Her current research engages with identity navigation in cosplay and drift car racing, patterns of trauma for women in prison, and student/community social movements and resistance within oppressive institutions.

Kristi Carey is a queer and mixed educational researcher, and is thankful to live as an uninvited guest on unceded Coast Salish territories. She has a background in educational studies and peace and conflict studies from Colgate University, where she also was deeply active in student-activist communities. She recently graduated with her MA from the Social Justice Institute at the University of British Columbia. In the now, she is grateful for moments of feeling, like finding a good sun spot during the winter, having just enough nut butter for morning toast, or waking up from a sneakily-taken couch nap.

Dr. Jesse Carr is the project coordinator for the Transfer Bridges to the Humanities Program at the University of Michigan–Ann Arbor, which aims to create accessible pathways between Michigan community colleges and the university. Dr. Carr's training is in American studies, with a focus on race, gender, and institutional or state-sanctioned violence. Dr. Carr previously worked at Beloit College as a Mellon postdoctoral fellow, managing the Decolonizing Pedagogies Project and the Graduate School Exploration Fellowship.

Dr. Rosalind Conerly is associate dean of students and director of the Black Community Services Center at Stanford University. She was the director of the Center for Black Cultural and Student Affairs and an adjunct professor in the Rossier School of Education at the University of Southern California. Dr. Conerly holds a bachelor's degree and a master's degree in education, both from the University of Nevada, Las Vegas, and a doctorate in education from the University of Southern California. Her interests include working with students of color to assist with their professional, identity, and personal development, as well as increasing the retention of underrepresented and first-generation college students. Her research is focused on the experiences of scholar practitioners that oversee cultural centers at predominantly white institutions.

Dr. Holly A. Foster is an assistant professor of student affairs administration / higher education in the Department of Educational Research and Administration at the University of Southern Mississippi.

Liane I. Hypolite is a Rossier dean's fellow in the Urban Education Policy PhD program at the University of Southern California's Rossier School of Education. She serves as a research assistant at the Pullias Center for Higher Education and the Center for Education, Identity, and Social Justice. Hypolite assists with research on topics related to college persistence, retention, and graduation. She is interested in understanding racial and economic integration, in addition to social and cultural capital as it relates equity across institutions of higher education. Her research interests include college supports that improve the success of first-generation, low-income students of color. Before attending USC, she served as the Dean of College and Career Advising at Codman Academy Charter Public School in Boston, Massachusetts, and has also worked at the national college access and success nonprofit Bottom Line helping students enter and graduate from college. She completed her bachelor's degree at Brandeis University, double majoring in psychology and sociology, and earned her master's in education policy and management at the Harvard Graduate School of Education.

Dr. Toby S. Jenkins is an associate professor of curriculum studies and director of the Museum of Education at the University of South Carolina. Her work focuses on culture as a politic of social survival, a tool of social change, and a transformative space of critical and creative pedagogy. Dr. Jenkins has authored four books focused on the evolving ideologies of culture, family, and education in contemporary society. *My Culture, My Color, My Self: Heritage, Resilience, and Community in the Lives of Young Adults* (2013) was listed by the Association of American University Press as one of the "Top 100 Books for Understanding Race Relations in the US." Dr. Jenkins has over 35 other publications, including journal articles, book chapters, books, and magazine articles. She has given over 50 presentations at national and international conferences. Before becoming a professor, Dr. Jenkins spent 10 years working as an administrator and diversity practitioner in higher education.

A. C. Johnson is a doctoral student of higher education administration in the Department of Educational Leadership, Policy, and Technology Studies at the University of Alabama. She currently serves as the editing graduate research assistant at the Office for Research and Service at the University of Alabama. Her research interests center historically Black colleges and universities, Black women in higher education, first-generation students, and P–20 educational access for underrepresented students. Before entering the field of higher education, she was an English professor in several diverse postsecondary contexts. A. C. earned her BS in psychology and her MA in English from Jacksonville State University, and although she has resided in many areas across the country, Birmingham, Alabama, is where she calls home.

Dr. Steve D. Mobley Jr. is assistant professor of higher education in the Department of Educational Leadership, Policy, and Technology Studies at the University of Alabama. His scholarship focuses on the contemporary placement of historically Black colleges and universities (HBCUs). Particularly, Dr. Mobley Jr.'s research underscores and highlights the understudied facets of HBCU communities, including issues surrounding race, social class, and student sexuality. He earned his BA in communication and culture from Howard University. Upon graduating from Howard he completed his master's in higher education management from the University of Pennsylvania, and earned his PhD in higher education from the University of Maryland.

Dr. Wilson Kwamogi Okello is an assistant professor in the Department of Educational Leadership at the University of North Carolina Wilmington. A scholar-artist, his research draws on Black feminist theories to think about the relationship between history, the body, and epistemology; anti-Blackness in educational contexts; and antideficit curriculum and pedagogy. His work has been published in venues such as the *Journal of College Student Development* and the *International Journal of Qualitative Studies in Education*. Wilson earned his PhD from Miami University, his master's degree from the University of Rhode Island, and a bachelor's degree from Youngstown State University.

Dr. Catherine M. Orr is professor and chair of the Critical Identity Studies Department at Beloit College in Beloit, Wisconsin, and co-principal investigator of the Mellon-funded Decolonizing Pedagogies Project. Her research focuses on gender and sexuality studies, social movements, and academic disciplinarity. She is coauthor (along with Ann Braithwaite) of the leading textbook *Everyday Women's and Gender Studies: Introductory Concepts*.

Dr. Lori D. Patton is the department chair of educational studies and professor of higher education and student affairs at The Ohio State University. Patton is best known for her important cross-cutting scholarship on African Americans in higher education, critical race theory, campus diversity initiatives on college campuses, girls and women of color in educational and social contexts, and college student development and graduate preparation. She is the immediate past president of the Association for the Study of Higher Education, has served on seven editorial boards for journals in the field of education, and was previously associate editor of the *International Journal of Qualitative Studies in Education*. She is coeditor of Critical *Perspectives on Black Women and College Success*. Her scholarship has also been widely adopted in higher education programs across the country.

Dr. R. Eric Platt is interim chair and associate professor of higher and adult education in the Department of Leadership at the University of Memphis. He holds a PhD in educational leadership and research/higher education administration from Louisiana State University. His research centers on the history of higher education in the American South. He is the author of *Sacrifice and Survival: Identity, Mission, and Jesuit Higher Education in the American South* (2014) and *Educating the Sons of Sugar: Jefferson College and the Creole Planter Class of South Louisiana* (2017).

Patrick Reynolds currently serves as a community director within the Office of Residential Life at Loyola University New Orleans. His scholarship interests include Black male success at predominately White institutions and first-generation low-income Black male students at PWIs. Prior to his work at Loyola University New Orleans he served as the community service coordinator with a dual report in residence life at Huntingdon College in Montgomery, Alabama. Patrick earned his MA in higher education administration from The University of Alabama and his BA in early childhood education from LaGrange College.

328 | Contributors

Sunni L. Solomon II is a doctoral candidate in the PhD in Higher Education Administration program at Morgan State University in Baltimore, Maryland. His research interests include the written and unwritten dynamics of faculty diversity at White institutions, the impacts of elitism on African American community cohesion, and the role of tradition in sustaining viable historically Black colleges and universities. Prior to enrolling at Morgan State University, he earned his BS in business administration with a marketing concentration from Cheyney University of Pennsylvania, and also possesses a master's degree in college student affairs from Eastern Illinois University.

Dr. D-L Stewart is a professor in the School of Education, co-coordinator of Student Affairs in Higher Education, codirector of the Race and Intersectional Studies for Educational Equity Center, and affiliated faculty in the Center for Women's Studies and Gender Research at Colorado State University. His scholarship focuses on higher education's history and philosophy, as well as institutional systems and structures that affect the postsecondary experiences, learning, growth, and becoming of minoritized students. He examines these topics through intersectional, critical, and poststructural frameworks that incorporate ableism, religious hegemony, and classism alongside racism, patriarchy, and queer/transantagonism.

Saran Stewart, PhD is an associate professor and program director of Higher Education and Student Affairs, and director of Global Education at the Neag School of Education at the University of Connecticut. Dr. Stewart's research examines issues in comparative education, decolonizing methodologies, critical/ inclusive pedagogy, and access and equity issues in higher education. She is a Salzburg Global fellow and the recipient of multiple awards, including the 2019 Vice-Chancellor's Award for Excellence from the University of the West Indies and the 2018 African Diaspora Emerging Scholar award by the Comparative and International Education Society. She is editor of *Decolonizing Qualitative Methodologies for and by the Caribbean* (2019) and coeditor of *Race, Equity, and the Learning Environment: The Global Relevance of Critical and Inclusive Pedagogies in Higher Education* (2016).

Dr. Armond R. Towns is an assistant professor in the Department of Rhetoric and Communication Studies at the University of Richmond. His research interests include the science and philosophy of race, (Black) philosophies of communication, (Black) new materialisms, decolonial theory, materialist media studies, and materialist rhetoric. His research can be found in *Souls, Social Identities, Women's Studies in Communication*, and *Communication and Critical/Cultural Studies*. He is currently completing a book manuscript that examines the relationship between media technologies, Darwinian evolutionary theories, and Blackness and whiteness.

Dr. Nicole Truesdell is a recovering academic who has been in higher education for the past 20 years as either a student, faculty member, or administrator—normally holding at least two of these positions at once. In these roles she has created programs, an office, and an institute that all focus on space making for populations marginalized within society. She has also worked with a UK community-based organization, Black South West Network, for the past 10 years as a grant writer, researcher, and strategical consultant.

Index

abolition, 65, 80–81, 201, 203–205, 208–10. *See also* emancipation; freedom
academic disciplines: boundary maintenance, 158; plantation politics and, 156. *See also* Black studies; criminology programs; ethnic studies; interdisciplinarity; interdisciplines; women's and gender studies (WGS)
access to higher education, 10, 15; completion rates and, 214–15; neoliberalism and, 123; slavery and, 279; through HBCUs, 80
acculturation, 65–66
Acoli, Sundiata, 300–301
Act for the Abolition of Slavery (1833), 65
activism: as rebellion, 4 (*see also* campus rebellions); rethinking, 135–36. *See also* Black Lives Matter movement; liberation struggles; Movement for Black Lives (M4BL); resistance; student protests
adaptation, 65–66
administration. *See* colleges and universities; institutional responses to student protests
admissions, 91, 93, 123, 214. *See also* affirmative action; enrollment

affinity spaces, 220. *See also* cultural centers
affirmative action, 49, 231–32, 237
Africa: proverb on history, 304–305; recruitment of immigrant students from, 49; Western ideas about, 125
African American Policy Forum, 206
agency, 78, 112, 190, 219, 232, 276, 283, 285
Ahmed, Sara, 47, 121–23, 191, 240, 315, 317
Aiello, Thomas, 89–90
Akans, 67
Alabama, 308–309
Alderman, Derek, 252
Allen, Chaunda Myretta, 190–92
allochronism, 17, 35–36, 142, 158, 160, 220
alumni, 21–22, 24, 90, 142, 217, 251–52, 266; racial/ethnic specific associations, 213
American Council on Education, 20, 28n14
American dream, 144–45
American grammar (Spiller's thesis on), 102–103
Amherst College, 109
Anderson, Ralph, 50, 51
Anderson-Levy, Lisa, 160–61, 164
anger, 22, 71–72, 249, 318. *See also* rage

anti-Blackness, 2–3; establishment of universities and, 121; in higher education, 6, 16–18, 22, 36–40; respectability politics and, 84; white supremacy and, 27n5. *See also* oppression; racism; violence
anticapitalist pedagogy, 70
antidiversity, 24, 141–67; Decolonizing Pedagogies Project, 143, 150, 161–67; decolonizing women's and gender studies, 143, 156–60; plantation political economy and, 141–48; as politics of equity and liberation, 148–55; use of term, 167n2
antiessentialist approaches, 85
antilynching movement, 107
antiracist praxis, 20, 24, 107, 142–43, 145, 159, 162–65, 189–93, 228, 275
Antwi, Phanuel, 21
apartheid, 88
appeasement, 145–47, 317–18
apprentice system in Caribbean, 65–66
Arapaho land, 120, 127
Argentina, 39
Armstrong, Samuel Chapman, 86, 88
Ashantis, 67
Asian Americans, 46, 216
assault, 104, 152–53
assimilation, 84, 100, 103, 108; rejection of, 109–11
Association for the Study of Higher Education (ASHE), 5–6
athletic-industrial complex, 38, 51. *See also* student-athletes
Attica prison rebellion, 301, 308
Austin, Sharon Wright, 141, 148
autonomy, 68, 103, 233

backlash, 21, 158, 251, 264, 285
Baldwin, James, 100

Baltimore, 284
Barbados, 58–60, 67
Baumgartner, Kabria, 110
Bazner, Kevin J., 21
Beatty, Cameron C., 84
Beck, Hubert Park, 287
Beckles, Hilary, 59, 65, 67
Bell, Derrick, 1–3, 25–26, 80, 173–74, 179, 189, 319
Bell, Shamell, 26n2
belonging, 203–204
Berry, Daina Ramey, 23
binary breaking, 156
Biondi, Martha, 122, 123
Black athletes. *See* student-athletes
Black Codes, 278, 309. *See also* slave codes
Black fungibility, 121, 132, 136n1
Black Liberation Army (BLA), 294, 299–301
Black Lives Matter movement: campus rebellions connected to, 1–2, 12–13, 135, 201; dance as resistance, 26n2; HBCUs and, 90; leaders of, 27n10; origins of, 9–11; transnational protests, 39–40; at University of Missouri, 210. *See also* Movement for Black Lives (M4BL)
"Black Menace," 78
Blackmon, Traci, 28n11
Black nationalism, 108–109, 300
Blackness: criminalization of, 152; ontological, 35, 42–43. *See also* anti-Blackness; identity; racial hierarchy
Black Panther Party (BPP), 112, 294, 299–301, 307
Black political literacy, 293–311
Black Power movement: HBCU students in, 88–89; higher education and, 108–12

Black Skin, White Masks (Fanon), 82
Black studies, 159; as act of insurrection, 18; cultural centers and, 217; emergence of, 108–109, 122; as redemption of Western society, 112–14
Black Trans Liberation Tuesday, 9
Black women: activist leadership, 9; as cultural center directors, 208; gendered analysis and, 23; racial violence against, 131; relationship between white women and, 23, 29n18, 158; survival under slavery, 65; violence against, 107, 131
Black Youth Project 100 (BYP100), 9, 11
Bland, Sandra, 90
Blue Ridge Rifles (at UNG), 262–63
bodies: Black, as site of power, 233; captive, 100–103; diversity workers as bodies of color, 47; legible to institutions, 163, 232, 239–43; space and, 124–26
Bogle, Paul, 67
boundary maintenance, 49–50, 158, 237, 278–80
Bourdieu, Pierre, 276
Bradshaw, Lauren Yarnell, 317
Brandzel, Amy, 157
Brattin, Rick, 29n16, 274
Brazil, 39
Bristol, Laurette, 63, 66, 283, 285
broken windows theory, 304
Brown, Amy E., 28n10
Brown, Dorothy, 263
Brown, M. Christopher, 79
Brown, Michael, 10–11, 26n1, 234
Brown, Wendy, 230
Brown v. Board of Education of Topeka, 111, 253
Burdziak, Alan, 227
Burton, Orisanmi, 22

Bussa's Rebellion, 67
Butler, Jonathan, 11, 235, 274
Butler, Malika, 84
Button, Andrea, 21

California, 280, 309
California Council of Cultural Centers in Higher Education, 220
Campaign magazine, 172
campus environments: culturally engaging, 203–205 (*see also* cultural centers); hostile, 176, 234–37, 242 (*see also* racism); safe houses, 210–14; safe spaces, 235–36
Campus Free Speech Act (University of Wisconsin), 282–83
campus police/security: racial targeting by, 17, 44, 279–80, 297; surveillance, 44; undercover, 133–34; violence against protestors, 130. *See also* police
campus rebellions: community organizing and, 3, 8–13, 135–36, 156; cultural center staff and, 201–203 (*see also* cultural centers); demands of (*see* student demands); global, 11–12; history of, 275; increase in, 171–72; intraracial tensions in, 90; meaning of, 315–19; plantation politics framework and, 1–26; student activist political subjectivity and, 227–44. *See also* activism; antidiversity; antiracist praxis; decolonization; institutional responses to student protests; rebellion; resistance; state responses to student protests; student protests
campus safety, 20, 50, 201
Candler, Allen, 252
capital, 7–8, 51; self-purchase and, 61
capitalism: higher education and, 17–18, 21–22; neoliberal, 37, 230,

capitalism *(continued)*
　316; protests as threat to, 230; racialism and, 121–24. *See also* anticapitalist pedagogy
capitalist subjectivity, 228, 238–39, 243
captive body, 100–103. *See also* enslaved Africans; slavery
carceral state, 228, 295–311
care, ethic of, 219
career advancement, 185, 207–208
Carey, Kristi, 21
Caribbean immigrants, 49
Caribbean region: plantation pedagogies in, 63–72; plantations in, 39; student movements, 68
Carmichael, Stokely, 108
Carolinas, 60
Carr, Jesse, 19, 29n18, 164
Carr, Julian, 131, 134, 257–58
Carruthers, Charlene, 9
Cartwright, Samuel, 99
"A Case for Reparations at the University of Chicago" (Jordan, Mount, and Parker), 14
Castro, Fidel, 111
Center for Strategic Diversity Leadership and Social Innovation, 175
Chapman, Maria Weston, 209
Charlottesville, Virginia, 250, 264
chattel slavery, 7, 42, 60–61, 85, 295–96
Chatterjee, Piya, 228
Chessman, Hollie, 28n13
Cheyenne land, 120, 127
Cheyney University, 78
Chicago BYP organizations, 9
chief diversity officers (CDOs): administrator support for, 175; emergence of, 174–76; plantation driver role and, 19–20, 47, 171, 173–74, 177–93, 315 (*see also*

overseer role); student demands for, 172–73. *See also* diversity and inclusion (D&I) initiatives
childbearing, 65
Chopp, Rebecca, 129
Chronicle of Higher Education, 172
citational practices, 158
#citationpolitics, 69
civility, 283
civil rights movement, 174, 201, 253, 284–85; HBCU students in, 88–89
Civil War, 78, 86, 131, 250–56, 259–67. *See also* Confederate iconography
Clark Atlanta University, 90
class system, 61–62, 65; elite students and, 277. *See also* elites; hierarchies
Click, Melissa, 45–46
Clifton, James M., 177–80
Clinton administration, 231
Cobbins, Elizabeth, 250
Code Noir. *See* slave codes
coevalness, 35
Cohen, Cathy, 9
COINTELPROs, 299–301. *See also* Federal Bureau of Investigation (FBI)
College of William & Mary, 136n2
colleges and universities: communities, relations with, 154; economic structures, 41–42; historical links to slavery, 14–15, 27n8, 36, 42, 120, 131–35, 142, 228, 235 (*see also* plantation politics); mystification and, 302; reputation and brand management, 19, 145–46, 245n6; responsibility for racist incidents, 123–24, 234–35; settler colonialism and, 121, 127 (*see also* settler colonialism); as sites of privilege, 12. *See also* cultural centers; diversity and

inclusion (D&I) initiatives; higher education; Historically Black Colleges and Universities (HBCUs); policies, campus; white institutions, predominantly/historically/traditionally
Colleton, John, 60
Collins, Addie Mae, 108
Colombia, 39
colonialism and empire, 17–18, 21–22, 229; Fanon's critique of, 111–12; plantation pedagogy and, 58, 63 (*see also* plantation pedagogies); subjectivities and, 239; white supremacy and, 37 (*see also* white supremacy). *See also* decolonization; settler colonialism
Colorado, 127, 280
color-blind racism, 145, 282
colorism, 40
Comer, Braxton Bragg, 261
communication, 48–49
communities, campus relations with, 154
community organizing: campus activism and, 3, 8–13, 135–36, 156. *See also* Black Liberation Army (BLA); Black Lives Matter movement; Black Panther Party (BPP); Black Power movement; Movement for Black Lives (M4BL)
compassion fatigue, 209
complaint, 317–18
completion rates, 214–15
compliance, 218–19
Concerned Student 1950 (group), 11, 46, 274
conductors, on Underground Railroad, 210–11
Conerly, Rosalind, 216, 220, 317
Confederate iconography, 21; establishment of campus memorials, 252–56; modern response to, 263–67; protests against removal of, 249–50; removal and/or contextualization of, 249–52, 256–67; in songs, 251, 253, 261; at Texas A&M University, 259–60; at University of Alabama, 260–62; at University of North Carolina Chapel Hill, 131–35, 136n4, 253, 257–59; at University of North Georgia, 262–63; at Washington and Lee University, 136n4. *See also* flags; Lost Cause movement
conformity, 218–19, 287
consciousness raising, 156
conservatives, 281, 304; appropriation of civil rights discourse, 135
control mechanisms, 7, 16–18, 45, 52, 173–74, 279; chief diversity officers and, 190–92; in response to student protests, 273–88; used in slavery, 99. *See also* criminal justice system; plantation drivers; slave codes; social control
Coombe, Robert, 128–29
cooptation, 164, 319
Coppini, Pompeo, 259
corporations, 48
Coulthard, Glen, 128, 142, 167n1
counseling services, 212–13, 240
COVID-19 pandemic, 249
Craig, Locke, 257
Crawford, Edward, Jr., 28n11
Crawley, Ashon, 243, 318
creativity, 113, 161, 180
Crenshaw, Kimberlé, 27n9
criminalization of Blackness, 152, 297
criminal justice system, 295–311
criminology programs, 302–11
crisis management, 19–21; chief diversity officers, 190–91; diversity as, 145–47

critical identity studies (CRIS), 143, 159–60, 166
critical race theory, 79–80
critical rage pedagogy, 71–72
Cross, William, 64
Cruse, Harold, 110, 111
Cuban Revolution, 68
Cullors, Patrisse, 9
culpability, 318
cultural centers, 199–221; abolitionists and, 201, 203–205, 208–10; allies and collaborators, 209–10; college completion and, 214–15; conductors, stationmasters, and stockholders, 210–11; development of identity and, 216–18; intersectional politics and, 205–209; as pathways to freedom, 218–21; programs, 216–18; as safe houses, 210–14; staff as family, 216–17; strategic activism, 201–203
culture wars, 231
Cunningham, Kevin, 90
curriculum: Eurocentric, 110; hidden, 84; industrial, 85–88, 316–17; knowledge and, 151; marginalized groups and, 154; workshops for decolonizing, 162
Cvetkovich, Ann, 240

Dache-Gerbino, Amalia, 232
Daily Tar Heel, 257–58
Dakota Access Pipeline, 129–30
Dartmouth College, 119
Darwin, Charles, 125, 136n3
Davis, Angela Y., 296, 309
Davis, James Earl, 79
Davis, Jefferson, 251
debt, student loan, 12, 298
decolonization, 68–73, 142–43, 148; "master's tools" and, 155, 242; of women's and gender studies, 156–60

Decolonizing Pedagogies Project, 143, 150, 161–67
deference, 104
deficit-based thinking, 151
dehumanization, 18, 20, 35–36, 319; plantation pedagogies and, 64; in prisons, 300; resistance to, 37, 84; social control and, 103; in traditionally white institutions, 173. *See also* humanity
Dei, George J. Sefa, 106
Demby, Gene, 236
democratization of higher education, 147
Denny, George, 261
Denver SWAT Team, 130
dependency, 38
desubjectification, 128
deviancy, 50–51
difference: hierarchies and, 155; as political branding, 236
Dillard University, 91, 176
discipline, 178, 181; power and, 240–41. *See also* punishment
disciplines, academic. *See* academic disciplines
dis-ease, 240
dispossession/displacement, 233
Diverse Issues in Higher Education, 172
diversity and inclusion (D&I) initiatives, 8, 14–16, 18–20, 119–36; activism and, 10; affirmative action and, 231–32; categories of, 128–29; Confederate iconography and, 252; cooptation of, 149–50; crisis management and appeasement, 145–47; critiques of, 232; discomfort and, 132–33; diversity management, 190–91, 232, 237; equality and, 202; equated with market, 126, 130; limits of, 136; as marker of progress, 232; mission

statements on, 15; neoliberalism and, 130; parity of representation and, 146; plantation political economy and, 141–48; plantation politics and, 126–35; racial violence and, 119–36; racism and capitalism, 121–24; in response to racist incidents, 234; siloed locations of, 147, 152, 165; staff (*see* chief diversity officers; diversity workers); student protests and, 242; symbolic role of, 175–76; Western constructs of space and, 121, 124–28. *See also* antidiversity; cultural centers; exclusion; inclusive excellence (IE)
DiversityInc, 145
diversity workers, 19–20, 24; as bodies of color, 47; career advancement, 185, 207–208; crisis management and, 147; roles of, 315. *See also* chief diversity officers (CDOs); diversity and inclusion (D&I) initiatives
Dixiecrats, 253
Doddington, David, 178
domination, 113, 149, 275–78, 284
double-consciousness, 15
Douglas, Stephen A., 14
Douglass, Frederick, 205, 214, 285, 293, 298
Drapetomania, 99
Dream Defenders, 4, 8, 11
drivers. *See* plantation drivers
Du Bois, W. E. B., 15, 80–81, 83–84, 87–88, 111
Duke University, 133, 264
Dumas, Michael, 17
Dunbar, Erica Armstrong, 205
Duncan, Garret Albert, 35
Durant, Thomas, 279, 282
Durant, Thomas J., 7, 42, 46, 50–52
Durkheim, Emile, 276
Duval, Dawn Riley, 28n10

economic structures, 41–42. *See also* funding for colleges and universities
education: after emancipation, 13–14; alternative modes of, 310–11 (*see also* Black political literacy); equality and, 38; hierarchies and, 61–62; legal right to, 78–79; prohibited under slavery, 85 (*see also* illiteracy); purpose of, 151–52, 154, 275–78, 285–86, 298–99, 315–19; as resistance, 274; as a right, 70. *See also* colleges and universities; higher education; knowledge
elites: affirmative action and, 49; exclusion and, 27n5, 185, 277; Ivy League institutions, 213, 277; knowledge, 66; language and, 48; plantations and, 41, 43, 46, 253; power and control, 18, 105–106, 141–42, 148–49, 277, 295–97; private institutions, 130; "Talented Tenth," 83–84. *See also* class system; hierarchies
Ellis, Eddie, 307
Elzie, Johnetta "Netta," 28n11
emancipation, 65, 102–103; chief diversity officers and, 189–93; education for formerly enslaved people, 85–88; legal right to education, 78–79. *See also* abolition; freedom
emancipatory pedagogical frameworks, 67–69, 285–88
emancipatory practices, 23–26
embodied knowledge, 106
emotional labor, 6–8; cultural center staff, 216; during racial crises, 20–21
emotions, 6; exploitation of, 62
empire. *See* colonialism and empire
employment. *See* labor
English language, 48–49

enrollment, 44, 48–49, 51, 109, 174, 176, 210, 236, 259. *See also* admissions; retention
enslaved Africans: compulsory illiteracy, 85, 293–94, 298; diaspora, 39; escape of, 99–100; as fixed capital, 51; isolation of, 63–64; as property, 100–103; self-purchase, 61. *See also* plantation as system; plantation drivers; slave codes; slave plantations; slavery
epistemic violence, 103–105, 107, 112, 114
Eppes, Frances, 264
equality and equity, 8, 10, 14, 38, 148–55. *See also* racial equity and equality
Ervin, Archie, 172
escape, 99–100, 104–105, 114, 311
ethical slippage, 82–83, 86
ethnic studies, 212, 217, 317. *See also* Black studies
Evans, John, 127
Evers, Medgar, 109
exclusion: assumption of, 120–21; of Black students, 15; Confederate iconography as symbol of, 254–55, 265–66; diversity workers' complicity in, 173; major incidents and, 152–53; patterns of, 150–53; resistance and, 148, 219. *See also* diversity and inclusion (D&I) initiatives; marginalization
experiential knowledge, 64
exploitation: of emotions, 62; neoliberalism and, 231; social control and, 103. *See also* labor exploitation
extension campuses, 48

facility, 48
faculty, Black, 8; campus rebellions and, 20; in Caribbean, 66; decolonizing pedagogy, 156; exploited labor of, 297–98 (*see also* labor exploitation); friendships among, 158
faith, 2
familial relationships, 216
Fanon, Frantz, 73, 82, 111–12
fatigue, 20–21, 209
Faust, Drew Gilpin, 178
FBI. *See* Federal Bureau of Investigation (FBI)
fear, 4, 39, 219, 278
Federal Bureau of Investigation (FBI), 133, 299; counterintelligence operations, 299–301, 303
#FeesMustFall, 12
Feldman, Jack, 45–46, 50
feminism: Black, 107, 142; racialized origins of term, 157. *See also* women's movement
Ferguson, Missouri, protests in, 3, 4, 10, 26n1, 234
Ferguson, Roderick, 227, 230, 238
#FergusonUprising, 10, 28n11
Ferreira da Silva, Denise, 125, 231–32, 244n3
Fifteenth Amendment, 251
financial assistance, 123
First Amendment, 280–82. *See also* free speech
first-generation college student programs, 213
Fisher, Abigail, 237
Fisher v. University of Texas, 237
Fisk University, 89, 279
flags: Alabama state, 260; Confederate, 212, 253–54, 256–58, 260; Mississippi state, 249–50; Phillip's Legion, 262. *See also* Confederate iconography
Florida, 309
Florida A&M University, 8
Florida State University, 8, 264

Floyd, George, 260
Foerster, Werner, 300
Folt, Carol, 132, 258–59
Foster, Gaines, 250
Foster, Holly A., 317
Foucault, Michel, 229
Fourteenth Amendment, 251
fragility, 21, 163–64
Frazier, E. Franklin, 81, 111
Free Alabama Movement (FAM), 308–309
Freedmen's Bureau, 13, 92n5
freedom, 99, 102–103, 200; cultural centers as pathways to, 218–21; knowledge and, 124. See also abolition; emancipation
freedom of expression, 266, 281–82
Freedom School movement, 275, 284–85
Freedom Summer, 275, 284–85
free speech, 44, 171, 236, 280–82, 284
Freire, Paolo, 66
French West Indies, 82
Friere, Paulo, 274–77, 283–84
Fuentes, Marisa J., 23
Fugitive Slave Act (1793), 99
fugitivity, 99–114, 318
Fulton, Sybrina, 90
funding for colleges and universities: administrative costs and, 147; criminology programs, 303; cultural centers, 206–207; importance of, 44; institutional responses to activism and, 273–75, 283, 285; radical programs, 297. See also resource allocation
futurity, 113

Gaines, Matthew, 259–60
Gainesville, Florida, 250
Gallman, Robert, 50, 51
Garvey, Marcus, 72
Garza, Alicia, 9

gender and sexuality centers, 213–14
gendered analysis, 23
gender studies. See women's and gender studies (WGS)
genocide, 40, 120, 122, 297, 317
Genovese, Eugene D., 41
Georgetown, 42
Ghana, 67
Gibson, Randall Lee, 252
Gilmore, Ruth Wilson, 296–97
Ginsberg, Benjamin, 147
Giroux, Henry A., 123
globalization, 48
global resistance, 11–12
Gold Coast, 67
Golden Drums (student organization), 299
Goldwater Institute, 280
Graham, Patience, 61
Grambling State University, 89
grassroots organizing, 156. See also activism; community organizing
Guattari, Félix, 238–40
Guinier, Lani, 49
Gumbs, Alexis Pauline, 106

Haidt, Johnathan, 236
Haitian Revolution, 39, 67
Hale, Sheffield, 265
Hall, Stuart, 305–306
Hamer, Jennifer, 37
Hamilton, Charles, 108
Hampton Institute, 89
Hampton Institute Model (Hampton-Tuskegee Idea), 85–88
harassment, 152–53, 171, 212, 304
Harding, Vincent, 163
Hare, Nathan, 111
Harney, Stefano, 25, 229, 242, 277
Harris, Cheryl, 100–101
Harris, Jessica, 206–207
Hartman, Saidiya, 3, 101
Harvard College, 9–10

Harvey, David, 232
hate crimes, 152–53
hate speech, 44, 281
hate symbols, 28n14, 212. *See also* Confederate iconography
HBCUs. *See* Historically Black Colleges and Universities (HBCUs)
Head, Payton, 234–35
Hearns, Elle, 9
Hegel, Friedrich, 125–26, 128
hegemony, 305–307, 310
Henderson, George, 111
heritage: cultural center celebrations, 217; regional, 249–50
Herschthal, Eric, 14–15
hidden curriculum, 84
hierarchies, 105, 233; difference and, 155; gendered, 145; power and, 46. *See also* class system; elites; racial hierarchy; status; white supremacy
Higginbotham, Evelyn Brooks, 84
higher education: centering Black lives in, 13–16; democratization of, 147; emancipatory practices, 23–26; gendered dynamics of, 23; globalization of, 40; humanity of Black lives in, 2; ideological warfare and, 13; instruments of insurrection in, 318–19; oppressive necessity of, 315–17; plantation politics and (*see* plantation politics); questionable sufficiency of, 317–18; systemic racism in, 13 (*see also* racism); value of, 273. *See also* colleges and universities; education
Higher Education Act (1965), 92n3
Hill, Dominique, 114
Hilton, Kitty, 68
hiring processes, 49–50
Historically Black Colleges and Universities (HBCUs): Blackness within, 82–83, 90–92; history of, 78–79, 91–92, 93n5; industrial curriculum, 85–88, 316–17; perceptions of, 79; queer and trans* students, 90–91; racist ideologies and, 80; respectability politics in, 83–85; social justice movements, 88–91; as "social settlements," 80–81; white supremacy and, 18, 77–93
historically white institutions. *See* white institutions, predominantly/historically/traditionally
house slaves, 46–47
housing, themed/special interest, 211–12
Howard University, 10, 89, 90
humanity, 2, 15, 17, 26; freedom and, 103; of marginalized populations, 171; recognition of, 110, 128. *See also* dehumanization
hunger strikes, 235, 274
hypervisibility, 215
Hypolite, Liane, 220, 317

"I, Too, Am Harvard," 9–10
identity: development of, 209, 216–18; exploitation of, 62; invalidation of, 236; as "problematic," 277; unlearning of, 63–65. *See also* Blackness; critical identity studies (CRIS); subjectivity
ideology, 305–307, 310
Illinois, 280–81
illiteracy, 79, 85, 293–94, 298
imperialism. *See* colonialism and empire
inclusive excellence (IE), 18–19, 172. *See also* diversity and inclusion (D&I) initiatives
indigenous land, 120, 127, 297. *See also* colonialism and empire; Native Indigenous peoples; settler colonialism

industrial education, 85–88, 316–17
information, transmission of, 48–49
innocence, 306–307
innovation, 161
institutionalization, 51–52, 165–66; as moral structure, 228
institutional responses to student protests, 2, 5, 13, 16, 133–34; backlash and, 21, 251, 265, 285; chief diversity officers and, 190–92; cleansing and erasure, 238–41, 244n1; economic and political aspects, 273–75, 283, 285; name changes to buildings, 229; neoliberal capitalism and, 230; scapegoating, 285; social control and, 280–88. *See also* diversity and inclusion (D&I) initiatives; policies, campus; repression
insubordinate practice, formation of, 103–14
insurrection, 39, 100; acts of, 107–109; Black studies programs as, 112–14; instruments of, 318–19. *See also* resistance; slave rebellions
intelligence, race and, 237
intelligentsia, 87–88
interdisciplinarity, 14; student identity and, 217; student movements and, 227–28
interdisciplines, 227–28, 239–42
interest convergence, 80–81; dilemma in, 192
interiority, 239–41
intersectionality, 14, 27n9, 72, 145, 156–57, 160; cultural centers and, 206–209, 214; lived experience, 228
isolation, 215
Ivy League institutions, 213, 277

Jacoby, Barbara, 287
Jamaica, 60, 66, 67

James, Joy, 302
Jenkins, Toby, 220, 317
Jenkins, Toby S., 20
Jim Crow South, 80, 251, 253–54
jobs. *See* labor
John, Beverly, 38, 43
Johns Hopkins University, 280, 284
Jones, Danye, 28n11
Jones, George Morgan, 252
Jones-Rogers, Stephanie, 157
Jordan, Caine, 14
Joshua, Deandre, 28n11
Judt, Tony, 240
justice, 16, 154. *See also* social justice movements at HBCUs

Kant, Immanuel, 125
Kelley, Robin, 241
Kelley, Robin D. G., 122
Kezar, Adrianna, 287
Kimbrough, Walter M., 176
King, Martin Luther, Jr., 109, 136
King, Tiffany Lethabo, 121
Kitwana, Bakari, 28n11
knowledge: curricula and, 151; embodied, 106; experiential, 64; as form of oppression, 72; freedom and, 124; liberation and, 299 (*see also* Black political literacy); monetization of, 297; plantation and "belief of what is thought to be true," 7, 42–43, 156; power and, 57–58; resistance and, 275; Western, establishment of universities and, 121, 124–26; white supremacy and, 73. *See also* epistemic violence
knowledge production, 114; alternative sources of, 303; decolonization and, 155–56, 160 (*see also* decolonization)
Koromantyns, 67
Ku Klux Klan, 254, 259

labor: job placement, 316; work ethic, 123. *See also* career advancement; diversity workers; faculty, Black; staff, Black
labor exploitation, 6, 14, 18–19, 22, 40, 62, 208, 228, 235–36; prisons and, 296–97, 309; university staff and faculty, 297–98
land grants, 142
Lang, Aaryn, 9
Lang, Clarence, 37
language, 48, 306–307, 309
la paperson, 25, 142, 148, 243
Latina/o cultural centers, 217
law enforcement. *See* campus police/security; criminal justice system; police
Law Enforcement Assistance Administration (LEAA), 303
Leakes, Julia, 14
Lee, Robert E., 251, 256–57, 264
legibility, 163, 232, 239–43
Legion of Black Collegians, 235
legislation: enfranchisement, 251; repressing protests, 29n16; in response to student activism, 273–74; as tool to repress rebellions, 20–22. *See also* state responses to student protests
Lewis, Mel Michelle, 158–59
liberal humanism, 230
liberalism, 149–50; hate crimes and, 153; interdisciplines and, 227–28
liberation struggles, 2, 7; Black radical prison movements, 294–311; in higher education, 199–221. *See also* activism
liberatory spaces, 165
Lincoln University, 78
Lipsitz, George, 232
literacy, 293–94; Black political literacy, 294–311
Lockhart, Dan Josiah, 178

Lockley, James, 178
Loftin, Richard Bowen, 235
#LoftinCantExplain, 245n5
Lorde, Audre, 113, 155, 166
Lost Cause movement, 250, 253–56. *See also* Confederate iconography
Louisiana, 279, 280–81
Louisiana State University, 251–52
Lukianoff, Greg, 236
lynching, 107

M4BL. *See* Movement for Black Lives (M4BL)
Mahmud, Tayyab, 230
Maira, Sunaina, 228
major incidents, 152–53
Manassas Industrial School, 285
Manhattan Community College, 299
manifest destiny, 127
Marable, Manning, 112
marginalization, 8, 109, 145, 150; diversity and inclusion efforts and, 20 (*see also* diversity and inclusion (D&I) initiatives); reversal of, 153–54, 156 (*see also* decolonization). *See also* exclusion
Marsha P. Johnson Institute, 9
Martin, Trayvon, 4, 8–9, 26n1, 90
Martinique, 82
Marx, Karl, 111, 167n1, 232
Marxism, 305
Marxist epistemology, 70
Masri, Bassem, 28n11
"master's tools," 155, 242
Matias, Cheryl, 38
Mayfield, Curtis, 294
McCarrel, MarShawn, 28n11
McCluskey-Titus, Phyllis, 207
McGowan, John, 133–34
McKinnies, Melissa, 28n11
McKittrick, Katherine, 3, 25, 37, 41, 124–25
McLaren, Peter, 71, 72

media: higher education, 172; negative publicity, 245n6; on student protests, 235–36. *See also* social media, mobilization using
Mellown, Robert, 261
memorialization, 131–34
Memphis, Tennessee, 250
mental health services, 12, 212–13, 240
mental illness, 245n9
meritocracy, 123, 144–45
Meyerhoff, Eli, 294
Meyerson, Debra, 190
Michalewicz, Rachel, 237
Michigan, 280, 309
microaggressions, 66, 151, 171, 212, 219
Middle Passage, 39
Miller, Elinor, 41
Miller, Shannon J., 158–59
mindsets, 156
Miseducation of the Negro (Woodson), 13
missionaries, 80–81
Mississippi prisons, 308, 309
Mississippi state flag, 249–50
Mitchell, Nick, 239, 241–42
Mizzou. *See* University of Missouri at Columbia (Mizzou)
Mobley Jr., Steve D., 18, 88
model minority myth, 40
Modyford, Thomas, 60
Moliere, N., 46
monetization, 123; of knowledge, 297
moral education, 73, 80–81
Morant Bay Rebellion, 67
Morehouse College, 90–91
Morgan, Phillip D., 179
Morgan State University, 91
Morril Act (1892), 92n5
Morrill Land-Grant Act (1862), 80, 92n4
Morrison, Toni, 83
Moten, Fred, 25, 229, 242, 277

motherhood, 66
Mount, Guy Emerson, 14
movement, freedom of, 45
Movement for Black Lives (M4BL), 25, 229; campus activism during, 2–5, 13, 16, 20; origins of, 9, 26n1; protests, 234. *See also* Black Lives Matter movement
Muhammad, Khalil Gibran, 297
multicultural humanism, 230
multiracial students, 40
Muntaqim, Jalil, 301
Museus, Samuel D., 203–204, 216
Mustaffa, Jalil Bishop, 242

Nagel, Mechthild, 190
name changes to buildings, 229
Nash, Diane, 89
National Association for the Advancement of Colored People, 299
National Association of Diversity Officers in Higher Education (NADOHE), 24, 172
National Conference on Race and Ethnicity (NCORE), 24
nationalist social movement, 174
National Strike Against Prison Slavery, 295, 308
National Student Clearinghouse Research Center, 215
National Underground Railroad Freedom Center, 203
Nation of Islam, 299
Native Indigenous peoples, 40–41; boarding schools, 316–17; building of higher education and, 36; genocide of, 40, 120, 297, 317; settler colonialism and, 120, 127–28; slavery and, 46
Native Student Alliance, 130
Nat Turner Rebellion (1831), 293
NcNair, Denise, 108

"Negro Problem," 78, 86
neocolonialism, 48
neoliberal capitalism, 37, 228–30, 316
neoliberal individualism, 241
neoliberalism, 228; diversity and, 43; emergence of universities and, 229; freedom and, 208; inclusion and, 123–24, 130; privatization and, 50; racist ideologies and, 37–38; resistance and, 288; rise of, 230–31; subjectivities and, 239; in US institutions, 40
networks, 9, 199–200, 218–20
Newfield, Christopher, 230, 232
New Hampshire, 280
Newman, Joshua, 254, 265
New Orleans, Louisiana, 250
Newton, Huey, 112
Newton, Isaac, 125
New York State prisons, 301–303, 307
niceness, 149–50, 153
Nicki, Andrea, 245n9
nigrescence model, 64
Nixon, Monica L., 190
Njoku, Nadrea, 66, 84
#NoDAPL, 130, 133
normality, 37
norms, 44–45; transmission of, 50; white, 26n5, 84, 148
North Carolina, 280–81
North Carolina Agricultural and Technical State University, 89
North Star, 214–15, 217–18
Northwestern University, 127

occupations, 316. *See also* labor
Ogbu, J. U., 92n2
Okello, Wilson Kwamogi, 18, 318
oligarchy, 61
Oliver, Liza, 266
oppression, 18; complicity in, 185–86, 189–90; forms of, 128; hate speech and, 281; in higher education, 199–200; internalized, 62, 66, 277; knowledge as, 72; plantation drivers and, 178; pressure and, 219; social control and, 103. *See also* anti-Blackness; racism
Organization of Afro-American Unity, 299
Orr, Catherine M., 160–61
Orr, Jackie, 240
otherness, 101
overseer role, 160–61. *See also* plantation drivers
"oversensitivity," 236
Oxbridge structure, 62

pan-African movements, 89
paradigm shifts, 25, 162–65
Parker, Eugene T., 175
Parker, Kai, 14
Passeron, Jean-Claude, 276
Patel, Leigh, 237
paternalism, 43–44, 80, 146, 236, 285
patriarchy, 23
Patton, Lori D., 66, 206–207, 216–17, 317
Peck, Jamie, 232
pedagogical labor, 6–8
pedagogy: emancipatory frameworks, 67–69, 285–88; radical frameworks, 23–24, 69–74; typology of, 59. *See also* decolonization; plantation pedagogies
Personal Responsibility and Work Opportunity Reconciliation Act, 231
personhood, 110. *See also* humanity; identity; subjectivity
phenotypic superiority, 40
Phibbah, 67–68
Phillips, Ulrich, 46–47
Phillip's Legion of Confederacy, 262

Pipeline Leadership Conference (2016), 129–30
plantation as system, 17, 41–42, 144; processual elements, 48–52; structural elements, 42–48
plantation drivers, 19–20, 46–47, 171, 173–74, 177–93, 315. *See also* overseer role
plantation pedagogies, 18, 57–74; as acculturation, adaptation, and survival lessons, 65–66; control and, 274; dismantling of, 69–75; in higher education, 61–63; as instruments of colonization, 63; as removal, isolation, and unlearning of self, 63–65; as resistance teaching, subversion planning, and emancipatory understanding, 67–69; slave society model, 59–60; social control as, 283–85
plantation political economy, 141–67, 295
plantation politics: antidiversity as intervention in, 141–67; Black political literacy in carceral university, 293–311; campus and state responses to student protest, 273–88; campus rebellions and, 1–26; chief diversity officers as plantation drivers, 171–93; defined, 3, 6–7, 121, 144, 148; as framework, 35–52; fugitivity and Black studies, 99–114; historically Black colleges and universities (HBCUs) and, 77–93; inclusion and, 119–36; Lost Cause (Confederate) iconography and, 249–67; student activist political subjectivity and, 227–44; universities and prisons as sites of, 293–311; university cultural centers and Underground Railroad, 199–221

Platt, R. Eric, 21, 317
Plessy v. Ferguson, 253
police: broken windows theory and, 304; surveillance, 231; violence by, 2, 7–11, 13, 260. *See also* campus police/security
policies, campus: power structures and, 62, 135, 142–43, 156; as tool to repress rebellions, 20–22, 273–88. *See also* institutional responses to student protests
political climate, 5–6; hostile, 231. *See also* state responses to student protests
political correctness, 231, 236
political economy, 141. *See also* economic structures; funding for colleges and universities; plantation political economy
political subjectivity, 227–44
Poon, OiYan, 40
Porter, Horace, 109
postracialism, 145; cultural centers and, 206–207, 220
poverty, 231. *See also* class system
power: Black bodies as site of, 233; chief diversity officers and, 192; control over others, 46–47; of cultural center staff, 201–203, 207; discipline and, 240–41; knowledge and, 57–58; of plantation drivers, 177–78, 182; rank and, 46; relationships of, 276; symbolic, 184; within university hierarchies, 62, 135, 142–43; whiteness and, 232. *See also* social control
Prairie View A&M University, 90
precarity, 166
Price, Vincent, 264
prison industrial complex: Black political literacy and, 294–311; rebellions and uprisings, 301, 303, 308–10

privatization, 50
privilege, 171; as deficit, 153; plantation drivers and, 178–79
professionalism, 283
profit, 147. See also capitalism; funding for colleges and universities
progress, diversity as marker of, 232
property: enslaved Blacks treated as, 279; space and, 124–26; white identity and, 100–103
psycho-affective realm, 111–12
psychological services, 212–13
public education, origins of, 14
publicity. See media
public universities: affirmative action in, 237; establishment of, 92n4; neoliberalism and, 230. See also colleges and universities; higher education
Puerto Rico, 39
punishment, 44, 66, 311. See also criminal justice system; discipline; sanctions
Puwar, Nirmal, 238

queer and trans* students, 9, 90–91

race, capital and labor, 7–8. See also capitalism; labor
race-conscious leadership, 191–93
racial economy, 41–42
racial equity and equality, 16; dismissal of, 21–22; inclusion and, 202; interest convergence and, 80–81. See also equality and equity
racial geographies, 37
racial hierarchy, 26n5, 145; colonization and, 46 (see also colonialism and empire); Confederate iconography and, 255; plantation system and, 40, 42–44, 46, 52, 278–79; slave codes and, 282. See also hierarchies; white supremacy
racial profiling, 152. See also campus police/security
racial purity, 254
racial solidarity, 46, 158
racism, 2, 174; campus incidents, 11, 29n15, 212, 234–35, 274; color-blind, 145; Confederate iconography and, 249–50; institutional accountability for, 20; institutionalized, 62; navigation of, 236; scientific, 99; systemic, 13, 77, 237, 282; at traditionally white institutions, 17. See also anti-Blackness; antiracist praxis; assault; harassment; microaggressions; oppression; violence
racist epistemologies, 35
radical community building, 243
radicality, 241
radical pedagogical frameworks, 23–24, 69–74
rage, 10, 70–72, 164. See also anger
rank, 46, 143
Reagan, Ronald, 230, 231
real estate, 124–25
rebellion: use of term, 4. See also campus rebellions; resistance; slave rebellions
Reconstruction era, 252–53, 295, 309
recruitment of students, 15
refuge, 200, 203, 210
religious education, 73
reparations, 7, 12
representation, 148, 306–307
repression, 20–22, 27n8; state, 301–302, 308; white supremacy and, 52. See also institutional responses to student protests; state responses to student protests

Reserve Officer's Training Corps (ROTC), 262–63
resilience, 2, 229, 236
resistance, 2–4, 7, 24; global, 11–12, 39–40; institutionalized dominance and, 275–78; low-profile forms of, 104–105; pedagogy of, 67–69, 73; prison rebellions, 301, 303, 308–10; self-management and, 229; student activist political subjectivity and, 227–44; student identity development and, 219–21; transformation and, 318. *See also* activism; campus rebellions; community organizing; insurrection; slave rebellions
resource allocation, 28, 176, 202, 219; as reward or punishment, 47–48. *See also* funding for colleges and universities
respectability politics, 80–86
restorative justice, 154
retention, 203–204, 210, 214–15. *See also* enrollment
revolutionary critical pedagogy, 59
revolutionary pedagogy, 71
risk taking, 202–203
Robertson, Carole, 109
Robinson, Cedric, 122
Rodney, Walter, 64, 73
Rodney riots, 68
Rolnik, Suely, 238–40
Ross, Lawrence Sullivan "Sully," 259–60
Rudolph, Frederick, 287
Ruscio, Kenneth, 257

safe houses, 210–14
safe spaces, 235–36
Saint Louis University, 10
Saint Mary's College, 119
Sakai, J., 245n7

San Antonio, Texas, 250
sanctions, 47–48, 219, 281–82, 284
sanctuary campuses, 154
Sand Creek massacre, 120, 127
San Jose State University, 212
San Juan, 11
Scalia, Antonin, 237
schooling, 107–108. *See also* education; higher education
school-to-prison pipeline, 308. *See also* prison industrial complex
scientific racism, 99
Scott, James C., 104
Scott, Rick, 8
Scully, Maureen, 190
Seale, Bobby, 112
Seals, Darren, 28n11
segregation, 79, 152
selfhood, 318–19
Semmes, Raphael, 251
sentiment, 43–44, 236
settler colonialism, 120–21, 127–28, 136n1, 236, 316–17. *See also* colonialism and empire
sexism, 23
sexuality and gender centers, 213–14
sexual violence, 107
Shahid, Kyra T., 104
Shakur, Assata, 298–301
Shakur, Zayd Malik, 300
Silent Sam statue (at UNC), 131–35, 136n4, 253
Silliman, Benjamin, 14–15
Simons, H. D., 92n2
skill building, 216–18
Slattery, Patrick, 259
slave codes, 22, 50–51, 152, 177, 273; Barbados (1661), 59–60; modern university and, 278–80; race and, 282; white dominance and, 284. *See also* enslaved Africans

slave plantations: characteristics of, 42; Confederate iconography and, 249–52; restrictions on movement, 38; social control, 278–80. *See also* plantation as system; plantation drivers; plantation politics

slave rebellions, 67; fear of, 39, 278; prohibition of literacy following, 293–94

slavery: afterlife of, 3, 7; barbarity of, 65–66; British American governance systems, 61; gender and, 23; goals of, 44; legacies of, 1, 25, 58, 189; use of terms related to, 26n4; white reliance on enslaved labor, 245n7; white women enslavers, 157. *See also* enslaved Africans; plantation politics

slave society model, 59–60

Smith, J. Goosby, 174

Smith, Linda Tuhiwai, 156

social control, 22, 274; deviancy and, 50–51; diversity as, 144; education and, 276–77; industrial education and, 85–88; over bodies, 103; as plantation pedagogy, 283–85; violence and, 43–44. *See also* control mechanisms; power

socialization, 50

social justice movements at HBCUs, 88–91

social media, mobilization using, 2, 11, 90, 146, 234

social policy. *See* legislation

social unit, positions in, 45–46. *See also* hierarchies

Sojoyner, Damien, 294, 303

solitary confinement, 301, 310

South Africa, 12, 39, 88

South America, 39

Southern Poverty Law Center, 250

Southern University, 89, 280

Southport Correctional Facility, 301

space: Black body and, 124–26; liberatory, 165; overregulation of, 44; Western constructs of, 121, 124–26, 136n1

Spelman College, 82, 90

Spencer, Richard, 281

spies, 133–34, 245n7, 300

Spillers, Hortense, 101–103

Squire, Dian D., 7, 17, 28n13, 120–21, 124, 141–42, 144, 147–48, 151, 156, 179, 190, 208, 255, 277–78, 315

staff, Black: campus rebellions and, 20; decolonizing pedagogy, 156; exploitation of, 19–20. *See also* cultural centers

Standing Rock, 130

Stand Your Ground laws, 8

statelessness, 64

state responses to student protests, 230, 273–75; legislative, 280–88; removal of Confederate iconography, 249–50. *See also* legislation; repression

stationmasters, on Underground Railroad, 210–11

status, 45–46, 152; cultural centers and, 207; of plantation drivers, 177–78. *See also* hierarchies

status quo, 154, 185, 237, 265

Stewart, Louis J., 177

Stewart, Maria, 100, 103, 105–106, 112

Stewart, Saran, 17–18

stockholders, Underground Railroad and, 210–11

Stone Mountain, Georgia, 250

Stono Rebellion (1739), 293

street dance activism, 26n2

strikes, 11, 210, 235, 274, 295, 308

student-athletes, 8, 44; athletic-industrial complex and, 38, 51; protests by, 210, 235, 274

student demands, 12, 28n13, 237, 274; for chief diversity officers, 172–73; institutional responses to, 191–92; perceived as complaints, 235–36
student groups, 44
student loan debt, 12, 298
student protests: of 1960s and 1970s, 2, 12, 122, 227, 299–301; Concerned Student 1950 (Mizzou), 233–37; cultural center staff and, 201–203 (see also cultural centers); economic and political power and, 273–75, 283, 285; against Lost Cause icons (see Confederate iconography). See also activism; campus rebellions; resistance
subjectivity, 114, 229, 245n8; capitalist, 228, 238–39, 243; political, 227–44; reconstituting, 111–12
submission, 18, 108, 193
subordination, 40, 42, 65, 81, 87, 104–107, 113, 208–209, 279, 282
subversion planning, 67–69
success, 38; college as path to, 208–209; defining, 318–19
sugar plantations, 59–60
Sullivan, Shannon, 82
support networks, 200. See also cultural centers
surveillance, 8, 10–11, 13, 44, 231; escape from, 99–100, 104–105, 311; rupturing, 105–106
survival, politics of, 221
survival lessons, 65–66
Sutton, Michael, 207
Sutton, Michael E., 176
systematic linkages, 50
systemic racism, 13, 77, 237, 282. See also racism

"Talented Tenth," 83–84

Tallahassee Community College, 8
technologies of production, 48, 52
Tennessee, 280
Teo, Thomas, 104
terror, 7, 44, 88, 101, 107, 112, 149, 200, 302, 308
Texas, 280–81, 284, 309
Texas A&M University, 259–60, 281
Texas Southern University, 281
Thatcher, Margaret, 230
themed/special interest housing, 211–12
The Third University (la paperson), 25
Thirteenth Amendment, 251, 295
Thistlewood, Thomas, 67–68
Tiffany stained glass, 260–62, 264
Till, Emmett, 108
time, 143. See also allochronism
time and place, 17, 35–36, 52, 179–80
time-space distinction, 121, 125–26, 136n3
tokenization, 123, 146, 238
tolerance, 236, 239, 241–42
Tometi, Opal, 9
torture, 301
Toscano, Pasquale, 257
Towns, Armond, 19, 317
toxic white femininity, 160
transformative justice, 154
transnational protests, 39–40
trans* students, 9, 90–91
Trinidad and Tobago, 63
Trollope, Anthony, 57–58, 61, 64, 73
troublemakers, 4, 24, 50
Truesdell, Nicole, 161, 164–65
Trump, Donald J., 5, 73
Tsesis, Alexander, 265
Tubman, Harriet, 199, 201, 205, 206, 208–209, 218
Tuchman, G., 245n6
Tuitt, Frank A., 12, 19–20, 36, 47, 51, 73, 120, 141, 147, 148, 277, 317

Tulane University, 252
Tuskegee University, 86
Tutu, Desmond, 218
TWIs (traditionally white institutions). *See* white institutions, predominantly/historically/traditionally
typecasting, career, 207–208

The Undercommons (Harney and Moten), 25
Underground (television show), 173
Underground Railroad, 199–202, 204–206, 210, 218
United Daughters of the Confederacy, 131, 132, 253, 257, 260–61
University of Alabama, 260–62, 264
University of Arizona, 119
University of California at Berkeley, 10, 110, 112
University of Cape Town, 12
University of Chicago, 14
University of Colorado Boulder, 119
University of Denver (DU), 119–21, 126–30, 132, 135
University of Georgia, 42, 252
University of Havana, 68
University of Illinois at Urbana-Champaign, 217
University of Maryland, 10
University of Mississippi, 251–53
University of Missouri at Columbia (Mizzou), 21, 29n16; Black student activism, 3–4, 11, 46, 210, 229, 233–42, 245nn4–6, 274; campus police, 227; One Mizzou (diversity initiative), 234
University of North Carolina at Chapel Hill (UNC), 10, 119–21, 126; *Silent Sam* statue, 131–35, 136n4, 253, 257–59

University of North Georgia, 262–65
University of Oklahoma, 111
University of Pennsylvania, 10
University of Puerto Rico, 11–12
University of Southern Mississippi (USM), 249
University of Texas, 237, 264
University of the West Indies, 62, 68
University of the Witwatersrand, 12
University of Wisconsin, 281–83
University of Wisconsin–Green Bay, 119
upward mobility, 38, 45, 144, 152, 302
US Immigration and Customs Enforcement, 304
Utah, 280

Vanderbilt University, 254
violence, 233; anti-Black racial, 8, 28n11, 37, 120, 131; governance and, 244n3; police, 2, 7–11, 13, 260; sexual, 107; social control and, 43–44; state, 301; structural, 4, 37. *See also* assault; epistemic violence; harassment
Violent Crime Control and Law Enforcement Act, 231
Virginia, 280; House of Delegates, 279
Virginia State University, 91
vision, 2
vocational training. *See* industrial education

Wade-Golden, Katrina C., 175, 186, 188
Walker, David, 100, 103, 105–106, 112
War of Yankee Aggression, 131. *See also* Civil War
Washington, Booker T., 86, 88
Washington, George, 256
Washington and Lee University, 256–57

Washington University, 10
Wayt, Lindsay, 28n13
Weber, Max, 276
welfare, 231
Wells, Ida B., 100, 103, 105–107, 112
Wesley, Cynthia, 109
Western society: Black studies as redemption of, 112–14; constructs of space, 121, 124–26, 136n1; critiques of institutionality, 135–36. *See also* colonialism and empire
White, Julie, 232
white anxiety, 4, 39, 278
white egos, 150
white fragility, 163–64
white institutions, predominantly/historically/traditionally: Black studies programs in, 112–13; decolonizing pedagogies at, 161–67; dehumanization in, 173; diversity and inclusion efforts, 19–20, 171–72, 174–75 (*see also* diversity and inclusion (D&I) initiatives); institutional fragility, 21; neoliberalism and, 123; racism at, 17 (*see also* racism); white supremacy in, 77
whiteness: centering and reinforcement of, 18–22; cooptation and, 164; decentering, 149–50, 153, 158–62, 165–66; depicted as humane, 17; diversity and, 18–20, 144–45; interrogation of, 287; ontological Blackness and, 35; oxymoronic, 43; plantation logics, 113; political subjectivity of students and, 238; power and, 232; "proper" English and, 48; as property, 100–103; toxic patterns of, 149–53; women's and gender studies and, 157. *See also* racial hierarchy
white norms, 26n5, 84, 148
white supremacy: capitalism and, 61; career typecasting and, 208; colonial competition and, 37; diversity and inclusion initiatives and, 18–20; HBCUs and, 18, 77–93; in higher education, 4, 16–18, 22, 316–17; internalization of, 283; knowledge and, 73; nationalism and, 171; normalization of, 255; patriarchy and, 23; plantation logics, 113; in political climate, 5–6; racist epistemologies and, 35; rallies supporting, 249–50, 281; reinforced by control mechanisms, 7, 52; struggles against, 3, 5–6, 12–13; underestimation of, 282; use of term, 26n5. *See also* racial hierarchy
white women: feminism and, 157; relationship between Black women and, 23, 29n18, 158; solidarity, 158; toxic white femininity, 160
Wilberforce University, 78
Wilder, Craig Steven, 7, 36, 228, 284, 285, 287, 297
Williams, Bianca C., 27n10, 28n13, 36, 51, 120, 141, 147, 148, 277, 315, 317
Williams, Damon A., 175, 186, 188
Williams, Joshua, 28n11
Williams, Robert F., 111
Williamsburg General Assembly, 124, 127, 136n2
Wilson, Darren, 10
Wilson, John, 257
Wilson, Rusan, 110
Wisconsin, 280–81
wokeness, 72
Wolfe, Tim, 11, 29n16

women. *See* Black women; white women
women's and gender studies (WGS), 143, 156–60
women's movement, 157. *See also* feminism
Woodson, Carter G., 13
work ethic, 123
Wynter, Sylvia, 125

X, Malcolm, 109, 302

Yale, 15, 42
Yates, Ashley, 28n11
Yates, Donald, 279
Yeamans, John, 60
Yiannopoulos, Milo, 136
Young, Michael, 260
Young Lords, 299

Zeppos, Nicholas, 255
Zimmerman, George, 8–9, 90
Zirin, Dave, 29n16

www.ingramcontent.com/pod-product-compliance
Lightning Source LLC
Chambersburg PA
CBHW020318180325
23536CB00047B/6